NEWFOUNDLAND

Placentia

Cape Briton

Corvo
Flores
Fayal   Terceirra
                    S. Michael
Azores

O   C   E   A   N

Madeira

Canary Is.
Gomera
Grand Canary

S   E   A

C. Blanco

artin
adaloupe
ominica

Cape Verde Is.

Mayo I.
Santiago I.   C. Verde

Rio Grande

of Trinidad
lf of Paria   GUINEA

Z I L

Queen Elizabeth I: the 'Armada Portrait' by George Gower

Richard Hakluyt

THE TUDOR VENTURERS

selected from

The principal Navigations, Voyages, Traffics
and Discoveries of the English Nation,
made by Sea or Over Land

and edited by

JOHN HAMPDEN

LONDON
THE FOLIO SOCIETY
MCMLXX

PRINTED IN GREAT BRITAIN
Printed and bound by W & J Mackay & Co Ltd, Chatham
Set in Van Dijck 12 point
Illustrations printed by D. H. Greaves Ltd, Scarborough
Binding design by Jeff Clements
Maps by K. C. Jordan FRGS

To
the memory of my father
FRANCIS JOHN HAMPDEN
Wanderer Mariner Teller of tales
J.H.

ACKNOWLEDGMENTS

The editor and publishers are indebted to the Hakluyt Society and the Cambridge University Press for permission to take the selections in this book from their edition of Hakluyt's *Voyages*; and to the following for permission to reproduce illustrations: His Grace the Duke of Bedford; the Trustees of the British Museum; Plymouth Art Gallery; Magdalene College, Cambridge; the Bodleian Library, Oxford; the Ashmolean Museum, Oxford; the National Portrait Gallery; the National Maritime Museum, Greenwich.

The editor is greatly indebted to Mrs Margaret Weston, Mrs Diane Crook and Miss Sybil Smith for their help in preparing this book, particularly in establishing the text.

J.H.

CONTENTS

The titles above have been supplied by the editor. Hakluyt's titles are given in the text.

ILLUSTRATIONS

INTRODUCTION: MEN AND SHIPS

Richard Hakluyt had one thing at least in common with his greater contemporaries, Francis Drake and William Shakespeare; he too was born into an age of vigorous national expansion which offered, for the first time in English history, all the conditions needed to give full scope to his distinctive talents. The age moved with him in providing great material for his *Voyages*, that 'prose epic of the English nation' which is his immortal monument. But he was not a secluded editor, sitting aloof and simply putting into a book any suitable narratives and documents which came his way. With as much zeal and pertinacity as Froissart he sought out the actors in great events. He made himself 'familiarly acquainted with the chiefest captains at sea, the greatest merchants and the best mariners of our nation', 'to learn of their discoveries and appreciate their motives'.

How he began, while still a boy at Westminster School, 'that fruitful nursery', he relates eloquently in his well-known Epistle Dedicatory to Sir Francis Walsingham with which this book opens. There were two Richard Hakluyts, cousins and members of an old family of landed gentry in Herefordshire, whose name was possibly Welsh in origin and most probably pronounced 'Hacklit'. The elder cousin was a lawyer of the Middle Temple, an economist, geographer and patriot, who was concerned to promote voyages of exploration in order to bring a much-needed increase in trade. He had the ear of the highest ministers of state and he had many friends with interests like his own. They included John Dee, the great geographer and holy-mouth, and the German-Flemish cartographer, Ortelius, whose atlas, the *Theatrum Orbis Terrarum* (1570), was widely used in England and Europe.

The younger Richard Hakluyt could not have had a better mentor than his cousin and after a fateful visit to his cousin's map- and book-strewn chambers there was no doubt of his vocation. He went up to Christ Church College, Oxford, as a Queen's scholar, in 1570, when he was about eighteen years old, he graduated M.A. in 1577 and he took orders in the Church of England. Meanwhile he read everything about voyages and travels which he could find in Greek, Latin, Italian, Spanish, Portuguese, French and English. He gave the first public lectures in Oxford on the new maps and globes which were being produced as knowledge grew. In 1582 he published his first book, *Divers Voyages touching the Discovery of America*. Then he went to Paris for five years, from 1583 to the year of the Armada, as chaplain to the English ambassador. There he learned much, from Portuguese refugees (Spain had annexed Portugal in 1580), and from French sea-captains who had shown vigorous, though often piratical, enterprise in the New World. There too he found that the English were scorned for playing an inadequate, or reputedly inadequate, part in European expansion overseas. While in Paris he wrote, at Sir Walter Raleigh's request, *A Discourse of Western Planting* (colonization), of which more must be said later. As soon as he came back to England he began to put together the records of English achievements for the first edition of *The Principal Navigations, Voyages and Discoveries of the English Nation, made by sea or overland . . . at any time within the compass of these 1500 years . . .* Despite 'the huge toil and little profit' of collecting, editing, writing or re-writing and translating, the book was published, in London, in 1589.

This book was a great achievement, but for Hakluyt it was only a beginning. He continued labouring 'to bring to light the ancient deeds and to preserve the recent exploits of the English nation for the honour and benefit of this commonwealth in which I live and breathe'. He was not the only writer on these themes, but the most able and diligent. '[He is] the most skilled man in research that I have ever known,' wrote Van Meteran in 1594. 'No man living is more eager in searching out the manner of voyages.' In three volumes, folio, in 1598, 1599 and 1600 he published the second, greatly enlarged edition of the *Principal Voyages*, the great work which is known as 'Hakluyt' and from which the present selection is taken.

The Church, one of the very few havens then open to a scholar, provided him with a livelihood without engrossing too much of his time. There is no reason to doubt that he was a good Protestant though not a zealot. A sincere, honest man, patriot, economist and historian as well as geographer, a patient scholar and at his best an eloquent writer, he won the patronage of Sir Philip Sidney, the intimate friendship of Sir Walter Raleigh, and the respect and admiration of many. He was made a prebendary of Bristol, where he was well known, in 1586, and rector of Wetheringsett, near Ipswich, in 1590. He made his home there for the rest of his life but was often away. About 1590 he married the oddly christened Douglas Cavendish, sister of the Thomas Cavendish who had made the second English voyage round the world in 1586–8. She bore him a son, Edmund, and she died in 1597. Five years later he married 'a comfortable widow' who outlived him. His services to the nation continued to be rewarded. He was made a prebendary of Westminster in 1603, and when he died in London in 1616, the year of Shakespeare's death, he was buried in Westminster Abbey, in a grave which is now unknown.

Richard Hakluyt was born not only into an expanding England, but into an expanding world and an expanding universe. The neat little universe of medieval faith, with a small earth at the centre, and sun, moon, planets and stars revolving round it to the music of the spheres, with heaven just above and hell just below, and angels and devils as frequent visitors to earth – this comfortable image was already beginning to crumble under the teachings of Copernicus and others, although it was not until the seventeenth century that they found general acceptance. It was widely realized that the world was round, long before Magellan's circumnavigation demonstrated it in 1519–22, but the existence of America and the Pacific Ocean was unsuspected before Spanish discoveries began at the end of the fifteenth century. Meanwhile man was beginning to peer through his newly-invented telescopes into the abyss of space, with all that that implied for feeling and belief.

For centuries the world known to the heirs of the Roman Empire had extended outside western Europe only to Iceland and perhaps Greenland, to the Middle East and northern Africa, with a legendary fringe of Russia, the steppes of Asia, India, the Spice Islands and Cathay. There had never, however, been an iron curtain between the west and the far east; trade had continued for hundreds of years, but with no direct contact. When the Venetian merchant, Marco Polo, came home in 1295 after spending twenty-three years with his father and uncle in the vast empire of Kublai Khan who ruled in Cambaluc (Pekin), his famous account of his travels worked a revolution in European thought: China became real. Not until 1579, however, was the book translated into English.

The first impulse to break out of the western world was, perhaps inevitably, commercial. In medieval Europe there was a great demand for spices, to make bad food palatable, and for silk and other oriental luxuries, but whether they came by the centuries-old Silk Road through central Asia, or by sea across the Indian Ocean to Egypt, they changed hands so often that their prices in Europe were extortionate. And when the land routes were closed by wars and Turkish conquests, the powerful city-state of Venice, the richest market in Europe, secured a monopoly of the trade through Egypt. Venice's closest rival, Genoa, made the first attempt to break the monopoly by opening an Atlantic sea-route to the east; the Genoese Ugolino di Vivaldo set out with two galleys in 1291. They were lost off the west African coast, and for a century the attempt was not repeated.

Then the Portuguese, at the dawn of their great age, took up the challenge under their enlightened Prince, Henry the Navigator. They had great difficulties and dangers to overcome. They had to build the first ocean-going ships, with Genoese help, and learn how to sail them.

They had to overcome the superstitious terrors of seamen who believed that a ship which sailed westward into the Atlantic would be swept over the edge of the world into an inconceivable abyss, and that the way south was barred by a zone so torrid that the sea boiled and no one could pass through it. But the Portuguese captains were not to be daunted. They had discovered Madeira and the Azores by 1351 and the Cape Verde islands before 1400. They ventured slowly further and further down the west African coast, rewarded by a rich trade in gold-dust, ivory and pepper. In 1487–8 Bartholomew Diaz rounded the Cape of Good Hope, and the way to India lay open.

Like the Spanish and the French, English seamen knew of the Portuguese achievements, and they must have heard the legends and rumours of the discovery of lands across the Atlantic by the Norseman Leif Ericsson in A.D. 1002 and by the Welsh Prince Madoc in the twelfth century. In 1480 an English ship of eighty tons, John Lloyd, master, sailed from Bristol to look for land beyond Ireland, but was driven back by foul weather. There may have been other ventures, earlier or later, which were unrecorded. In 1497 the Venetian navigator, John Cabot, licensed by Henry VII, commanding a Bristol ship, discovered North America near Nova Scotia, and claimed that he had reached Asia. On his next voyage he vanished without trace, but this did not deter Bristol seamen from visiting North America and the Newfoundland fisheries. In 1509 his son, Sebastian Cabot, claimed to have discovered the North-west Passage into the Pacific, having probably sailed into Hudson's Bay, and then turned south as far as Florida. On his return, he said later, 'I found great tumults among the people and preparations for wars in Scotland, by reason whereof there was no more consideration had to this voyage. Whereupon I went into Spain . . .'

Meanwhile the Genoese visionary, Christopher Columbus, was nursing his delusion that a short westward voyage across the Atlantic would bring him to Asia. One of the great 'ifs' of history is the differ-ence it would have made to the world if his appeal to Henry VII had resulted in his sailing in command of an English expedition, though the prevailing winds would probably have taken him to North America. But it was Isabella of Castile who gave him the ships and men to discover his 'Indies' in 1492.

The Pope Alexander VI had already divided all the new lands between Portugal and Spain, and the two countries signed the Treaty of Tordesillas in 1494, under which all America except Brazil (settled by the Portuguese in 1500) was to be Spanish, and all the new dis-coveries in Africa and the far east were to be Portuguese – although the Spanish occupied the Philippines in 1564. These monopolies were increasingly resented and broken by the French, the English and other European seamen, sometimes in trading vessels, more often in well-armed privateers, so that hostility grew.

The pace of Iberian expansion quickened. By 1500 the Portuguese had begun to trade with India; by 1511 they had reached the coveted Spice Islands, the Moluccas; and by 1516 they were trading with Cathay, China. In 1519 a Spanish expedition commanded by the Portuguese Ferdinand Magellan set out to sail round the world. After discovering his straits and crossing the Pacific for the first time, he was killed by natives in the Philippines, but his flagship came home.

In the first half of the sixteenth century the Spaniards carried Christianity to exterminate the Caribbean islanders (except for the fierce Caribs) and to destroy the Aztec and Inca civilizations, and they began importing African slaves to work their mines and plantations. Slaves soon became scarce and expensive, partly because so many escaped to freedom in the jungles, and this provided a profitable trade for such interlopers as John Hawkins.

When that arch-bureaucrat Philip II came to the throne of Spain in 1556 and married Mary of England he bestrode the narrow world like a colossus. In Europe his possessions included the whole of Spain, Sardinia and Sicily, much of Italy and Austria, and the Netherlands, while unprecedented wealth poured into his coffers from the New World. When he annexed Portugal and the Portuguese empire in 1580 it looked as though no one could stand against the overweening power of Catholic Spain. But the Protestant Netherlands and Protestant England did so.

Although the English were at first left far behind by the Portuguese and Spaniards they never entirely abandoned oceanic enterprise; they made a few voyages to West Africa, Brazil and North America. The chief obstacles were religious and social upheavals at home and commercial apathy. For centuries wool had provided the main export trade, as the Lord Chancellor's woolsack still testifies, and so long as the trade with Europe flourished the London merchants, in particular, saw no point in looking elsewhere. By the reign of Edward VI, however, it had declined so much that his ministers invited Sebastian Cabot, by then Pilot-major of Spain, to return and advise them on finding new markets. There followed the Willoughby-Chancellor expedition of 1553 in search of the North-east Passage round Asia to China, which resulted in a new trade with Russia. Furthermore, intrepid merchants crossed Russia and the Caspian Sea to begin a hazardous but profitable trade with Persia, which continued until the Turkish invasions closed the route. Meanwhile the trade with West Africa grew, despite clashes with the Portuguese, and fishermen regularly visited the Newfoundland cod fisheries. All this 'put shipping to work', trained deep-sea sailors, encouraged the building of ocean-going ships and began to change public opinion.

It was only a beginning, however. When Elizabeth came to the throne in 1558 England was still a minor European power, recently defeated by France, poor, insecure, and dangerously divided by religious faction. There was nothing to show that before the end of the century this country would have emerged as a leading maritime nation whose future clearly lay upon the seas.

The process of change was inevitably confused. Many of the most significant and interesting of the seamen's successes and failures are recounted in the following pages, often by eyewitnesses, often with the eloquence natural to Elizabethan prose. There is no need to enumerate them here. Motives were very mixed: patriotism, love of adventure, a sincere longing to carry the Gospel to peoples who had never heard it, hatred of Spaniards and 'popery', and an eager desire for wealth and fame. In Drake and others all these motives were united. The most powerful common factor was that every venture was expected to bring home a profit, whether it was a single small ship, fitted out to capture a Spanish prize or two by a West Country gentle-man who had sold half his estate to raise the money, or a powerful naval expedition, commissioned by the Queen, with her own warships in the van, and financed by a syndicate of Privy Councillors, great noblemen, courtiers, rich merchants of London and Plymouth, and the Queen herself. Even John Davis, the most disinterested and scientific, and probably the most able of Elizabethan explorers, was reduced to catching fish in the Arctic to pay his expenses.

Among merchants, sea-captains and politicians there was a steadily growing ferment of ideas, arguments and plans, with a number of publicists fertilizing the discussions, most notably Dee and Hakluyt. Dr John Dee, was the leading mathematician, geographer and astrologer of the day. He had the ear of the Queen and her chief ministers. It was he, a Welshman, who coined the phrase 'the British Empire'. Richard Hakluyt too played a very important part. He was the greatest publicist of the day, not only through his collections of 'voyages' but through his numerous writings, translations, memoranda and private conversa-tions.

A few major aims predominated. First was the search for a North-east or North-west Passage, a search which was to cost many lives and defeat all explorers for another three hundred years. Its attractions were very great, since either Passage would have provided a short cut to Cathay, Cipangu and the Spice Islands, which would enable England to trade with them direct without crossing the Portuguese and Spanish zones. The geographers underestimated the difficulties of the Arctic ice and believed that there were clear sea-passages around both continents, trending southwards into warmer waters.

Another widely accepted myth was the *Terra Australis Incognita*. Contemporary maps and globes showed a great unknown continent in the south Pacific, separated from South America only by the Straits of Magellan and containing, among other fabled kingdoms, the land of Ophir, from which King Solomon drew his wealth. The English regarded this as outside the Spanish and Portuguese zones, so that if they could discover it they could legitimately establish an empire there. In fact Drake showed, on his voyage round the world, that the continent did not exist, or at least was not where the maps showed it, but the myth lingered until Captain Cook destroyed it in the eighteenth century.

Plans for settlements overseas were another recurrent theme, always with the hope of finding a territory rich in gold, silver and jewels, and if possible spices as well. Linked with these were plans to establish a naval base at a strategic point where it could command the sea-routes by which American treasure poured into Spain. Many sites were mooted in turn – the *Terra Australis*, the Pacific coast of South America, the Straits of Magellan (inhospitable as they were), the Atlantic coast of South America, the Spanish main (the Caribbean mainland, not the sea), a West Indian island, or the neighbourhood of Florida. These were much discussed but none was even attempted.

Much more far-sighted, and in the end productive, were the schemes 'for western planting' – for colonization, in the true sense, on the coast of North America, which England claimed through the Cabots' discoveries. Here the prime movers were not merchants or privateers looking for a quick profit but three West Country gentlemen: Sir Humphrey Gilbert, his half-brother Sir Walter Raleigh and his cousin Sir Richard Grenville, with constant encouragement from the two Hakluyts, John Dee and others. Gilbert mooted the idea as early as 1565. Richard Hakluyt's first collection, *Divers Voyages touching the discovery of America* (1582), was in support, and in 1584 he wrote a persuasive memorandum (first published in 1877), *A particular discourse concerning the great necessity and manifold commodities that are like to grow to this realm of England by the western discoveries lately attempted*. The advocates of western planting expected great commodities. It was to restore the national balance of payments by decreasing imports and increasing exports, and to relieve the alarming unemployment by finding new homes overseas for the unemployed.

The Queen did not subsidise the project, but she gave Gilbert a comprehensive charter to discover and govern new lands, and he put all the money he had into the first venture. The ship carrying the colonists and their stores sank with all hands off Nova Scotia, and on his return voyage Gilbert himself went down in his own ship, reminding his crew to the last that 'We are as near to heaven by sea as by land.'

Raleigh then obtained a similar charter. The expedition which he sent out in 1584 discovered what is now South Carolina and described it as an earthly paradise, which he named Virginia in compliment to the Queen. There followed several inefficient and ill-fated attempts at settlement, soon to be postponed and not to succeed until 1607, four years after Elizabeth's death.

It was the Armada campaign which enforced this postponement, and it was indeed the constantly changing relations between England and Spain which conditioned all Elizabethan maritime enterprise. When Elizabeth came to her insecure throne in 1558 she was most anxious to avoid offending Spain and until 1585 both she and Philip II wanted to avoid war, but that did not exclude many changes in policy and feeling.

In 1558 the Anglo-Spanish alliance of 1489 was still in full force, many English merchants were established in Spain, some of them trading with the New World, and trade with Spain was far too valuable to be lightly jeopardized. English intruders in the Caribbean were mainly peaceful until the treacherous defeat of John Hawkins at San Juan de Ulua in 1568 showed that peaceful trading was almost impossible and permanently embittered English seamen. Drake took his first revenge by his highly profitable raid on the treasure-trains in Panama in 1572–3, which gave fresh impetus to privateering in the Caribbean. His voyage round the world, from which the *Golden Hind* returned with her holds stuffed with Spanish treasure, made him the most famous sea-captain in Europe, a national hero and a rich man, and convinced a host of adventurers that plundering Spanish ships and settlements in the New World was the quickest way to wealth. Often they failed, sunk or captured, or defeated by mutiny or disease, but the game went on, to reach its heyday between 1585 and 1603. Meanwhile the relations between the two countries worsened. Religious fanaticism grew intense, Philip sent troops to support the Catholic rebels in Ireland and Elizabeth sent help to the Protestant rebels in the Spanish Netherlands, Spain took a hand in English Catholic plots to murder Elizabeth and put Mary Queen of Scots on the throne, and English privateers ravaged Spanish colonies. Yet almost to the day on which the Invincible Armada set sail for England Elizabeth clung to the hope of avoiding war and often fretted her sea-dogs by vetoing their plans. It was Philip who precipitated the downfall of Spanish pride.

Drake's brilliant career as navigator, privateer and naval commander brought dismay to Spain and inspiration to England. The achievement of John Hawkins was far less sensational but equally important. After the battle of San Juan he too fought his private war with Philip II, by building the kind of warships which he and Drake and others saw to be needed for the inevitable trial of national strength. The Royal Navy was the monarch's private property and Elizabeth had inherited a small, out-of-date fleet, including only twenty-two ships of more than a hundred tons, which had been rotted by neglect and by gross corruption in the Navy Board and the dockyards – a corruption continued into her own reign. Lord Burghley, himself an honest man, recognized the honesty, and the expertise, of Hawkins, whom he appointed Treasurer of the Navy in 1577.

The typical medieval ships of northern Europe were the 'round ships', with a keel-length only about twice their beam, square-rigged on their two or three masts, pot-bellied, clumsy, and reluctant to answer the helm. Fore and aft they had tall castles which could be filled with soldiers, and in a naval battle the ships were simply floating forts to be grappled so that the soldiers could fight it out hand-to-hand. They had no heavy guns. Such ships were quite unsuitable for ocean voyaging, as the ponderous *Jesus of Lübeck* showed Hawkins and Drake conclusively before she came to her end at San Juan de Ulua. The Portuguese and Spaniards had developed the galleon, with a keel-length three times the beam, or more, and with lower castles and lateen sails on the mizzen and bonaventure mizzen masts. Henry VIII had initiated the arming of ships with heavy guns, not sited in the already top-heavy castles but firing through gun-ports in the sides, and Hawkins adopted this vital principle in fighting galleons, which he succeeded in building in the teeth of opposition from the rest of the Navy Board. His ships, with their low forecastles, sailed closer to the wind than any others, were quicker in manoeuvre and were armed to shatter enemy ships at long range, not to grapple and board. The *Revenge* was the prototype, built in 1577, a galleon of 500 tons, 92 feet in length, 32 feet in the beam, 15 feet in depth, with a heavy armament of some forty guns. Drake chose her for his flagship against the Armada, and it was in her that Grenville fought his last fight.

In time of war, however, the Royal Navy never faced the enemy alone. Any other ship might volunteer or be pressed into service, and it was fortunate for England that while Hawkins was building a Navy the number of privateers and well-armed ocean-going merchantmen steadily increased, most or all of them practised in attacking Spanish ships or fighting their way through the pirate-infested Mediterranean. The fleet which harried the Armada up the Channel was such a *levée en masse* as England was not to see again until the little ships went to Dunkirk.

To the Elizabethans building ships was less difficult than maintaining experienced crews, largely because the wastage from disease was so terrible. The seamen were packed together, for months or years at a stretch, in cramped, uncomfortable, verminous quarters which must have been almost unbearable in the tropics, with no sanitation, no rules of hygiene, no understanding of diet and disease. Provisions were often scanty and bad. Naturally they varied from ship to ship, and they were supplemented whenever possible by fresh fish and shell-fish and fresh or salted penguins, seals and any other edible creature; but in the main they consisted of salt beef, pork and fish, cheese and biscuit, with occasional delicacies added, with water (often foul), beer and wine. Victuallers, notoriously dishonest, were apt to supply meat that was already putrid, beer that already stank, and short measure in everything. Disease was rampant: food poisoning, dysentery, typhus, fevers and above all, on every long voyage, 'the plague of the sea and the spoil of mariners', scurvy. Sir Richard Hawkins estimated that in twenty years scurvy had killed ten thousand English seamen. It was common for more than half the crew to die on a voyage, and many a ship must have been lost because the survivors were too few and too weak to work her. In the battle with the Armada less than a hundred men were killed by enemy action, while thousands died of food poisoning and plague. Yet men may often have been better off aboard ship than begging a living in disease-ridden dockside slums. Moreover there was often the chance of plunder, which might be considerable. A third of it was usually shared out among the crew, according to their rank, while the rest went to the owners and victuallers.

The sailors were for the most part ignorant, superstitious and mercurial, prone to vacillate between cowardice and bravado or the most stubborn courage, and notoriously difficult to manage. 'I know sailors to be the most envious people of the world, and so unruly without government', said Drake. Mutiny and desertion were common. The Master, responsible for navigating the ship and directing the crew, had been bred a seaman, but the Captain, who was in command, might be a landsman with little or no knowledge of the sea, and friction between them would be aggravated if the ship carried gentlemen adventurers, a privileged class who did no work and showed their contempt for the sailors. A force of several ships was usually controlled, not by the Captain-General, despite his title, but by a council of senior officers, and any captain who disagreed with their decisions was likely to leave the fleet and often did; or his crew might compel him to do so. Maps and charts were often inaccurate and sometimes lacking. Compass, cross-staff, back-staff, quadrant and astrolabe were in use, and latitude might be found fairly accurately, but there was no way of calculating longitude. When a ship was out of sight of known land its position was largely a matter of guess-work based on experience. As the century progressed there was much discussion and improvement of navigational methods, but every ocean voyage was still to some extent a venture into the unknown.

Yet dangerous, grim and brutish as life at sea often was, it had the lure of great adventure and possible profit, and something of the panoply of romance, the colourful 'bravery' so dear to Elizabethans; the gaily-painted scroll-work of the ships' hulls, the decoration of sails, banners and pennants, the musicians playing while the captain dined, the trumpets that sang to battle. . . . Apparently crews could always be found, and sea-captains, famous or unknown, to lead them. Only 'fortunate Drake', 'the master-thief of the unknown world', seems to have combined in himself nearly all the qualities which the sea demanded; his greed and arrogance were eclipsed by his genius for seamanship and leadership, his inexhaustible courage and resource and his humanity to his prisoners. Few captains were as shrewd and prudent as Sir John Hawkins, as reckless as Sir Richard Grenville, as scientific as John Davis, as tough as that muscular ex-pirate, Sir Martin Frobisher, as accomplished and haughty as Sir Walter Raleigh, or as matter-of-fact as Roger Bodenham – and few as insane as Thomas Windham. But there were many others who played their parts, well or ill. The age shaped them and they shaped England's future. They often came to unhappy ends. But they were fortunate, as we are, that they had such a chronicler as Richard Hakluyt.

The *Voyages* are an imposing monument to his devotion; the twelve portly volumes of the Hakluyt Society's standard edition must comprise something like one and a quarter million words. This great length has evidently daunted scholars. Many other Elizabethan texts have been edited in the fullest detail, and the labours of generations of patient editors have explained almost every reference, every strange word. The *Voyages* have been passed over. Even the compilers of the great *Oxford English Dictionary* seem to have given scanty attention to Hakluyt's vocabulary. There is no glossary to the *Voyages* as a whole, and indeed there are some corrupt phonetic renderings of remote foreign words and place-names which might always defy interpretation. The present editor regrets that he has not found an explanation of every word and reference which the reader might like explained, but these failures are not numerous enough, it is hoped, to lessen the reader's enjoyment.

One omission calls for special comment. No attempt has been made to give the present-day value of sixteenth-century money, English or Spanish, because no generally accepted figure can be given. In his life of *Sir Francis Drake*, 1951, page 46, the great authority on the Tudor seamen, Dr James A. Williamson, states that £40,000, Elizabethan, was worth 'about a million of our modern money', but no doubt some economists would dispute this, and obviously there is the further problem of inflation since 1951.

The *Voyages* vary a great deal. Some are very long and prosy, some very short. Some are as pedantic as Clement Adams! Some are crude extracts from ships' logs kept by master-mariners for whom the sword was mightier than the pen. Some are the work of accomplished writers such as Raleigh and Hakluyt, some have an unconscious eloquence and evocative power. Most of them bear the hall-mark of personal experience. This selection contains less than a tenth of the original work. The *Voyages* included have been chosen for their intrinsic interest and readability, whether they are of great historical importance or provide vivid side-lights on the time. They cover every quarter of the globe into which Tudor seamen ventured before 1600. The spelling and the use of capitals have been modernized, and paragraphs of inordinate length have been broken up, but idiom and syntax have not been altered or the inconsistencies characteristic of Elizabethan writing. No attempt has been made to 'improve' Hakluyt and the full flavour of the originals has been retained.

J.H.

1969

NOTE ON BOOKS

The principal navigations, voyages, traffics and discoveries of the English nation . . . by Richard Hakluyt, the second edition, revised and very much enlarged, was first published in three volumes, folio, in 1598, 1599 and 1600. The standard modern edition, in the original spelling, is that of the Hakluyt Society, 12 volumes, 1903–5. There is a good edition in Everyman's Library, 8 volumes, 1907; reprinted 1962. Important narratives not in 'Hakluyt' include *Sir Francis Drake Revived*, by Philip Nichols and others, 1626; in *Sir Francis Drake's Raid on the Treasure Trains*, edited by Janet and John Hampden, Folio Society, 1954: *The World Encompassed by Sir Francis Drake*, 1628; edited by N. M. Penzer, with contemporary documents and a long essay by Sir Richard Carnac Temple, 1926: *The observations of Sir Richard Hawkins, Knight, in his voyage to the South Sea, anno domini 1593*, 1622; edited by James A. Williamson, 1933.

There is a short life of Hakluyt, by James A. Williamson, in *Richard Hakluyt and his successors*, edited by Edward Lynam, 1946.

The very numerous modern works on the Elizabethan seamen include *The Age of Drake*, by James A. Williamson, 5th edition, 1966; *The Expansion of Elizabethan England*, by A. L. Rowse, 1955; *Hawkins of Plymouth*, by James A. Williamson, 1949; *The defeat of John Hawkins*, by Rayner Unwin, 1960; *Sir Francis Drake*, by Christopher Lloyd, 1957; *Drake's Voyages*, by Kenneth R. Andrews, 1967; *The Defeat of the Spanish Armada*, by Garrett Mattingly, 1959; *The Spanish Armada*, by Michael Lewis, 1960; *Sir Walter Raleigh*, by Norman Lloyd Williams, 1962; *Sir Richard Grenville of the Revenge*, by A. L. Rowse, 1940.

J.H.

THE EPISTLE DEDICATORY
IN THE FIRST EDITION, 1589

This dedication, given here for its autobiographical, historical and literary interest, was not reprinted in the much enlarged second edition, three volumes folio, of 1598, 1599 and 1600, in which the first volume is dedicated to Lord Charles Howard, Lord High Admiral of England, and the second and third volumes are dedicated to Sir Robert Cecil. It is this second edition, The principal navigations, voiages, traffiques and discoveries of the English nation . . ., *which is commonly known as 'Hakluyt'. All the 'voyages' in this book are taken from it.*

To the Right Honourable Sir Francis Walsingham, Knight, Principal Secretary to Her Majesty, Chancellor of the Duchy of Lancaster, and one of Her Majesty's Most Honourable Privy Council.

RIGHT Honourable, I do remember that being a youth, and one of Her Majesty's scholars at Westminster, that fruitful nursery, it was my hap to visit the chamber of Mr Richard Hakluyt, my cousin, a gentleman of the Middle Temple, well known unto you, at a time when I found lying open upon his board certain books of cosmography, with a universal map. He, seeing me somewhat curious in view thereof, began to instruct my ignorance by showing me the division of the earth into three parts after the old account, and then, according to the latter and better distribution, into more. He pointed with his wand to all the known seas, gulfs, bays, straits, capes, rivers, empires, kingdoms, dukedoms and territories of each part, with declaration also of their special commodities and particular wants which, by the benefit of traffic and intercourse of merchants, are plentifully supplied. From the map he brought me to the Bible and, turning to the 107th Psalm, directed me to the 23rd and 24th verses, where I read that they which go down to the sea in ships and occupy by the great waters, they see the works of the Lord and His wonders in the deep, etc. Which words of the Prophet, together with my cousin's discourse (things of high and rare delight to my young nature), took in me so deep an impression that I constantly resolved, if ever I were preferred to the university, where better time and more convenient place might be ministered for these studies, I would, by God's assistance, prosecute that knowledge and kind of literature, the doors whereof (after a sort) were so happily opened before me.

According to which my resolution when, not long after, I was removed to Christ Church in Oxford, my exercises of duty first performed, I fell to my intended course, and by degrees read over whatsoever printed or written discoveries and voyages I found extant either in the Greek, Latin, Italian, Spanish, Portugal, French, or English languages, and in my public lectures was the first that produced and showed both the old imperfectly composed and the new lately reformed maps, globes, spheres, and other instruments of this art for demonstration in the common schools, to the singular pleasure and general contentment of my auditory.

In continuance of time, and by reason principally of my insight in this study, I grew familiarly acquainted with the chiefest captains at sea, the greatest merchants and the best mariners of our nation: by which means having gotten somewhat more than common knowledge, I passed at length the narrow seas into France with Sir Edward Stafford, Her Majesty's careful and discreet ligier [ambassador], where, during my five years abroad with him in his dangerous and chargeable residency in Her Highness' service, I both heard in speech and read in books other nations miraculously extolled for their discoveries and notable enterprises by sea, but the English of all others, for their sluggish security and continual neglect of the like attempts, especially in so long and happy a time of peace, either ignominiously reported or exceedingly condemned; which singular opportunity if some other people our neighbours had been blessed with, their protestations are often and vehement, they would far otherwise have used.

And that the truth and evidence hereof may better appear, these are the very words of Popiliniere in his book called *L'Admiral de France*, and printed at Paris. Folio 73, pages 1, 2. The occasion of his speech is the commendation of the Rhodians, who being (as we are) islanders, were excellent in navigation, whereupon he wondereth much that the English should not surpass in that quality, in this sort:

'Ce qui m'a fait autrefois rechercher les occasions, qui empêchent que les Anglais, qui ont d'esprit, de moyens et valeur assez pour s'acquérir un grand honneur parmi tous les Chrétiens, ne se font plus valoir sur l'élément qui leur est et doit être plus naturel qu'à autres peuples: qui leur doivent céder en la structure, accommodement et police de navires, comme j'ai vu en plusieurs endroits parmi eux.'

Thus both hearing and reading the obloquy of our nation and finding few or none of our own men able to reply herein; and further, not seeing any man to have care to recommend to the world the industrious labours and painful travels of our countrymen; for stopping the mouths of the reproachers, myself being the last winter returned from France with the Honourable The Lady Sheffield, for her passing good behaviour highly esteemed in all the French Court, determined notwithstanding all difficulties to undertake the burden of that work wherein all others pretended either ignorance, or lack of leisure, or want of sufficient argument, whereas (to speak truly) the huge toil and the small profit to ensue were the chief causes of the refusal. I call the work a burden in consideration that these voyages lay so dispersed, scattered, and hidden in several hucksters' hands that I now wonder at myself, to see how I was able to endure the delays, curiosity, and backwardness of many from whom I was to receive my originals: so that I have just cause to make that complaint of the maliciousness of divers in our time which Pliny made of the men of his age:

'At nos elaborata iis abscondere atque supprimere cupimus, et fraudare vitam etiam alienis bonis, etc.'★

To harp no longer upon this string and to speak a word of that just commendation which our nation do indeed deserve, it cannot be denied, but as in all former ages, they have been men full of activity, stirrers abroad, and searchers of the remote parts of the world, so in this most famous and peerless Government of Her Most Excellent Majesty, Her subjects through the special assistance and blessing of God, in searching the most opposite corners and quarters of the world and, to speak plainly, in compassing the vast globe of the earth more than once,† have excelled all the nations and people of the earth. For which of the kings of this land before Her Majesty had their banners ever seen in the Caspian Sea? Which of them hath ever dealt with the Emperor of Persia as Her Majesty hath done, and obtained for Her merchants large and loving privileges? Who ever saw before this regiment an English ligier in the stately porch of the Grand Signor at Constantinople? Who ever found English consuls and agents at Tripoli in Syria, at Aleppo, at Babylon [Cairo], at Balsara, and, which is more, who ever heard of Englishmen at Goa before now? What English ships did heretofore ever anchor in the mighty River of Plate, pass and repass the unpassable (in former opinion) Strait of Magellan, range along the coast of Chile, Peru, and all the backside of Nova Hispania further than any Christian ever passed, traverse the mighty breadth of the South Sea, land upon the Luzons [Philippines] in despite of the enemy,

★ 'But we indeed want to cover up and conceal their efforts, and even to rob the world of other men's good works etc.'
† By Francis Drake in 1577–80 and by Thomas Cavendish in 1586–8.

enter into alliance, amity and traffic with the Princes of the Moluccas and the Isle of Java, double the famous Cape of Bona Speranza, arrive at the Isle of St Helena, and, last of all, return home most richly laden with the commodities of China, as the subjects of this now flourishing Monarchy have done?

Lucius Florus, in the very end of his history *De Gestis Romanorum*, recordeth as a wonderful miracle that the Seres (which I take to be the people of Cathay or China) sent Ambassadors to Rome to entreat friendship, as moved with the fame of the majesty of the Roman Empire. And have not we as good cause to admire that the Kings of the Moluccas and Java Major have desired the favour of Her Majesty, and the commerce and traffic of her people? Is it not as strange that the born naturals of Japan and the Philippines are here to be seen, agreeing with our climate, speaking our language, and informing us of the state of their eastern habitations? For mine own part, I take it as a pledge of God's further favour both unto us and them: to them especially, unto whose doors I doubt not in time shall be by us carried the incomparable treasure of the truth of Christianity and of the Gospel, while we use and exercise common trade with their merchants. I must confess to have read in the excellent history entitled, *Origins* of Joannes Goropius, a testimony of King Henry the VIII, a Prince of noble memory, whose intention was once, if death had not prevented him, to have done some singular thing in this case; whose words, speaking of his dealing to that end with himself, he being a stranger and his history rare, I thought good in this place verbatim to record:

'Ante viginti et plus eo annos ab Henrico Knevetto Equite Anglo nomine Regis Henrici arram accepi, qua convenerat, Regio sumptu me totam Asiam, quod Turcorum et Persarum Regum commendationes, et legationes admitterentur, peragraturum. Ab his enim duobus Asiae principibus facile se impetraturum sperabat, ut non solum tuto mihi per ipsorum fines liceret ire, sed ut commendatione etiam ipsorum ad confinia quoque daretur penetrare. Sumptus quidem non exiguus erat futurus, sed tanta erat principi cognoscendi aviditas, ut nullis pecuniis ad hoc iter necessariis se diceret parsurum. O Dignum Regia Majestate animum, O me foelicem, si Deus non ante et Knevettum & Regem abstulisset, quam reversus ab hac peregrinatione fuissem, etc.'*

* 'Some twenty or more years before, I had received a pledge – as far as that was possible – from Henry Knevett, English knight, in the name of King Henry, that I should travel throughout Asia at the king's expense. The king was at that time receiving letters of commendation and embassies from the kings of the Turks and the Persians, and he hoped that he would easily be able to obtain for me from these two kings not only right of passage through their own territories, but also at their request the opportunity of penetrating as far as the territories of their

But as the purpose of David the King to build a house and temple to God was accepted, although Solomon performed it, so I make no question but that the zeal in this matter of the aforesaid most renowned Prince may seem no less worthy (in his kind) of acceptation, although reserved for the person of our Solomon, Her Gracious Majesty, whom I fear not to pronounce to have received the same heroical spirit and most honourable disposition as an inheritance from her famous father.

Now whereas I have always noted your wisdom to have had a special care of the honour of Her Majesty, the good reputation of our country and the advancing of navigation, the very walls of this our Island, as the oracle is reported to have spoken of the sea forces of Athens: and whereas I acknowledge in all dutiful sort how honourably both by your letter and speech I have been animated in this and other my travails, I see myself bound to make presentment of this work to yourself as the fruits of your own encouragements and the manifestation both of my unfeigned service to my Prince and country, and of my particular duty to your honour: which I have done with the less suspicion either of not satisfying the world, or of not answering your own expectation in that according to your order it hath passed the sight and partly also the censure of the learned physician, Master Doctor James, a man many ways very notably qualified.

And thus beseeching God, the giver of all true honour and wisdom, to increase both these blessings in you, with continuance of health, strength, happiness, and whatsoever good thing else yourself can wish, I humbly take my leave. London, the 17 of November.

Your Honour's most humble, always to be commanded,

RICHARD HAKLUYT

neighbours. The expense indeed would be no small matter, but the king was so eager for knowledge that he declared he would spare no money necessary for this journey. Oh mind worthy of kingly majesty, oh happy me, if God had not taken from this world both Knevett and the King before I returned from my wanderings.'

WILLIAM HAWKINS REACHES BRAZIL

Richard Hakluyt

The Portuguese discovered Brazil in 1500–2, the only part of South America not claimed by the Spaniards; they established a few settlements along the coast and claimed a monopoly of trade, here and also on the Guinea coast, which William Hawkins visited en route. There was a valuable trade in brazil wood, which was used in dyeing and which gave its name to the country. Hawkins was among the interlopers who disputed the monopoly, but if he had to fight the Portuguese his son John Hawkins was too cautious to say so, or Hakluyt was too cautious to record it.

A brief relation of two sundry voyages made by the Worshipful Master William Hawkins of Plymouth, father to Sir John Hawkins, Knight, late treasurer of Her Majesty's Navy, in the years 1530 and 1532.

OLD Master William Hawkins of Plymouth, a man for his wisdom, valour, experience and skill in sea-causes much esteemed, and beloved of King Henry VIII, and being one of the principal sea-captains in the West parts of England in his time, not contented with the short voyages commonly then made only to the known coasts of Europe, armed out a tall and goodly ship of his own of the burden of 250 tons, called the *Paul of Plymouth*, wherewith he made three long and famous voyages unto the coast of Brazil, a thing in those days very rare, especially to our nation. In the course of which voyages he touched at the River of Sestos upon the coast of Guinea, where he trafficked with the negroes and took of them elephants' teeth and other commodities which the place yieldeth. And so arriving on the coast of Brazil, he used there such discretion and behaved himself so wisely with those savage people that he grew into great familiarity and friendship with them. Insomuch that in his second voyage one of the savage kings of the country of Brazil was contented to take ship with him, and to be transported hither into England: whereunto Master Hawkins agreed, leaving behind in the country as a pledge for his safety and return again one Martin Cockeram of Plymouth. This

Brazilian King, being arrived, was brought up to London and presented to King Henry VIII, lying as then at Whitehall: at the sight of whom the King and all the nobility did not a little marvel, and not without cause; for in his cheeks were holes made according to their savage manner, and therein small bones were planted standing an inch out from the said holes, which in his own country was reputed for a great bravery. He had also another hole in his nether lip wherein was set a precious stone about the bigness of a pea. All his apparel, behaviour and gesture were very strange to the beholders.

Having remained here the space almost of a whole year, and the King with his sight fully satisfied, Master Hawkins, according to his promise and appointment, purposed to convey him again into his country: but it fell out in the way that by change of air and alteration of diet the said savage King died at sea, which was feared would turn to the loss of the life of Martin Cockeram, his pledge. Nevertheless the savages, being fully persuaded of the honest dealing of our men with their Prince, restored again the said pledge without any harm to him or any man of the company: which pledge of theirs they brought home again into England, with their ship freighted and furnished with the commodities of the country. Which Martin Cockeram, by the witness of Sir John Hawkins, being an officer in the town of Plymouth, was living within these few years.

THE NEW FOUND LAND

Richard Hakluyt

The Venetian navigator, John Cabot, commanding an English ship out of Bristol under licence from Henry VII, discovered Newfoundland, or Nova Scotia, and the very valuable cod fisheries, in 1497. Very soon the banks were being fished regularly by fishermen of several nations and voyages to Newfoundland were frequent. Sir Humphrey Gilbert annexed it in 1583 but it was not colonised for another hundred years.

The reference to cannibalism in this account seems to be the only one in Hakluyt, but it may not have been very uncommon, since ships' crews often found themselves dying of starvation.

The voyage of Master Hore and divers other gentlemen to Newfoundland and Cape Briton, in the year 1536, and in the 28th year of King Henry the Eighth.

ONE, Master Hore of London, a man of goodly stature and of great courage and given to the study of cosmography, in the 28th year of King Henry the Eighth and in the year of Our Lord 1536, encouraged divers gentlemen and others, being assisted by the King's favour and good countenance, to accompany him in a voyage of discovery upon the northwest parts of America: wherein his persuasions took such effect that within short space many gentlemen of the Inns of Court, and of the Chancery, and divers others of good worship, desirous to see the strange things of the world, very willingly entered into the action with him, some of whose names were as followeth: Master Weeks, a gentleman of the West country of five hundred marks by the year living, Master Tuck, a gentleman of Kent, Master Tuckfield, Master Thomas Butts, the son of Sir William Butts Knight, of Norfolk, which was lately living and from whose mouth I wrote most of this relation, Master Hardy, Master Byron, Master Carter, Master Wright, Master Rastal, Sergeant Rastal's brother, Master Ridley, and divers other, which all were in the admiral★ called the *Trinity*, a ship of seven score tons, wherein Master Hore himself was embarked.

★ The 'admiral' was the flagship. The commander of the expedition was usually called 'Captain-general'.

In the other ship, whose name was the *Minion*, went a very learned and virtuous gentleman, one Master Armigil Wade, afterwards Clerk of the Councils of King Henry the Eighth and King Edward the Sixth, father to the Worshipful Master William Wade, now Clerk of the Privy Council, Master Oliver Daubeny, merchant of London, Master Joy, afterward Gentleman of the King's Chapel, with divers other of good account. The whole number that went in the two tall ships aforesaid, to wit, the *Trinity* and the *Minion*, were about six score persons, whereof thirty were gentlemen, which all we mustered in warlike manner at Gravesend, and after the receiving of the sacrament they embarked themselves in the end of April, 1536.

From the time of their setting out from Gravesend they were very long at sea, to wit, above two months, and never touched any land until they came to part of the West Indies about Cape Briton, shaping their course thence north-eastwards until they came to the island of Penguin, which is very full of rocks and stones, whereon they went and found it full of great fowls, white and grey, as big as geese, and they saw infinite numbers of their eggs. They drave a great number of the fowls into their boats upon their sails, and took up many of their eggs; the fowls they flead [skinned] and their skins were very like honeycombs full of holes being flead off: they dressed and eat them and found them to be very good and nourishing meat. They saw also store of bears, both black and white, of whom they killed some and took them for no bad food.

Master Oliver Daubeny, which (as it is before mentioned) was in this voyage and in the *Minion*, told Master Richard Hakluyt of the Middle Temple these things following: to wit, that after their arrival in Newfoundland, and having been there certain days at anchor and not having yet seen any of the natural people of the country, the same Daubeny, walking one day on the hatches, spied a boat with savages of those parts rowing down the bay toward them to gaze upon the ship and our people, and taking view of their coming aloof, he called to such as were under the hatches and willed them to come up if they would see the natural people of the country that they had so long and so much desired to see: whereupon they came up and took view of the savages rowing toward them and their ship, and upon the view they manned out a ship-boat to meet them and to take them. But they, spying our ship-boat making towards them, returned with main force and fled into an island that lay up in the bay or river there, and our men pursued them into the island and the savages fled and escaped: but our men found a fire and the side of a bear on a wooden spit left at the same by the savages that were fled.

There in the same place they found a boot of leather garnished on the outward side of the calf with certain brave trails, as it were of raw silk, and also found a certain great warm mitten: and these carried with them they returned to their ship, not finding the savages, nor seeing anything else besides the soil and the things growing in the same, which chiefly were store of fir and pine trees.

And further, the said Master Daubeny told him that lying there they grew into great want of victuals and that there they found small relief, [not] more than that they had from the nest of an osprey that brought hourly to her young great plenty of divers sorts of fishes. But such was the famine that increased amongst them from day to day that they were forced to seek to relieve themselves of raw herbs and roots that they sought on the main: but the famine increasing and the relief of herbs being to little purpose to satisfy their insatiable hunger, in the fields and deserts here and there the fellow killed his mate while he stopped to take up a root for his relief, and cutting out pieces of his body whom he had murdered broiled the same on the coals and greedily devoured them.

By this mean the company decreased, and the officers knew not what was become of them. And it fortuned that one of the company, driven with hunger to seek abroad for relief, found out in the fields the savour of broiled flesh, and fell out with one for that he would suffer him and his fellows to starve, enjoying plenty as he thought: and this matter growing to cruel speeches, he that had the broiled meat burst out into these words, 'If thou wouldst needs know, the broiled meat that I had was a piece of such a man's buttock'.

The report of this brought to the ship, the Captain found what became of those that were missing and was persuaded that some of them were neither devoured with wild beasts nor yet destroyed with savages. And hereupon he stood up and made a notable oration, containing how much these dealings offended the Almighty, and vouched the Scriptures from first to last what God had in cases of distress done for them that called upon him, and told them that the power of the Almighty was then no less than in all former time it had been: and added that if it had not pleased God to have holpen them in that distress that it had been better to have perished in body, and to have lived everlastingly, than to have relieved for a poor time their mortal bodies, and to be condemned everlastingly both body and soul to the unquenchable fire of hell. And thus having ended to that effect he began to exhort to repentance, and besought all the company to pray that it might please God to look upon their miserable present state and for His own mercy to relieve the same.

The famine increasing, and the inconvenience of the men that were missing being found, they agreed amongst themselves rather than all should perish to cast lots who should be killed. And such was the mercy of God that the same night there arrived a French ship in that part, well furnished with victual, and such was the policy of the English that they became masters of the same, and changing ships and victualling them they set sail to come into England.

In their journey they were so far northwards that they saw mighty islands of ice in the summer season on which were hawks and other fowls to rest themselves, being weary of flying overfar from the main. They saw also certain great white fowls with red bills and red legs, somewhat bigger than herons, which they supposed to be storks. They arrived at St Ives in Cornwall about the end of October. From thence they departed unto a certain castle belonging to Sir John Luttrell, where Master Thomas Butts and Master Rastal and other gentlemen of the voyage were very friendly entertained. After that they came to the Earl of Bath at Bath, and thence to Bristol, so to London.

Master Butts was so changed in the voyage with hunger and misery that Sir William, his father, and my lady, his mother, knew him not to be their son until they found a secret mark which was a wart upon one of his knees, as he told me, Richard Hakluyt of Oxford, himself, to whom I rode 200 miles only to learn the whole truth of this voyage from his own mouth as being the only man now alive that was in this discovery.

Certain months after those Frenchmen came into England and made complaint to King Henry the Eighth: the King, causing the matter to be examined, and finding the great distress of his subjects and the causes of the dealing so with the French, was so moved with pity that he punished not his subjects, but of his own purse made full and royal recompense unto the French.

In this distress of famine the English did somewhat relieve their vital spirits by drinking at the springs the fresh water out of certain wooden cups out of which they had drunk their aqua composita before.

Map of the World by Rumold Mercator, 1587

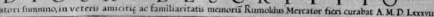

DIOSA DESCRIPTIO

...tori summino, in veteris amicitię ac familiaritatis memoriā Rumoldus Mercator fieri curabat A. M. D. Lxxxvii

proprio motu, anno uno eclipticem permeat obliquè aequinoctialem secās & ad 13. cui rsus utrumq; polum recedens, ubi tropicus Cancri & Capricorni notantur. Meridiani sunt sectionem quaeuis & polos mundi descripti, ideo Meridiani dicti, quod in illo constitute a quisub eodem in eodem hemisphaerio duobus polis terminato habitent. mutationi quaeue accidentia in regiones & diuersas sphaerae partes afferant. andi. Meridia m & longitudinis siue horarum differentiam duorum quorumlibet locorum indicant. Con graphi initium longitudinum in meridiano qui per occidentalissimam insulam Canariarum orientem longitudinem computant, quia proprius astrorum motus per quem longitudines occasu in ortum tendit. Differentia autem longitudinis duorum locorum, ex distantiameri ex aequinoctiali patescit, cognoscitur. Vt si Meridiani illorum 30. gradibus in aequatore à se entia longitudinis eorum 30. gradum & duorum horarum differentia, sit ut cum in occi cima, in orientali erit duodecima, duobus enim horis sol ab orientaltoris meridiano perue ridianum meridio atenim 24. horis totum globum terrae ambit. Praeterea diuiduntur admodum aequinoctialis, & numerantur ab aequinoctiali utrinque ad polum 90, Arcticum designant latitudinem borealem, uersus Antarcticum uero meridionalem, et quot eodemq; hemisphaerio polis terminatae sunt loca diuersae latitudinis, eandem semper eodem nt aut cum unus computat horam 8. cum dimidia, reliqui omnes tantundē numerant. Paral siores uocant, quia eorum planities non per centrum mundi transit, ansi à Meridiani gradibat

designanturiuxta eorum latitudinem, sic tropici duo, Cancri & Capricorni, gradum latitudinis 23. cum dimidio in meridianis omnibus occupant. Arcticus autem & Antarcticus circuli 66. cum dimidio, qui circuli zonas quinq; com prehendunt, inter duos tropicos sitam, torridam uocant quod sol perpetuo supra eā uersosi omnia libiorreat & in tensum calorem afferat duae inter tropicos et Arcticū Antarcticum q; temperatae dicuntur, quod melio modo inter calidissimam & frigidissimam se habeant, reliquae intra Arcticā unā & intra Antarcticum altera, frigidae sunt ut pote à sole remotissimae. Rursum quia in diuersa latitudine etiam diuersa sit quantitas dici, unicuiq; distiorum sint uni uersam latitudinem ab aequinoctiali ad polum usq; per certos aliquot Parallelos, in quibus primam latitudinem notat in qua maxima dies maxima q; nox super perpetuam aequalitate, quae est in aequinoctiali quadrante unius horae crescit secunda illam in qua dimidia horae, tertius in qua tribus quadrantibus et sic deinceps donec parallelorū nicitas per fenibor as tantum differentias consider at tandem etiam per horas integras, dies, hebdomedes, menses, ita ut sub po lo unus tantum dies unaq; nox totum anni emetiantur. Inter hos parallelos constituerunt Veteres quina; spatia quae climata appellarunt, primum à tertio parallelo ad quintum usq; secundum hinc ad 7. tertium ad 9. quartum ad 11 quintum ad 13. Hucusq; putabant orbem habitari, uterius non propter intensū frigus, ab aequi noctiali etiam usq; ad tertium utrinq; per allelum, quod est medium torridae zonae, propter nimium aestum inhabitabilem crede bant, posteriores triesc lmat uersus polum addiderunt, at tandem inuentum est totam undique terram habitabilem esse, & sub aequinoctiali temperatiorem opinione calorem esse propter breuiorem Solis praesentiam, ut qui perpetuo 12. tantum horis supra horizontem manet, in frigidissima autem zone propter longissimos dies aestate calidiorem opinione aeteme esse, noctuq; propter uentorum raritatem ac debilitatem minus infrigidari. Vale & fructe.

A VOYAGE TO THE LEVANT

Roger Bodenham

English merchant-adventurers had long coveted a share of trade with the Mediterranean and especially with the Levant. There they could sell English woollens and load highly profitable cargoes of such Far Eastern spices, scents, silks and other luxuries as the great fleet of Venetian galleys brought every year to Southampton, Sandwich, London and Antwerp. Italian city-states whose wealth and power were built mainly on this trade did not welcome rivals; when a Bristol ship made the first English attempt to trade with the Levant in 1458 it was looted by the Genoese, and Turkish conquests in the eastern Mediterranean at the beginning of the sixteenth century added an even greater menace, as Roger Bodenham discovered.

The voyage of Master Bodenham with the great bark *Aucher* to Candia and Chios, in the year 1550.

IN the year 1550, the 13th of November, I, Roger Bodenham, Captain of the bark *Aucher*, entered the said ship at Gravesend for my voyage to the islands of Candia [Crete] and Chios in the Levant. The Master of my ship was one, William Sherwood. From thence we departed to Tilbury Hope, and there remained with contrary winds until the 6th of January, 1551. The 6th of January the Master came to Tilbury, and I had provided a skilful pilot to carry me over the land's end whose name was Master Wood, and with all speed I vailed down that night ten miles to take the tide in the morning, which happily I did, and that night came to Dover and there came to an anchor, and there remained until Tuesday, meeting with the worthy Knight, Sir Anthony Aucher, owner of the said ship.

The 11th day we arrived in Plymouth, and the 13th in the morning we set forward on our voyage with a prosperous wind, and the 16th we had sight of Cape Finisterre on the coast of Spain.

The 30th we arrived at Cadiz, and there discharged certain merchandise and took others aboard.

The 20th of February we departed from Cadiz, and passed the Straits of Gibraltar that night, and the 25th we came to the isle of Majorca, and stayed there five days with contrary winds.

The 1st of March we had sight of Sardinia, and the 5th of the said month we arrived at Messina in Sicilia and there discharged much goods, and remained there until Good Friday in Lent.

The chief merchant that laded the said bark *Aucher* was a merchant stranger called Anselm Salvago, and because the time was then very dangerous and no going into Levant, especially to Chios, without a safe conduct from the Turk, the said Anselm promised the owner, Sir Anthony Aucher, that we should receive the same at Messina. But I was posted from thence to Candia, and there I was answered that I should send to Chios and there I should have my safe conduct. I was forced to send one, and he had his answer that the Turk would give none, willing me to look what was best for me to do, which was no small trouble to me considering I was bound to deliver the goods that were in the ship at Chios or send them at mine adventure [risk]. The merchants, without care of the loss of the ship, would have compelled me to go or send their goods at mine adventure, the which I denied, and said plainly I would not go because the Turk's galleys were come forth to go against Malta, but by the French King's means he was persuaded to leave Malta and to go to Tripoli in Barbary, which by the French he won.

In this time there were in Candia certain Turks' vessels, called skyrasas, which had brought wheat thither to sell and were ready to depart for Turkey. And they departed in the morning betimes, carrying news that I would not go forth. The same night I prepared beforehand what I thought good without making any man privy until I saw time. Then I had no small business to cause my mariners to venture with the ship in such a manifest danger. Nevertheless I won them to go all with me, except three which I set on land, and with all diligence I was ready to set forth about eight of the clock at night, being a fair moonshine night, and went out. Then my three mariners made such requests unto the rest of my men to come aboard as I was constrained to take them in. And so with good wind we put into the archipelago, and being among the islands the wind scanted and I was forced to anchor at an island called Mykonos, where I tarried ten or twelve days, having a Greek pilot to carry the ship to Chios.

In this mean season there came many small boats with mizen sails to go for Chios with divers goods to sell, and the pilot requested me that I would let them go in my company, to which I yielded. After the said days expired I weighed and set sail for the island of Chios, with which place I fell in the afternoon, whereupon I cast to seaward again to come with the island in the morning betimes. The foresaid small vessels which came in my company departed from me to win the shore, to get in ye night, but upon a sudden they espied three foists★ of Turks

★ A foist was a small light galley with eighteen to twenty oars a side and two masts.

coming upon them to spoil them. My pilot, having a son in one of those small vessels, entreated me to cast about towards them, which at his request I did, and being something far from them I caused my gunner to shoot a demi-culverin at a foist that was ready to enter one of the boats. This was so happy a shot that it made the Turk to fall astern of the boat and to leave him, by the which means he escaped.

Then they all came to me and requested that they might hang at my stern until daylight, by which time I came before the Mole of Chios, and sent my boat on land to the merchants of that place to send for their goods out of hand, or else I would return back with all to Candia and they should fetch their goods there. But in fine, what by persuasion of my merchants' Englishmen and those of Chios I was entreated to come into the harbour, and had a safe assurance for twenty days against the Turks' army, with a bond of the city in the sum of 12,000 ducats. So I made haste and sold such goods as I had to Turks that came thither, and put all in order with as much speed as I could, fearing the coming of the Turks' navy, of the which the Chief of the city knew right well.

So upon the sudden they called me of great friendship and in secret told me I had no way to save myself but to be gone, for, said they, we be not able to defend you that are not able to help ourselves, for the Turk where he cometh taketh what he will and leaveth what he list, but the Chief of the Turks set order that none shall do any harm to the people or to their goods. This was such news to me that indeed I was at my wits end, and was brought into many imaginations how to do, for that the wind was contrary. In fine, I determined to go forth. But the merchants Englishmen and other, regarding more their gains than the ship, hindered me very much in my purpose of going forth, and made the mariners to come to me to demand their wages to be paid them out of hand, and to have a time to employ the same there. But God provided so for me that I paid them their money that night, and then charged them that if they would not set the ship forth I would make them to answer the same in England with danger of their heads. Many were married in England and had somewhat to lose; those did stick to me. I had twelve gunners: the master gunner, who was a mad-brained fellow, and the owner's servant had a parlament between themselves, and he upon the same came up to me with his sword drawn, swearing that he had promised the owner, Sir Anthony Aucher, to live and die in the said ship against all that should offer any harm to the ship, and that he would fight with the whole army of the Turks and never yield: with this fellow I had much to-do, but at the last I made him confess his fault and follow mine advice.

Thus with much labour I got out of the mole of Chios into the sea by warping forth, with the help of Genoese boats and a French boat that was in the mole, and being out God sent me a special gale of wind to go my way. Then I caused a piece to be shot off for some of my men that were yet in the town, and with much ado they came aboard, and then I set sail a little before one of the clock and I made all the sail I could, and about half an hour past two of the clock there came seven galleys into Chios to stay the ship: and the admiral of them was in a great rage because she was gone. Whereupon they put some of the best in prison, and took all the men of the three ships which I left in the port and put them into the galleys. They would have followed after me but that the townsmen found means they did not. The next day came thither a hundred more of galleys and there tarried for their whole company, which being together were about two hundred and fifty sail, taking their voyage for to surprise the island of Malta.*

The next day after I departed I had the sight of Candia, but I was two days after or ever I could get in, where I thought myself out of their danger. There I continued until the Turks' army was past, who came within the sight of the town. There was preparation made as though the Turks had come thither. There be in that island of Candia many banished men that live continually in the mountains; they came down to serve to the number of four or five thousand. They are good archers, every one with his bow and arrows, a sword and a dagger, with long hair, and boots that reach up to their groin, and a shirt of mail hanging the one half before and the other half behind. These were sent away again as soon as the army was past. They would drink wine out of all measure.

Then the army being past, I laded my ship with wines and other things: and so after I had that which I left in Chios I departed for Messina. In the way I found about Zante certain galliots of Turks lying aboard of certain vessels of Venice laden with muscatels. I rescued them, and had but a barrel of wine for my powder and shot. And within a few days after I came to Messina. I had in my ship a Spanish pilot called Noblezia which I took in at Cadiz at my coming forth: he went with me all this voyage into the Levant without wages, of goodwill that he bare me and the ship. He stood me in good stead until I came back again to Cadiz, and then I needed no pilot.

And so from thence I came to London with the ship and goods in safety, God be praised. And all those mariners that were in my said ship, which were, besides boys, threescore and ten, for the most part were within five or six years after able to take charge, and did. Richard Chancellor, who first discovered Russia, was with me in that voyage,

* This was not for the famous siege of Malta, in 1565, when the Knights of St John and the Maltese heroically repulsed a great Turkish force.

and Matthew Baker, who afterward became the Queen's Majesty's Chief Shipwright.

After Bodenham's dangerous voyage no further attempt was made to revive the trade with the Levant for another thirty years, and Bodenham joined the large colony of English merchants living in Spain. Like many others he took a Spanish name and a Spanish wife, and avoided religious difficulties by conforming, outwardly at least, with Catholic practice. One great advantage was that he was licensed to trade with Spanish America. He probably went also with the Spanish expedition to the Philippines in 1567. Once he was captured by Turkish pirates, who infested the Mediterranean and sometimes ventured into the Atlantic, but was fortunate enough to be ransomed. 'I pd for my bodye seven hunderd duckatts,' he wrote to a friend, 'wch a ffriend of myne layd out for me and how I shall paye it ageyne god knowis.' He became an English spy in Spain, as his extant letters to Burghley and Walsingham prove.

THE FIRST VOYAGE TO GUINEA AND BENIN

Anonymous

The Portuguese reached Guinea in 1446, in the progress down the west coast of Africa which brought them increasing trade in gold dust, pepper and ivory. It was more than a century before the English tried to break into the market, and the first attempt, made in the first year of Queen Mary, was one of the most peculiarly ill-fated of Tudor voyages.

The first voyage to Guinea and Benin

IN the year of our Lord 1553, the twelfth day of August, sailed from Portsmouth two goodly ships, the *Primrose* and the *Lion*, with a pinnace called the *Moon*, being all well furnished as well with men of the lustiest sort to the number of seven score as also with ordnance and victuals requisite to such a voyage: having also two Captains, the one a stranger [foreigner] called Anthony Anes Pinteado, a Portugal, born in a town named the Port of Portugal [Oporto], a wise, discreet and sober man, who for his cunning in sailing, being as well an expert pilot as a politic Captain, was sometime in great favour with the King of Portugal, and to whom the coasts of Brazil and Guinea★ were committed to be kept from the Frenchmen, to whom he was a terror on the sea in those parts, and was furthermore a gentleman of the King his master's house. But as fortune in manner never favoureth but flattereth, never promiseth but deceiveth, never raiseth but casteth down again : and as great wealth and favour have always companions, emulation and envy, he was after many adversities and quarrels made against him enforced to come into England, where in this golden voyage he was evil matched with an unequal companion, an unlike match of most sundry qualities and conditions, with virtues few or none adorned.

Thus departed these noble ships under sail on their voyage; but first Captain Wyndham, putting forth of his ship at Portsmouth, a kinsman of one of the head merchants, and showing herein a muster of the tragical parts he had conceived in his brain, and with such small

★ The Portuguese were the first to explore the coasts of West Africa (1415–88) and Brazil (1500) and they claimed a monopoly of trade which was disputed by the English, French and Dutch.

beginnings nourished so monstrous a birth that more happy, yea and blessed was that young man being left behind than if he had been taken with them, as some do wish he had done the like by theirs.

Thus sailed they on their voyage until they came to the island of Madeira, where they took in certain wines for the store of their ships and paid for them as they agreed of the price. At these islands they met with a great galleon of the King of Portugal, full of men and ordnance, yet such as could not have prevailed if it had attempted to withstand or resist our ships, for the which cause it was set forth not only to let [hinder] and interrupt these our ships of their purposed voyage but all other that should attempt the like: yet chiefly to frustrate our voyage. For the King of Portugal was sinisterly informed that our ships were armed to [attack] his castle in Mina [in the Gold Coast] in those parts, whereas nothing less was meant.

After that our ships departed from the island of Madeira forward on their voyage began this worthy Captain Pinteado's sorrow, as a man tormented with the company of a terrible hydra who hitherto flattered with him and made him a fair countenance and show of love. Then did he [Wyndham] take upon him to command all alone, setting nought both by Captain Pinteado and the rest of the merchants' factors, sometimes with opprobrious words and sometimes with threatenings most shamefully abusing them, taking from Pinteado the service of the boys and certain mariners that were assigned him by the order and direction of the worshipful merchants, and leaving him as a common mariner, which is the greatest despite and grief that can be to a Portugal or Spaniard, to be diminished of their honour, which they esteem above all riches.

Thus sailing forward on their voyage they came to the Islands of Canary, continuing their course from thence until they arrived at the island of St Nicholas, where they victualled themselves with fresh meat of the flesh of wild goats, whereof is great plenty in that island and in manner of nothing else. From hence, following on their course and tarrying here and there at the desert islands in the way, because they would not come too timely to the country of Guinea for the heat, and tarrying somewhat too long (for what can be well ministered in a commonwealth where inequality with tyranny will rule alone?) they came at the length to the first land of the country of Guinea, where they fell with [reached] the great river of Sestos, where they might for their merchandises have laden their ships with the grains of that country, which is a very hot fruit and much like unto a fig as it groweth on the tree. For as the figs are full of small seeds, so is the said fruit full of grains which are loose within the cod, having in the midst thereof a hole on every side. This kind of spice is much used in cold countries and may there be sold for great advantage for exchange of other wares. But our men, by the persuasion or rather enforcement of this tragical Captain, not regarding and setting light by that commodity in comparison of ye fine gold they thirsted, sailed an hundred leagues further until they came to the golden land, where, not attempting to come near the castle pertaining to the King of Portugal, which was within the river of Mina, they made sale of their ware only on this side and beyond it for the gold of that country to the quantity of an hundred and fifty pounds weight, there being in case that they might have despatched all their ware for gold if the untame brain of Wyndham had or could have given ear to the counsel and experience of Pinteado. For when that Wyndham, not satisfied with the gold which he had, and more might have had if he had tarried about the Mina, commanding the said Pinteado (for so he took upon him) to lead the ships to Benin, being under the Equinoctial line and an hundred and fifty leagues beyond the Mina, where he looked to have their ships laden with pepper. Being counselled of the said Pinteado considering the late time of the year for that time to go no further, but to make sale of their wares such as they had for gold, whereby they might have been great gainers, Wyndham not assenting hereunto fell into a sudden rage, reviling the said Pinteado, calling him Jew, with other opprobrious words, saying, 'This whoreson Jew hath promised to bring us to such places as are not, or as he cannot bring us unto: but if he do not I will cut off his ears and nail them to the mast.'

Pinteado gave the foresaid counsel to go no further for the safeguard of the men and their lives, which they should put in danger if they came too late for the rossia, which is their winter, not for cold but for smothering heat, with close and cloudy air and storming weather of such putrifying quality that it rotted the coats off their backs: or else for coming too soon for the scorching heat of the sun, which caused them to linger in the way. But of force and not of will brought he the ships before the river of Benin, where, riding at an anchor, they sent their pinnace up into the river 50 or 60 leagues, from whence certain of the merchants with Captain Pinteado, Francisco, a Portugal, Nicholas Lambart, gentleman, and other merchants were conducted to the Court where the King remained, ten leagues from the riverside, whither when they came they were brought with a great company to the presence of the King, who, being a black Moor (although not so black as the rest) sat in a great huge hall, long and wide, the walls made of earth, without windows, the roof of thin boards, open in sundry places like unto louvers to let in the air.

And here to speak of the great reverence they give to their King, it is such that if we would give as much to Our Saviour Christ we should remove from our heads many plagues which we daily deserve for our contempt and impiety. So it is, therefore, that when his noblemen are in his presence they never look him in the face, but sit cowering, as we upon our knees, so they upon their buttocks, with their elbows upon their knees and their hands before their faces, not looking up until the King command them. And when they are coming toward the King as far as they do see him they do show such reverence, sitting on the ground with their faces covered as before. Likewise, when they depart from him they turn not their backs toward him but go creeping backward with like reverence.

And now to speak somewhat of the communication that was between the King and our men, you shall first understand that he himself could speak the Portugal tongue which he had learned of a child. Therefore after he had commanded our men to stand up and demanded of them the cause of their coming into that country, they answered by Pinteado that they were merchants travelling into those parties for the commodities of his country for exchange of wares which they had brought from their countries, being such as should be no less commodious for him and his people. The King then having of old lying in a certain storehouse 30 or 40 kintals of pepper (every kintal being an hundredweight) willed them to look upon the same, and again to bring him a sight of such merchandises as they had brought with them. And thereupon sent with the Captain and the merchants certain of his men to conduct them to the water's side, with other to bring the ware from the pinnace to the Court; who when they were returned and the wares seen, the King grew to this end with the merchants to provide in thirty days the lading of all their ships with pepper. And in case their merchandises would not extend to the value of so much pepper he promised to credit them to their next return, and thereupon sent [to] the country round about to gather pepper, causing the same to be brought to the Court: so that within the space of thirty days they had gathered fourscore ton of pepper.

In the mean season our men, partly having no rule of themselves, but eating without measure of the fruits of the country and drinking the wine of the palm trees that droppeth in the night from the cut of the branches of the same, and in such extreme heat running continually into the water, not used before to such sudden and vehement alterations (than the which nothing is more dangerous) were thereby brought into swellings and agues; insomuch that the later time of the year coming on, caused them to die sometimes three and sometimes four or five in a day.

Then Wyndham, perceiving the time of the thirty days to be expired and his men dying so fast, sent to the Court in post to Captain

Pinteado and the rest to come away and to tarry no longer. But Pinteado with the rest wrote back to him again, certifying him of the great quantity of pepper they had already gathered, and looked daily for much more; desiring him furthermore to remember the great praise and name they should win if they came home prosperously, and what shame of the contrary.

With which answer Wyndham not satisfied and, many of their men dying daily, willed and commanded them again either to come away forthwith or else threatened to leave them behind. When Pinteado heard this answer, thinking to persuade him with reason, he took his way from the Court toward the ships, being conducted thither with men by the King's commandment.

In the mean season Wyndham, all raging, brake up Pinteado's cabin, brake open his chests, spoiled such provision of cold stilled waters and suckets [preserved fruits] as he had provided for his health, and left him nothing, neither of his instruments to sail by nor yet of his apparel: and in the meantime falling sick himself died also. Whose death Pinteado, coming aboard, lamented as much as if he had been the dearest friend he had in the world. But certain of the mariners and other officers did spit in his face, some calling him Jew, saying that he had brought them thither to kill them, and some drawing their swords at him making a show to slay him.

Then he perceiving that they would needs away desired them to tarry that he might fetch the rest of the merchants that were left at the Court, but they would not grant this request. Then desired he them to give him the ship-boat, with as much of an old sail as might serve for the same, promising them therewith to bring Nicholas Lambert and the rest into England, but all was in vain. Then wrote he a letter to the Court to the merchants informing them of all the matter, and promising them if God would lend him life to return with all haste to fetch them. And thus was Pinteado kept ashipboard against his will, thrust among the boys of the ship, not used like a man nor yet like an honest boy, but glad to find favour at the cook's hand. Then departed they, leaving one of their ships behind them, which they sunk for lack of men to carry her.

After this, within six or seven days sailing, died also Pinteado for very pensiveness and thought that struck him to the heart. A man worthy to serve any prince, and most vilely used. And of sevenscore men came home to Plymouth scarcely forty, and of them many died. And that no man should suspect these words which I have said in commendation of Pinteado, to be spoken upon favour otherwise than truth, I have thought good to add hereunto the copy of the letters which the King of Portugal and the Infant, his brother, wrote unto him to reconcile him,* at such time as upon the King his Master's displeasure (and not for any other crime or offence as may appear by the said letters) he was only for poverty enforced to come into England, where he first persuaded our merchants to attempt the said voyages to Guinea.

But as the King of Portugal too late repented him that he had so punished Pinteado upon malicious informations of such as envied the man's good fortune; even so may it hereby appear that in some cases even lions themselves may either be hindered by the contempt, or aided by the help of the poor mice, according unto the fable of Aesop.

This voyage began a profitable English trade with West Africa. Queen Mary forbade it, but it continued surreptitiously until 1558, when Elizabeth legalized it. There was much fighting, because the Portuguese tried to maintain the monopoly which they claimed.

* Not included in this selection.

RICHARD CHANCELLOR IN RUSSIA

Clement Adams

Many sixteenth-century geographers, navigators and merchants cherished the belief that there was a North-east Passage around the north of Asia which would provide a short and easy route to the fabled riches of Cathay and Cipangu (China and Japan) and beyond them to the Spice Islands in the East Indies. No one apparently suspected the severity of the Arctic climate, but English and then Dutch sea-captains, and others later, discovered it to their cost. It was not until 1878–9 that the passage was made at last, by the Swedish navigator, N. A. E. Nordenskjöld. But the English attempt had one great and permanent result: the establishment of direct contact between England and Russia.

The new navigation and discovery of the Kingdom of Muscovy by the north-east, in the year 1553: enterprised by Sir Hugh Willoughby, Knight, and performed by Richard Chancellor Pilot-Major of the voyage: written in Latin by Clement Adams [Schoolmaster to the Queen's henchmen, as he received it at the mouth of the said Richard Chancellor].

AT what time our merchants perceived the commodities and ware of England to be in small request with the countries and people about us and near unto us, and that those merchandises which strangers in the time and memory of our ancestors did earnestly seek and desire were now neglected, and the price thereof abated, although by us carried to their own ports, and all foreign merchandises in great accompt and their prices wonderfully raised: certain grave citizens of London, and men of great wisdom, and careful for the good of their country, began to think with themselves how this mischief might be remedied.

Neither was a remedy (as it then appeared) wanting to their desires for the avoiding of so great an inconvenience: for seeing that the wealth of the Spaniards and Portingals, by the discovery and search of new trades and countries was marvellously increased, supposing the same to be a course and mean for them also to obtain the like, they thereupon resolved upon a new and strange navigation.

And whereas at the same time one, Sebastian Cabot,* a man in those days very renowned, happened to be in London, they began first of all to deal and consult diligently with him, and after much speech and conference together it was at last concluded that three ships should be prepared and furnished out for the search and discovery of the northern part of the world, to open a way and passage to our men for travel to new and unknown kingdoms.

And whereas many things seemed necessary to be regarded in this so hard and difficult a matter, they first made choice of certain grave and wise persons, in manner of a senate or company, which should lay their heads together and give their judgments, and provide things requisite and profitable for all occasions. By this company it was thought expedient that a certain sum of money should publicly be collected to serve for the furnishing of so many ships. And lest any private man should be too much oppressed and charged, a course was taken that every man willing to be of the Society should disburse the portion of twenty and five pounds apiece; so that in short time by this means, the sum of six thousand pounds being gathered, the three ships were bought, the most part whereof they provided to be newly built and trimmed [viz. the *Bona Esperanza*, 120 tons, Sir Hugh Willoughby, Captain-general of the fleet; the *Edward Bonaventure*, 160 tons, Richard Chancellor, Captain, and Pilot-general of the fleet; the *Bona Confidentia*, 90 tons, Cornelius Durforth, Master].

But in this action I wot not whether I may more admire the care of the merchants or the diligence of the shipwrights. For the merchants, they get very strong and well seasoned planks for the building; the shipwrights, they with daily travail and their greatest skill do fit them for the dispatch of the ships. They caulk them, pitch them, and among the rest they make one most staunch and firm by an excellent and ingenious invention. For they had heard that in certain parts of the Ocean a kind of worm is bred which many times pierceth and eateth through the strongest oak that is; and therefore that the mariners and the rest to be employed in this voyage might be free and safe from this danger, they cover a piece of the keel of the ship with thin sheets of lead. And having thus built the ships and furnished them with armour and artillery, then followed a second care no less troublesome and necessary than the former, namely the provision of victuals, which was to be made according to the time and length of the voyage. And whereas they afore determined to have the east part of the world sailed unto, and yet that the sea towards the same was not open

* Sebastian Cabot, Pilot-Major of Spain and one of the most famous navigators of the time, had returned to England in 1548 at the request of Edward VI's ministers, to advise them on finding new markets.

except they kept the Northern tract,★ whereas yet it was doubtful whether there were any passage yea or no, they resolved to victual the ships for eighteen months, which they did for this reason. For our men being to pass that huge and cold part of the world, they wisely foreseeing it, allow them six months' victual to sail to the place, so much more to remain there if the extremity of the winter hindered their return, and so much more also for the time of their coming home.

Now this provision being made and carried aboard, with armour and munition of all sorts, sufficient Captains and Governors of so great an enterprise were as yet wanting. To which office and place, although many men (and some void of experience) offered themselves, yet one, Sir Hugh Willoughby, a most valiant gentleman and well born, very earnestly requested to have that care and charge committed unto him; of whom before all others, both by reason of his goodly personage (for he was of a tall stature) as also for his singular skill in the services of war, the company of the merchants made greatest accompt: so that at the last they concluded and made choice of him for the General of this voyage, and appointed to him the Admiral, with authority and command over all the rest. And for the government of other ships, although divers men seemed willing and made offers of themselves thereunto, yet by a common consent one, Richard Chancellor, a man of great

★ A North-east passage would enable English ships to reach the Far East without clashing with the Portuguese and Spaniards.

estimation for many good parts of wit in him, was elected, in whom alone great hope for the performance of this business rested. This man was brought up by one, Master Henry Sidney, a noble young gentleman and very much beloved of King Edward [VI], who at this time coming to the place where the merchants were gathered together began a very eloquent speech or oration, and spake to them after this manner following.

'My very worshipful friends, I cannot but greatly commend your present godly and virtuous intention, in the serious enterprising (for the singular love you bear to your country) a matter which (I hope) will prove profitable for this nation and honourable to this our land. Which intention of yours we also of the nobility are ready to our power to help and further; neither do we hold anything so dear and precious unto us which we will not willingly forego and lay out in so commendable a cause. But principally I rejoice in myself, that I have nourished and maintained that wit which is like by some means and in some measure to profit and stead [help] you in this worthy action.

'But yet I would not have you ignorant of this one thing, that I do now part with Chancellor, not because I make little reckoning of the man or that his maintenance is burdenous and chargeable unto me, but that you might conceive and understand my goodwill and promptitude for the furtherance of this business, and that the authority and estimation which he deserveth may be given him. You know the man by report, I by experience; you by words, I by deeds; you by speech and company, but I, by the daily trial of his life, have a full and perfect knowledge of him. And you are also to remember into how many perils for your sakes and his country's love he is now to run: whereof it is requisite that we be not unmindful, if it please God to send him good success. We commit a little money to the chance and hazard of fortune; he commits his life (a thing to a man of all things most dear) to the raging sea and the uncertainties of many dangers. We shall here live and rest at home quietly with our friends and acquaintance; but he, in the meantime labouring to keep the ignorant and unruly mariners in good order and obedience, with how many cares shall he trouble and vex himself, with how many troubles shall he break himself, and how many disquietings shall he be forced to sustain? We shall keep our own coasts and country; he shall seek strange and unknown kingdoms. He shall commit his safety to barbarous and cruel people and shall hazard his life amongst the monstrous and terrible beasts of the sea.

'Wherefore, in respect of the greatness of the dangers and the excellence of his charge, you are to favour and love the man thus

departing from us. And if it fall so happily out that he return again, it
is your part and duty also liberally to reward him.'

 After that this noble young gentleman had delivered this or some
suchlike speech, much more eloquently than I can possibly report it,
the company then present began one to look upon another, one to
question and confer with another. And some (to whom the virtue and
sufficiency of the man was known) began secretly to rejoice with themselves, and to conceive a special hope that the man would prove in time
very rare and excellent, and that his virtues, already appearing and
shining to the world, would grow to the great honour and advancement of this kingdom.

After all this, the company growing to some silence, it seemed good
to them that were of greatest gravity amongst them to enquire, search
and seek what might be learned and known concerning the easterly
part or tract of the world. For which cause two Tartarians, which were
then of the King's stable, were sent for, and an interpreter was gotten
to be present, by whom they were demanded touching their country
and the manners of their nation. But they were able to answer nothing
to the purpose, being indeed more acquainted (as one there merrily
and openly said) to toss pots than to learn the states and dispositions
of people.

But after much ado and many things passed about this matter, they
grew at last to this issue, to set down and appoint a time for the
departure of the ships; because divers were of opinion that a great part
of the best time of the year was already spent, and if the delay grew
longer the way would be stopped and barred by the force of the ice and
the cold climate. And therefore it was thought best by the opinion of
them all that by the twentieth day of May the Captains and mariners
should take shipping and depart from Radcliff [on London river] upon
the ebb, if it pleased God. They, having saluted their acquaintance, one
his wife, another his children, another his kinsfolks, and another his
friends dearer than his kinsfolks, were present and ready at the day
appointed: and, having weighed anchor, they departed with the turning of the water and, sailing easily, came first to Greenwich. The
greater ships are towed down with boats and oars, and the mariners,
being all apparelled in watchet or sky-coloured cloth, rowed amain and
made way with diligence.

And being come near to Greenwich (where the Court then lay)
presently, upon the news thereof, the courtiers came running out, and
the common people flocked together, standing very thick upon the
shore: the Privy Council they looked out at the windows of the Court,
and the rest ran up to the tops of the towers. The ships hereupon

discharged their ordnance and shoot off their pieces after the manner of war, and of the sea, insomuch that the tops of the hills sounded therewith, the valleys and the waters gave an echo, and the mariners they shouted in such sort that the sky rang again with the noise thereof. One stood in the poop of the ship, and by his gesture bids farewell to his friends in the best manner he could. Another walks upon the hatches, another climbs the shrouds, another stands upon the main-yard, and another in the top of the ship. To be short, it was a very triumph (after a sort) in all respects to the beholders. But (alas) the good King Edward (in respect of whom principally all this was pre-pared) he only by reason of his sickness was absent from this show, and not long after the departure of these ships the lamentable and most sorrowful accident of his death followed.

But to proceed in the matter.

The ships, going down with the tide, came at last to Woolwich, where they stayed and cast anchor, with purpose to depart therehence again as soon as the turning of the water and a better wind should draw them to set sail. After this they departed and came to Harwich, in which port they stayed long, not without great loss and consuming of time. Yet at the last with a good wind they hoisted up sail and com-mitted themselves to the sea, giving their last adieu to their native country, which they knew not whether they should ever return to see again or not. Many of them looked oftentimes back and could not refrain from tears, considering into what hazards they were to fall, and what uncertainties of the sea they were to make trial of.

Amongst the rest, Richard Chancellor, the Captain of the *Edward Bonaventure*, was not a little grieved with the fear of wanting victuals, part whereof was found to be corrupt and putrified at Harwich, and the hogsheads of wine also leaked and were not staunch. His natural and fatherly affection also somewhat troubled him, for he left behind him his two little sons, which were in the case of orphans if he sped not well. The estate also of his company moved him to care, being in the former respects after a sort unhappy, and were to abide with him-self every good or bad accident.

But in the meantime, while his mind was thus tormented with the multiplicity of sorrows and cares, after many days sailing they kenned land afar off, whereunto the pilots directed the ships. And being come to it they land, and find it to be Rost Island, where they stayed certain days; and afterwards set sail again and, proceeding towards the North, they espied certain other islands, which were called the Cross of Islands. From which places, when they were a little departed, Sir Hugh Willoughby, the General, a man of good foresight and providence in all his actions, erected and set out his flag, by which he called together the chiefest men of the other ships that by the help and assistance of their counsels the order of the government and conduction of the ships in the whole voyage might be the better: who being come together accordingly, they concluded and agreed that if any great tempest should arise at any time, and happen to disperse and scatter them, every ship should endeavour his best to go to Wardhouse [Vardö], a haven or castle of some name in the Kingdom of Norway, and that they that arrived there first in safety should stay and expect the coming of the rest.

The very same day in the afternoon, about four of the clock, so great a tempest suddenly arose and the seas were so outrageous that the ships could not keep their intended course, but some were perforce driven one way and some another way, to their great peril and hazard. The General, with his loudest voice, cried out to Richard Chancellor and earnestly requested him not to go far from him. But he neither would nor could keep company with him, if he sailed still so fast, for the Admiral was of better sail than his ship. But the said Admiral (I know not by what means) bearing all his sails, was carried away with so great force and swiftness that not long after he was quite out of sight, and the third ship also, with the same storm and like rage, was dispersed and lost us.

The ship-boat of the Admiral (striking against the ship) was overwhelmed in the sight and view of the mariners of the *Bonaventure*: and as for them that are already returned and arrived, they know nothing of the rest of the ships what was become of them.

But if it be so, that any miserable mishap have overtaken them, if the rage and fury of the sea have devoured those good men, or if as yet they live and wander up and down in strange countries, I must needs say they were men worthy of better fortune; and if they be living, let us wish them safety and a good return. But if the cruelty of death hath taken hold of them God send them a Christian grave and sepulchre.*

Now Richard Chancellor, with his ship and company, being thus left alone, and become very pensive, heavy and sorrowful by this dispersion of the fleet, he (according to the order before taken) shapeth his course for Wardhouse in Norway, there to expect and abide the arrival of the rest of the ships. And being come thither, and having stayed there the space of seven days and looked in vain for their coming, he determined at length to proceed alone in the purposed voyage. And as he was preparing himself to depart it happened that he fell in company and speech with certain Scottish men, who, having understanding of his intention and wishing well to his actions, began

* The lost ships were found later in the Lapland ice, with Sir Hugh Willoughby and their crews aboard them, frozen to death.

earnestly to dissuade him from the further prosecution of the discovery by amplifying the dangers which he was to fall into, and omitted no reason that might serve to that purpose. But he, holding nothing so ignominious and reproachful as inconstancy and levity of mind, and persuading himself that a man of valour could not commit a more dishonourable part than for fear of danger to avoid and shun great attempts, was nothing at all changed or discouraged with the speechs and words of the Scots, remaining stedfast and immutable in his first resolution, determining either to bring that to pass which was intended or else to die the death.

And as for them which were with Master Chancellor in his ship, although they had great cause of discomfort by the loss of their company (whom the foresaid tempest had separated from them) and were not a little troubled with cogitations and perturbations of mind in respect of their doubtful course, yet, notwithstanding, they were of such consent and agreement of mind with Master Chancellor that they were resolute, and prepared under his direction and government to make proof and trial of all adventures without all fear or mistrust of future dangers. Which constancy of mind in all the company did exceedingly increase their Captain's carefulness; for he, being swallowed up with like goodwill and love towards them, feared lest through any error of his the safety of the company should be endangered.

To conclude, when they saw their desire and hope of the arrival of the rest of the ships to be every day more and more frustrated they provided to sea again, and Master Chancellor held on his course towards that unknown part of the world, and sailed so far that he came at last to the place where he found no night at all, but a continual light and brightness of the sun shining clearly upon the huge and mighty sea. And having the benefit of this perpetual light for certain days, at the length it pleased God to bring them into a certain great bay, which was of one hundred miles or thereabout over. Whereinto they entered and somewhat far within it cast anchor, and looking every way about them it happened that they espied afar off a certain fisher boat, which Master Chancellor, accompanied with a few of his men, went towards to commune with the fishermen that were in it, and to know of them what country it was, and what people, and of what manner of living they were. But they, being amazed with the strange greatness of his ship (for in those parts before that time they had never seen the like), began presently to avoid and to flee: but he, still following them, at last overtook them, and being come to them they (being in great fear, as men half dead) prostrated themselves before him, offering to kiss his feet. But he (according to his great and singular courtesy) looked pleasantly upon them, comforting them by signs and gestures, refusing those duties and reverences of theirs, and taking them up in all loving sort from the ground. And it is strange to consider how much favour afterwards in that place this humanity of his did purchase to himself. For they, being dismissed, spread by and by a report abroad of the arrival of a strange nation of a singular gentleness and courtesy. Whereupon the common people came together, offering to these new-come guests victuals freely, and not refusing to traffic with them, except they had been bound by a certain religious use and custom not to buy any foreign commodities without the knowledge and consent of the King.

By this time our men had learned that this country was called Russia, or Muscovy, and that Ivan★ Vasiliwich (which was at that time their King's name) ruled and governed far and wide in those places. And the barbarous Russes asked likewise of our men whence they were, and what they came for. Whereunto answer was made that they were Englishmen sent into those coasts from the most excellent King Edward the Sixth, having from him in commandment certain things to deliver to their King, and seeking nothing else but his amity and friendship, and traffic with his people, whereby they doubted not but that great commodity and profit would grow to the subjects of both kingdoms.

The barbarians heard these things very gladly, and promised their aid and furtherance to acquaint their King out of hand with so honest and a reasonable request.

In the meantime Master Chancellor entreated victuals for his money of the Governor of that place (who, together with others, came aboard him), and required hostages of them likewise for the more assurance of safety to himself and his company. To whom the Governors answered that they knew not in that case the will of their King, but yet were willing in such things as they might lawfully do to pleasure him; which was as then to afford him the benefit of victuals.

Now, while these things were adoing they secretly sent a messenger unto the Emperor to certify him of the arrival of a strange nation, and withall to know his pleasure concerning them. Which message was very welcome unto him, insomuch that voluntarily he invited them to come to his Court: but if by reason of the tediousness of so long a journey they thought it not best so to do, then he granted liberty to his subjects to bargain and to traffic with them; and further promised that if it would please them to come to him, he himself would bear the whole charges of post horses.

In the meantime the Governors of the place deferred the matter from day to day, pretending divers excuses, and saying one while that

★ Ivan IV ('Ivan the Terrible'), 1533–84.

the consent of all the Governors, and another while that the great and weighty affairs of the kingdom, compelled them to defer their answer. And this they did of purpose, so long to protract the time until the messenger (sent before to the King) did return with relation of his will and pleasure.

But Master Chancellor (seeing himself held in this suspense with long and vain expectation, and thinking that of intention to delude him they posted the matter off so often) was very instant with them to perform their promise, which if they would not do, he told them that he would depart and proceed in his voyage. So that the Muscovites (although as yet they knew not the mind of their King) yet fearing the departure indeed of our men who had such wares and commodities as they greatly desired, they at last resolved to furnish our people with all things necessary, and to conduct them by land to the presence of their King.

And so Master Chancellor began his journey, which was very long and most troublesome, wherein he had the use of certain sleds, which in that country are very common for they are carried themselves upon sleds, and all their carriages are in the same sort, the people almost not knowing any other manner of carriage, the cause whereof is the exceeding hardness of the ground congealed in the winter time by the force of the cold, which in those places is very extreme and horrible, whereof hereafter we will say something.

But now, they having passed the greater part of their journey, met at last with the sledman (of whom I spake before) sent to the King secretly from the Justices or Governors, who by some ill hap had lost his way and had gone to the sea side, which is near to the country of the Tartars, thinking there to have found our ship. But having long erred and wandered out of his way, at the last in his direct return he met (as he was coming) our Captain on the way. To whom he by and by delivered the Emperor's letters, which were written to him with all courtesy and in the most loving manner that could be: wherein express commandment was given that post horses should be gotten for him and the rest of his company without any money. Which thing was of all the Russians in the rest of their journey so willingly done that they began to quarrel, yea, and to fight also, in striving and contending which of them should put their post horses to the sled.

So that after much ado and great pains taken in this long and weary journey (for they had travelled very near fifteen hundred miles) Master Chancellor came at last to Moscow, the chief city of the kingdom and the seat of the King: of which city, and of the Emperor himself, and of the principal cities of Muscovy, we will speak immediately more at large in this discourse.

OF MUSCOVY, WHICH IS ALSO CALLED RUSSIA

Muscovy, which hath the name also of Russia the White, is a very large and spacious country, every way bounded with divers nations. Towards the south and the east it is compassed with Tartaria: the northern side of it stretcheth to the Scythian Ocean: upon the west part border the Lappians, a rude and savage nation living in woods, whose language is not known to any other people. Next unto these, more towards the South, is Swecia [Sweden], then Finlandia, then Livonia, and last of all Lithuania.

This country of Muscovy hath also very many and great rivers in it, and is marsh ground in many places. And as for the rivers, the greatest and most famous amongst all the rest is that which the Russes in their own tongue call Volga, but others know it by the name of Rha. Next unto it in fame is Tanais, which they call Don; and the third Boristhenes, which at this day they call Dnieper. Two of these, to wit, Rha and Boristhenes, issuing both out of one fountain, run very far through the land. Rha, receiving many other pleasant rivers into it, and running from the very head or spring of it towards the East, after many crooked turnings and windings dischargeth itself and all the other waters and rivers that fall into it by divers passages into the Caspian Sea. Tanais, springing from a fountain of great name in those parts and growing great near to his head, spreads itself at length very largely and makes a great lake: and then, growing narrow again, doth so run for certain miles until it fall into another lake, which they call Ivan: and therehence, fetching a very crooked course, comes very near to the river Volga: but, disdaining as it were the company of any other river, doth there turn itself again from Volga and runs toward the South and falls at last into the Lake of Moeotis. Boristhenes, which comes from the same head that Rha doth (as we said before) carrieth both itself and other waters that are near unto it towards the South, not refusing the mixture of other small rivers: and running by many great and large countries falls at last into Pontus Euxinus. Besides these rivers are also in Muscovy certain lakes and pools. The lakes breed fish by the celestial influence. And amongst them all the chiefest and most principal is called Bealozera, which is very famous by reason of a very strong tower built in it, wherein the kings of Muscovy reserve and repose their treasure in all time of war and danger.

Touching the Riphean mountains, whereupon the snow lieth continually and where hence in times past it was thought that Tanais the river did spring, and that the rest of the wonders of nature which the Grecians feigned and invented of old were there to be seen, our men which lately came from thence neither saw them nor yet have brought home any perfect relation of them, although they remained there for the space of three months and had gotten in that time some intelligence of the language of Muscovy. The whole country is plain and champion, and few hills in it: and towards the North it hath very large and spacious woods wherein is great store of fir trees, a wood very necessary and fit for the building of houses.

There are also wild beasts bred in those woods, as buffs, bears, and black wolves, and another kind of beast unknown to us but called by them rossomakka. And the nature of the same is very rare and wonderful, for when it is great with young and ready to bring forth it seeketh out some narrow place between two stakes, and so going through them presseth itself, and by that means is eased of her burden, which otherwise could not be done. They hunt their buffs for the most part ahorseback, but their bears afoot, with wooden forks.

The north parts of the country are reported to be so cold that the very ice or water which distilleth out of the moist wood which they lay upon the fire is presently congealed and frozen; the diversity growing suddenly to be so great that in one and the selfsame firebrand a man shall see both fire and ice. When the winter doth once begin there it doth still more and more increase by a perpetuity of cold: neither doth that cold slake until the force of the sunbeams doth dissolve the cold and make glad the earth returning to it again.

Our mariners which we left in the ship in the meantime to keep it, in their going up only from their cabins to the hatches had their breath oftentimes so suddenly taken away that they eftsoons fell down as men very near dead, so great is the sharpness of that cold climate. But as for the south parts of the country, they are somewhat more temperate.

OF MOSCOW, THE CHIEF CITY OF THE KINGDOM, AND OF THE EMPEROR THEREOF

It remaineth that a larger discourse be made of Moscow, the principal city of that country, and of the Prince also, as before we have promised. The Empire and Government of the King is very large, and his wealth at this time exceeding great. And because the city of Moscow is the chiefest of all the rest it seemeth of itself to challenge the first place in this discourse. Our men say that in bigness it is as great as the City of London, with the suburbs thereof. There are many and great buildings in it, but for beauty and fairness nothing comparable to ours. There are many towns and villages also, but built out of order and with no handsomeness. Their streets and ways are not paved with stone as ours are; the walls of their houses are of wood; the roofs for the most part are covered with shingle boards.

There is hard by the city a very fair castle, strong, and furnished with artillery, whereunto the city is joined directly towards the north with a brick wall: the walls also of the castle are built with brick, and are in breadth or thickness eighteen foot. This castle hath on the one side a dry ditch, on the other side the river Moskva, whereby it is made almost inexpugnable. The same Moskva, trending towards the east, doth admit into it the company of the river Oka.

In the castle aforesaid there are in number nine churches, or chapels, not altogether unhandsome, which are used and kept by certain religious men, over whom there is after a sort a Patriarch, or Governor, and with him other Reverend Fathers, all which for the greater part dwell within the castle. As for the King's court and palace, it is not of the neatest, only in form it is foursquare and of low building, much surpassed and excelled by the beauty and elegance of the houses of the Kings of England. The windows are very narrowly built, and some of them by glass, some other by lattices, admit the light. And whereas the palaces of our Princes are decked and adorned with hangings of cloth of gold, there is none such there. They build and join to all their walls benches, and that not only in the Court of the Emperor but in all private men's houses.

Now after that they had remained about twelve days in the city there was then a messenger sent unto them to bring them to the King's house: and they, being after a sort wearied with their long stay, were very ready and willing so to do. And being entered within the gates of the Court there sat a very honourable company of courtiers, to the number of one hundred, all apparelled in cloth of gold down to their ankles. And therehence being conducted into the chamber of presence our men began to wonder at the majesty of the Emperor. His seat was aloft in a very royal throne, having on his head a diadem, or crown of gold, apparelled with a robe all of goldsmith's work, and in his hand he held a sceptre garnished and beset with precious stones. And besides all other notes and appearances of honour there was a majesty in his countenance proportionable with the excellence of his estate. On the one side of him stood his Chief Secretary, on the other side the great Commander of Silence, both of them arrayed also in cloth of gold. And then there sat the Council of one hundred and fifty in number, all in like sort arrayed and of great state.

This so honourable an assembly, so great a majesty of the Emperor and of the place, might very well have amazed our men and have dashed them out of countenance: but notwithstanding Master Chancellor, being therewithal nothing dismayed, saluted, and did his duty to the Emperor after the manner of England, and withal delivered unto him the letters of our King, Edward the Sixth. The Emperor, having taken and read the letters, began a little to question with them and to ask them of the welfare of our King: whereunto our men answered him directly and in few words. Hereupon our men presented some thing to the Emperor by the Chief Secretary, which at the delivery of it put off his hat, being before all the time covered. And so the Emperor, having invited them to dinner, dismissed them from his presence. And going into the chamber of him that was Master of the Requests to the Emperor, and having stayed there the space of two hours, at the last the messenger commeth and calleth them to dinner.

They go, and being conducted into the Golden Court (for so they call it, although not very fair) they find the Emperor sitting upon an high and stately seat, apparelled with a robe of silver, and with another diadem on his head. Our men, being placed over against him, sit down. In the midst of the room stood a mighty cupboard upon a square foot, whereupon stood also a round board, in manner of a diamond, broad beneath and towards the top narrow, and every step rose up more narrow than another. Upon this cupboard was placed the Emperor's plate, which was so much that the very cupboard itself was scant able to sustain the weight of it. The better part of all the vessels and goblets was made of very fine gold: and amongst the rest, there were four pots of very large bigness which did adorn the rest of the plate in great measure, for they were so high that they thought them at the least five foot long. There were also upon this cupboard certain silver casks, not much differing from the quantity of our firkins, wherein was reserved the Emperor's drink. On each side of the Hall stood four tables, each of them laid and covered with very clean table-cloths, whereunto the company ascended by three steps or degrees, all which were filled with the assembly present. The guests were all apparelled with linen without and with rich skins within, and so did notably set out this royal feast. The Emperor, when he takes any bread or knife in his hand, doth first of all cross himself upon his forehead. They that are in special favour with the Emperor sit upon the same bench with him, but somewhat far from him. And before the coming in of the meat the Emperor himself, according to an ancient custom of the kings of Muscovy, doth first bestow a piece of bread upon every one of his guests, with a loud pronunciation of his title and honour, in this manner: 'The Great Duke of Muscovy and Chief Emperor of Russia, John Basiliwich (and then the officer nameth the guest) doth give thee bread.' Whereupon all the guests rise up, and by and by sit down again.

This done, the Gentleman Usher of the Hall comes in, with a notable company of servants carrying the dishes, and, having done his reverence to the Emperor, puts a young swan in a golden platter upon the table, and immediately takes it thence again, delivering it to the carver, and seven other of his fellows, to be cut up: which, being performed, the meat is then distributed to the guests with the like pomp and ceremonies. In the meantime the Gentleman Usher receives his bread, and tasteth to the Emperor, and afterward, having done his reverence, he departeth. Touching the rest of the dishes, because they were brought in out of order, our men can report no certainty. But this is true, that all the furniture of dishes and drinking vessels which were then for the use of a hundred guests was all of pure gold, and the tables were so laden with vessels of gold that there was no room for some to stand upon them.

We may not forget that there were 140 servitors arrayed in cloth of gold that in the dinner time changed thrice their habit and apparel, which servitors are in like sort served with bread from the Emperor, as the rest of the guests. Last of all, dinner being ended and candles brought in (for by this time night was come) the Emperor calleth all his guests and noble men by their names, in such sort that it seems miraculous that a Prince, otherwise occupied in great matters of estate, should so well remember so many and sundry particular names. The Russes told our men that the reason thereof, as also of the bestowing of bread in that manner, was to the end that the Emperor might keep the knowledge of his own household: and withal, that such as are under his displeasure might by this means be known.

OF THE DISCIPLINE OF WAR AMONG THE RUSSES

Whensoever the injuries of their neighbours do call the King forth to battle he never armeth a less number against the enemy than 300 thousand soldiers, 100 thousand whereof he carrieth out into the field with him, and leaveth the rest in garrison in some fit places for the better safety of his Empire. He presseth no husbandman nor merchant, for the country is so populous that these being left at home the youth of the realm is sufficient for all his wars. As many as go out to warfare do provide all things of their own cost. They fight not on foot, but altogether on horseback; their armour is a coat of mail and a helmet; the coat of mail without is gilded, or else adorned with silk, although it pertain to a common soldier; they have a great pride in showing their wealth: they use bows and arrows, as the Turks do; they carry lances also into the field. They ride with a short stirrup after the manner of the Turks.

They are a kind of people most sparing in diet, and most patient in extremity of cold above all others: for when the ground is covered with snow and is grown terrible and hard with the frost, this Russe hangs up his mantle, or soldier's coat, against that part from whence the

wind and snow drives, and so making a little fire lieth down with his
back towards the weather. This mantle of his serves him for his bed,
wall, house and all. His drink is cold water of the river, mingled with
oatmeal, and this is all his good cheer, and he thinketh himself well
and daintily fed therewith, and so sitteth down by his fire, and upon the
hard ground, roasteth as it were his weary sides thus daintily stuffed:
the hard ground is his feather bed, and some block or stone his pillow:
and as for his horse, he is as it were a chamberfellow with his master,
faring both alike.

How justly may this barbarous and rude Russe condemn the
daintiness and niceness of our Captains who, living in a soil and air
much more temperate, yet commonly use furred boots and cloaks?
But thus much of the furniture of their common soldiers. But those
that are of higher degrees come into the field a little better provided.
As for the furniture of the Emperor himself, it is then above all other
times most notable. The coverings of his tent for the most part are all
of gold, adorned with stones of great price, and with the curious work-
manship of plumasiers.

As often as they are to skirmish with the enemy they go forth without any order at all: they make no wings, nor military divisions of their
men, as we do, but lying for the most part in ambush do suddenly set
upon the enemy. Their horses can well abstain two whole days from
any meat: they feed upon the barks of trees and the most tender
branches in all the time of war. And this scant and miserable manner
of living both the horse and his master can well endure, sometimes for
the space of two months, lusty and in good state of body.

If any man behave himself valiantly in the field to the contentation
of the Emperor he bestoweth upon him in recompense of his service
some farm, or so much ground as he and his may live upon, which
notwithstanding after his death returneth again to the Emperor if he
die without a male issue. For although his daughters be never so many
yet no part of that inheritance comes to them, except peradventure
the Emperor of his goodness give some portion of the land amongst
them to bestow them withal. As for the man, whosoever he be, that is
in this sort rewarded by the Emperor's liberality, he is bound in a great
sum to maintain so many soldiers for the war, when need shall require,
as that land in the opinion of the Emperor is able to maintain. And all
those to whom any land falls by inheritance are in no better condition;
for if they die without any male issue all their lands fall into the hands
of the Emperor. And, moreover, if there be any rich man amongst them
who in his own person is unfit for the wars, and yet hath such wealth
that thereby many noblemen and warriors might be maintained, if
any of the courtiers present his name to the Emperor, the unhappy man

is by-and-by sent for and in that instant deprived of all his riches which with great pains and travail all his lifetime he had gotten together, except perhaps some small portion thereof be left him to maintain his wife, children and family.

But all this is done of all the people so willingly at the Emperor's commandment that a man would think they rather make restitution of other men's goods than give that which is their own to other men. Now the Emperor having taken these goods into his hands bestoweth them among his courtiers according to their deserts: and oftener that a man is sent to the wars the more the favour he thinketh is borne to him by the Emperor, although he go upon his own charge, as I said before. So great is the obedience of all men generally to their Prince.

OF THE AMBASSADORS OF THE EMPEROR OF MUSCOVY

The Muscovite, with no less pomp and magnificence than that which we have spoken of, sends his Ambassadors to foreign Princes in the affairs of estate. For while our men were abiding in the city of Moscow there were two Ambassadors sent to the King of Poland, accompanied with 500 notable horses, and the greater part of the men were arrayed in cloth of gold and of silk, and the worst apparel was of garments of blue colour, to speak nothing of the trappings of the horses, which were adorned with gold and silver and very curiously embroidered: they had also with them one hundred white and fair spare horses, to use them at such times as any weariness came upon them. But now the time requireth me to speak briefly of other cities of the Muscovites, and of the wares and commodities that the country yieldeth.

NOVGOROD

Next unto Moscow the city of Novgorod is reputed the chiefest of Russia; for although it be in majesty inferior to it, yet in greatness it goeth beyond it. It is the chiefest and greatest mart town of all Muscovy: and albeit the Emperor's seat is not there, but at Moscow, yet the commodiousness of the river, falling into that gulf which is called Sinus Finnicus [Gulf of Finland], whereby it is well frequented by merchants, makes it more famous than Moscow itself.

This town excels all the rest in the commodities of flax and hemp: it yields also hides, honey and wax. The Flemings there sometimes had a house of merchandise, but by reason that they used the like ill dealing there, which they did with us, they lost their privileges, a restitution whereof they earnestly sued for at the time that our men were there. But those Flemings, hearing of the arrival of our men in those parts, wrote their letters to the Emperor against them, accusing them for pirates and rovers, wishing him to detain and imprison them:

which things, when they were known of our men, they conceived fear that they should never have returned home. But the Emperor, believing rather the King's letters which our men brought than the lying and false suggestions of the Flemings, used no ill entreaty towards them.

YAROSLAVL

Yaroslavl also is a town of some good fame for the commodities of hides, tallow and corn, which it yields in great abundance. Cakes of wax are there also to be sold, although other places have greater store. This Yaroslavl is distant from Moscow about two hundred miles; and betwixt them are many populous villages. Their fields yield such store of corn that in conveying it towards Moscow, sometimes in a forenoon, a man shall see seven hundred or eight hundred sleds going and coming, laden with corn and salt fish. The people come a thousand miles to Moscow to buy that corn and then carry it away upon sleds; and these are those people that dwell in the north parts, where the cold is so terrible that no corn doth grow there, or if it spring up it never comes to ripeness. The commodities that they bring with them are salt fish, skins and hides.

VOLOGDA

Vologda, being from Moscow 550 miles, yields the commodities of hemp and flax also, although the greatest store of flax is sold at Novgorod.

PLESCO

The town of Plesco is frequented by merchants for the good store of honey and wax that it yieldeth.

KHOLMOGORY

The north parts of Russia yield very rare and precious skins, and amongst the rest those principally which we call sables, worn about the necks of our noble women and ladies. It hath also martens' skins, white, black and red fox skins, skins of hares and ermins, and others which they call and term barbarously as beavers, minks and minivers. The sea adjoining breeds a certain beast which they call the morse [walrus], which seeketh his food upon the rocks, climbing up with the help of his teeth. The Russians use to take them for the great virtue that is in their teeth, whereof they make as great account as we do of the elephant's tooth.

These commodities they carry upon deer's backs to the town of Lampas; and from thence to Kholmogory, and there in the winter time are kept great fairs for the sale of them. This city of Kholmogory serves all the country about it with salt, and salt fish. The Russians also of the north parts send thither oil, which they call train, which they make in a river called Una, although it be also made elsewhere: and here they use to boil the water of the sea, whereof they make very great store of salt.

OF CONTROVERSIES IN LAW, AND HOW THEY ARE ENDED

Having hitherto spoken so much of the chiefest cities of Russia, as the matter required, it remaineth that we speak somewhat of the laws that the Muscovites do use, as far forth as the same are come to our knowledge. If any controversy arise among them they first make their landlords judges in the matter, and if they cannot end it then they prefer it to the magistrate. The plaintiff craveth of the said magistrate that he may have leave to enter law against his adversary; and having obtained it, the officer fetcheth the defendant and beateth him on the legs till he bring forth a surety for him: but if he be not of such credit as to procure a surety, then are his hands by an officer tied to his neck and he is beaten all the way till he come before the Judge. The Judge then asketh him (as for example in the matter of debt) whether he oweth anything to the plaintiff. If he denies it, then saith the Judge, 'How canst thou deny it?' The defendant answereth, 'By an oath': thereupon the officer is commanded to cease from beating of him until the matter be further tried.

They have no lawyers, but every man is his own advocate, and both the complaint of the accuser and the answer of the defendant are in manner of petition delivered to the Emperor, entreating justice at his hands. The Emperor himself heareth every great controversy, and upon the hearing of it giveth judgement, and that with great equity, which I take to be a thing worthy of special commendation in the majesty of a Prince. But although he do this with a good purpose of mind, yet the corrupt magistrates do wonderfully pervert the same: but if the Emperor take them in any fault he doth punish them most severely.

Now at the last, when each party hath defended his cause with his best reasons, the Judge demandeth of the accuser whether he hath any more to say for himself. He answereth that he will try the matter in fight by his champion, or else entreateth that in fight betwixt themselves the matter may be ended: which, being granted, they both fight it out: or if both of them or either of them seem unfit for that kind of trial, then they have public champions to be hired, which live by ending of quarrels. These champions are armed with iron axes and spears, and fight on foot, and he whose champion is overcome is by-and-by taken and imprisoned, and terribly handled, until he agree with his adversary. But if either of them be of any good calling and degree, and do challenge one another to fight, the Judge granteth it: in which case they may not use public champions. And he that is of any good birth doth contemn the other if he be basely born and will not fight with him.

If a poor man happen to grow in debt his creditor takes him and maketh him pay the debt in working either to himself or to some other man, whose wages he taketh up. And there are some among them that use willingly to make themselves, their wives, and children, bond-slaves unto rich men to have a little money at the first into their hands, and so for ever after content themselves with meat and drink; so little accompt do they make of liberty.

OF PUNISHMENTS UPON THIEVES

If any man be taken upon committing of theft he is imprisoned, and often beaten, but not hanged for the first offence, as the manner is with us: and this they call the law of mercy. He that offendeth the second time hath his nose cut off, and is burnt in the forehead with a hot iron. The third time he is hanged. There are many cutpurses among them, and if the rigour of the Prince did not cut them off they could not be avoided.

OF THEIR RELIGION

They maintain the opinions of the Greek Church: they suffer no graven images of saints in their churches, but their pictures painted in tables [on flat surfaces] they have in great abundance, which they do adore and offer unto, and burn wax candles before them, and cast holy water upon them, without other honour. They say that our images which are set up in churches and carved have no divinity in them. In their private houses they have images for their household saints, and for the most part they are put in the darkest place of the house: he that comes into his neighbour's house doth first salute his saints although he see them not. If any form or stool stand in his way he oftentimes beateth his brow upon the same, and often ducking down with his head and body worshipeth the chief image.

The habit and attire of the priests and of the laymen doth nothing at all differ. As for marriage, it is forbidden to no man; only this is received and held amongst them for a rule and custom, that if a priest's wife do die he may not marry again, nor take a second wife; and therefore they of secular priests, as they call them, are made monks, to whom then chastity for ever is commanded.

Their divine service is all done and said in their own language that every man may understand it. They receive the Lord's Supper with leavened bread, and after the consecration they carry it about the church in a saucer, and prohibit no man from receiving and taking of it that is willing so to do. They use both the Old and the New Testament, and read both in their own language, but so confusedly that they themselves that do read understand not what themselves do say: and while any part of either Testament is read there is liberty given by custom to prattle, talk, and make a noise; but in the time of the rest of the service they use very great silence and reverence and behave themselves very modestly and in good sort.

As touching the Lord's Prayer, the tenth man amongst them knows it not; and for the Articles of our faith and the Ten Commandments no man, or at the least very few of them, do either know them or can say them: their opinion is that such secret and holy things as they are should not rashly and imprudently be communicated with the common people. They hold for a maxim amongst them that the old Law and the Commandments also are abolished by the death and blood of Christ. All studies and letters of humanity they utterly refuse: concerning the Latin, Greek, and Hebrew tongues they are altogether ignorant in them.

Every year they celebrate four several fasts, which they call according to the names of the saints. The first begins with them at the time that our Lent begins. The second is called amongst them the fast of St Peter. The third is taken from the day of the Virgin Mary. And the fourth and last begins upon St Philip's day. But as we begin our Lent upon Wednesday, so they begin theirs upon the Sunday. Upon the Saturday they eat flesh. Whensoever any of those fasting feasts do draw near, look what week doth immediately go before them, the same week they live altogether upon white meats, and in their common language they call those weeks the Fast of Butter.

In the time of their fasts the neighbours everywhere go from one to another and visit one another, and kiss one another with kisses of peace in token of their mutual love and Christian concord: and then also they do more often than at any other time go to the Holy Communion.

When seven days are past from the beginning of the fast, then they do often either go to their churches, or keep themselves at home, and use often prayer: and for that seven-night they eat nothing but herbs; but after that seven-night's fast is once past then they return to their old intemperancy of drinking, for they are notable tosspots. As for the keeping of their fasting days, they do it very straightly, neither do they eat anything besides herbs and salt fish as long as those fasting days do endure: but upon every Wednesday and Friday in every week throughout the year they fast.

There are very many monasteries of the Order of St Benedict amongst them, to which many great livings, for their maintenance, do belong; for the friars and the monks do at the least possess the third part of the livings throughout the whole Muscovite Empire. To those monks that are of this order there is amongst them a perpetual prohibition that they may eat no flesh; and therefore their meat is only salt fish, milk, and butter: neither is it permitted them by the laws and customs of their religion to eat any fresh fish at all: and at those four fasting times, whereof we spake before, they eat no fish at all; only they live with herbs and cucumbers, which they do continually for that purpose cause and take order to grow and spring for their use and diet.

As for their drink, it is very weak and small. For the discharge of their office they do every day say service, and that early in the mornings before day: and they do in such sort and with such observation begin their service that they will be sure to make an end of it before day: and about nine of the clock in the morning they celebrate the Communion. When they have so done they go to dinner, and after dinner they go again to service, and the like also after supper: and in the meantime, while they are at dinner, there is some exposition or interpretation of the Gospel used.

Whensoever any Abbot of any monastery dieth, the Emperor taketh all his household stuff, beasts, flocks of sheep, gold, silver, and all that he hath: or else he that is to succeed him in his place and dignity doth redeem all those things, and buyeth them of the Emperor for money.

Their churches are built of timber, and the towers of their churches for the most part are covered with shingle boards. At the doors of their churches they usually build some entrance or porch as we do, and in their churchyards they erect a certain house of wood, wherein they set up their bells, wherein sometimes they have but one, in some two, and in some also three.

There is one use and custom amongst them which is strange and rare, but yet it is very ridiculous, and that is this. When any man dieth amongst them, they take the dead body and put it in a coffin or chest, and in the hand of the corpse they put a little scroll, and in the same there are these words written, that the same man died a Russe of Russes, having received the faith, and died in the same. This writing or letter they say they send to St Peter, who receiving it (as they affirm) reads it, and by-and-by admits him into heaven, and that his glory and place is higher and greater than the glory of the Christians of the Latin Church, reputing themselves to be followers of a more sincere faith and religion than they. They hold opinion that we are but half Christians, and themselves only to be the true and perfect church. These are the foolish and childish dotages of such ignorant barbarians.

OF THE MUSCOVITES THAT ARE IDOLATERS, DWELLING NEAR TO TARTARY

There is a certain part of Muscovy, bordering upon the countries of the Tartars, wherein those Muscovites that dwell are very great idolaters. They have one famous idol amongst them which they call the Golden Old Wife, and they have a custom that whensoever any plague or any calamity doth afflict the country, as hunger, war, or such like, then they go to consult with their idol, which they do after this manner. They fall down prostrate before the idol and pray unto it, and put in the presence of the same a cymbal; and about the same certain persons stand which are chosen amongst them by lot; upon their cymbal they place a silver toad and sound the cymbal, and to whomsoever of those lotted persons that toad goeth he is taken, and by-and-by slain. And immediately, I know not by what illusions of the devil, or idol, he is again restored to life and then doth reveal and deliver the causes of the present calamity. And by this means, knowing how to pacify the idol, they are delivered from the imminent danger.

OF THE FORM OF THEIR PRIVATE HOUSES, AND OF THE APPAREL OF THE PEOPLE

The common houses of the country are everywhere built of beams of fir tree: the lower beams do so receive the round hollowness of the uppermost that by the means of the building thereupon they resist and expel all winds that blow, and where the timber is joined together, there they stop the chinks with moss. The form and fashion of their houses in all places is foursquare, with straight and narrow windows, whereby with a transparent casement, made or covered with skin like to parchment, they receive the light. The roofs of their houses are made of boards covered without with ye bark of trees: within their houses they have benches or grees [steps] hard by their walls, which commonly they sleep upon, for the common people know not the use of beds. They have stoves wherein in the morning they make a fire, and the same fire doth either moderately warm or make very hot the whole house.

The apparel of the people for the most part is made of wool, their caps are peaked like unto a rick or diamond, broad beneath and sharp upward. In the manner of making whereof there is a sign and representation of nobility; for the loftier or higher their caps are, the greater is their birth supposed to be, and the greater reverence is given them by the common people.

THE CONCLUSION TO QUEEN MARY

These are the things, Most Excellent Queen, which your subjects newly returned from Russia have brought home concerning the state of that country. Wherefore if Your Majesty shall be favourable and grant a continuance of the travel, there is no doubt but that the honour and renown of your name will be spread amongst those nations whereunto three only noble personages from the very creation have had access, to whom no man hath been comparable.

The Tsar welcomed the English because Russian trade with Europe had been monopolized by the merchants of the Hanseatic League, who were high-handed and extortionate. Chancellor returned to London in 1554 with a letter from the Tsar to Edward VI (who had meanwhile been succeeded by Queen Mary), expressing his willingness to authorize 'free mart with all free liberties' for the English in Russia. To exploit this a company was formed in 1555, with a royal charter and the grand title of Merchant Adventurers of England for the Discovery of Lands, Territories, Isles, Dominions and Seignories unknown. It was the first English joint-stock company, with a capital of £6,000 in £25 shares and Sebastian Cabot as Governor. It soon became known as the Muscovy Company.

'And now [in 1569] the English began more confidently to survey those [eastern] countries, carrying their merchandises up the river Dwina in boats made of one whole piece of tree, which they rowed and towed up the stream with hawsers as far as Vologda and from thence by land seven days' journey to Yaroslav and then by the Volga. . . . thirty days and as many nights' journey down the river to Astrakhana. And from Astrakhana (where they built ships) they did by a very great and memorable adventure many times cross the Caspian sea . . . to Teheran and Casbin, cities of Persia, in hope at length to discover Cathay, but the wars . . . interrupted this laudable enterprise . . .' – William Camden: *Annals.*

All this opened a new and presently profitable market for English woollen goods, and broke the Hanseatic monopoly in Russian cordage, pitch and timber, which were increasingly needed as English maritime enterprise developed. It stimulated the quest for new lands, and trained seamen for the ocean voyages.

JOHN HAWKINS' FIRST VOYAGE
TO THE SPANISH MAIN

Anonymous

John Hawkins, knighted in 1588, was the son of William Hawkins and the Hawkins family of Plymouth was one of the richest and most famous of Elizabethan families of merchant-adventurers. The iniquitous trade in African slaves, begun by the Portuguese and Spaniards, troubled the consciences of some Elizabethans but not of the majority. Unfortunately it was highly profitable (Hawkins is said to have made sixty per cent on his second voyage) because of the urgent demand in Spanish America for slaves to work mines and plantations. The Spanish government claimed a monopoly but since there was a great shortage the Spanish colonists were often eager to buy surreptitiously from foreign interlopers.

The first voyage of the Right Worshipful and valiant Knight, Sir John Hawkins, sometimes Treasurer of Her Majesty's Navy Royal, made to the West Indies 1562.

MASTER John Hawkins, having made divers voyages to the [Spanish] isles of the Canaries and there by his good and upright dealing being grown in love and favour with the people, informed himself amongst them by diligent inquisition of the state of the West India, whereof he had received some knowledge by the instructions of his father but increased the same by the advertisements and reports of that people. And being amongst other particulars assured that the negroes were very good merchandise in Hispaniola, and that store of negroes might easily be had upon the coast of Guinea, resolved with himself to make trial thereof and communicated that device with his worshipful friends of London: namely, with Sir Lionel Ducket, Sir Thomas Lodge, Master Gonson, his father-in-law, Sir William Winter, Master Bromfield, and others. All which persons liked so well of his intention that they became liberal contributors and adventurers in the action. For which purpose there were three good ships immediately provided: the one called the *Salomon* of the burden of 120 tons, wherein Master Hawkins himself went as General: the second the *Swallow* of 100 tons, wherein went for Captain Master

AETATIS SVAE LVIII
Ano Dni 1591

Sir John Hawkins: painting by unknown artist, 1591

Thomas Hampton: and the third the *Jonas*, a bark of 40 tons, wherein the Master supplied the Captain's room: in which small fleet Master Hawkins took with him not above 100 men for fear of sickness and other inconveniences, whereunto men in long voyages are commonly subject.

With this company he put off and departed from the coast of England in the month of October, 1562, and in his course touched first at Teneriffe where he received friendly entertainment. From thence he passed to Sierra Leone, upon the coast of Guinea, which place by the people of the country is called Tagarin, where he stayed some good time and got into his possession, partly by the sword and partly by other means, to the number of 300 negroes at the least, besides other merchandises which that country yieldeth. With this prey he sailed over the Ocean Sea unto the island of Hispaniola, and arrived first at the port of Isabella: and there he had reasonable utterance of his English commodities, as also of some part of his negroes, trusting the Spaniards no further than that by his own strength he was able still to master them. From the port of Isabella he went to Puerto de Plata, where he made like sales, standing always upon his guard. From thence also he sailed to Monte Christi, another port on the north side of Hispaniola and the last place of his touching, where he had peaceable traffic and made vent of the whole number of his negroes: for which he received in those three places by way of exchange such quantity of merchandise that he did not only lade his own three ships with hides, ginger, sugars and some quantity of pearls, but he freighted also two other hulks with hides and other like commodities, which he sent into Spain. And thus leaving the island he returned and disembarked, passing out by the islands of the Caicos without further entering into the Bay of Mexico, in this his first voyage to the West India. And so, with prosperous success and much gain to himself and the aforesaid adventurers, he came home, and arrived in the month of September, 1563.

THE BATTLE OF SAN JUAN

John Hawkins

Like so many other Elizabethan expeditions this was financed by a syndicate, formed for the occasion and consisting of merchants, courtiers, Privy Councillors and the Queen's Majesty herself. The Royal Navy was the monarch's private property and as Elizabeth was always acutely short of money she hired out naval ships for commercial and privateering expeditions. The Jesus of Lubeck *and the* Minion *were her ships. Hawkins acted under the Queen's orders and flew the royal standard at his peak, but, as he knew, she would not hesitate to disown him if this suited her. Hence the diplomatic caution of his narrative, written no doubt with one eye on the Privy Council and the other on the Spanish ambassador.*

The third troublesome voyage made with the *Jesus of Lubeck*, the *Minion*, and four other ships, to the parts of Guinea and the West Indies, in the years 1567 and 1568, by Master John Hawkins.

THE ships departed from Plymouth the second day of October, Anno 1567, and had reasonable weather until the seventh day, at which time forty leagues north from Cape Finisterre there arose an extreme storm, which continued four days in such a sort that the fleet was dispersed and all our great boats lost, and the *Jesus* our chief ship in such case as not thought able to serve the voyage: whereupon in the same storm we set our course homeward, determining to give over the voyage. But the eleventh day of the same month the wind changed with fair weather, whereby we were animated to follow our enterprise, and so did, directing our course with the islands of the Canaries, where according to an order before prescribed all our ships before dispersed met at one of those Islands, called Gomera, where we took water, and departed from thence the fourth day of November towards the coast of Guinea, and arrived at Cape Verde the eighteenth of November, where we landed 150 men hoping to obtain some negroes, where we got but few and those with great hurt and damage to our men, which chiefly proceeded of their envenomed arrows. And although in the beginning they seemed to be but small hurts yet there hardly escaped any that had blood drawn of them, but died in strange sort, with their mouths shut some ten days before they died and after their wounds were whole; where I myself had one of the greatest wounds yet, thanks be to God, escaped.

From thence we passed the time upon the coast of Guinea, searching with all diligence the rivers from Rio Grande unto Sierra Leone till the twelfth of January, in which time we had not gotten together a hundred and fifty negroes: yet notwithstanding [nevertheless] the sickness of our men and the late time of the year commanded us away. And thus, having nothing wherewith to seek the coast of the West Indies, I was with the rest of our company in consultation to go to the coast of the Mine [in West Africa], hoping there to have obtained some gold for our wares and thereby to have defrayed our charge.

But even in that present instant there came to us a negro, sent from a king oppressed by other kings his neighbours, desiring our aid, with promise that as many negroes as by these wars might be obtained, as well of his part as of ours, should be at our pleasure. Whereupon we concluded to give aid and sent 120 of our men which, the 15th of January, assaulted a town of the negroes of our ally's adversaries which had in it 8,000 inhabitants, being very strongly impaled and fenced after their manner, but it was so well defended that our men prevailed not but lost six men and forty hurt; so that our men sent forthwith to me for more help. Whereupon, considering that the good success of this enterprise might highly further the commodity of our voyage, I went myself, and with the help of the king of our side assaulted the town, both by land and sea, and very hardly with fire (their houses being covered with dry palm leaves) obtained the town, put the inhabitants to flight, where we took 250 persons, men, women and children, and by our friend the king of our side there were taken 600 prisoners, whereof we hoped to have had our choice: but the negro (in which nation is seldom or never found truth) meant nothing less; for that night he removed his camp and prisoners so that we were fain to content us with those few which we had gotten ourselves.

Now had we obtained between four and five hundred negroes, wherewith we thought it somewhat reasonable to seek the coast of the West Indies, and there for our negroes and other our merchandise we hoped to obtain whereof to countervail our charges with some gains, whereunto we proceeded with all diligence, furnished our watering, took fuel, and departed the coast of Guinea the third of February, continuing at sea with a passage more hard than before hath been accustomed till the 27th day of March, which day we had sight of an island, called Dominica, upon the coast of the West Indies in fourteen degrees. From thence we coasted from place to place, making our traffic with the Spaniards as we might, somewhat hardly because the king had straitly commanded all his Governors in those parts by no means to suffer any trade to be made with us.

Notwithstanding, we had reasonable trade and courteous entertainment from the isle of Margarita unto Cartagena without anything greatly worth the noting, saving at Capo de la Vela, in a town called Rio de la Hacha (from whence come all the pearls) the treasurer, who had the charge there, would by no means agree to any trade or suffer us to take water; he had fortified his town with divers bulwarks in all places where it might be entered, and furnished himself with an hundred harquebusiers, so that he thought by famine to have enforced us to have put aland our negroes: of which purpose he had not greatly failed unless we had by force entered the town: which (after we could by no means obtain his favour) we were enforced to do, and so with two hundred men brake in upon their bulwarks and entered the town with the loss only of two men of our parts, and no hurt done to the Spaniards, because after their volley of shot discharged they all fled.

Thus having the town with some circumstance, as partly by the Spaniards' desire of negroes and partly by friendship of the Treasurer, we obtained a secret trade: whereupon the Spaniards resorted to us by night and bought of us to the number of 200 negroes. In all other places where we traded the Spaniards inhabitants were glad of us and traded willingly.

At Cartagena, the last town we thought to have seen on the coast, we could by no means obtain to deal with any Spaniard, the Governor was so straight. And because our trade was so near finished we thought not good either to adventure any landing or to detract further time, but in peace departed from thence the 24th of July hoping to have escaped the time of their storms, which then soon after began to reign, the which they call furicanos. But passing by the West end of Cuba towards the coast of Florida there happened to us the 12th day of August an extreme storm, which continued by the space of four days, which so beat the *Jesus* that we cut down all her higher buildings;★ her rudder also was sore shaken and withal [she] was in so extreme a leak that we were rather upon the point to leave her than to keep her any longer, yet hoping to bring all to good pass we sought the coast of Florida, where

★ The *Jesus of Lubeck* was a dilapidated old ship which Henry VIII had bought second-hand from the Hanseatic League in 1544. She had a high forecastle and aftercastle ('buildings') which caused her to roll dangerously, straining her structure. One of the ship's company recorded that in this storm she sprang leaks 'so big as a man's arm' and 'the living fish did swim' in her hold 'as in the sea.' Hawkins knew her to be unseaworthy, but he could not avoid hiring her when the Queen commanded it, and she was at least a very imposing ship and had commodious holds. During this storm the *William and John* left the fleet and made her own way home.

we found no place nor haven for our ships because of the shallowness of the coast.

Thus, being in greater despair and taken with a new storm which continued other three days, we were enforced to take for our succour the port which serveth the city of Mexico called Saint John de Ulua, which standeth in 19 degrees: in seeking of which port we took in our three ships which carried passengers to the number of an hundred, which passengers we hoped should be a mean to us the better to obtain victuals for our money and a quiet place for the repairing of our fleet. Shortly after this, the 16th of September, we entered the port of Saint John de Ulua and in our entry the Spaniards, thinking us to be the fleet of Spain, the chief officers of the country came aboard us, which being deceived of their expectation were greatly dismayed: but immediately when they saw our demand was nothing but victuals were recomforted.

I found also in the same port twelve ships which had in them by report two hundred thousand pounds in gold and silver, all which (being in my possession, with the king's island* as also the passengers before in my way thitherward stayed) I set at liberty, without the taking from them the weight of a groat: only because I would not be delayed of my dispatch I stayed two men of estimation and sent post immediately to Mexico, which was two hundred miles from us, to the Presidents and Council there, showing them of our arrival there by the force of weather and the necessity of the repair of our ships and victuals, which wants we required as friends to King Philip to be furnished of for our money: and that the Presidents and Council there should with all convenient speed take order that at the arrival of the Spanish fleet, which was daily looked for, there might no cause of quarrel rise between us and them but for the better maintenance of amity their commandment might be had in that behalf.

This message being sent away, the sixteenth day of September [1568] at night, being the very day of our arrival, in the next morning, which was the seventeenth day of the same month, we saw open of [outside] the haven thirteen great ships; and understanding them to be the fleet of Spain I sent immediately to advertise the General of the Fleet of my being there, doing him to understand that before I would suffer them to enter the port there should some order of conditions pass between us for our safe being there and maintenance of peace.

Now it is to be understood that this port is made by a little island of stones not three foot above the water in the highest place and but a bow-shot of length any way. This island standeth from the mainland

* The small island, with guns mounted on it, which commanded the harbour and the entrances to it.

two bow-shots or more, also it is to be understood that there is not in all this coast any other place for ships to arrive in safety because the north wind hath there such violence that unless the ships be very safely moored with their anchors fastened upon this island there is no remedy for these north winds but death. Also the place of the haven was so little that of necessity the ships must ride one aboard the other, so that we could not give place to them nor they to us.

And here I began to bewail that which after followed, 'For now,' said I, 'I am in two dangers, and forced to receive the one of them'. That was, either I must have kept out the fleet from entering the port, the which with God's help I was very well able to do, or else suffer them to enter in with their accustomed treason, which they never fail to execute where they may have opportunity to compass it by any means. If I had kept them out then had there been present shipwreck of all the fleet which amounted in value to 6,000,000, which was in value of our money 1,800,000 pounds, which I considered I was not able to answer, fearing the Queen's Majesty's indignation in so weighty a matter. Thus with myself revolving the doubts I thought rather better to abide the jut of the uncertainty than the certainty. The uncertain doubt I account was their treason, which by good policy I hoped might be prevented, and therefore as choosing the least mischief I proceeded to conditions.

Now was our first messenger come and returned from the fleet with report of the arrival of a Viceroy,* so that he had authority both in all this Province of Mexico (otherwise called *Nueva España*) and in the sea, who sent us word that we should send our conditions which of his part should (for the better maintenance of amity between the Princes) be both favourably granted and faithfully performed, with many fair words how passing the coast of the Indies he had understood of our honest behaviour towards the inhabitants where we had to do, as well elsewhere as in the same port, the which I let pass.

Thus following our demand we required victuals for our money and licence to sell as much ware as might furnish our wants, and that there might be of either part twelve gentlemen as hostages for the maintenance of peace: and that the island for our better safety might be in our own possession during our abode there, and such ordnance as was planted in the same island, which were eleven pieces of brass: and that no Spaniard might land in the island with any kind of weapon. These conditions at the first he somewhat misliked, chiefly the guard of the island to be in our own keeping, which if they had had we had soon known our fare, for with the first north wind they had cut our cables

* The newly appointed Viceroy, Don Martin Enriquez. He ranked second only to the King.

and our ships had gone ashore. But in the end he concluded to our request, bringing the twelve hostages to ten, which with all speed of either part were received, with a writing from the Viceroy signed with his hand and sealed with his seal of all the conditions concluded, and forthwith a trumpet blown with commandment that none of either part should be mean to violate the peace upon pain of death: and further it was concluded that the two Generals of the fleets should meet and give faith each to other for the performance of the premises, which was so done.

Thus at the end of three days all was concluded and the fleet entered the port, saluting one another as the manner of the sea doth require. Thus, as I said before, Thursday we entered the port, Friday we saw the fleet, and on Monday at night they entered the port. Then we laboured two days placing the English ships by themselves and the Spanish ships by themselves, the Captains of each part and inferior men of their parts promising great amity of all sides: which even as with all fidelity it was meant on our part, so the Spaniards meant nothing less on their parts, but from the mainland had furnished themselves with a supply of men to the number of 1,000, and meant the next Thursday, being the 23rd of September, at dinner time to set upon us on all sides.

The same Thursday in the morning, the treason being at hand, some appearance showed as shifting of weapon from ship to ship, planting and bending of ordnance from the ships to the island where our men warded, passing to and fro of companies of men more than required for their necessary business, and many other ill likelihoods which caused us to have a vehement suspicion, and therewithal sent to the Viceroy to enquire what was meant by it, which sent immediately straight commandment to unplant all things suspicious, and also sent word that he in the faith of a Viceroy would be our defence from all villainies.

Yet we being not satisfied with this answer, because we suspected a great number of men to be hid in a great ship of 900 tons which was moored next unto the *Minion,* sent again to the Viceroy the master* of the *Jesus* which had the Spanish tongue and required to be satisfied if any such thing were or not. The Viceroy now seeing that the treason must be discovered forthwith stayed our master, blew the trumpet, and of all sides set upon us. Our men which warded ashore being stricken with sudden fear gave place, fled, and sought to recover succour of the ships. The Spaniards, being before provided for the purpose, landed in all places in multitudes from their ships, which they might easily do without boats, and slew all our men ashore without mercy; a few of them escaped aboard the *Jesus.* The great ship which had by the estimation

* Robert Barrett. He was burned at the stake in Seville.

three hundred men placed on her secretly immediately fell aboard the *Minion*, but by God's appointment in the time of the suspicion we had, which was only one half hour, the *Minion* was made ready to avoid, and so releasing her headfasts and haling away by the sternfasts she was gotten out. Thus with God's help she defended the violence of the first brunt of these three hundred men.

The *Minion* being passed out they came aboard the *Jesus*, which also with very much ado and the loss of many of our men were defended and kept out. Then there were also two other ships that assaulted the *Jesus* at the same instant so that she had hard getting loose, but yet with some time we had cut our headfasts and gotten out by the sternfasts. Now when the *Jesus* and the *Minion* were gotten about two ships' length from the Spanish fleet the fight began so hot on all sides that within one hour the admiral of the Spaniards was supposed to be sunk, their vice-admiral burned, and one other of their principal ships supposed to be sunk, so that the ships were little able to annoy us.

Then it is to be understood that all the ordnance upon the island was in the Spaniards' hands, which did us so great annoyance that it cut all the masts and yards of the *Jesus* in such sort that there was no hope to carry her away; also it sunk our small ships. Whereupon we determined to place the *Jesus* on that side of the *Minion* that she might abide all the battery from the land and so be a defence for the *Minion* till night, and then to take such relief of victual and other necessaries from the *Jesus* as the time would suffer us and to leave her.

As we were thus determining and had placed the *Minion* from the shot of the land, suddenly the Spaniards had fired two great ships which were coming directly with us, and having no means to avoid the fire it bred among our men a marvellous fear, so that some said, 'Let us depart with the *Minion*,' others said, 'Let us see whither the wind will carry the fire from us'. But to be short, the *Minion*'s men, which had always their sails in a readiness, thought to make sure work, and so without either consent of the Captain or Master cut their sail, so that very hardly I was received into the *Minion*.

The most part of the men that were left alive in the *Jesus* made shift and followed the *Minion* in a small boat: the rest which the little boat was not able to receive were enforced to abide the mercy of the Spaniards (which I doubt was very little). So with the *Minion* only and the *Judith* (a small bark of 50 tons) we escaped, which bark the same night forsook us in our great misery.* We were now removed with the

* Drake was in command of the *Judith*. It is impossible now to say whether Drake deliberately deserted Hawkins (as he seems to think) or whether his battered little ship was driven helplessly out to sea during the night. She reached Plymouth on January 20th, 1569, five days before Hawkins reached Mount's Bay.

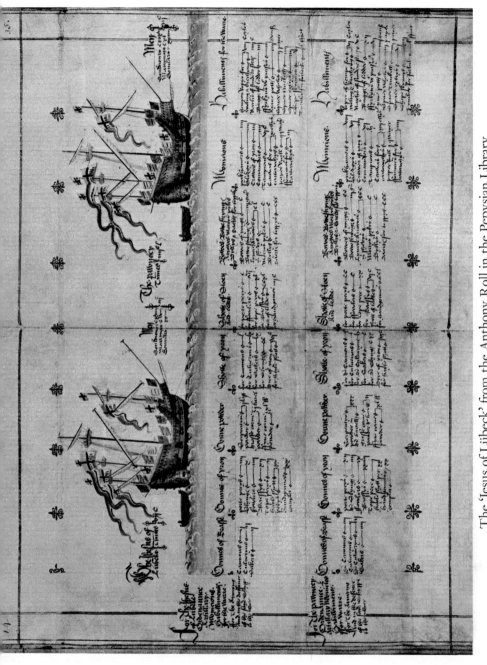

The 'Jesus of Lübeck' from the Anthony Roll in the Pepysian Library

Minion from the Spanish ships two bowshots, and there rode all that night. The next morning we recovered an island a mile from the Spaniards where there took us a north wind, and being left only with two anchors and two cables (for in this conflict we lost three cables and two anchors) we thought always upon death which ever was present, but God preserved us to a longer time.

The weather waxed reasonable and the Saturday we set sail, and having a great number of men and little victuals our hope of life waxed less and less: some desired to yield to the Spaniards, some rather desired to obtain a place where they might give themselves to the infidels, and some had rather abide with a little pittance the mercy of God at sea.

So thus with many sorrowful hearts we wandered in an unknown sea by the space of fourteen days till hunger enforced us to seek the land, for hides were thought very good meat, rats, cats, mice and dogs, none escaped that might be gotten, parrots and monkeys that were had in great price were thought there very profitable if they served the turn one dinner. Thus in the end the 8th day of October we came to the land in the bottom of the same Bay of Mexico, in 23 degrees and a half, where we hoped to have found inhabitants of the Spaniards, relief of victuals, and place for the repair of our ship, which was so sore beaten with shot from our enemies and bruised with shooting off our own ordnance, that our weary and weak arms were scarce able to defend and keep out water. But all things happened to the contrary, for we found neither people, victual, nor haven of relief, but a place where having fair weather with some peril we might land a boat. Our people being forced with hunger desired to be set on land, whereunto I consented.

And such as were willing to land I put them apart, and such as were desirous to go homewards I put apart, so that they were indifferently parted a hundred of one side and a hundred of the other side: these hundred men we set aland with all diligence in this little place before-said, which being landed, we determined there to take in fresh water, and so with our little remain of victuals to take the sea.

The next day, having aland with me fifty of our hundred men that remained, for the speedier preparing of our water aboard, there arose an extreme storm so that in three days we could by no means repair aboard our ship. The ship also was in such peril that every hour we looked for shipwreck.

But yet God again had mercy on us and sent fair weather. We had aboard our water and departed the 16th day of October, after which day we had fair and prosperous weather till the 16th day of November, which day, God be praised, we were clear from the coast of the Indies and out of the channel and Gulf of Bahama, which is between the Cape of Florida and the islands of Lucayo.

After this, growing near to the cold country, our men being oppressed with famine died continually, and they that were left grew into such weakness that we were scantly able to manage our ship, and the wind being always ill for us to recover England we determined to go with Galicia in Spain, with intent there to relieve our company and other extreme wants. And being arrived the last day of December in a place near unto Vigo, called Pontevedra, our men with excess of fresh meat grew into miserable diseases and died a great part of them. This matter was borne out as long as it might be, but in the end although there were none of our men suffered to go aland, yet by access of the Spaniards our feebleness was known to them. Whereupon they ceased not to seek by all means to betray us, but with all speed possible we departed to Vigo, where we had some help of certain English ships and twelve fresh men, wherewith we repaired our wants as we might, and departing the 20th day of January, 1568, arrived in Mounts Bay in Cornwall the 25th of the same month, praised be God therefore.

If all the miseries and troublesome affairs of this sorrowful voyage should be perfectly and thoroughly written there should need a painful man with his pen and as great a time as he had that wrote the lives and deaths of the Martyrs.

It is clear from the Viceroy's report of the battle that he never intended to keep his word. To him Hawkins was a heretic and a pirate, an enemy of God who had outrageously insulted the majesty of Spain, and there could be no question of keeping faith with him. The Elizabethan seamen never forgot or forgave this treachery and the Spanish cruelty to their prisoners, and henceforward Drake and Hawkins, the most formidable of the Elizabethan sea-captains, fought their private war with Philip II. 'The military and sea-faring men all over England', wrote William Camden, 'fretted and demanded war against the Spaniards.'

A POWDER-MAKER'S ADVENTURES
Job Hortop

Two of the English seamen captured by the Spaniards after the Battle of San Juan not only survived, and ultimately escaped, but wrote or dictated the story of their adventures. One was Job Hortop, the other was Miles Philips, and both narratives are in Hakluyt. Hortop's is the more interesting; he had an observant eye for his surroundings, and particularly for picturesque detail, which was all too rare among Elizabethan seamen.

The travails of Job Hortop, which Sir John Hawkins set on land within the Bay of Mexico, after his departure from the haven of St John de Ulua in Nueva España, the 8th of October, 1568.

NOT untruly nor without cause, said Job, the faithful servant of God (whom the sacred Scriptures tell us to have dwelt in the land of Hus) that man being born of a woman, living a short time, is replenished with many miseries: which some know by reading of histories, many by the view of others' calamities, and I by experience in myself, as this present treatise ensuing shall show.

It is not unknown unto many that I, Job Hortop, powder-maker, was born at Bourne, a town in Lincolnshire, from my age of twelve years brought up in Redriff, near London, with Master Francis Lee, who was the Queen's Majesty's powder-maker, whom I served until I was pressed to go on the 3rd voyage to the West Indies with the Right Worshipful Sir John Hawkins, who appointed me to be one of the gunners in Her Majesty's ship called the *Jesus of Lubeck*, who set sail from Plymouth in the month of October, 1567, having with him another ship of Her Majesty called the *Minion*, and four ships of his own, namely the *Angel*, the *Swallow*, the *Judith* and the *William and John*. He directed his Vice-Admiral that if foul weather did separate them to meet at the island of Teneriffe. After which by the space of seven days and seven nights we had such storms at sea that we lost our long boats and a pinnace, with some men. Coming to the isle of Teneriffe there our General heard that his Vice-Admiral with the *Swallow* and the *William and John* were at the island called Gomera, where, finding his Vice-Admiral, he anchored, took in fresh water, and set sail for Cape Blankco, where in the way we took a Portugal caravel laden with fish called mullets.

From thence we sailed to Cape Verde. In our course thither we met a Frenchman of Rochelle, called Captain Bland, who had taken a Portugal caravel, whom our Vice-Admiral chased and took. Captain Drake, now Sir Francis Drake, was made Master and Captain of the caravel, and so we kept our way till we came to Cape Verde, and there we anchored, took our boats and set soldiers on shore. Our General was the first that leapt on land and with him Captain Dudley. There we took certain negroes, but not without damage to ourselves, for our General, Captain Dudley, and eight other of our company were hurt with poisoned arrows: about nine days after the eight that were wounded died. Our General was taught by a negro to draw the poison out of his wound with a clove of garlic whereby he was cured. From thence we went to Sierra Leone, where be monstrous fishes called sharks which will devour men. I amongst others was sent in the *Angel* with two pinnaces into the river called Calousa to seek two caravels that were there trading with the negroes; we took one of them with the negroes and brought them away.

In this river in ye night time we had one of our pinnaces bulged by a sea-horse [walrus] so that our men swimming about the river were all taken into the other pinnaces, except two that took hold one of another and were carried away by the sea-horse. This monster hath the just proportion of a horse saving that his legs be short, his teeth very great and a span in length: he useth in the night to go on land into the woods seeking at unawares to devour the negroes in their cabins, whom they by their vigilance prevent and kill him in this manner. The negroes keep watch and diligently attend their coming, and when they are gone into the woods they forthwith lay a great tree overthwart the way so that at their return, for that their legs be so short, they cannot go over it; then the negroes set upon them with their bows, arrows and darts, and so destroy them.

From thence we entered the river called the Casserroes, where there were other caravels trading with the negroes, and them we took. In this island, betwixt the river and the main, trees grow with oysters upon them. There grow palmetto trees, which be as high as a ship's main mast and on their tops grow nuts [from which come] wine and oil, which they call palmetto wine and palmetto oil. The plantain tree also groweth in that country; the tree is as big as a man's thigh and as high as a fir pole, the leaves thereof be long and broad, and on the top grow the fruit which are called plantanos: they are crooked and a cubit long, and as big as a man's wrist; they grow on clusters: when they be ripe they be very good and dainty to eat; sugar is not more delicate in taste than they be.

From thence with the *Angel*, the *Judith* and the two pinnaces we sailed to Sierra Leone, where our General at that time was, who with the captains and soldiers went up into the river called Taggarin to take a town of the negroes, where he found three kings of that country with fifty thousand negroes besieging the same town, which they could not take in many years before, when they had warred with it. Our General made a breach, entered and valiantly took the town, wherein were found five Portugals which yielded themselves to his mercy and he saved their lives. We took and carried thence for traffic to the West Indies 500 negroes. The three kings drove 7,000 negroes into the sea at low water at the point of the land, where they were all drowned in the ooze for that they could not take their canoes to save themselves. We returned back again in our pinnaces to the ships, and there took in fresh water and made ready sail towards Rio Grande. At our coming thither we entered with the *Angel*, the *Judith* and the two pinnaces, and found there seven Portugal caravels which made great fight with us. In the end by God's help we won the victory and drove them to the shore, from whence the negroes they fled, and we fetched the caravels from the shore into the river. The next morning Master Francis Drake with his caravel, the *Swallow*, and the *William and John* came into the river with Captain Dudley and his soldiers, who landed being but a hundred soldiers, and fought with seven thousand negroes, burned the town, and returned to our General with the loss of one man.

In that place there be many musk-cats which breed in hollow trees: the negroes take them in a net and put them in a cage and nourish them very daintily, and take the musk from them with a spoon.

Now we directed our course from Guinea towards the West Indies.

And by the way died Captain Dudley.

In sailing towards the Indies the first land that we escried was the island called Dominica, where at our coming we anchored and took in fresh water and wood for our provision: which done, we sailed towards the island called Margarita, where our General, in despite of the Spaniards, anchored, landed and took in fresh victuals. A mile off the island there is a rock in the sea wherein do breed many fowls like unto barnacles [geese]: in the night we went out in our boats and with cudgels we killed many of them and brought them with many of their eggs aboard with us. Their eggs be as big as turkey's eggs, and speckled like them. We did eat them and found them very good meat.

From thence we sailed to Burburata, which is in the mainland of the West Indies: there we came in, moored our ships and tarried two months, trimming and dressing our ships, and in the meantime traded with certain Spaniards of that country. There our General sent us unto a town called Placentia (which stood on a high hill) to have entreated a Bishop that dwelt there for his favour and friendship in their laws, who, hearing of our coming, for fear forsook ye town.

On our way up the hill to Placentia we found a monstrous venomous worm with two heads; his body was as big as a man's arm and a yard long. Our Master, Robert Barrett, did cut him in sunder with his sword, and it made it as black as if it were coloured with ink.

Here be many tigers, monstrous and furious beasts, which by subtlety devour and destroy many men. They use the traded ways, and will show themselves twice or thrice to the travellers, and so depart secretly, lurking till they be past, then suddenly and at un-awares they leap upon them and devour them. They had so used two of our company had not one of them looked behind. Our General sent three ships unto the island called Curaçao to make provision for the rest, where they remained until his coming. He sent from thence the *Angel* and the *Judith* to Rio de Hacha, where we anchored before the town. The Spaniards shot three pieces at us from the shore, whom we requited with two of ours and shot through the Governor's house. We weighed anchor and anchored again without shot of the town, where we rode five days in despite of the Spaniards and their shot. In the mean space there came a caravel of advice from S. Domingo, whom with the *Angel* and the *Judith* we chased and drove to the shore. We fetched him from thence in spite of 200 Spaniards' harquebus shot, and anchored again before the town and rid there with them till our General's coming, who anchored, landed his men, and valiantly took the town with the loss of one man whose name was Thomas Surgeon.

We landed and planted on the shore for our safeties our field ordnance: we drove the Spaniards up into the country above two leagues, whereby they were enforced to trade with our General, to whom he sold most part of his negroes.

In this river we killed a monstrous lagarto or crocodile, in this port at sunset. Seven of us went in the pinnace up into the river carrying with us a dog, unto whom with ropeyarn we bound a great hook of steel with a chain that had a swivel which we put under the dog's belly, the point of the hook coming over his back fast bound, as aforesaid. We put him overboard and veered out our rope by little and little, rowing away with our boat. The lagarto came and presently swallowed up the dog, then did we row hard till we had choked him; he plunged and made a wonderful stir in the water: we leapt on shore and haled him on land. He was 23 feet by the rule, headed like a hog, in body like a serpent, full of scales as broad as a saucer; his tail long and full of knots as big as a falcon shot: he hath four legs, his feet have long nails like unto a dragon. We opened him, took out his guts, flayed him, dried his skin and stuffed it with straw, meaning to have brought it home had not the ship been cast away. This monster will carry away and devour both man and horse.

From hence we shaped our course to Santa Martha where we landed, traded, and sold certain negroes. There two of our company killed a monstrous adder going towards his cave with a coney in his mouth; his body was as big as any man's thigh and seven foot long; upon his tail he had sixteen knots, every one as big as a great walnut, which they say do show his age: his colour was green and yellow. They opened him and found two coneys in his belly.

From thence we sailed to Carthagena, where we went in, moored our ships and would have traded with them but they durst not for fear of the King. We brought up the *Minion* against the castle and shot at the castle and town. Then we landed in an island where were many gardens: there in a cave we found certain botijos of wine which we brought away with us, in recompense whereof our General commanded to be set on shore woollen and linen cloth to the value thereof.

From hence by foul weather we were forced to seek the port of Saint John de Ulua. In our way thwart of Campeachy we met with a Spaniard, a small ship, who was bound for Santo Domingo. He had in him a Spaniard called Augustin de Villa Nueva, who was the man that betrayed all the noblemen in the Indies and caused them to be beheaded, wherefore he with two friars fled to Santo Domingo: them we took and brought with us into the port of Saint John de Ulua. Our General made great account of him and used him like a nobleman: howbeit in the end he was one of them that betrayed us.

When we had moored our ships and landed we mounted the ordnance that we found there in the island, and for our safety kept watch and ward. The next day after we discovered the Spanish fleet, whereof Luçon, a Spaniard, was General: with him came a Spaniard called Don Martin Henriquez, whom the King of Spain sent to be his Viceroy of the Indies. He sent a pinnace with a flag of truce unto our General to know of what country those ships were that rode there in the King of Spain's port; who said, they were the Queen of England's ships, which came in there for victuals for their money: 'Wherefore if your General will come in here he shall give me victuals and all other necessaries, and I will go out on the one side of the port and he shall come in on the other side.' The Spaniard returned for answer that he was a Viceroy and had a thousand men, and therefore he would come in. Our General said, 'If he be a Viceroy I represent my Queen's person and I am a Viceroy as well as he; and if he have a thousand men, my powder and shot will take the better place.'

Then the Viceroy, after council among themselves, yielded to our General's demand, swearing by his King and his Crown, by his commission and authority that he had from his King, that he would perform it, and thereupon pledges were given on both parts. Our General, bearing a godly and Christian mind, void of fraud and deceit, judged the Spaniards to have done the like, delivered to them six gentlemen, not doubting to have received the like from them. But the faithless Spaniards in costly apparel gave of the basest of their company, as afterwards it was well known. These things finished, proclamation was made on both sides that on pain of death no occasion should be given whereby any quarrel should grow to the breach of the league, and then they peaceably entered the port with great triumph on both sides.

The Spaniards presently brought a great hulk, a ship of six hundred, and moored her by the side of the *Minion*, and they cut out ports in their other ships planting their ordnance towards us. In the night they filled the hulk with men to lay the *Minion* aboard, as the sequel did show, which made our General doubtful of their dealings.

Wherefore, for that he could speak the Spanish tongue, he sent Robert Barrett aboard the Viceroy to know his meaning in those dealings, who willed him with his company to come in to him, whom he commanded presently to be set in the bilboes [in chains]: and forthwith a cornet (for a watchword among the false Spaniards) was sounded for the enterprising of their pretended treason against our General, whom Augustine de Villa Nova, sitting at dinner with him, should then presently have killed with a poniard which he had privily in his sleeve, which was espied and prevented by one, John Chamberlain, who took the poniard out of his sleeve. Our General hastily rose up and commanded him to be put prisoner in the steward's room and to be kept with two men. The faithless Spaniards, thinking all things to their desire had been finished, suddenly sounded a trumpet, and therewith three hundred Spaniards entered the *Minion*, whereat our General with a loud and fierce voice called unto us, saying, 'God and Saint George, upon those traitorous villains and rescue the *Minion*. I trust in God the day shall be ours.'

And with that the mariners and soldiers leapt out of the *Jesus of Lubeck* into the *Minion* and beat out the Spaniards, and with a shot out of her fired the Spaniards' Vice-Admiral, where the most part of 300 Spaniards were spoiled and blown overboard with powder. Their Admiral also was on fire half an hour. We cut our cables, wound off our ships, and presently fought with them. They came upon us on every side and continued the fight from ten of the clock until it was night. They killed all our men that were on shore in the island, saving three, which by swimming got aboard the *Jesus of Lubeck*. They sunk the

General's ship called the *Angel*, and took the *Swallow*: the Spaniards' Admiral had above threescore shot through her; many of his men were spoiled: four other of their ships were sunk. There were in that fleet and that came from the shore to rescue them fifteen hundred: we slew of them five hundred and forty as we were credibly informed by a note that came to Mexico. In this fight the *Jesus of Lubeck* had five shot through her mainmast: her foremast was struck in sunder under the hounds with a chain shot, and her hull was wonderfully pierced with shot, therefore it was impossible to bring her away. They set two of their ships on fire intending therewith to have burnt the *Jesus of Lubeck*, which we prevented by cutting our cables in the halse and winding off by our stern-fast.

The *Minion* was forced to set sail and stand off from us and come to an anchor without shot of the island. Our General courageously cheered up his soldiers and gunners and called to Samuel, his page, for a cup of beer, who brought it him in a silver cup, and he drinking to all men willed the gunners to stand by their ordnance lustily like men. He had no sooner set the cup out of his hand but a demi-culverin shot struck away the cup and a cooper's plane that stood by the mainmast, and ran out on the other side of the ship; which nothing dismayed our General, for he ceased not to encourage us, saying, 'Fear nothing, for God, who hath preserved me from this shot will also deliver us from these traitors and villains.'

Then Captain Bland, meaning to have turned out of the port, had his mainmast struck overboard with a chain shot that came from the shore, wherefore he anchored, fired his ship, took his pinnace with all his men, and came aboard the *Jesus of Lubeck* to our General, who said unto him that he thought he would not have run away from him. He answered that he was not minded to have run away from him, but his intent was to have turned up and to have laid the weathermost ship of the Spanish fleet aboard and fired his ship in hope therewith to have set on fire the Spanish fleet. He said if he had done so he had done well. With this night came on. Our General commanded the *Minion* for safe-guard of her masts to be brought under the *Jesus of Lubeck*'s lee. He willed Master Francis Drake to come in with the *Judith*, and to lay the *Minion* aboard to take in men and other things needful and to go out, and so he did.

At night when the wind came off the shore we set sail and went out in despite of the Spaniards and their shot, where we anchored with two anchors under the island, the wind being northerly, which was wonderful dangerous and we feared every hour to be driven with [on] the lee shore. In the end, when the wind came larger we weighed anchor and set sail, seeking the river of Panuco for water, whereof we had very little, and victuals were so scarce that we were driven to eat hides, cats, rats, parrots, monkeys and dogs; wherefore our General was forced to divide his company into two parts, for there was a mutiny among them for want of victuals. And some said that they had rather be on the shore to shift for themselves amongst the enemies than to starve on shipboard. He asked them who would go on shore and who would tarry on shipboard; those that would go on shore he willed to go on foremast, and those that would tarry on baft-mast. Fourscore and sixteen of us were willing to depart. Our General gave unto every one of us six yards of roan cloth, and money to them that demanded it. When we were landed he came unto us, where friendly embracing every one of us he was greatly grieved that he was forced to leave us behind him. He counselled us to serve God and to love one another, and thus courteously he gave us a sorrowful farewell and promised if God sent him safe home he would do what he could that so many of us as lived should by some means be brought into England, and so he did.

Since my return into England I have heard that many misliked that he left us so behind him and brought away negroes; but the reason is this, for them he might have had victuals or any other thing needful, if by foul weather he had been driven upon the islands, which for gold nor silver he could not have had.

And thus our General departed to his ship and we remained on land, where for our safeties, fearing the wild Indians that were about us, we kept watch all night, and at sun rising marched on our way, three and three in a rank, until that we came into a field under a grove, where the Indians came upon us, asking us what people we were and how we came there. Two of our company, namely Anthony Goddard and John Cornish, for that they could speak the Spanish tongue, went to them and said we were Englishmen that never came in that country before, and that we had fought with the Spaniards and for that we lacked victuals our General set us on shore. They asked us whither we intended to go; we said to Panuco. The Captain of the Indians willed us to give unto them some of our clothes and shirts, which we did. Then he bade us give them all, but we would not so do, whereupon John Cornish was then slain with an arrow which an Indian boy that stood by the Captain shot at him; wherefore he stroke the boy on the neck with his bow that he lay for dead, and willed us to follow him, who brought us into a great field where we found fresh water. He bad us sit down about the pond and drink, and he with his company would go in the mean space to kill five or six deer and bring them us. We tarried there till three of the clock, but they came not. There one of our company, whose name was John Cooke, with four other departed from us into a grove to seek relief, where presently they were taken by the Indians and stript as naked as ever they were born, and so returned to us.

Then we divided ourselves into two parts, half to Anthony Goddard and the rest to James Collier, and thus severally we sought for Panuco. Anthony Goddard with his company bid us farewell; they passed a river where the Indians robbed many of them of their clothes, and so passing on their way came to a stony hill where they stayed. James Collier with his company that day passed the same river and were also robbed, and one of them slain by chance. We came that night unto the hill where Anthony Goddard and his company rested; there we remained till morning, and then we marched all together from thence, entering between two groves, where the Indians robbed us of all our clothes and left us naked; they hurt many, and killed eight of us. Three days after we came to another river, there the Indians showed us the way to Panuco, and so left us. We passed the river into the wilderness where we made wreaths of green grass which we wound about our bodies, to keep us from the sun and gnats of that country.

We travelled there seven days and seven nights before we came to Panuco, feeding on nothing but roots and guavas, a fruit like figs. At our coming to the river of Panuco two Spanish horsemen came over unto us in a canoe. They asked us how long we had been in the wilderness, and where our General was, for they knew us to be of the company that had fought with their countrymen. We told them seven days and seven nights, and for lack of victuals our General set us on shore, and he was gone away with his ships. They returned to their Governor, who sent them with five canoes to bring us all over, which done they set us in array where a hundred horsemen with their lances came forcibly upon us, but did not hurt us. They carried us prisoners to Panuco, where we remained one night. In the river of Panuco there is a fish like a calf, the Spaniards call it a mallatin; he hath a stone in his head which the Indians use for the disease of the colic. In the night he cometh on land and eateth grass. I have eaten of it and it eateth not much unlike to bacon.

From thence we were sent to Mexico, which is 90 leagues from Panuco. In our way thither, 20 leagues from the sea side, I did see white crabs running up and down the sands; I have eaten of them and they be very good meat. There groweth a fruit which the Spaniards call avocados; it is proportioned like an egg and as black as a coal, having a stone in it, and it is an excellent good fruit. There also groweth a strange tree which they call magueys [aloe]; it serveth them to many uses; below by the root they make a hole whereat they do take out of it twice every day a certain kind of liquor which they seethe in a great kettle till the third part be consumed and that it wax thick, it is as sweet as any honey and they do eat it. Within twenty days after that they have taken all the liquor from it it withereth, and they cut it down and use it as we use our hemp here in England, which done, they convert it to many uses. Of some part they make mantles, ropes and thread; of the ends they make needles to sew their saddles, panels, and other furniture for their horses; of the rest they make tiles to cover their houses, and they put it to many other purposes.

And thus we came to Mexico, which is seven or eight miles about, seated in a great fen, environed with four hills. It hath but two ways of entrance, and it is full of creeks in the which in their canoes they pass from place to place, and to the islands there within. In the Indies ordinarily three times a year be wonderful earthquakes which put the people in great fear and danger. During the time of two years that I was in Mexico I saw them six times. When they come they throw down trees, houses and churches. There is a city twenty-five leagues from Mexico called Tlaxcalla which is inhabited with a hundred thousand Indians. They go in white shirts, linen breeches and long mantles, and the women wear about them a garment much like unto a flannel petticoat. The King's palace was the first place we were brought unto in Mexico, where without we were willed to sit down. Much people, men, women and children came wandering about us, many lamented our misery, and some of their clergy asked us if we were Christians. We said, we praised God, we were as good Christians as they. They asked how they might know that; we said by our confessions.

From thence we were carried in a canoe to a tanner's house which standeth a little from the city. The next morning two friars and two priests came thither to us, and willed us to bless ourselves, and say our prayers in the Latin tongue that they might understand us. Many of our company did so, whereupon they returned to the Viceroy and told him that we were good Christians and that they liked us well, and then they brought us much relief, with clothes. Our sick men were sent to their hospitals where many were cured, and many died. From the tanner's house we were led to a gentleman's place where upon pain of death we were charged to abide and not to come into the city; thither we had all things necessary brought us. On Sundays and holy days much people came and brought us great relief.

The Viceroy practised to hang us and caused a pair of new gallows to be set up to have executed us, whereunto the noblemen of that country would not consent but prayed him to stay until the ship of advice brought news from the King of Spain what should be done with us, for they said they could not find anything by us whereby they might lawfully put us to death.

The Viceroy then commanded us to be sent to an island thereby, and he sent for the Bishop of Mexico, who sent four priests to the island to examine and confess us, who said that the Viceroy would burn us when we were examined and confessed, according to the laws of the country. They returned to the Bishop and told him that we were very good Christians. The Bishop certified the Viceroy of our examinations and confessions, and said that we were good Christians, therefore he would not meddle with us. Then the Viceroy sent for our Master, R. Barrett, whom he kept prisoner in his palace until the fleet was departed for Spain. The rest of us he sent to a town seven leagues from Mexico, called Tescuco, to card wool among the Indian slaves, which drudgery we disdained and concluded to beat our masters, and so we did. Wherefore they sent to the Viceroy, desiring him for God's sake and our Lady's to send for us for they would not keep us any longer; they said that we were devils and no men.

The Viceroy sent for us and imprisoned us in a house in Mexico. From thence he sent Anthony Goddard and some other of our company with him into Spain with Luçon, the General that took us. The rest of us stayed in Mexico two years after, and then were sent prisoners into Spain, with Don Juan de Velasco de Varre, Admiral and General of the Spanish fleet, who carried with him in his ship to be presented to the King of Spain the anatomy of a giant, which was sent from China to Mexico, to the Viceroy, Don Martin Henriquez, to be sent to the King of Spain for a great wonder. It did appear by the anatomy that he was of a monstrous size, the skull of his head was near as big as half a bushel, his neck-bones, shoulder-plates, arm-bones and all other lineaments of his other parts were huge and monstrous to behold, the shank of his leg from the ankle to the knee was as long as from any man's ankle up to his waist, and of bigness accordingly.

At this time and in this ship were also sent to be presented to the King of Spain two chests full of earth with ginger growing in them, which were also sent from China to be sent to the King of Spain. The ginger runneth in the ground like to liquorice, the blades grow out of it in length and proportion like unto the blades of wild garlic, which they cut every fifteen days. They use to water them twice a day, as we do our herbs here in England; they put the blades in their pottage and use them in their other meats, whose excellent savour and taste is very delightful and procureth a good appetite.

When we were shipped in the port of S. John de Ulua the General called our Master, Robert Barrett, and us with him, into his cabin and asked us if we would fight against Englishmen if we met them at the sea. We said that we would not fight against our Crown, but if we met with any other we would do what we were able. He said if we had said otherwise he would not have believed us, and for that we should be the better used and have allowance as other men had: and he gave a charge to every one of us, according unto our knowledge. Robert Barrett was placed with the pilot, I was put in the gunners' room, William Cawse with the boatswain, John Beare with the quartermasters, Edward Rider and Geoffrey Giles with the ordinary mariners, Richard the Master's boy attended on him and the pilot. Shortly after we departed from the port of S. John de Ulua with all the fleet of Spain for the port called Havana. We were 26 days sailing thither. There we came in, anchored, took in fresh water, and stayed 16 days for the fleet of Nombre de Dios, which is the fleet that brings the treasure from Peru.

The General of that fleet was called Diego Flores de Valdes. After his coming, when he had watered his ships, both the fleets joined in one, and Don Juan de Velasco de Varre was the first fifteen days General of both the fleets, who turning through the channel of Bahama his pilot had like to have cast away all the fleet upon the Cape called Canaveral, which was prevented by me, Job Hortop, and our Master, Robert Barrett; for I, being in the second watch, escried land and called to Robert Barrett, bidding him look overboard, for I saw land under the lee bow of the ship. He called to the boatswain and bid him fly the foresail sheet, and lay the helm upon the lee and cast the ship about. When we were cast about we were but in seven fathom water. We shot off a piece, giving advice to the fleet to cast about, and so they did. For this we were beloved of the General and all the fleet.

The General was in a great rage and swore by the King that he would hang his pilot, for he said that twice before he had almost cast away the Admiral. When it was day he commanded a piece to be shot off to call to council. The other Admiral in his ship came up to him and asked what the matter was. He said that his pilot had cast away his ship and all the fleet had it not been for two of the Englishmen, and therefore he would hang him. The other Admiral with many fair words persuaded him to the contrary.

When we came in the height [of the latitude] of Bermuda we discovered a monster in the sea who showed himself three times unto us from the middle upwards, in which parts he was proportioned like a man, of the complexion of a mulatto or tawny Indian. The General did command one of his clerks to put it in writing, and he certified the King and his nobles thereof. Presently after this for the space of sixteen days we had wonderful foul weather, and then God sent us a fair wind until such time as we discovered the island called Fayal.

On S. James' day we made rockets, wheels, and other fireworks to make pastime that night, as it is the order of the Spaniards. When we came near the land our Master, Robert Barrett, conferred with us to take the pinnace one night, when we came on the island called Terceira, to free ourselves from the danger and bondage that we were going into, whereunto we agreed. None had any pinnace astern then but our ship, which gave great courage to our enterprise. We prepared a bag of bread and a botijo of water which would have served us nine days, and provided ourselves to go. Our Master borrowed a small compass of the Master gunner of the ship, who lent it him but suspected his intent and closely made the General privy to it, who for a time dissembled the matter. In the end seeing our pretence he called R. Barrett, commanding his head to be put in the stocks and a great pair of iron bolts on his legs, and the rest of us to be set in the stocks by the legs. Then he willed a piece to be shot off, and he sent the pinnace for the other Admiral and all the captains, masters and pilots of both fleets to come aboard of him. He commanded the mainyard to be struck down and to put two pulleys, on every yardarm one; the hangman was called, and we were willed to confess ourselves, for he swore by the King that he would hang us.

When the other Admiral and the rest were come aboard he called them into his council-chamber and told them that he would hang the Master of the Englishmen and all his company. The Admiral, whose name was Diego Flores de Valdes, asked him wherefore. He said that we had determined to rise in the night with the pinnace, and with a ball of firework to set the ship on fire and go our ways. Therefore, said he, 'I will have you, the Captains, Masters and Pilots, to set your hands unto that, for I swear by the King that I will hang them'. Diego Flores de Valdes answered, 'I, nor the Captains, Masters, and Pilots will not set our hands to that', for he said if he had been prisoner as we were he would have done the like himself. He counselled him to keep us fast in prison till he came into Spain, and then send us to the Contractation House in Seville, where if we had deserved death the law would pass on us, for he would not have it said that in such a fleet as that was, six men and a boy should take the pinnace and go away, and so he returned to his ship again.

When he was gone the General came to the mainmast to us and swore by the King that we should not come out of the stocks till we came into Spain. Within sixteen days after we came over the bar of S. Lucar, and came up to the hurcados, then he put us into a pinnace in the stocks and sent us prisoners to the Contractation House in Seville. From thence after one year we brake prison on S. Stephen's day at night. Seven of our company escaped, Robert Barrett, I, Job Hortop, John Emery, Humphrey Roberts and John Gilbert were taken and brought back to the Contractation House, where we remained in the stocks till twelve tide [? the twelve days of Christmas] was past.

Then our keeper put up a petition to the Judge of the Contractation House that we might be sent to the great prison house in Seville, for that we broke prison, whereupon we were presently led thither, where we remained one month, and then from thence to the Castle of the Inquisition House in Triana, where we continued one year: which expired, they brought us out in procession, every one of us having a candle in his hand and the coat with S. Andrew's cross on our backs. They brought us up on an high scaffold that was set up in the place of S. Francis, which is in the chief street of Seville. There they set us down upon benches, every one in his degree, and against us on another scaffold sat all the Judges and the clergy on their benches. The people wondered and gazed on us, some pitying our cases, other said, burn those heretics. When we had sat there two hours we had a sermon made to us; after which one called Bresinia, secretary to the Inquisition, went up into the pulpit with the process, and called Robert Barrett and John Gilbert, whom two familiars of the Inquisition brought from the scaffold before the Judges, where the secretary read the sentence, which was that they should be burnt, and so they returned to the scaffold and were burnt.

Then I, Job Hortop, and John Bone were called and brought to the place, as before, where we heard our sentence, which was that we should go to the galleys and there row at the oar's end ten years, and then to be brought back to the Inquisition house to have the coat with S. Andrew's cross put on our backs, and from thence to go to the everlasting prison remediless, and so we were returned from the scaffold from whence we came.

Thomas Marks and Thomas Ellis were called, and had sentence to serve in the galleys eight years, and Humphrey Roberts and John Emery to serve five years, and so were returned to the benches on the scaffold, where we sat till four of clock in the afternoon. Then we were led again to the Inquisition House from whence we were brought.

The next day, in the morning, Bresinia, the treasurer, came thither to us and delivered to every one of us his sentence in writing. I with the rest were sent to the galleys, where we were chained four and four together. Every man's daily allowance was 26 ounces of coarse, black biscuit and water, our clothing for the whole year two shirts, two pair of breeches of coarse canvas, a red coat of coarse cloth, soon on and soon off, and a gown of hair with a friar's hood. Our lodging was on the bare boards and banks of the galleys, our heads and beards were shaven every month; hunger, thirst, cold and stripes we lacked none, till our several times expired.

And after the time of twelve years, for I served two years above my sentence, I was sent back to the Inquisition House in Seville, and there having put on the coat with S. Andrew's cross I was sent to the ever-lasting prison remediless, where I wore the coat four years; and then upon great suit I had it taken off for 50 ducats, which Hernando de Soria, treasurer of the King's mint, lent me, whom I served for it as a drudge seven years, and until the month of October last, 1590. And then I came from Seville to S. Lucar, where I made means to come away in a flyboat that was laden with wines and salt, which were Fleming's goods, the King of Spain's subjects, dwelling in Seville, married to Spanish women and sworn to their King. In this month of October last, departing from S. Lucar at sea, off the southernmost cape, we met an English ship, called the galleon *Dudley*, who took the Fleming, and me out of him, and brought me to Portsmouth, where they set me on land the 2nd day of December last past, 1590. From thence I was sent by Master Muns, the Lieutenant of Portsmouth, with letters to the Right Honourable the Earl of Sussex, who commanded his secretary to take my name and examination, how long I had been out of England, and with whom I went, which he did. And on Christmas Even I took my leave of his honour and came to Redriff.

THE COMPUTATION OF MY IMPRISONMENT

I suffered imprisonment in Mexico, two years.
In the Contractation house in Seville, one year.
In the Inquisition House in Triana, one year.
I was in the galleys, twelve years.
In the everlasting prison remediless, with the coat with S. Andrew's
cross on my back, four years.
And at liberty I served as a drudge Hernando de Soria three years,
which is the full complement of 23 years.
Since my departure from England until this time of my return I was
five times in great danger of death, besides the many perils I was in
in the galleys.
First, in the port of S. John de Ulua, where being on shore with many
other of our company, which were all slain saving I and two other
that by swimming got aboard the *Jesus of Lubeck.*
Secondly, when we were robbed by the wild Indians.
Thirdly after we came to Mexico, the Viceroy would have hanged us.
Fourthly, because he could not have his mind to hang us he would have
burnt us.
Fifthly, the General that brought us into Spain would have hanged us
at sea.

Thus, having truly set down unto you my travels, misery and dangers, endured the space of twenty-three years, I end.

TRAVELLING IN NEW SPAIN

Henry Hawks

Like his friend, Roger Bodenham, Hawks settled in Spain, took a Spanish name and married a Spanish wife. He traded with New Spain, profitably no doubt, until he fell into the hands of the Inquisition there. He escaped to Spain and then to England.

A relation of the commodities of Nova Hispania, and the manners of the inhabitants, written by Henry Hawks, Merchant, which lived five years in the said country, and drew the same at the request of Mr Richard Hakluyt, Esquire, of Eiton in the County of Hereford, 1572.

SAINT JOHN DE ULUA is an island not high above the water, where now the Spaniards, upon Mr John Hawkins being there, are in making a strong fort. In this place all the ships that come out of Spain with goods for these parts do unlade, for they have none other port so good as this is. The coming into this place hath three channels, and the best of all is the northernmost, which goeth by the mainland: and on every side of the channels there are many small rocks as big as a small barrel; they will make men stand in doubt of them, but there is no fear of them. There is another island thereby, called the Island of Sacrifices, where the Spaniards did in times past unlade their goods; and for that, they say, there are upon it spirits or devils, it is not frequented as it hath been. In these places the north wind hath so great dominion that oftentimes it destroyeth many ships and barks. This place is given to great sickness. These islands stand in eighteen degrees and a half, and about the same is great plenty of fish.

Five leagues from St John de Ulua is a fair river. It lieth northwest from the port, and goeth to a little town of the Spaniards called Vera Cruz, and with small vessels or barks, which they call frigates, they carry all their merchandise which cometh out of Spain to the said town; and in like manner bring all the gold, silver, cochineal, hides, and all other things that the ships carry into Spain unto them. And the goods being in Vera Cruz they carry them to Mexico, and to Pueblo de los Angeles, Sacatecas, and Saint Martin, and divers other places so far within the country that some of them are 700 miles off, and some more and some less, all upon horses, mules, and in wains drawn with oxen, and in carts drawn with mules.

In this town of Vera Cruz within these twenty years, when women were brought to bed the children new born incontinently died: which is not so now in these days, God be thanked.

This town is inclined to many kind of diseases by reason of the great heat and a certain gnat or fly, which they call a mosquito, which biteth both men and women in their sleep; and as soon as they are bitten incontinently the flesh swelleth as though they had been bitten with some venomous worm. And this mosquito or gnat doth most follow such as are newly come into the country. Many there are that die of this annoyance.

This town is situated upon the river aforesaid, and compassed with woods of divers manners and sorts, and many fruits, as oranges and lemons, guavas, and divers others, and birds in them, popinjays both small and great, and some of them as big as a raven, and their tails as long as the tail of a pheasant. There are also many other kind of birds of purple colour, and small monkeys, marvellous proper.

This hot or sick country continueth five and forty miles towards the city of Mexico. And the five and forty miles being passed, then there is a temperate country and full of tillage: but they water all their corn with rivers which they turn in upon it. And they gather their wheat twice a year. And if they should not water the ground where their corn is sown the country is so hot it would burn all.

Before you come to Mexico there is a great town called Tlaxcala, which hath in it above 16,000 households. All the inhabitants thereof are free by the kings of Spain; for these were the occasion that Mexico was won in so short time, and with so little loss of men. Wherefore they are all gentlemen and pay no tribute to the king. In this town is all the cochineal growing.

Mexico is a great city. It hath more than fifty thousand households, whereof there are not past five or six thousand houses of Spaniards: all the other are the people of the country which live under the Spaniards' laws. There are in this city stately buildings, and many monasteries of friars and nuns which the Spaniards have made. And the building of the Indians is somewhat beautiful outwardly, and within full of small chambers with very small windows, which is not so comely as the building of the Spaniards. This city standeth in the midst of a great lake and the water goeth through all or the most part of the streets: and there come small boats, which they call canoes, and in them they bring all things necessary, as wood, and coals, and grass for their horses, stones and lime to build, and corn.

This city is subject to many earthquakes which oftentimes cast down houses and kill people. This city is very well provided of water to drink, and with all manner of victuals, as fruits, flesh and fish, bread, hens and capons, guinea cocks and hens, and all other fowl. There are in this city every week three fairs or markets which are frequented with many people, as well Spaniards as the people of the country. There are in these fairs or markets all manner of things that may be invented to sell, and specially things of the country. The one of these fairs is upon the Monday, which is called St Hypolitos' fair, and St James his fair is upon the Thursday, and upon Saturday is St John's fair. In this city is always the King's Governor or Viceroy, and there are kept the Terms and Parliaments. And although there be other places of justice yet this is above all; so that all men may appeal unto this place, and may not appeal from this city, but only into Spain before the King: and it must be for a certain sum; and if it be under that sum then there is no appellation from them. Many rivers fall into this lake which the city standeth in; but there was never any place found whither it goeth out.

The Indians know a way to drown the city, and within these three years they would have practised the same; but they which should have been the doers of it were hanged, and ever since the city hath been well watched both day and night for fear lest at some time they might be deceived; for the Indians love not the Spaniards. Round about the town there are very many gardens and orchards of the fruits of the country, marvellous fair, where the people have great recreation. The men of this city are marvellous vicious; and in like manner the women are dishonest of their bodies, more than they are in other cities or towns in this country.

There are near about this city of Mexico many rivers and standing waters which have in them a monstrous kind of fish [an alligator], which is marvellous ravening and a great devourer of men and cattle. He is wont to sleep upon the dry land many times, and if there come in the meantime any man or beast and wake or disquiet him he speedeth well if he get from him. He is like unto a serpent saving that he doth not fly, neither hath he wings.

There is west out of Mexico a port town which is on the south sea, called Puerto de Acapulco, whereas there are ships which they have ordinarily for the navigation of China, which they have newly found. This port is threescore leagues from Mexico.

There is another port town which is called Culiacan, on the south sea, which lieth west and by north out of Mexico and is 200 leagues from the same. And there the Spaniards made two ships to go seek the strait or gulf which, as they say, is between the Newfoundland and

Greenland; and they call it the Englishmen's strait:* which as yet was never fully found. They say that strait lieth not far from the mainland of China, which the Spaniards account to be marvellous rich.

Toward the north from Mexico there are great store of silver mines. There is greater quantity of silver found in these mines toward the north than there is in any other parts: and as the most men of experience said always, they find the richer mines the more northerly. These mines are commonly upon great hills and stony ground, marvellous hard to be laboured and wrought.

Out of some of the mines the Indians find a certain kind of earth of divers colours, wherewith they paint themselves in times of their dances and other pastimes which they use.

In this country of Nova Hispania there are also mines of gold, although the gold be commonly found in rivers or very near unto rivers. And now in these days there is not so much gold found as there hath been heretofore.

There are many great rivers and great store of fish in them, not like unto our kinds of fish. And there are marvellous great woods, and as fair trees as may be seen of divers sorts, and especially fir trees that may mast any ship that goeth upon the sea, oaks and pineapples, and another tree which they call mesquite; it beareth a fruit like unto a peascod, marvellous sweet, which the wild people gather and keep it all the year and eat it instead of bread.

The Spaniards have notice of seven cities which old men of the Indians show them should lie towards the northwest from Mexico. They have used, and use daily, much diligence in seeking of them but they cannot find any one of them. They say that the witchcraft of the Indians is such that when they come by these towns they cast a mist upon them so that they cannot see them.

They have understanding of another city which they call Copalla: and in like manner, at my being in the country, they have used much labour and diligence in the seeking of it. They have found the lake on which it should stand, and a canoe, the head whereof was wrought with copper curiously, and could not find nor see any man nor the town which to their understanding should stand on the same water, or very near the same.

There is a great number of beasts or kine in the country of Cibola which were never brought thither by the Spaniards, but breed naturally in the country. They are like unto our oxen saving that they have long hair, like a lion, and short horns, and they have upon their

* It was well known that the English were persistently seeking a North-west Passage round America which would enable them to bypass the Spanish possessions and take a short cut to the fabulous riches of the Far East.

shoulders a bunch like a camel which is higher than the rest of their body. They are marvellous wild and swift in running. They call them the beasts or kine of Cibola.

This Cibola is a city which the Spaniards found now of late without any people in the same, goodly buildings, fair chimneys, windows made of stone and timber excellently wrought, fair wells with wheels to draw their water, and a place where they had buried their dead people, with many fair stones upon the graves. And the Captain would not suffer his soldiers to break up any part of these graves, saying he would come another time to do it.

They asked certain people which they met whither the people of this city were gone; and they made answer they were gone down a river which was thereby, very great, and there had builded a city which was more for their commodity.

This Captain, lacking things necessary for himself and his men, was fain to return back again without finding any treasure according to his expectation: neither found they but few people, although they found beaten ways which had been much haunted and frequented. The Captain at his coming back again had a great check of the Governor because he had not gone forwards and seen the end of that river.

They have in the country, far from the seaside, standing waters which are salt: and in the months of April and May the water of them congealeth into salt, which salt is all taken for the king's use and profit.

Their dogs are all crooked backed, as many as are of the country breed, and cannot run fast. Their faces are like the face of a pig or an hog, with sharp noses.

In certain provinces which are called Guatemala and Soconusco there is growing great store of cacao, which is a berry like unto an almond: it is the best merchandise that is in all the Indies. The Indians make drink of it, and in like manner meat to eat. It goeth currently for money in any market or fair, and may buy any flesh, fish, bread or cheese, or other things.

There are many kind of fruits of the country which are very good, as plantains, sapotes, guavas, pineapples, aluacatas, tunas, mammees, lemons, oranges, walnuts, very small and hard with little meat in them, grapes which the Spaniards brought into the country, and also wild grapes which are of the country and are very small, quinces, peaches, figs, and but few apples and very small, and no pears: but there are melons and calabash or gourds.

There is much honey, both of bees and also of a kind of tree which they call maguey. This honey of maguey is not so sweet as the other honey is, but it is better to be eaten only with bread than the other is.

And the tree serveth for many things as the leaves make thread to sew any kind of bags, and are good to cover and thatch houses, and for divers other things.

They have in divers places of the country many hot springs of water; as above all other, I have seen one in the province of Mechuacan. In a plain field without any mountain there is a spring which hath much water, and it is so hot that if a whole quarter of beef be cast into it, within an half hour it will be as well sodden [boiled] as it will be over a fire in half a day. I have seen half a sheep cast in, and immediately it hath been sodden and I have eaten part of it.

There are many hares, and some conies. There are no partridges, but abundance of quails.

They have great store of fish in the South sea, and many oysters, and very great. The people do open the oysters and take out the meat of them and dry it as they do any other kind of fish, and keep them all the year: and when the times serve they send them abroad into the country to sell, as all other fish. They have no salmon, nor trout, nor peal, nor carp, tench, nor pike in all the country.

There are in the country mighty high mountains and hills, and snow upon them: they commonly burn; and twice every day they cast out much smoke and ashes at certain open places which are in the tops of them.

There is among the wild people much manna. I have gathered of the same and have eaten it and it is good; for the apothecaries send their servants at certain times to gather of the same for purgations, and other uses.

There are in the mountains many wild hogs which all men may kill, and lions and tigers; which tigers do much harm to men that travel in the wilderness.

In this country, not long since, there were two poor men that found a marvellous rich mine. And when these men went to make a register of the same (according to the law and custom) before the King's officers they thought this mine not meet for such men as they were; and violently took the said mine for the king, and gave no part thereof unto the two poor men. And within certain days the King's officers resorted thither to labour in the mine, and they found two great mighty hills were come together; so they found no place to work in. And in the time while I was among them, which was five years, there was a poor shepherd who, keeping his sheep, happened to find a well of quicksilver; and he went in like manner to manifest the same, as the custom and manner is. The King's officers dealt in like order as they did with the two poor men that found the rich mine, taking it quite from the shepherd. But when they went to fetch home the quicksilver, or part thereof, they could never find it again. So these things have been declared unto the King, who hath given commandment that nothing being found in the fields, as mines and suchlike, shall be taken away from any man. And many other things have been done in this country which men might count for great marvels.

There is great abundance of sugar here, and they make divers conserves, and very good, and send them into Peru, where they sell them marvellous well because they make none in those parts.

The people of the country are of a good stature, tawny coloured, broad-faced, flat-nosed, and given much to drink both wine of Spain and also a certain kind of wine which they make with honey of magueys and roots, and other things which they use to put into the same. They call the same wine pulco. They are soon drunk and given to much beastliness and void of all goodness. In their drunkenness they use and commit sodomy; and with their mothers and daughters they have their pleasures and pastimes. Whereupon they are defended from the drinking of wines upon pains of money, as well he that selleth the wines as the Indian that drinketh the same. And if this commandment were not, all the wine in Spain and in France were not sufficient for the West Indies only.

They are of much simplicity and great cowards, void of all valour, and are great witches. They use divers times to talk with the devil, to whom they do certain sacrifices and oblations: many times they have been taken with the same, and I have seen them most cruelly punished for that offence.

The people are given to learn all manner of occupations and sciences, which for the most part they learned since the coming of the Spaniards. I say all manner of arts. They are very artificial [skilful] in making of images with feathers, or the proportion or figure of any man in all kind of manner as he is. The fineness and excellency of this is wonderful, that a barbarous people as they are should give themselves to so fine an art as this is. They are goldsmiths, blacksmiths, and coppersmiths, carpenters, masons, shoemakers, tailors, sadlers, embroiderers, and of all other kind of sciences. And they will do work so good cheap that poor young men that go out of Spain to get their living are not set on work: which is the occasion there are many idle people in the country. For the Indian will live all the week with less than one groat; which the Spaniard cannot do, nor any man else.

They say that they came of the lineage of an old man which came thither in a boat of wood, which they call a canoe. But they cannot tell whether it were before the flood or after, neither can they give any reason of the flood, nor from whence they came. And when the Spaniards came first among them they did certain sacrifice to an image made in stone of their own invention. The stone was set upon a great hill which they made of bricks of earth: they call it their Cowa. And certain days in the year they did sacrifice certain old men and young children; and only believed in the sun and the moon, saying that from them they had all things that were needful for them. They have in these parts great store of cotton-wool with which they make a manner of linen cloth which the Indians wear, both men and women, and it serveth for shirts and smocks and all other kind of garments which they wear upon their bodies: and the Spaniards use it to all such purposes, especially such as cannot buy other. And if it were not for this kind of cloth, all manner of cloth that goeth out of Spain, I say linen cloth, would be sold out of all measure.

The wild people go naked, without anything upon them. The women wear the skin of a deer before their privities, and nothing else upon all their bodies. They have no care for anything, but only from day to day for that which they have need to eat. They are big men, and likewise the women. They shoot bows which they make of a cherry tree, and their arrows are of cane, with a sharp flint stone in the end of the same: they will pierce any coat of mail, and they kill deer, and cranes, and wild geese, ducks and other fowl, and worms, and snakes, and divers other vermin, which they eat. They live very long, for I have seen men that have been an hundred years of age. They have but very little hair in their face, nor on their bodies.

The Indians have the friars in great reverence: the occasion is that by them and by their means they are free and out of bondage, which was so ordained by Charles the Emperor: which is the occasion that now there is not so much gold and silver coming into Europe as there was while the Indians were slaves. For when they were in bondage they could not choose but do their task every day, and bring their masters so much metal out of their mines; but now they must be well paid and much entreated to have them work. So it hath been, and is a great hindrance to the owners of the mines, and to the King's quinto or custom.

There are many mines of copper in great quantity, whereof they spend in the country as much as serveth their turns. There is some gold in it, but not so much as will pay the costs of the fining. The quantity of it is such, and the mines are so far from the sea, that it will not be worth the freight to carry it into Spain. On the other side, the King's officers will give no licence to make ordnance thereof; whereupon the mines lie unlaboured and of no valuation.

There is much lead in the country, so that with it they cover churches and other religious houses: wherefore they shall not need any of our lead as they have had need thereof in times past.

The pomp and liberality of the owners of the mines is marvellous to behold: the apparel both of them and of their wives is more to be compared to the apparel of noble persons than otherwise. If their wives go out of their houses, as unto the church or any other place, they go out with great majesty, and with as many men and maids as though she were the wife of some noble man. I will assure you I have seen a miner's wife go to the church with an hundred men, and twenty gentle-women and maids. They keep open house; who will may come to eat their meat. They call men with a bell to come to dinner and supper. They are princes in keeping of their houses, and bountiful in all manner of things.

A good owner of mines must have at the least an hundred slaves to carry and to stamp his metals; he must have many mules, and men to keep the mines; he must have mills to stamp his metals; he must have many wains and oxen to bring home wood to fine the ore; he must have much quicksilver, and a marvellous quantity of salt-brine for the metals; and he must be at many other charges. And as for this charge of quicksilver, it is a new invention which they find more profitable than to fine their ore with lead. Howbeit, the same is very costly, for there is never a hundred [weight] of quicksilver but costeth at the least threescore pounds sterling. And the mines fall daily in decay, and of less value; and the occasion is, the few Indians that men have to labour their mines.

There is in Nova Hispania a marvellous increase of cattle, which daily do increase, and they are of a greater growth than ours are. You may have a great steer that hath an hundredweight of tallow in his belly for sixteen shillings; and some one man hath 20,000 head of cattle of his own. They sell the hides unto the merchants, who lade into Spain as many as may be well spared. They spend many in the country in shoes and boots, and in the mines: and as the country is great, so is the increase of the cattle wonderful. In the Island of Santo Domingo they commonly kill the beasts for their hides and tallow, and the fowls eat the carcases: and so they do in Cuba and Porto Rico, whereas there is much sugar, and cana fistula, which daily they send into Spain. They have great increase of sheep in like manner, and daily do intend to increase them. They have much wool, and as good as the wool of Spain. They make cloth as much as serveth the country for the common people, and send much cloth into Peru. I have seen cloth made in the city of Mexico which hath been sold for ten pesos a vare, which is almost four pounds English, and the vare is less than our yard. They have woad growing in the country, and alum, and brazil, and divers other things to dye withal, so that they make all colours. In Peru they make no cloth; but hereafter our cloth will be little set by in these parts unless it be some fine cloth. The wools are commonly four shillings every roue, which is five and twenty pounds. And in some places of the country that are far from the places whereas they make cloth it is worth nothing, and doth serve but only to make beds for men to lie on.

They make hats, as many as do serve the country, very fine and good, and sell them better cheap than they can be brought out of Spain, and in like manner send them into Peru.

Many people are set on work both in the one and in the other. They spin their wool as we do, and instead of oil they have hog's grease. They twist not their thread so much as we do, neither work so fine a thread. They make no Kerseys, but they make much cloth which is coarse, and sell it for less than 12 pence the vare. It is called sail.

They have much silk, and make all manner of sorts thereof, as taffetas, satins, velvets of all colours, and they are as good as the silks of Spain saving that the colours are not so perfect: but the blacks are better than the blacks that come out of Spain.

They have many horses, and mares, and mules, which the Spaniards brought thither. They have as good jennets as any are in Spain, and better cheap than they be in Spain. And with their mules they carry all their goods from place to place.

There is rain usually in this country from the month of May to the midst of October, every day, which time they call their winter by reason of the said waters. And if it were not for the waters which fall in these hot seasons their maize, which is the greatest part of their sustenance, would be destroyed. This maize is the greatest maintenance which the Indian hath, and also all the common people of the Spaniards. And their horses and mules which labour cannot be without the same. This grain is substantial, and increaseth much blood. If the miners should be without it they could not labour their mines; for all their servants eat none other bread, but only of this maize, and it is made in cakes, as they make oaten cakes in some places of England.

The Indians pay tribute, being of the age of 20 years, 4 shillings of money and an hanege of maize, which is worth 4 shillings more unto the King every year. This is paid in all Nova Hispania of as many as be of the age of 20 years, saving the city of Tlaxcala, which was made free because the citizens thereof were the occasion that Cortes took Mexico in so little a time. And although at the first they were freed from payment of tribute, yet the Spaniards now begin to usurp upon them, and make them to till a great field of maize at their own costs every year for the King, which is as beneficial unto him and as great cost unto them as though they paid their tribute, as the others do.

The ships which go out of Spain with goods for Peru go to Nombre de Dios and there discharge the said goods; and from thence they be carried over the neck of a land unto a port town in the South sea, called Panama, which is 17 leagues distant from Nombre de Dios. And there they do ship their goods again, and so from thence go to Peru. They are in going thither three months, and they come back again in 20 days. They have seldom foul weather, and few ships are lost in the South sea. Four years past, to wit 1568, there was a ship made out of Peru to seek Solomon's Islands,* and they came somewhat to the south of the equinoctial and found an island with many black people in such number that the Spaniards durst not go on land among them. And because they had been long upon the voyage their people were very weak, and so went not on land to know what commodity was upon it. And for want of victuals they arrived in Nova Hispania in a port called Puerto de Navidad, and thence returned back again unto Peru, where they were evil entreated because they had not known more of the same island.

They have in this port of Navidad ordinarily their ships which go to the Islands of China, which are certain islands which they have found within these 7 years. They have brought from thence gold, and much cinnamon, and dishes of earth, and cups of the same, so fine that every man that may have a piece of them will give the weight of silver for it. There was a mariner that brought a pearl as big as a dove's egg from thence, and a stone for which the Viceroy would have given 3,000 ducats. Many things they bring from thence most excellent. There are many of these islands, and the Spaniards have not many of them as yet; for the Portugals disturb them much and combat with them every day, saying it is part of their conquest, and to the mainland they cannot come at any hand. There are goodly people in them, and they are great mariners, richly apparelled in cloth of gold, and silver, and silk of all sorts, and go apparelled after the manner of the Turks. This report make such as come from thence. The men of the mainland have certain traffic with some of these islanders, and come thither in a kind of ship which they have with one sail, and bring of such merchandise as they have need of. And of these things there have been brought into Nova Hispania both cloth of gold and silver, and divers manners of silks, and works of gold and silver, marvellous to be seen. So by their saying there is not such a country in the whole world. The mainland is from the islands 190 leagues; and the islands are not far from the Moluccas northwards. And the people of those islands, which the Spaniards have, say that if they would bring their wives and children that then they should have among them what they would have. So

* The Spaniards believed these islands to be near the land of Ophir, from which King Solomon had obtained his riches.

there go women daily, and the King payeth all the charges of the married men and their wives that go to those islands. And there is no doubt but the trade will be marvellous rich in time to come. It was my fortune to be in company with one, Diego Gutieres, who was the first pilot that ever went to that country of the Philippines. He maketh report of many strange things in that country, as well riches as other, and saith, 'If there be any Paradise upon earth it is in that country': and addeth that sitting under a tree, you shall have such sweet smells, with such great content and pleasure, that you shall remember nothing, neither wife, nor children, nor have any kind of appetite to eat or drink, the odoriferous smells will be so sweet. This man hath good livings in Nova Hispania, notwithstanding he will return thither with his wife and children, and as for treasure there is abundance, as he maketh mention. In this country of Nova Hispania there are many bucks and does, but they have not so long horns as they have here in England. The Spaniards kill them with hand-guns and with greyhounds, and the Indians kill them with their bows and arrows, and with the skins they make chamois, such as we in England make doublets and hose of, as good as the skins that are dressed in Flanders, and likewise they make marvellous good Spanish leather of them. There is a bird which is like unto a raven, but he hath some of his feathers white: there is such abundance of them that they eat all the corrupt and dead flesh which is in the country. Otherwise the abundance of carrion is so much that it would make a marvellous corrupt air in all the country, and be so noisome that no man could abide it. Therefore it is commanded there shall none of them be killed. These birds are always about cities and towns where there is much flesh killed.

The Indians are much favoured by the Justices of the country, and they call them their orphans. And if any Spaniard should happen to do any of them harm, or to wrong him in taking anything from him, as many times they do, or to strike any of them, being in any town where justice is, they are as well punished for the same as if they had done it one Spaniard to another. When a Spaniard is far from Mexico or any place of justice, thinking to do with the poor Indian what he list, considering he is so far from any place of remedy, he maketh the Indian do what he commandeth him, and if he will not do it he beateth and misuseth him according to his own appetite. The Indian holdeth his peace until he find an opportunity, and then taketh a neighbour with him and goeth to Mexico, although it be 20 leagues off, and maketh his complaint. This his complaint is immediately heard, and although it be a knight, or a right good gentleman, he is forthwith sent for and punished both by his goods and also his person is imprisoned, at the pleasure of the Justice. This is the occasion that the Indians are so tame and civil as they are. And if they should not have this favour the Spaniards would soon dispatch all the Indians, or the Indians would kill them. But they may call them dogs, and use other evil words as much as they will, and the Indian must needs put it up and go his way.

The poor Indians will go every day two or three leagues to a fair or market with a child upon their necks, with as much fruit or roots, or some kind of ware, as cotton-wool, or caddis of all colours, as shall be not past worth a penny: and they will maintain themselves upon the same. For they live with a marvellous small matter.

They are in such poverty that if you need to ride into the country you shall have an Indian to go with you all the day, with your bed upon his back, for one royal of plate: and this you shall have from one town to another. Here you are to understand that all men that travel by the way are always wont to carry their beds with them. They are great thieves and will steal all that they may, and you shall have no recompense at their hands.

The garments of the women are in this manner. The uppermost part is made almost like to a woman's smock, saving that it is as broad above as beneath, and hath no sleeves but holes on each side one to put out their arms. It is made of linen cloth made of cotton-wool, and filled full of flowers, of red cadis and blue and other colours. This garment cometh down to the knees, and then they have another cloth made after the same manner, and that goeth round about their waist and reacheth to their shoes, and over this a white fine sheet upon their heads which goeth down half the leg. Their hair is made up round with an hair lace about their head. And the men have a small pair of breeches of the same cotton-wool, and their shirts which hang over their breeches and a broad girdle about their middles, and a sheet with flowers upon their backs and with a knot upon one shoulder, and an hat upon their heads, and a pair of shoes. And this is all their apparel, although it be a cacique, which they use in all the country.

The walls of the houses of the Indians are but plain, but the stones are laid so close that you shall not well perceive the joints between one stone and another, they are so finely cut: and by the means that the stones are so workmanly done and finely joined together there is some beauty in their walls. They are marvellous small and light, as pumice stones. They make their doors very little so that there can go in but one man at a time. Their windows and rooms within their houses are small, and one room they have reserved for their friends when they come to talk one with another, and that is always fair matted and kept marvellous clean and hanged full of images, and their chairs standing there to sit in. They eat their meat upon the ground, and sleep on the ground upon a mat without any bed, both the gentlemen and other.

The Indians strike their fire with one stick in another, as well the tame people as the wild. For they know not how to do it with an iron and a stone.

In Nova Hispania every 10 or 12 leagues they have a contrary speech saving only about Mexico; so there is a number of speeches in the country.

Montezuma, which was the last King of this country, was one of the richest princes which have been seen in our time or long before. He had all kind of beasts which were then in the country, and all manner of birds and fishes, and all manner of worms which creep upon the earth, and all trees and flowers and herbs, all fashioned in silver and gold, which was the greatest part of all his treasure, and in these things had he great joy, as the old Indians report. And unto this day they say that the treasure of Montezuma is hidden and that the Spaniards have it not. This King would give none of his people freedom, nor forgive any of them that should pay him tribute though he were never so poor. For if it had been told him that one of his tributaries was poor and that he was not able to pay his tribute according to the custom, then he would have him bound to bring at such times as tributes should be paid a quill full of lice, saying he would have none free but himself. He had as many wives or concubines as he would have, and such as liked him. Always whensoever he went out of his Court to pass the time he was borne upon four of his noblemen's shoulders set upon a table, some say of gold, and very richly dressed with feathers of divers and many colours and flowers. He washed all his body every day, were it never so cold. And unto this day so do all the Indians, and especially the women.

The Spaniards keep the Indians in great subjection. They may have in their houses no sword nor dagger, nor knife with any point, nor may wear upon them any manner of arms, neither may they ride upon any horse nor mules in any saddle nor bridle, neither may they drink wine, which they take for the greatest pain of all. They have attempted divers times to make insurrections but they have been overthrown immediately by their own great and beastly cowardliness.

There remain some among the wild people that unto this day eat one another. I have seen the bones of a Spaniard that have been as clean burnished as though it had been done by men that had no other occupation. And many times people are carried away by them, but they never come again, whether they be men or women.

They have in the sea islands of red salt in great abundance, where they lade it from place to place about the sea coast: and they spend very much salt with salting their hides, and fish: and in their mines they occupy great quantity. They have much alum, and as good as any that is in all the Levant, so that they need none of that commodity. They have also of their own growing much cana fistula, and much sarsaparilla, which is marvellous good for many kind of diseases.

There are in Florida many gerfalcons, and many other kind of hawks which the gentlemen of Nova Hispania send for every year. The Spaniards have two forts there, chiefly to keep out the Frenchmen from planting there.

OXENHAM'S RAID ON PANAMA

Lopez Vaz

After the Battle of San Juan Francis Drake made two or three voyages to the isthmus of Panama, to plunder and to learn more of the Spanish treasure routes. Great quantities of gold, silver and precious stones from Chile and Peru were taken across the isthmus to Nombre de Dios, whence they were shipped to Spain. In 1572-3, by one of the most remarkable commando raids in history, he captured one of the mule-trains conveying the treasure and sailed home heavily laden with plunder. This was the beginning of his wealth and fame. Unfortunately the only account of Drake's raid in Hakluyt, by Lopez Vaz, is too garbled for inclusion here; the full account was not published until 1626.

John Oxenham served under Drake on this raid. Together they climbed a great tree on the isthmus from which they looked down on the Pacific Ocean, the first Englishmen to see it, 'silent, upon a peak in Darien'. They both resolved to sail an English ship on the Pacific.

The only known account of Oxenham's raid is this by Lopez Vaz, given below, but Spanish documents which supplement it have now been discovered, and a full account of these is given by Dr James A. Williamson in The Age of Drake. *Oxenham (spelt 'Oxnam' in the original) sailed from Plymouth on April 9th, 1576, not 1575 as stated by Vaz. He had a ship of about a hundred tons and another smaller ship, with two prefabricated pinnaces in their holds. He lacked Drake's genius and good luck.*

The voyage of John Oxenham of Plymouth to the West India and over the Strait of Darien into the South Sea. Anno 1575 . . . [written and recorded by one Lopez Vaz, a Portugal born in the city of Elvas, in manner follow: which Portugal, with the discourse about him, was taken at the River of Plate by the ships set forth by the Right Honourable The Earl of Cumberland in the year 1586.]

THERE was another Englishman who, hearing of the spoil that Francis Drake had done upon the coast of Nova Hispania and of his good adventure and safe return home, was thereby provoked to undertake the like enterprise with a ship of 140 tons and 70 men, and came thither, and had also conference with the foresaid negroes:*, and hearing that the gold and silver which came upon the mules from Panama to Nombre de Dios was now conducted with soldiers he determined to do that which never any man before enterprised, and landed in that place where Francis Drake before had had his conference with the negroes. This man covered his ship after he had brought her aground with boughs of trees, and hid his great ordnance in the ground: and so, not leaving any man in his ship, he took two small pieces of ordnance, and his calivers, and good store of victuals, and so went with the negroes about twelve leagues into the mainland to a river that goeth to the South Sea, and there he cut wood and made a pinnace which was five and forty foot by the keel. And having made this pinnace he went into the South Sea, carrying six negroes with him to be his guides, and so went to the Island of Pearls [in February 1577], which is five and twenty leagues from Panama, which is in the way that they come from Peru to Panama, and there he was ten days without showing himself to any man to see if he might get any ship that came from Peru.

At last there came a small bark by which came from Peru, from a place called Quito, which he took and found in her sixty thousand pesos of gold and much victuals. But not contenting himself with this prize he stayed long without sending away his prize or any of the men, and in the end of six days after he took another bark which came from Lima, in which he took an hundred thousand pesos of silver in bars, with the which he thought to have gone and entered the river, but first he went into the islands to see if he could find any pearls, where he found a few, and so returned to his pinnace again. And so sailing to the river from whence he came, and coming near to the mouth of the said river, he sent away the two prizes that he took, and with his pinnace he went up the river.

The negroes that dwelt in the Island of Pearls, the same night that he went from them, went in canoes to Panama, and the Governor within two days sent four barks, 100 men, 25 in every one, and negroes to row with the Captain, John de Ortega, which went to the Island of Pearls and there had intelligence which way the Englishmen were gone, and following them he met by the way the ships which the Englishmen had taken, of whom he learned that the Englishmen were gone up the river. And he going thither, when he came to the mouth of the river the Captain of Panama knew not which way to take because there were three partitions in the river to go up in, and being determined to go up the greatest of the three rivers he saw coming down a lesser river many feathers of hens which the Englishmen had pulled to eat. And

* The Cimaroons, escaped slaves who had made independent, well-organized settlements deep in the forests and were constantly at war with the Spaniards. They had been of great help to Drake.

being glad thereof, he went up that river where he saw the feathers, and after that he had been in that river four days he descried the Englishmen's pinnace upon the sands; and coming to her there were no more than six Englishmen, whereof they killed one and the other five escaped away, and in the pinnace he found nothing but victuals.

But this Captain of Panama, not herewith satisfied, determined to seek out the Englishmen by land, and leaving twenty men in his pinnaces he, with 80 shot, went up the country. He had not gone half a league but he found a house made of boughs, where they found all the Englishmen's goods, and the gold and silver also, and carrying it back to their pinnaces the Spaniards were determined to go away without following the Englishmen any further.

But at the end of three days the English Captain came to the river with all his men and above 200 negroes, and set upon the Spaniards with great fury. But the Spaniards, having the advantage of trees which they stood behind, did easily prevail, and killed eleven Englishmen and five negroes, and took other seven Englishmen alive, but of the Spaniards two were slain and five sore hurt.

Among other things, the Spaniards enquired of the Englishmen which they took why they went not away in fifteen days' liberty which they had. They answered that their Captain had commanded them to carry all that gold and silver which they had to the place where they had left their ship, and they had promised him to carry it although they made three or four journeys of it, for he promised to give them part of it besides their wages; but the mariners would have it by and by [at once]: and so their Captain, being angry because they would not take his word, fell out with them and they with him, insomuch that one of the company would have killed the Captain, so that the Captain would not have them to carry the treasure but said he would seek negroes to carry it. And so he went and sought for negroes, and bringing those negroes to carry it he met with the five Englishmen that he had left in his pinnace which ran from the Spaniards, and the rest also which ran from the house, and they told him what the Spaniards had done. And then, making friendship with all his men, he promised them half of all the treasure if they got it from the Spaniards, and the negroes promised to help him with their bows and arrows, and thereupon they came to seek the Spaniards. And now that some of his company were killed and taken he thought it best to return to his ship and to pass back for England. The Spanish Captain hearing this, having buried the dead bodies and having gotten all things into his barks, and taking the Englishmen and their pinnace with him, he returned to Panama: so the voyage of that Englishman did not prosper with him as he thought it would have done.

Now when the four barks were come to Panama they sent advice also to Nombre de Dios, and they of Nombre de Dios sent also from them other four barks which (as the Spaniards say) found the English ship where she was hid and brought her to Nombre de Dios. And that the Viceroy of Peru, not thinking it good to suffer fifty Englishmen to remain in the country, sent a servant of his, called Diego de Frees, with a hundred and fifty shot into the mountains to seek them out, who found them making of certain canoes to go into the North Sea, and there to take some bark or other. Some of them were sick and were taken, and the rest fled with the negroes, who in the end betrayed them to the Spaniards so that they were brought to Panama. And the Justice of Panama asked the English Captain whether he had the Queen's licence, or the licence of any other Prince or Lord for his attempt. And he answered he had none, whereupon he and all his company were condemned to die, and so were all executed saving the Captain, the Master, the Pilot, and five boys which were carried to Lima, and there the Captain was executed with the other two, but the boys be yet living.*

The King of Spain, having intelligence of these matters, sent 300 men of war against those negroes which had assisted those Englishmen, which before were slaves unto the Spaniards and, as before is said, fled from their masters unto those mountains and so joined themselves to the Englishmen, to the end they might the better revenge themselves on the Spaniards.

At the first coming of these 300 soldiers they took many of the negroes and executed great justice upon them. But after a season the negroes grew wise and wary and prevented the Spaniards, so that none of them could be taken.

The Spaniards of that country marvelled much at this one thing, to see that since the conquering of this land there have been many Frenchmen that have come to those countries but never saw Englishmen there but only those two [Drake and Oxenham] of whom I have spoken. And although there have many Frenchmen been on the coast yet never durst they put foot upon land, only those two Englishmen adventured it and did such exploits as are before remembered.

All these things coming to the hearing of the King of Spain he provided two galleys well appointed to keep those coasts: and the first year they took six or seven French ships. And after that this was known there were no more Englishmen or Frenchmen of war that durst

* There was a story, which Sir Richard Hawkins brought home from Peru twenty years later, that Oxenham's ruin was due to entanglement with a Spanish lady whom he had taken prisoner, and Charles Kingsley made much of this in *Westward Ho!* There is no evidence to support the story.

adventure to approach the coast until this present year 1586 that the aforesaid Francis Drake, with a strong fleet of 24 ships, arrived there and made spoil of Santo Domingo, Carthagena and S. Augustine, things that are known to all the world. But it is likely that if the King of Spain lives he will in time provide sufficient remedy to keep his countries and subjects from the invasion of other nations.

FROBISHER'S FIRST VOYAGE TO THE NORTH-WEST

George Best

There was a wide-spread belief in a North-west Passage round North America, which would provide a short cut to the riches of the Far East without clashing with the Spaniards and Portuguese, and Sebastian Cabot claimed to have found the eastern entrance to it in 1509. This was thought to be just north of New-foundland. There were always seamen and others eager to seek the passage, but for years no one could make the attempt. The charter of the Muscovy Company gave them a monopoly of navigation to the north-west (as well as the north-east) and they would neither undertake nor permit the venture. At last in 1575 an enthusiast for the idea, a rich London merchant named Michael Lok, obtained an order from the Queen that the Company must give way. He raised funds in the City, and under Martin Frobisher's command a small expedition was organized, with the Queen's approval but no government support.

CAPTAIN FROBISHER, as well for that he is thoroughly furnished of the knowledge of the sphere and all other skills appertaining to the art of navigation, as also for the confirmation he
hath of the same by many years' experience both by sea and land, and
being persuaded of a new and nearer passage to Cataya [China] than
by Capo de Buona Speranca, which the Portugals yearly use: he began
first with himself to devise, and then with his friends to confer, and
laid a plain plat unto them [showed them on a chart] that that voyage
was not only possible by the north-west but also he could prove easy to
be performed. And further, he determined and resolved with himself
to go make full proof thereof and to accomplish or bring true certifi-
cate of the truth, or else never to return again, knowing this to be the
only thing of the world that was left yet undone, whereby a notable
mind might be made famous and fortunate.

But although his will were great to perform this notable voyage,
whereof he had conceived in his mind a great hope by sundry sure
reasons and secret intelligence which here for sundry causes I leave
untouched, yet he wanted altogether means and ability to set forward
and perform the same. Long time he conferred with his private friends
of these secrets, and made also many offers for the performing of the
same in effect unto sundry merchants of our country above 15 years

Sir Martin Frobisher by Cornelius Ketel, 1577

before he attempted the same, as by good witness shall well appear (albeit some evil willers which challenge to themselves the fruits of other men's labours have greatly injured him in the reports of the same, saying that they have been the first authors of that action, and that they have learned him the way which themselves as yet have never gone) but perceiving that hardly he was hearkened unto of the merchants, which never regard virtue without sure, certain, and present gains, he repaired to the Court (from whence, as from the fountain of our Commonwealth, all good causes have their chief increase and maintenance) and there laid open to many great estates and learned men the plot and sum of his device.

And amongst many honourable minds which favoured his honest and commendable enterprise he was specially bound and beholding to the Right Honourable Ambrose Dudley, Earl of Warwick, whose favourable mind and good disposition hath always been ready to countenance and advance all honest actions with the authors and executers of the same. And so by means of my lord his honourable countenance he received some comfort of his cause, and by little and little with no small expense and pain brought his cause to some perfection, and had drawn together so many adventurers and such sums of money as might well defray a reasonable charge to furnish himself to sea withal.

He prepared two small barks of twenty and five and twenty tons apiece, wherein he intended to accomplish his pretended voyage. Wherefore, being furnished with the foresaid two barks, and one small pinnace of ten ton burden, having therein victuals and other necessaries for twelve months' provision, he departed upon the said voyage from Blackwall the 15th of June, Anno Domini 1576.

One of the barks wherein he went was named the *Gabriel*, and the other the *Michael*: and sailing north-west from England upon the 11th of July he had sight of an high and ragged land, which he judged to be Frisland [Greenland] (whereof some authors have made mention) but durst not approach the same by reason of the great store of ice that lay alongst the coast, and the great mists that troubled them not a little. Not far from thence he lost company of his small pinnace, which by means of the great storm he supposed to be swallowed up of the sea, wherein he lost only four men.

Also the other bark, named the *Michael*, mistrusting the matter, conveyed themselves privily away from him and returned home, with great report that he was cast away.

The worthy Captain, notwithstanding these discomforts, although his mast was sprung and his topmast blown overboard with extreme foul weather, continued his course towards the north-west, knowing that the sea at length must needs have an ending and that some land should have a beginning that way; and determined therefore at the least to bring true proof what land and sea the same might be so far to the north-westwards, beyond any man that hath heretofore discovered. And the twentieth of July he had sight of an high land, which he called Queen Elizabeth's Foreland, after Her Majesty's name. And sailing more northerly alongst that coast he descried another foreland with a great gut, bay, or passage, divided as it were two mainlands or continents asunder. There he met with store of exceeding great ice all this coast along, and coveting still to continue his course to the northwards was always by contrary wind detained overthwart these straits, and could not get beyond.

Within few days after he perceived the ice to be well consumed and gone, either there engulfed in by some swift currents or indraughts, carried more to the southwards of the same straits, or else conveyed some other way: wherefore he determined to make proof of this place to see how far that gut had continuance, and whether he might carry himself through the same into some open sea on the backside, whereof he conceived no small hope, and so entered the same the one and twentieth of July and passed above fifty leagues therein, as he reported, having upon either hand a great main or continent. And that land upon his right hand as he sailed westward he judged to be the continent of Asia, and there to be divided from the firm of America which lieth upon the left hand over against the same.

This place he named after his name, Frobisher's Straits, like as Magellanus at the south-west end of the world, having discovered the passage to the South Sea (where America is divided from the continent of that land which lieth under the South Pole)* and called the same straits, Magellan's Straits.

* It was widely believed that there was a vast undiscovered southern continent,

After he had passed 60 leagues into this foresaid strait he went ashore and found signs where fire had been made. He saw mighty deer that seemed to be mankind [male], which ran at him, and hardly he escaped with his life in a narrow way where he was fain to use defence and policy to save his life.

In this place he saw and perceived sundry tokens of the peoples resorting thither. And being ashore upon the top of a hill he perceived a number of small things fleeting in the sea afar off, which he supposed to be porpoises or seals, or some kind of strange fish; but coming nearer he discovered them to be men in small boats made of leather. And before he could descend down from the hill certain of those people had almost cut off his boat from him, having stolen secretly behind the rocks for that purpose, where he speedily hasted to his boat and bent himself to his halberd, and narrowly escaped the danger and saved his boat.

Afterwards he had sundry conferences with them, and they came aboard his ship and brought him salmon and raw flesh and fish, and greedily devoured the same before our men's faces. And to show their agility they tried many masteries upon the ropes of the ship after our mariners' fashion, and appeared to be very strong of their arms and nimble of their bodies. They exchanged coats of seals and bears' skins, and such like, with our men; and received bells, looking glasses and other toys in recompense thereof again. After great courtesy and many meetings our mariners, contrary to their Captain's direction, began more easily to trust them; and five of our men going ashore were by them intercepted with their boat and were never since heard of to this day again; so that the Captain, being destitute of boat, bark and all company, had scarcely sufficient number to conduct back his bark again.

He could now neither convey himself ashore to rescue his men (if he had been able) for want of a boat; and again, the subtle traitors were so wary as they would after that never come within our men's danger. The Captain notwithstanding desirous to bring some token from thence of his being there was greatly discontented that he had not before apprehended some of them: and therefore to deceive the deceivers he wrought a pretty policy; for knowing well how they greatly delighted in our toys, and specially in bells, he rang a pretty lowbell, making signs that he would give him the same that would come and fetch it. And because they would not come within his danger for fear he flung one bell unto them, which of purpose he threw short that it might fall into the sea and be lost. And to make them more greedy of

Terra Australis Incognita, which was separated from South America only by the Straits of Magellan.

the matter he rang a louder bell, so that in the end one of them came
near the ship side to receive the bell, which, when he thought to take
at the Captain's hand, he was thereby taken himself; for the Captain,
being readily provided, let the bell fall and caught the man fast, and
plucked him with main force, boat and all, into his bark out of the sea.
Whereupon when he found himself in captivity, for very choler and
disdain he bit his tongue in twain within his mouth: notwithstanding,
he died not thereof, but lived until he came in England, and then he
died of cold which he had taken at sea.

Now with this new prey (which was a sufficient witness of the Captain's far and tedious travel towards the unknown parts of the world,
as did well appear by this strange infidel, whose like was never seen,
read, nor heard of before, and whose language was neither known nor
understood of any) the said Captain Frobisher returned homeward,
and arrived in England in Harwich the 2nd of October following, and
thence came to London 1576, where he was highly commended of all
men for his great and notable attempt, but specially famous for the
great hope he brought of the passage to Cataya.

And it is especially to be remembered that at their first arrival in
those parts there lay so great store of ice all the coast along so thick
together that hardly his boat could pass unto the shore. At length,
after divers attempts, he commanded his company if by any possible
means they could get ashore to bring him whatsoever thing they could
first find, whether it were living or dead, stock or stone, in token of
Christian possession, which thereby he took in behalf of the Queen's
most excellent Majesty, thinking that thereby he might justify the
having and enjoying of the same things that grew in these unknown
parts.

Some of his company brought flowers, some green grass; and one
brought a piece of black stone much like to a sea-coal in colour, which
by the weight seemed to be some kind of metal or mineral. This was a
thing of no account in the judgment of the Captain at the first sight;
and yet for novelty it was kept in respect of the place from whence it
came.

After his arrival in London, being demanded of sundry his friends
what thing he had brought them home out of that country, he had
nothing left to present them withal but a piece of this black stone. And
it fortuned a gentlewoman, one of the adventurers' wives, to have a
piece thereof, which by chance she threw and burned in the fire so
long that at the length, being taken forth and quenched in a little
vinegar, it glistened with a bright marcasite of gold. Whereupon, the
matter being called in some question, it was brought to certain gold-
finers in London to make assay thereof, who gave out that it held gold,

and that very richly for the quantity. Afterwards, the same gold-finers promised great matters thereof if there were any store to be found, and offered themselves to adventure for the searching of those parts from whence the same was brought. Some that had great hope of the matter sought secretly to have a lease at Her Majesty's hands of those places, whereby to enjoy the mass of so great a public profit unto their own private gains.

In conclusion, the hope of more of the same gold ore to be found kindled a greater opinion in the hearts of many to advance the voyage again. Whereupon preparation was made for a new voyage against the year following, and the Captain more specially directed by commission for the searching more of this gold ore than for the searching any further discovery of the passage. And being well accompanied with divers resolute and forward gentlemen, Her Majesty then lying at the Right Honourable the Lord of Warwick's house in Essex, he came to take his leave, and kissing Her Highness hands, with gracious countenance and comfortable words departed toward his charge.

Frobisher discovered the Straits which still bear his name and persuaded himself or at least persuaded others that he had found the North-west Passage. It was soon widely believed also (on slender and possibly false evidence) that he had found gold. Michael Lok formed the Company of Cathay to exploit these two discoveries, a gold fever seized the City, and merchants, courtiers and the Queen herself hastened to take shares. Frobisher made his second voyage in 1577, with one of the Queen's ships, the Aid and two small barks; he gave up the quest for the North-west Passage and came back laden with ore. The gold fever was at its height, obscuring judgment, although some assayers declared that there was no gold in the ore. A fleet of fifteen ships was hastily organized, Lok put all his private fortune into the venture and Frobisher sailed again early in 1578. When he returned with heavy cargoes of ore it had already been shown to be worthless. The Company of Cathay went bankrupt; the 'venturers' refused to pay up their shares; everyone, including even Frobisher, rounded on the misguided but honest Michael Lok, and he went to a debtor's prison.

THE CAPTIVITY OF JOHN FOXE

Anonymous

John Foxe was one of the most remarkable of those few slaves who, like Job Hortop, were tough enough to survive the ghastly life of the galleys and clever and determined enough to escape. His story is a grim reminder of Turkish dominance in the eastern Mediterranean in the sixteenth century.

The worthy enterprise of John Foxe, an Englishman, in delivering 266 Christians out of the captivity of the Turks at Alexandria, the 3 of January, 1577.

AMONG our merchants here in England it is a common voyage to traffic into Spain: Whereunto a ship, being called *The Three Half Moons*, manned with 38 men and well fenced with munitions the better to encounter their enemies withal, and having wind and tide, set from Portsmouth 1563, and bended her journey toward Seville, a city in Spain, intending there to traffic with them. And falling near the Straits they perceived themselves to be beset round with eight galleys of the Turks, in such wise that there was no way for them to fly or escape away, but that either they must yield or else be sunk. Which the owner perceiving manfully encouraged his company, exhorting them valiantly to show their manhood, showing them that God was their God and not their enemies, requesting them also not to faint in seeing such a heap of their enemies ready to devour them: putting them in mind also that if it were God's pleasure to give them into their enemies' hands it was not they that ought to show one displeasant look or countenance there against; but to take it patiently, and not to prescribe a day and time for their deliverance, as the citizens of Bethulia did, but to put themselves under His mercy. And again, if it were His mind and good will to show His mighty power by them, if their enemies were ten times so many they were not able to stand in their hands; putting them likewise in mind of the old and ancient worthiness of their countrymen who in the hardest extremities have always most prevailed and gone away conquerors, yea, and where it hath been almost impossible. Such (quoth he) hath been the valiantness of our countrymen, and such hath been the mighty power of our God.

With other like encouragements, exhorting them to behave themselves manfully, they fell all on their knees making their prayers briefly unto God: who, being all risen up again, perceived their enemies by their signs and defiances bent to the spoil, whose mercy was nothing else but cruelty, whereupon every man took him to his weapon.

Then stood up one, Grove, the master, being a comely man, with his sword and target, holding them up in defiance against his enemies. So likewise stood up the owner, the master's mate, boatswain, purser, and every man well appointed. Now likewise sounded up the drums, trumpets and flutes, which would have encouraged any man, had he never so little heart or courage in him.

Then taketh him to his charge John Foxe, the gunner, in the disposing of his pieces in order to the best effect and sending his bullets towards the Turks, who likewise bestowed their pieces thrice as fast toward the Christians. But shortly they drew near so that the bowmen fell to their charge in sending forth their arrows so thick amongst the galleys, and also in doubling their shot so sore upon the galleys, that there were twice so many of the Turks slain as the number of the Christians were in all. But the Turks discharged twice as fast against the Christians, and so long, that the ship was very sore stricken and bruised under water. Which the Turks perceiving, made the more haste to come aboard the ship: which, ere they could do, many a Turk bought it dearly with the loss of their lives. Yet was all in vain, and boarded they were, where they found so hot a skirmish that it had been better they had not meddled with the feast. For the Englishmen showed themselves men indeed in working manfully with their brown-bills and halberds; where the owner, master, boatswain and their company stood to it so lustily that the Turks were half dismayed. But chiefly the boatswain showed himself valiant above the rest, for he fared amongst the Turks like a wood lion. For there was none of them that either could or durst stand in his face till at the last there came a shot from the Turks which brake his whistle asunder and smote him on the breast so that he fell down, bidding them farewell and to be of good comfort, encouraging them likewise to win praise by death rather than to live captives in misery and shame. Which they hearing, indeed intended to have done, as it appeared by their skirmish. But the press and store of the Turks was so great that they were not able long to endure, but were so overpressed that they could not wield their weapons: by reason whereof they must needs be taken, which none of them intended to have been but rather to have died; except only the master's mate, who shrunk from the skirmish like a notable coward, esteeming neither the value of his name nor accounting of the present example of his fellows, nor having respect to the miseries whereunto he should be put.

But in fine, so it was that the Turks were victors, whereof they had no great cause to rejoice or triumph. Then would it have grieved any hard heart to see these infidels so violently intreating the Christians, not having any respect of their manhood which they had tasted of, nor yet respecting their own state, how they might have met with such a booty as might have given them the overthrow. But no remorse hereof, or anything else, doth bridle their fierce and tyrannous dealing but that the Christians must needs to the galleys to serve in new offices: and they were no sooner in them but their garments were pulled over their ears and torn from their backs, and they set to the oars.

I will make no mention of their miseries, being now under their enemies' raging stripes. I think there is no man will judge their fare good, or their bodies unladen of stripes, and not pestered with too much heat and also with too much cold. But I will go to my purpose, which is to show the end of those, being in mere misery, which continually do call on God with a steadfast hope that He will deliver them and with a sure faith that He can do it.

Nigh to the city of Alexandria, being a haven town and under the dominion of the Turks, there is a road, being made very fencible with strong walls, whereinto the Turks do customably bring their galleys on shore every year in the winter season, and there do trim them and lay them up against the springtime. In which road there is a prison wherein the captives and such prisoners as serve in the galleys are put for all that time until the seas be calm and passable for the galleys, every prisoner being most grievously laden with irons on their legs, to their great pain and sore disabling of them to any labour taking. Into which prison were these Christians put and fast warded all the winter season.

But ere it was long the Master and the owner, by means of friends, were redeemed: the rest abiding still by the misery while that they were all (through reason of their ill usage and worse fare miserably starved) saving one, John Foxe, who (as some men can abide harder and more misery than other some can, so can some likewise make more shift and work more devices to help their state and living than other some can do) being somewhat skilful in the craft of a barber, by reason thereof made great shift in helping his fare now and then with a good meal. Insomuch till at the last God sent him favour in the sight of the keeper of the prison, so that he had leave to go in and out to the road at his pleasure, paying a certain stipend unto the keeper and wearing a lock about his leg. Which liberty likewise six more had upon like sufferance; who, by reason of their long imprisonment, not being feared or suspected to start aside or that they would work the Turks any mischief, had liberty to go in and out at the said road in such manner as this John Foxe did, with irons on their legs, and to return again at night.

In the year of our Lord 1577, in the winter season, the galleys happily coming to their accustomed harbour and being discharged of all their masts, sails, and other such furnitures as unto galleys do appertain, and all the masters and mariners of them being then nested in their own homes, there remained in the prison of the said road two hundred threescore and eight Christian prisoners who had been taken by the Turks' force, and were of sixteen sundry nations. Among which there were three Englishmen, whereof one was named John Foxe of Woodbridge in Suffolk, the other William Wickney of Portsmouth, in the County of Southampton, and the third Robert Moore of Harwich, in the County of Essex. Which John Foxe, having been thirteen or fourteen years under their gentle entreatance, and being too too weary thereof, minding his escape, weighed with himself by what means it might be brought to pass: and continually pondering with himself thereof, took a good heart unto him in hope that God would not be always scourging His children, and never ceased to pray Him to further his pretended enterprise if that it should redound to His glory.

Not far from the road, and somewhat from thence at one side of the City, there was a certain victualling house which one Peter Unticaro had hired, paying also a certain fee unto the keeper of the road. This Peter Unticaro was a Spaniard born and a Christian, and had been prisoner about thirty years, and never practised any means to escape, but kept himself quiet without touch or suspect of any conspiracy; until that now this John Foxe, using much thither, they brake one to another their minds concerning the restraint of their liberty and imprisonment. So that this John Foxe, at length opening unto this Unticaro the device which he would fain put into practice, made privy one more to this their intent. Which three debated of this matter at such times as they could compass to meet together: insomuch that at seven weeks' end they had sufficiently concluded how the matter should be if it pleased God to further them thereto. Who, making five more privy to this their device whom they thought they might safely trust, determined in three nights after to accomplish their deliberate purpose. Whereupon the same John Foxe and Peter Unticaro and the other six appointed to meet all together in the prison the next day, being the last day of December, where this John Foxe certified the rest of the prisoners what their intent and device was, and how and when they minded to bring their purpose to pass: who thereunto persuaded them without much ado to further their device. Which the same John Foxe seeing, delivered unto them a sort of files which he had gathered together for this purpose by the means of Peter Unticaro, charging them that every man should be ready discharged of his irons by eight of the clock on the next day at night.

On the next day at night this said John Foxe and his six other companions, being all come to the house of Peter Unticaro, passing the time away in mirth for fear of suspect till the night came on so that it was time for them to put in practice their device, sent Peter Unticaro to the master of the road in the name of one of the masters of the city with whom this keeper was acquainted and at whose request he also would come at the first; who desired him to take the pains to meet him there, promising him that he would bring him back again. The keeper agreed to go with him, willing the warders not to bar the gate, saying that he would not stay long but would come again with all speed.

In the mean season the other seven had provided them of such weapons as they could get in that house: and John Foxe took him to an old rusty sword blade, without either hilt or pommel, which he made to serve his turn in bending the hand end of the sword instead of a pommel, and the other had got such spits and glaives as they found in the house.

The keeper now being come unto the house and perceiving no light nor hearing any noise straightway suspected the matter, and, returning backward, John Foxe standing behind the corner of the house, stepped forth unto him; who, perceiving it to be John Foxe, said, 'O Foxe, what have I deserved of thee that thou shouldst seek my death?'

'Thou villain,' quoth Foxe, 'hast been a bloodsucker of many a Christian's blood, and now thou shalt know what thou hast deserved at my hands.' Wherewith he lift up his bright shining sword of ten years' rust and stroke him so main a blow as therewithal his head clave asunder, so that he fell stark dead to the ground. Whereupon Peter Unticaro went in and certified the rest how the case stood with the keeper; who came presently forth, and some with their spits ran him through, and the other with their glaives hewed him in sunder, cut off his head, and mangled him so that no man should discern what he was.

Then marched they toward the road whereinto they entered softly, where were six warders, whom one of them asked, saying, who was there? Quoth Foxe and his company, 'All friends'. Which, when they were all within, proved contrary, for, quoth Foxe, 'My masters, here is not to every man a man, wherefore look you play your parts'. Who so behaved themselves indeed that they had dispatched these six quickly. Then John Foxe, intending not to be barred of his enterprise and minding to work surely in that which he went about, barred the gate surely and planted a cannon against it.

Then entered they into the gaoler's lodge, where they found the keys of the fortress and prison by his bedside, and there had they all better weapons. In this chamber was a chest wherein was a rich treasure and all in ducats, which this Peter Unticaro and two more opening stuffed themselves so full as they could between their shirts and their skin: which John Foxe would not once touch, and said that it was his and their liberty which he sought for, to the honour of his God, and not to make a mart of the wicked treasure of the infidels. Yet did these words sink nothing into their stomachs, they did it for a good intent. So did Saul save the fattest oxen to offer unto the Lord, and they to serve their own turn. But neither did Saul escape the wrath of God therefore, neither had these that thing which they desired so and did thirst after. Such is God's justice. He that they put their trust in to deliver them from the tyrannous hands of their enemies, he (I say) could supply their want of necessaries.

Now these eight being armed with such weapons as they thought well of, thinking themselves sufficient champions to encounter a stronger enemy, and coming unto the prison, Foxe opened the gates and doors thereof and called forth all the prisoners, whom he set some to ramming up the gate, some to the dressing up of a certain galley which was the best in all the road and was called the *Captain of Alexandria*, whereinto some carried masts, sails, oars, and other such furniture as doth belong unto a galley.

At the prison were certain warders whom John Foxe and his company slew; in the killing of whom there were eight more of the Turks which perceived them and got them to the top of the prison: unto whom John Foxe and his company were fain to come by ladders, where they found a hot skirmish. For some of them were there slain, some wounded, and some but scarred and not hurt. As John Foxe was thrice shot through his apparel and not hurt, Peter Unticaro and the other two that had armed them with the ducats were slain, as not able to wield themselves, being so pestered with the weight and uneasy carrying of the wicked and profane treasure: and also divers Christians were as well hurt about that skirmish, as Turks slain.

Amongst the Turks was one thrust through, who (let us not say that it was ill fortune) fell off from the top of the prison wall and made such a lowing that the inhabitants thereabout (as here and there scattering stood a house or two) came and dawed him [brought him back to consciousness] so that they understood the case, how that the prisoners were paying their ransoms: wherewith they raised both Alexandria, which lay on the west side of the road, and a castle which was at the city's end, next to the road, and also another fortress which lay on the north side of the road, so that now they had no way to escape but one, which by man's reason (the two holds [forts] lying so upon the mouth of the road) might seem impossible to be a way for them. So was the Red Sea impossible for the Israelites to pass through, the hills and rocks lay so on the one side, and their enemy compassed them on the other. So was it impossible that the walls of Jericho should fall down, being neither undermined nor yet rammed at with engines, nor yet any man's wisdom, policy, or help set or put thereunto. Such impossibilities can our God make possible. He that held the lions' jaws from renting Daniel asunder, yea, or yet from once touching him to his hurt, cannot He hold the roaring cannons of this hellish force? He that kept the fire's rage in the hot burning oven from the three children that praised His name, cannot He keep the fire's flaming blasts from among His elect?

Now is the road fraught with lusty soldiers, labourers, and mariners who are fain to stand to their tackling in setting to every man his hand, some to the carrying in of victuals, some munitions, some oars, and some one thing, some another, but most are keeping their enemy from the wall of the road. But to be short, there was no time misspent, no man idle, nor any man's labour ill bestowed or in vain. So that in short time this galley was ready trimmed up, whereinto every man leaped in all haste, hoisting up the sails lustily, yielding themselves to His mercy and grace, in whose hands are both wind and weather.

Now is this galley on float and out of the safety of the road: now have the two castles full power upon the galley, now is there no remedy but to sink: how can it be avoided? The cannons let fly from both sides, and the galley is even in the midst and between them both. What man can devise to save it? There is no man but would think it must needs be sunk.

There was not one of them that feared the shot which went thundering round about their ears, nor yet were once scarred or touched, with five and forty shot which came from the castles. Here did God hold forth His buckler, He shieldeth now this galley and hath tried their faith to the uttermost. Now cometh His special help: yea, even when man thinks them past all help then cometh He himself down from heaven with His mighty power, then is His present remedy most ready pressed. For they sail away, being not once touched with the glance of a shot, and are quickly out of the Turkish cannons' reach. Then might they see them coming down by heaps to the water side in companies like unto swarms of bees, making show to come after them with galleys in bustling themselves to dress up the galleys, which would be a swift piece of work for them to do for that they had neither oars, masts, sails, gables, nor anything else ready in any galley.

But yet they are carrying them into them, some into one galley and some into another, so that, being such a confusion amongst them without any certain guide, it were a thing impossible to overtake them. Besides that, there was no man that would take charge of a galley, the weather was so rough and there was such an amazedness amongst them. And verily I think their God was amazed thereat: it could not be but he must blush for shame, he can speak never a word for dullness much less can he help them in such an extremity. Well, howsoever it is, he is very much to blame, to suffer them to receive such a jibe. But howsoever their God behaved himself, our God showed Himself a God indeed, and that He was the only living God: for the seas were swift under His faithful which made the enemies aghast to behold them, a skilfuller pilot leads them, and their mariners bestir them lustily: but the Turks had neither mariners, pilot, nor any skilfull Master that was in a readiness at this pinch.

When the Christians were safe out of the enemy's coast John Foxe called to them all, willing them to be thankful unto Almighty God for their delivery and most humbly to fall down upon their knees, beseeching Him to aid them unto their friends' land and not to bring them into another danger sith He had most mightily delivered them from so great a thraldom and bondage.

Thus, when every man had made his petition they fell straightway to their labour with the oars, in helping one another when they were wearied, and with great labour striving to come to some Christian land as near as they could guess by the stars. But the winds were so diverse, one while driving them this way, another while that way, that they were now in a new maze, thinking that God had forsaken them and left them to a greater danger.

And forasmuch as there were no victuals now left in the galley it might have been a cause to them (if they had been the Israelites) to have murmured against their God. But they knew how that their God, who had delivered them out of Egypt, was such a loving and merciful God as that He would not suffer them to be confounded in whom He had wrought so great a wonder: but what calamity soever they sustained they knew it was but for their further trial, and also (in putting them in mind of their further misery) to cause them not to triumph and glory in themselves therefore. Having (I say) no victuals in the galley it might seem that one misery continually fell upon another's neck. But to be brief, the famine grew to be so great that in 28 days, wherein they were on the sea, there died eight persons, to the astonishment of all the rest.

So it fell out that upon the 29 day after they set from Alexandria they fell on the isle of Candie, and landed at Gallipoli where they were made much of by the abbot and monks there, who caused them to stay there while they were well refreshed and eased. They kept there the sword wherewith John Foxe had killed the keeper, esteeming it as a most precious jewel, and hung it up for a monument.

When they thought good, having leave to depart from thence, they sailed along the coast till they arrived at Taranto, where they sold their galley and divided it, every man having a part thereof. The Turks, receiving so shameful a foil at their hand, pursued the Christians and scoured the seas where they could imagine that they had bent their course. And the Christians had departed from thence on the one day in the morning, and seven galleys of the Turks came thither that night, as it was certified by those who followed Foxe and his company, fearing lest they should have been met with. And then they came afoot to Naples, where they departed asunder, every man taking him to his next way home.

From whence John Foxe took his journey unto Rome, where he was well entertained of an Englishman, who presented his worthy deed unto the Pope, who rewarded him liberally and gave him his letters unto the King of Spain, where he was very well entertained of him there, who for this his most worthy enterprise gave him in fee twenty pence a day. From whence, being desirous to come into his own country, he came thither at such time as he conveniently could, which was in the year of Our Lord God, 1579. Who being come into England went unto the Court and showed all his travel unto the Council. Who, considering of the state of this man, in that he had spent and lost a great part of his youth in thraldom and bondage, extended to him their liberality to help to maintain him now in age, to their right honour, and to the encouragement of all true-hearted Christians.

AN EMBASSY TO MOROCCO
Edmund Hogan

Trade could make a bridge even between Christians and Muslims, sworn enemies though they were. In 1551, the fourth year of Edward VI, a syndicate of London merchants initiated English trade with Morocco (Barbary). They sent a ship, commanded by Thomas Windham, to Santa Cruz (now Agadir) on the Atlantic coast, and the trade in saltpetre, fruit, sugar, etc, which he established became permanent. 'The Portugals were much offended,' says Hakluyt, 'and gave out that if they took us in those parts they would use us as their mortal enemies.' The trade continued, and was confirmed by this embassy.

The Ambassage of Master Edmund Hogan, one of the sworn Esquires of Her Majesty's person, from Her Highness to Mully Abdelmelech, Emperor of Morocco, and King of Fez and Sus: in the year 1577, written by himself.

I, EDMUND HOGAN, being appointed Ambassador from the Queen's Majesty to the above-named Emperor and King, Mully Abdelmelech, departed with my company and servants from London the two and twenty day of April, 1577, being embarked in the good ship called the *Galleon of London*, and arrived in Azafi, a port of Barbary, the one and twenty day of May next following. Immediately I sent Lionel Edgerton ashore with my letters directed to John Williams and John Bampton, who dispatched a *trottero* [messenger] to Morocco to know the King's pleasure for my repair to the Court, which letters came to their hands on the Thursday night.

They with all speed gave the King understanding of it, who being glad thereof speeded the next day certain captains with soldiers and tents, with other provision, to Azafi: so that upon Whitsunday at night the said captains, with John Bampton, Robert Washborne, and Robert Lion, and the King's officers, came late to Azafi.

In the meantime I remained aboard, and caused some of the goods to be discharged for lightening of the ship, and I wrote in my letter that I would not land till I knew the King's pleasure.

The 22nd day, being Saturday, the *Make-speed* arrived in the road about two of the clock in the afternoon.

The 27th day, being Whitsunday, came aboard the galleon John Bampton and others, giving me to understand how much the King rejoiced of my safe arrival, coming from the Queen's Majesty, and how that for my safe conduct to the Court he had sent four captains and an hundred soldiers well appointed, with a horse furnished which he used himself to ride on with all other furniture accordingly: they wished me also to come on land in the best order I could, as well for myself as my men, which I did having to the number of ten men, whereof three were trumpeters.

The ships, being four, appointed themselves in the best order they could for the best show, and shot off all their ordnance to the value of twenty marks in powder.

At my coming ashore I found all the soldiers well appointed on horseback, the captains and the Governor of the town standing as near the waterside as they could, with a jennet of the King's, and received me from the boat declaring how glad His Majesty was of my safe arrival, coming from the Queen's Majesty, my mistress, and that he had sent them to attend upon me, it being his pleasure that I should tarry there on shore five or six days for my refreshing.

So being mounted upon the jennet they conducted me through the town into a fair field upon the seaside, where was a tent provided for me, and all the ground spread with Turkey carpets, and the castle discharged a peal of ordnance, and all things necessary were brought into my tent, where I both took my table and lodging and had other convenient tents for my servants.

The soldiers environed the tents, and watched about us day and night as long as I lay there, although I sought my speedier dispatch.

On the Wednesday towards night I took my horse and travelled ten miles to the first place of water that we could find, and there pitched our tents till the next morning, and so travelled till ten of the clock and then pitched our tents till four, and so travelled as long as daylight would suffer, about 26 miles that day.

The next day, being Friday, I travelled in like order but eight and twenty miles at the most, and by a river being about six miles within sight of the city of Morocco we pitched our tents.

Immediately after came all our English merchants and the French on horseback to meet me, and before night there came an alcaide from the King with fifty men and divers mules laden with victual and banquet for my supper, declaring unto me how glad the King showed himself to hear of the Queen's Majesty, and that his pleasure was I should be received into his country as never any Christian the like: and desired to know what time the next day I would come into his city, because he would that all the Christians, as also his nobility, should meet me, and willed John Bampton to be with him early in the morning, which he did.

About seven of the clock, being accompanied with the French and English merchants and a great number of soldiers, I passed towards the city, and by that time I had travelled two miles there met me all the Christians of the Spaniards and Portugals to receive me, which I know was more by the King's commandment than of any goodwills of themselves: for some of them, although they speak me fair, hung down their heads like dogs, and especially the Portugals, and I countenanced them accordingly.

So I passed on till I came within two English miles of the city, and then John Bampton returned, showing me that the King was so glad of my coming that he could not devise to do too much to show the goodwill that he did owe to the Queen's Majesty and her realm.

His counsellors met me without the gates, and at the entry of the gates his footmen and guard were placed on both sides of my horse, and so brought me to the King's palace.

The King sat in his chair with his Council about him, as well the Moors as the Elchies, and, according to his order given unto me before, I there declared my message in Spanish and made delivery of the Queen's Majesty's letters, and all that I spake at that present in Spanish he caused one of his Elchies to declare the same to the Moors present in the Larbe tongue.

Which done, he answered me again in Spanish, yielding to the Queen's Majesty great thanks, and offering himself and his country to be at Her Grace's commandment, and then commanded certain of his counsellors to conduct me to my lodging, not being far from the Court.

The house was fair after the fashion of that country, being daily well furnished with all kind of victual at the King's charge.

The same night he sent for me to the Court, and I had conference with him about the space of two hours, where I throughly declared the charge committed unto me from Her Majesty, finding him conformable, willing to pleasure and not to urge Her Majesty with any demands more than conveniently she might willingly consent unto, he knowing that out of his country the realm of England might be better served with lacks than he in comparison from us.

Further, he gave me to understand that the King of Spain had sent unto him for a licence that an ambassador of his might come into his country, and had made great means that if the Queen's Majesty of England sent any unto him that he would not give him any credit or entertainment, 'Albeit,' (said he) 'I know what the King of Spain is, and what the Queen of England and Her realm is; for I neither like of him nor of his religion, being so governed by the Inquisition that he can do nothing of himself.

'Therefore when he cometh upon the licence which I have granted he shall well see how little account I will make of him and Spain, and how greatly I will extol you for the Queen's Majesty of England.

'He shall not come to my presence as you have done, and shall daily; for I mind to accept of you as my companion and one of my house, whereas he shall attend twenty days after he hath done his message.'

After the end of this speech I delivered Sir Thomas Gresham's* letters, when as he took me by the hand and led me down a long court to a palace where there ran a fair fountain of water, and there sitting himself in a chair he commanded me to sit down in another, and there called for such simple musicians as he had.

Then I presented him with a great bass lute which he most thankfully accepted, and then he was desirous to hear of the musicians, and I told him that there was great care had to provide them and that I did not doubt but upon my return they should come with the first ship. He is willing to give them good entertainment with provision of victual, and to let them live according to their law and conscience, wherein he urgeth none to the contrary.

I find him to be one that liveth greatly in the fear of God, being well exercised in the Scriptures, as well in the Old Testament as also in the New, and he beareth a greater affection to our nation than to others because of our religion, which forbiddeth worship of idols, and the Moors called him the Christian King.

The same night, being the first of June, I continued with him till twelve of the clock, and he seemed to have so good liking of me that he took from his girdle a short dagger, being set with 200 stones, rubies and turkis, and did bestow it upon me, and so I, being conducted, returned to my lodging for that time.

The next day, because he knew it to be Sunday and our Sabbath day, he did let me rest. But on the Monday in the afternoon he sent for me, and I had conference with him again, and music.

Likewise on the Tuesday by three of the clock he sent for me into his garden, finding him laid upon a silk bed complaining of a sore leg: yet after long conference he walked into another orchard, where as having a fair banqueting-house and a great water, and a new galley in it, he went aboard the galley and took me with him and passed the space of two or three hours, showing the great experience he had in galleys, wherein (as he said) he had exercised himself eighteen years in his youth.

* Sir Thomas Gresham (1519?–79), financier, economist and crown agent, founded the Royal Exchange and Gresham College. He often advised Elizabeth on financial matters.

After supper he showed me his horses and other commodities that he had about his house, and since that night I have not seen him, for that he hath kept in with his sore leg, but he hath sent to me daily.

The 13th of June at six of the clock at night I had again audience of the King, and I continued with him till midnight, having debated as well for the Queen's commission as for the well dealing with her merchants for their traffic here in these parts, saying he would do much more for the Queen's Majesty and the realm, offering that all English ships with her subjects may with good security enter into his ports and dominions, as well in trade of merchandise as for victual and water, as also in time of war with any her enemies to bring in prizes and to make sales as occasion should serve, or else to depart again with them at their pleasure.

Likewise for all English ships that shall pass along his coast of Barbary, and through the straits into the Levant seas, that he would grant safe conduct that the said ships and merchants with their goods might pass into the Levant seas, and so to the Turks dominions and the King of Algiers as his own, and that he would write to the Turk and to the King of Algiers his letters for the well using of our ships and goods.

Also that hereafter no Englishmen that by any means may be taken captives shall be sold within any of his dominions: whereupon I declared that the Queen's Majesty, accepting of these his offers, was pleased to confirm the intercourse and trade of our merchants within this his country, as also to pleasure him with such commodities as he should have need of to furnish the necessities and wants of his country in trade of merchandise, so as he required nothing contrary to her honour and law, and the breach of league with the Christian princes her neighbours.

The same night I presented the King with the case of combs, and desired His Majesty to have special regard that the ships might be laden back again, for that I found little store of saltpetre in readiness in John Bampton's hands. He answered me that I should have all the assistance therein that he could, but that in Sus he thought to have some store in his house there, as also that the mountaineers [people of the mountains] had made much in a readiness: I requested that he would send down, which he promised to do.

The eighteenth day I was with him again and so continued there till night, and he showed me his house with pastime in ducking with water-spaniels, and baiting bulls with his English dogs.

At this time I moved him again for the sending down to Sus, which he granted to do, and the 24th day there departed Alcaide Mammie, with Lionel Edgerton and Rowland Guy to Sus, and carried with them for our accompts and his company the King's letters to his brother, Muly Hammet, and Alcaide Shauan, and the Viceroy.

The 23rd day the King sent me out of Morocco to his garden, called Shersbonare, with his guard and Alcaide Mamoute, and the 24th at night I came to the Court to see a Morris dance, and a play of his Elchies. He promised me audience the next day, being Tuesday, but he put it off till Thursday: and the Thursday at night I was sent for to the King after supper, and then he sent Alcaide Rodwan and Alcaide Gowry to confer with me, but after a little talk I desired to be brought to the King for my dispatch. And being brought to him I preferred two bills of John Bamptons which he had made for provision of saltpetre, also two bills for the quiet traffic of our English merchants, and bills for sugars to be made for the Jews, as well for the debts past, as hereafter, and for good order in the ingenios [sugar mills]. Also I moved him again for the saltpetre and other dispatches, which he referred to be agreed upon by the two Alcaides. But the Friday, being the 20th, the Alcaides could not intend it, and upon Saturday Alcaide Rodwan fell sick, so on Sunday we made means to the King, and that afternoon I was sent for to confer upon the bargain with the Alcaides and others, but did not agree.

Upon Tuesday I wrote a letter to the King for my dispatch, and the same afternoon I was called again to the Court, and referred all things to the King, accepting his offer of saltpetre.

That night again the King had me into his galley, and the spaniels did hunt the duck.

The Thursday I was appointed to weigh the 300 kintals gross of saltpetre, and that afternoon the tabybe came unto me to my lodging, showing me that the King was offended with John Bampton for divers causes.

The Sunday night late, being the 7th of July, I got the King to forgive all to John Bampton, and the King promised me to speak again with me upon Monday.

Upon Tuesday I wrote to him again for my dispatch, and then he sent Fray Lewes to me and said that he had order to write.

Upon Wednesday I wrote again, and he sent me word that upon Thursday I should come and be dispatched so that I should depart upon Friday without fail, being the twelfth of July.

So the Friday after, according to the King's order and appointment, I went to the Court, and whereas motion and petition was made for the confirmation of the demands which I had preferred they were all granted, and likewise the privileges which were on the behalf of our English merchants requested were with great favour and readiness yielded unto. And whereas the Jews there resident were to our men in certain round sums indebted, the Emperor's pleasure and command-ment was that they should without further excuse or delay pay and discharge the same. And thus at length I was dismissed with great honour and special countenance, such as hath not ordinarily been shewed to other Ambassadors of the Christians.

And touching the private affairs intreated upon betwixt Her Majesty and the Emperor, I had letters from him to satisfy Her Highness there-in. So to conclude, having received the like honourable conduct from his Court as I had for my part at my first landing I embarked myself with my foresaid company, and arriving not long after in England I repaired to Her Majesty's Court, and ended my ambassage to Her Highness' good liking, with relation of my service performed.

A VOYAGE TO INDIA

Thomas Stevens

The writer of the following letter was an English Jesuit, educated at Winchester and at St Andrew's College, Rome, who went as a missionary to the 'East Indies', which then included India. Until his death in 1619 he lived in Goa, on the west coast of India, which was a Portuguese colony from 1503 to 1961.

A letter written from Goa, the principal city of all the East Indies, by one Thomas Stevens, an Englishman, and sent to his father, Master Thomas Stevens: anno 1579.

AFTER most humble commendations: These shall be to crave your daily blessing, with like commendations unto my mother; and withal, to certify you of my being, according to your will and my duty. I wrote unto you, taking my journey from Italy to Portugal, which letters I think are come to your hands, so that, presuming thereupon, I think I have the less need at this time to tell you the cause of my departing, which nevertheless in one word I may conclude if I do but name obedience.

I came to Lisbon toward the end of March, eight days before the departure of the ships, so late that if they had not been stayed about some weighty matters they had been long gone before our coming, insomuch that there were others ordained to go in our places that the king's provision and ours also might not be in vain. Nevertheless our sudden coming took place, and the fourth of April five ships departed for Goa, wherein, besides shipmen and soldiers, there were a great number of children which in the seas bear out better than men, and no marvel when that many women also pass very well. The setting forth from the port I need not to tell how solemn it is, with trumpets and shooting of ordnance, you may easily imagine it considering that they go in the manner of war. The tenth of the foresaid month we came to the sight of Porto Santo near unto Madeira, where an English ship set upon ours (which was then also alone) with a few shots, which did no harm, but after that our ship had laid out her greatest ordnance they straight departed as they came. The English ship was very fair and great, which I was sorry to see so ill occupied, for she went roving about so that we saw her again at the Canary Isles, unto the which we came the thirteenth of the said month, and good leisure we had to wonder at the high mountain of the Island Teneriffe, for we wandered between that and Grand Canary four days by reason of contrary winds: and briefly, such evil weather we had until the fourteenth of May that they despaired to compass the Cape of Good Hope that year.

Nevertheless, taking our voyage between Guinea and the Islands of Cape Verde, without seeing of any land at all, we arrived at length unto the coast of Guinea, which the Portuguese so call chiefly that part of the burning zone which is from the sixth degree unto the Equinoctial, in which parts they suffered so many inconveniences of heats and lack of winds that they think themselves happy when they have passed it; for sometimes the ship standeth there almost by the space of many days, sometime she goeth, but in such order that it were almost as good to stand still. And the greatest part of this coast not clear, but thick and cloudy, full of thunder and lightning, and rain so unwholesome that if the water stand a little while all is full of worms, and falling on the meat, which is hanged up, it maketh it straight full of worms.

Along all that coast we often times saw a thing swimming upon the water like a cockscomb (which they call a ship of Guinea) but the colour much fairer; which comb standeth upon a thing almost like the swimmer of a fish in colour and bigness, and beareth underneath in the water strings which save it from turning over. This thing is so poisonous that a man cannot touch it without great peril.

In this coast, that is to say from the sixth degree unto the Equinoctial, we spent no less than thirty days, partly with contrary winds, partly with calm. The thirtieth of May we passed the Equinoctial with contentation, directing our course as well as we could to pass the promontory, but in all that gulf, and in all the way beside, we found so often calms that the expertest mariners wondered at it. And in places where are always wont to be most horrible tempests we found most quiet calms, which was very troublesome to those ships which be the greatest of all other and cannot go without good winds. Insomuch, that when it is tempest almost intolerable for other ships and maketh them main all their sails, these hoist up and sail excellent well, unless the waters be too too furious, which seldom happened in our navigation.

You shall understand that, being past the line, they cannot straightway go the next way to the promontory; but, according to the wind, they draw always as near South as they can to put themselves in the latitude of the point, which is 35 degrees and an half, and then they take their course towards the East and so compass the point. But the wind served us so that at 33 degrees we did direct our course toward the point or promontory of Good Hope.

You know that it is hard to sail from East to West, or contrary, because there is no fixed point in all the sky whereby they may direct their course, wherefore I shall tell you what helps God provided for these men. There is not a fowl that appeareth, or sign in the air, or in the sea, which they have not written which have made the voyages heretofore. Wherefore, partly by their own experience, and pondering withal what space the ship was able to make with such a wind, and such direction, and partly by the experience of others whose books and navigations they have, they guess whereabouts they be, touching degrees of longitude, for of latitude they be always sure. But the greatest and best industry of all is to mark the variation of the needle or compass, which in the Meridian of the Island of S. Michael, which is one of the Azores in the latitude of Lisbon, is just North, and thence swerveth towards the East so much that betwixt the Meridian aforesaid and the point of Africa it carrieth three or four quarters of 32. And again in the point of Africa, a little beyond the point that is called Cape das Agulias (in English the needles) it returneth again unto the North, and that place passed it swerveth again toward the West, as it did before proportionally.

As touching our first signs, the nearer we came to the people of Africa the more strange kinds of fowls appeared, insomuch that when we came within no less than thirty leagues (almost an hundred miles) and six hundred miles as we thought from any island, as good as three thousand fowls of sundry kinds followed our ship; some of them so great that their wings being opened from one point to the other contained seven spans, as the Mariners said. A marvellous thing to see how God provided so that in so wide a sea these fowls are all fat, and nothing wanteth them. The Portuguese have named them all according to some propriety which they have: some they call Rushtails because their tails be not proportionable to their bodies but long and small like a rush, some forked tails because they be very broad and forked, some Velvet sleeves because they have wings of the colour of velvet and bow them as a man boweth his elbow. This bird is always welcome, for he appeareth nearest the Cape. I should never make an end if I should tell all particulars: but it shall suffice briefly to touch a few, which yet shall be sufficient, if you mark them, to give occasion to glorify Almighty God in his wonderful works, and such variety in his creatures. And to speak somewhat of fishes in all places of calm, especially in the burning Zone, near the line (for without we never saw any) there waited on our ship fishes as long as a man, which they call Tuberones. They come to eat such things as from the ship fall into the sea, not refusing men themselves if they light upon them. And if they find any meat tied in the sea they take it for theirs. These have waiting on them six or seven small fishes (which never depart) with gardes blue and green round about their bodies, like comely serving men: and they go two or three before him, and some on every side. Moreover, they have other fishes which cleave always unto their body, and seem to take such superfluities as grow about them, and they are said to enter into their bodies also to purge them if they need. The Mariners in time past have eaten of them, but since they have seen them eat men their stomachs abhor them. Nevertheless, they draw them up with great hooks and kill of them as many as they can, thinking that they have made a great revenge.

There is another kind of fish, as big almost as a herring, which hath wings and flieth, and they are together in great number. These have two enemies, the one in the sea, the other in the air. In the sea the fish which is called Albocore, as big as a salmon, followeth them with great swiftness to take them. This poor fish not being able [to] swim fast, for he hath no fins but swimmeth with moving of his tail, shutting his wings, lifteth himself above the water and flieth not very high: the Albocore seeing that, although he have no wings, yet he giveth a great leap out of the water and sometimes catcheth him, or else he keepeth himself under the water going that way on as fast as he flieth. And when the fish, being weary of the air or thinking himself out of danger, returneth into the water, the Albocore meeteth with him: but sometimes his other enemy, the sea-crow, catcheth him before he falleth.

With these and like sights, but always making our supplications to

God for good weather and salvation of the ship, we came at length unto the point, so famous and feared of all men: but we found there no tempest, only great waves, where our Pilot was a little overseen. For whereas commonly all other never come within sight of land, but seeing signs ordinary and finding bottom go their way sure and safe, he, thinking himself to have wind at will, shot so nigh the land that the wind, turning into the South, and the waves being exceeding great, rolled us so near the land that the ship stood in less than 14 fathoms of water, no more than six miles from the Cape, which is called Das Agulias. And there we stood as utterly cast away; for under us were rocks of main stone so sharp and cutting that no anchor could hold the ship, the shore so evil that nothing could take land, and the land itself so full of Tigers, and people that are savage and killers of all strangers, that we had no hope of life nor comfort, but only in God and a good conscience. Notwithstanding, after we had lost anchors, hoisting up the sails for to get the ship a coast in some safer place, or when it should please God, it pleased His mercy suddenly, where no man looked for help, to fill our sails with wind from the land, and so we escaped, thanks be to God.

And the day following, being in the place where they are always wont to catch fish, we also fell a-fishing, and so many they took that they served all the ship for that day, and part of the next. And one of them pulled up a coral of great bigness and price. For there they say (as we saw by experience) that the corals do grow in the manner of stalks upon the rocks in the bottom, and wax hard and red.

The day of peril was the nine and twentieth of July. And you shall understand that, the Cape passed, there be two ways to India: one within the Isle of S. Laurence, which they take willingly because they refresh themselves at Mozambique a fortnight or a month, not without great need, and thence in a month more land in Goa. The other is without the Isle of S. Laurence, which they take when they set forth so late, and come so late to the point that they have no time to take the foresaid Mozambique, and then they go heavily because in this way they take no port. And by reason of the long navigation, and want of food and water, they fall into sundry diseases, their gums wax great and swell and they are fain to cut them away; their legs swell, and all the body becometh sore and so benumbed that they can not stir hand nor foot, and so they die for weakness. Others fall into fluxes and agues and die thereby. And this way it was our chance to make. Yet, though we had more than one hundred and fifty sick, there died not past seven and twenty; which loss they esteemed not much in respect of other times. Though some of ours were diseased in this sort, yet, thanks be to God, I had my health all the way, contrary to the expectation of many. God send me my health so well in the land, if it may be to His honour and service.

This way is full of privy rocks and quicksands so that sometimes we durst not sail by night, but by the providence of God we saw nothing, nor never found bottom until we came to the coast of India. When we had passed again the line, and were come to the third degree or somewhat more, we saw crabs swimming on the water that were red as though they had been sodden [boiled]: but this was no sign of land. After, about the eleventh degree, the space of many days, more than ten thousand fishes by estimation followed round about our ship, whereof we caught so many that for fifteen days we did eat nothing else, and they served our turn very well; for at this time we had neither meat nor almost anything else to eat, our navigation growing so long that it drew near to seven months, whereas commonly they go it in five, I mean when they sail the inner way. But these fishes were not sign of land but rather of deep sea.

At length we took a couple of birds, which were a kind of Hawks, whereof they joyed much thinking that they had been of India, but indeed they were of Arabia as we found afterward. And we that thought we had been near India were in the same latitude near Zocotoro, an Isle in the mouth of the Red Sea. But there God sent us great winds from the northeast or northnortheast, whereupon unwillingly they bare up toward the East, and thus we went ten days without seeing sign of land, whereby they perceived their error. For they had directed their course before always Northeast, coveting to multiply degrees of latitude, but partly the difference of the needle, and most of all the running seas, which at that time ran northwest, had drawn us to this other danger, had not God sent us this wind, which at length waxed larger and restored us to our right course. These running seas be so perilous that they deceive the most part of the governors, and some be so little curious, contenting themselves with ordinary experience, that they care not to seek out any means to know when they swerve, neither by the compass nor by any other trial.

The first sign of land were certain fowls which they knew to be of India; the second, boughs of palms and sedges; the third, snakes swimming on the water, and a substance which they call by the name of a coin of money, as broad and as round as a groat, wonderfully printed and stamped of nature like unto some coin. And these two last signs be so certain that the next day after, if the wind serve, they see land, which we did to our great joy, when all our water (for you know they make no beer in those parts) and victuals began to fail us. And to Goa we came the four and twentieth day of October, there being received with passing great charity.

The people be tawny, but not disfigured in their lips and noses as the Moors and Kaffirs of Ethiopia. They that be not of reputation, or at least the most part, go naked, saving an apron of a span long, and as much in breadth before them, and a lace two fingers broad before them, girded about with a string and no more: and thus they think them as well as we with all our trimming. Of the fruits and trees that be here I cannot now speak for I should make another letter as long as this. For hitherto I have not seen a tree here whose like I have seen in Europe, the vine excepted, which nevertheless here is to no purpose, so that all the wines are brought out of Portugal. The drink of this country is good water, or wine of the palm-tree, or of a fruit called cocos. And this shall suffice for this time.

If God send me my health I shall have opportunity to write to you once again. Now the length of my letter compelleth me to take my leave: and thus I wish your most prosperous health.

From Goa the tenth of November, 1579.
Your loving son,
Thomas Stevens.

DRAKE'S VOYAGE ROUND
THE WORLD

Anonymous

Since this was Drake's most sensational and controversial achievement there are many contemporary accounts of it, some very favourable to him, some very hostile. The narrative which follows, the only one in Hakluyt, is carefully favourable and it was added mysteriously to Hakluyt's first edition of 1589 after all the rest of the book had been printed.

The ships in the expedition were the Pelican, *later renamed the* Golden Hind, *100 tons, Captain-General Francis Drake; the* Elizabeth, *80 tons, Captain John Winter; the* Marigold, *30 tons, Captain John Thomas; the* Swan, *a fly-boat, 50 tons, Captain John Chester; the* Christopher, *a pinnace, 15 tons, Captain Thomas Moone. They were manned with '164 able and sufficient men'—gentlemen adventurers (including Drake's friend, Thomas Doughty), seamen, archers, musicians and others.*

The shareholders most probably included the Queen; the Lord High Admiral; the Earl of Leicester; Sir Francis Walsingham; Sir William Winter, surveyor of the Navy; John Hawkins and Drake himself. His instructions are unknown; they may have been to find likely sites for a settlement in South America and to return by the North-west Passage or the Moluccas. But most probably his own intention was to plunder the Spaniards and the Queen may have privately endorsed this.

The famous voyage of Sir Francis Drake into the South Sea, and therehence about the whole globe of the earth, begun in the year of Our Lord 1577.

THE 15 day of November, in the year of our Lord 1577, Master Francis Drake, with a fleet of five ships and barks, and to the number of 164 men, gentlemen and sailors, departed from Plymouth, giving out his pretended voyage for Alexandria.* But the wind falling contrary, he was forced the next morning to put into Falmouth Haven, in Cornwall, where such and so terrible a tempest took us as few men have seen the like, and was indeed so vehement

---

* This had been publicly announced, in the (probably vain) attempt to delude the Spanish spies.

that all our ships were like to have gone to wrack. But it pleased God to preserve us from that extremity, and to afflict us only for that present with these two particulars: the mast of our admiral, which was the *Pelican*, was cut overboard for the safeguard of the ship, and the *Marigold* was driven ashore, and somewhat bruised. For the repairing of which damages we returned again to Plymouth; and having recovered those harms, and brought the ships again to good state, we set forth the second time from Plymouth, and set sail the 13 day of December following.

The 25 day of the same month we fell with the Cape Cantin, upon the coast of Barbary; and coasting along, the 27 day we found an island called Mogador, lying one mile distant from the main. Between which island and the main we found a very good and safe harbour for our ships to ride in, as also very good entrance, and void of any danger. On this island our General erected a pinnace, whereof he brought out of England with him four already framed [prefabricated].

While these things were in doing, there came to the water's side some of the inhabitants of the country, shewing forth their flags of truce; which being seen of our General, he sent his ship's boat to the shore to know what they would. They being willing to come aboard, our men left there one man of our company for a pledge, and brought two of theirs aboard our ship; which by signs shewed our General that the next day they would bring some provision, as sheep, capons, and hens, and such like. Whereupon our General bestowed amongst them some linen cloth and shoes, and a javelin, which they very joyfully received, and departed for that time.

The next morning they failed not to come again to the water's side. And our General again setting out our boat, one of our men leaping over-rashly ashore, and offering friendly to embrace them, they set violent hands on him, offering a dagger to his throat if he had made any resistance; and so laying him on a horse carried him away.* So that a man cannot be too circumspect and wary of himself among such miscreants. Our pinnace being finished, we departed from this place the 30 and last day of December, and coasting along the shore we did descry, not contrary to our expectation, certain *canters*, which were Spanish fishermen; to whom we gave chase and took three of them. And proceeding further we met with three caravels, and took them also.

The 17 day of January we arrived at Cape Blanco, where we found a ship riding at anchor, within the Cape, and but two simple mariners

* This man, John Fry, was released as soon as the Moors discovered that he was English, not Portuguese, and 'by the King's favour he was sent home into England not long after, in an English merchant's ship'. – *The World Encompassed.*

Ship Model, possibly 'The Golden Hind', early seventeenth century

in her. Which ship we took and carried her further into the harbour, where we remained four days; and in that space our General mustered and trained his men on land in warlike manner, to make them fit for all occasions. In this place we took of the fishermen such necessaries as we wanted, and they could yield us; and leaving here one of our little barks, called the *Benedict*, we took with us one of theirs which they called *canters*, being of the burden of 40 tons or thereabouts.

All these things being finished we departed this harbour the 22 of January, carrying along with us one of the Portugal caravels, which was bound to the islands of Cape Verde for salt, whereof good store is made in one of those islands. The master or pilot of that caravel did advertise our General that upon one of those islands, called Mayo, there was great store of dried cabritos [goats], which a few inhabitants there dwelling did yearly make ready for such of the king's ships as did there touch, being bound for his country of Brazil or elsewhere. We fell with this island the 27 of January, but the inhabitants would in no case traffic with us, being thereof forbidden by the king's edict. Yet the next day our General sent to view the island, and the likelihoods that might be there of provision of victuals, about threescore and two men under the conduct and government of Master Winter and Master Doughty. And marching towards the chief place of habitation in this island (as by the Portugal we were informed), having travelled to the mountains the space of three miles, and arriving there somewhat before the daybreak, we arrested ourselves, to see day before us. Which appearing, we found the inhabitants to be fled; but the place, by reason that it was manured, we found to be more fruitful than the other part, especially the valleys among the hills.

Here we gave ourselves a little refreshing, as by very ripe and sweet grapes, which the fruitfulness of the earth at that season of the year yielded us; and that season being with us the depth of winter, it may seem strange that those fruits were then there growing. But the reason thereof is this, because they being between the tropic and the equinoctial, the sun passeth twice in the year through their zenith over their heads, by means whereof they have two summers; and being so near the heat of the line they never lose the heat of the sun so much, but the fruits have their increase and continuance in the midst of winter. The island is wonderfully stored with goats and wild hens; and it hath salt also, without labour, save only that the people gather it into heaps; which continually in great quantity is increased upon the sands by the flowing of the sea, and the receiving heat of the sun kerning [drying] the same. So that of the increase thereof they keep a continual traffic with their neighbours.

Amongst other things we found here a kind of fruit called *cocos*,

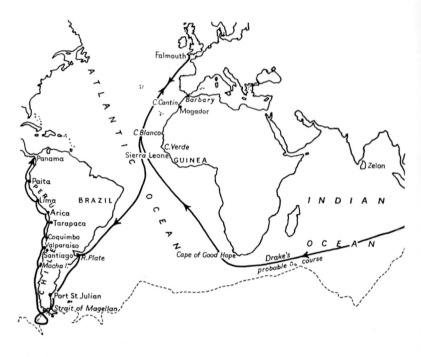

which because it is not commonly known with us in England, I thought good to make some description of it. The tree beareth no leaves nor branches, but at the very top the fruit groweth in clusters, hard at the top of the stem of the tree, as big every several fruit as a man's head; but having taken off the uttermost bark, which you shall find to be very full of strings or sinews, as I may term them, you shall come to a hard shell, which may hold in quantity of liquor a pint commonly, or some a quart, and some less. Within that shell, of the thickness of half-an-inch good, you shall have a kind of hard substance and very white, no less good and sweet than almonds; within that again, a certain clear liquor, which being drunk, you shall not only find it very delicate and sweet, but most comfortable and cordial.

After we had satisfied ourselves with some of these fruits, we marched further into the island, and saw great store of *cabritos* alive, which were so chased by the inhabitants that we could do no good towards our provision; but they had laid out, as it were to stop our mouths withal, certain old dried *cabritos,* which being but ill, and small and few, we made no account of. Being returned to our ships, our General departed hence the 31 of this month, and sailed by the island of Santiago, but far enough from the danger of the inhabitants, who shot and discharged at us three pieces; but they all fell short of us, and

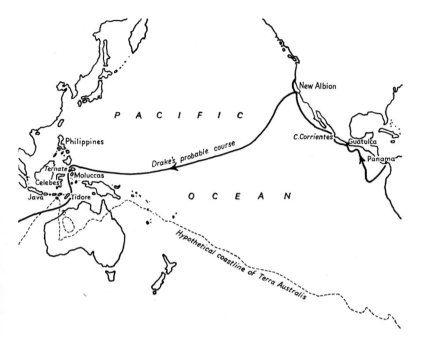

did us no harm. The island is fair and large, and, as it seemeth, rich and fruitful, and inhabited by the Portugals; but the mountains and high places of the island are said to be possessed by the Moors, who having been slaves to the Portugals, to ease themselves, made escape to the desert places of the island, where they abide with great strength.

Being before this island, we espied two ships under sail, to the one of which we gave chase, and in the end boarded her with a ship-boat without resistance; which we found to be a good prize, and she yielded unto us good store of wine. Which prize our General committed to the custody of Master Doughty; and retaining the pilot, sent the rest away with his pinnace, giving them a butt of wine and some victuals, and their wearing clothes, and so they departed. The same night we came with the island called by the Portugals *Ilha do Fogo*, that is, the burning island; in the north side whereof is a consuming fire. The matter is said to be of sulphur, but, notwithstanding, it is like to be a commodious island, because the Portugals have built, and do inhabit there. Upon the south side thereof lieth a most pleasant and sweet island, the trees whereof are always green and fair to look upon; in respect whereof they call it *Ilha Brava*, that is, the brave island. From the banks thereof into the sea do run in many places reasonable streams of fresh waters easy to come by, but there was no convenient road for our ships; for such was the depth that no ground could be had for anchoring. And it is reported that ground was never found in that place; so that the tops of *Fogo* burn not so high in the air, but the roots of *Brava* are quenched as low in the sea.

Being departed from these islands, we drew towards the line, where we were becalmed the space of three weeks, but yet subject to divers great storms, terrible lightnings and much thunder. But with this misery we had the commodity of great store of fish, as dolphins, bonitos, and flying-fishes, whereof some fell into our ships; wherehence they could not rise again for want of moisture, for when their wings are dry they cannot fly.

From the first day of our departure from the islands of Cape Verde, we sailed 54 days without sight of land. And the first land that we fell with was the coast of Brazil, which we saw the fifth of April, in the height of 33 degrees towards the pole Antarctic. And being discovered at sea by the inhabitants of the country, they made upon the coast great fires for a sacrifice (as we learned) to the devils; about which they use conjurations, making heaps of sand, and other ceremonies, that when any ship shall go about to stay upon their coast, not only sands may be gathered together in shoals in every place, but also that storms and tempests may arise, to the casting away of ships and men, whereof, as it is reported, there have been divers experiments.

The 7 day in a mighty great storm, both of lightning, rain, and thunder, we lost the *canter*, which we called the *Christopher*. But the eleventh day after, by our General's great care in dispersing his ships, we found her again; and the place where we met our General called the Cape of Joy, where every ship took in some water. Here we found a good temperature and sweet air, a very fair and pleasant country with an exceeding fruitful soil, where were great store of large and mighty deer, but we came not to the sight of any people; but travelling further into the country we perceived the footing of people in the clay ground, shewing that they were men of great stature.

Being returned to our ships we weighed anchor, and ran somewhat further, and harboured ourselves between the rock and the main; where by means of the rock that brake the force of the sea, we rid very safe. And upon this rock we killed for our provision certain sea-wolves, commonly called with us seals. From hence we went our course to 36 degrees, and entered the great river of Plate, and ran into 54 and $53\frac{1}{2}$ fathoms of fresh water, where we filled our water by the ship's side; but our General finding here no good harbourough, as he thought he should, bare out again to sea the 27 of April, and in bearing out we lost sight of our fly-boat, wherein Master Doughty was.

But we, sailing along, found a fair and reasonable good bay, wherein were many and the same profitable islands; one whereof had so many seals as would at the least have laden all our ships, and the rest of the islands are, as it were, laden with fowls, which is wonderful to see, and they of divers sorts. It is a place very plentiful of victuals, and hath in it no want of fresh water. Our General, after certain days of his abode in this place, being on shore in an island, the people of the country shewed themselves unto him, leaping and dancing, and entered into traffic with him; but they would not receive anything at any man's hands, but the same must be cast upon the ground. They are of clean, comely, and strong bodies, swift on foot, and seem to be very active.

The 18 day of May, our General thought it needful to have a care of such ships as were absent; and therefore endeavouring to seek the fly-boat wherein Master Doughty was, we espied her again the next day. And whereas certain of our ships were sent to discover the coast and to search an harbour, the *Marigold* and the *canter* being employed in that business, came unto us and gave us understanding of a safe harbour that they had found. Wherewith all our ships bare, and entered it; where we watered and made new provision of victuals, as by seals, whereof we slew to the number of 200 or 300 in the space of an hour. Here our General in the admiral rid close aboard the fly-boat, and took out of her all the provision of victuals and what else was in her, and hauling her to the land, set fire to her, and so burnt her to save the iron work.

Which being a-doing, there came down of the country certain of the people naked, saving only about their waist the skin of some beast, with the fur or hair on, and something also wreathed on their heads. Their faces were painted with divers colours, and some of them had on their heads the similitude of horns, every man his bow, which was an ell in length, and a couple of arrows. They were very agile people and quick to deliver, and seemed not to be ignorant in the feats of wars, as by their order of ranging a few men might appear. These people would not of a long time receive anything at our hands; yet at length our General being ashore, and they dancing after their accustomed manner about him, and he once turning his back towards them, one leaped suddenly to him, and took his cap with his gold band off his head, and ran a little distance from him, and shared it with his fellow, the cap to the one, and the band to the other.

Having despatched all our business in this place, we departed and set sail. And immediately upon our setting forth we lost our *canter*, which was absent three or four days; but when our General had her again, he took out the necessaries, and so gave her over, near to the Cape of Good Hope. The next day after, being the 20 of June, we harboured ourselves again in a very good harbourough, called by

Magellan, Port St Julian, where we found a gibbet standing upon the main; which we supposed to be the place where Magellan did execution upon some of his disobedient and rebellious company.*

The two and twentieth day our General went ashore to the main, and in his company John Thomas, and Robert Winterhie, Oliver the master gunner, John Brewer, Thomas Hood, and Thomas Drake [Francis Drake's brother]. And entering on land, they presently met with two or three of the country people. And Robert Winterhie having in his hands a bow and arrows, went about to make a shoot of pleasure, and, in his draught, his bowstring brake; which the rude savages taking as a token of war, began to bend the force of their bows against our company, and drove them to their shifts very narrowly.

In this port our General began to enquire diligently of the actions of Master Thomas Doughty, and found them not to be such as he looked for, but tending rather to contention or mutiny, or some other disorder, whereby, without redress, the success of the voyage might greatly have been hazarded. Whereupon the company was called together and made acquainted with the particulars of the cause, which were found, partly by Master Doughty's own confession, and partly by the evidence of the fact, to be true. Which when our General saw, although his private affection to Master Doughty, as he then in the presence of us all sacredly protested, was great, yet the care he had of the state of the voyage, of the expectation of her Majesty, and of the honour of his country did more touch him, as indeed it ought, than the private respect of one man. So that the cause being thoroughly heard, and all things done in good order as near as might be to the course of our laws in England, it was concluded that Master Doughty should receive punishment according to the quality of the offence. And he, seeing no remedy but patience for himself, desired before his death to receive the communion, which he did at the hands of Master Fletcher, our minister, and our General himself accompanied him in that holy action. Which being done, and the place of execution made ready, he having embraced our General, and taken his leave of all the company, with prayers for the Queen's Majesty and our realm, in quiet sort laid his head to the block, where he ended his life.†

* Ferdinand Magellan, a Portuguese navigator, commanded a Spanish expedition of five ships which sailed in 1519 to find a western route to the 'Spice Islands,' the Moluccas. At Port St Julian he dealt with a mutiny as drastically as Drake dealt with Doughty. He discovered the Straits which bear his name, and he named the Pacific Ocean. He was killed by natives in the Philippines, but one of his ships, the first to sail round the world, reached Spain in 1522.
† The execution of Thomas Doughty was the most questionable act of Drake's controversial career. The account given here is very carefully favourable to Drake; other accounts give a very different impression. It can be argued that

This being done, our General made divers speeches to the whole company, persuading us to unity, obedience, love, and regard of our voyage; and for the better confirmation thereof, willed every man the next Sunday following to prepare himself to receive the communion, as Christian brethren and friends ought to do, which was done in very reverent sort; and so with good contentment every man went about his business.

The 17 day of August we departed the port of St Julian, and the 20 day we fell with the Strait or Fret of Magellan, going into the South Sea; at the cape or headland whereof we found the body of a dead man, whose flesh was clean consumed. The 21 day we entered the Strait, which we found to have many turnings, and as it were shuttings-up, as if there were no passage at all. By means whereof we had the wind often against us; so that some of the fleet, recovering a cape or point of land, others should be forced to turn back again, and to come to an anchor where they could. In this Strait there be many fair harbours, with store of fresh water. But yet they lack their best commodity, for the water there is of such depth, that no man shall find ground to anchor in, except it be in some narrow river or corner, or between some rocks; so that if any extreme blasts or contrary winds do come, whereunto the place is much subject, it carrieth with it no small danger.

The land on both sides is very huge and mountainous; the lower mountains whereof, although they be monstrous and wonderful to look upon for their height, yet there are others which in height exceed them in a strange manner, reaching themselves above their fellows so high, that between them did appear three regions of clouds. These mountains are covered with snow. At both the southerly and easterly parts of the Strait there are islands, among which the sea hath his indraught into the Straits, even as it hath in the main entrance of the fret.★ This Strait is extreme cold, with frost and snow continually; the trees seem to stoop with the burden of the weather, and yet are green continually, and many good and sweet herbs do very plentifully grow and increase under them. The breadth of the Strait is in some places a

---

★ Here Drake changed the name of his ship from *Pelican* to *Golden Hind*. The latter was the crest of his patron, Sir Christopher Hatton, who was high in the Queen's favour, and Drake must have known that he would need a champion at court on his return.

Magellan took 37 days to pass through the Straits, Drake 16 days, Cavendish 51 and Sir Richard Hawkins 46 days.

there was no justification for the execution, and that Drake was actuated only by venomous personal hatred of his former friend; it can be argued, at the other extreme, that Drake did the only thing which could save the expedition from mutiny and disaster. It is very unlikely that the truth will ever be established.

league, in some other places two leagues and three leagues, and in some other four leagues; but the narrowest place hath a league over.

The 24 of August we arrived at an island in the Straits, where we found great store of fowl [penguins] which could not fly, of the bigness of geese; whereof we killed in less than one day 3,000, and victualled ourselves throughly therewith. The 6 day of September we entered the South Sea at the cape or head shore. The 7 day we were driven by a great storm★ from the entering into the South Sea, 200 leagues and odd in longitude, and one degree to the southward of the Strait; in which height, and so many leagues to the westward, the 15 day of September, fell out the eclipse of the moon at the hour of six of the clock at night. But neither did the ecliptical conflict of the moon impair our state, nor her clearing again amend us a whit; but the accustomed eclipse of the sea continued in his force, we being darkened more than the moon sevenfold.

From the bay which we called the Bay of Severing of Friends, we were driven back to the southward of the Straits in 57 degrees and a tierce; in which height we came to an anchor among the islands, having there fresh and very good water, with herbs of singular virtue. Not far from hence we entered another bay, where we found people, both men and women, in their canoes naked, and ranging from one island to another to seek their meat; who entered traffic with us for such things as they had. We returning hence northward again, found the 3 of October three islands, in one of which was such plenty of birds as is scant credible to report. The 8 day of October we lost sight of one of our consorts, wherein Master *Winter* was; who, as then we supposed, was put by a storm into the Straits again. Which at our return home we found to be true, and he not perished, as some of our company feared. Thus being come into the height of the Straits again, we ran, supposing the coast of Chile to lie as the general maps have described it, namely north-west; which we found to lie and trend to the north-east and eastwards. Whereby it appeareth that this part of Chile hath not been truly hitherto discovered, or at the least not truly reported, for the space of twelve degrees at the least; being set down either of purpose to deceive, or of ignorant conjecture.

We continuing our course, fell the 29 of November with an island called La Mocha, where we cast anchor; and our General, hoising out our boat, went with ten of our company to shore, where we found people, whom the cruel and extreme dealings of the Spaniards have forced, for their own safety and liberty, to flee from the main, and to fortify

★ In this storm the *Marigold* sank with all hands. The *Elizabeth*, Captain Winter, returned home, reaching England on June 2nd, 1579. Winter claimed that his crew compelled him to return. Other statements say that the decision was his own.

VERA TOTIVS EX
Descriptio D. Franc Draci qui 5. navibus probè instructis, ex Anglia solvens 13
cęteris partim flammis, partim fluctibus correptis, in Angliam rediit 27 Septe
Angli, qui eundem Draci cursum ferè tenuit etiam ex Anglia per universum
quinto Septembris 1588. in patriæ portum Plimmouth, undè prius ex

Portus Novæ
Albionis

Drake's and Cavendish's Circumnavigations: engraved by Jodocus Hondius, *c.* 1590

themselves in this island. We being on land, the people came down to us to the water side with show of great courtesy, bringing to us potatoes, roots, and two very fat sheep; which our General received, and gave them other things for them, and had promise to have water there. But the next day repairing again to the shore, and sending two men a-land with barrels to fill water, the people taking them for Spaniards (to whom they use to show no favour if they take them) laid violent hands on them, and, as we think, slew them.*

Our General seeing this, stayed here no longer, but weighed anchor, and set sail towards the coast of Chile. And drawing towards it, we met near to the shore an Indian in a *canoa*, who thinking us to have been Spaniards, came to us and told us, that at a place called Santiago, there was a great Spanish ship laden from the kingdom of Peru; for which good news our General gave him divers trifles. Whereof he was glad, and went along with us and brought us to the place, which is called the port of Valparaiso.

When we came thither we found, indeed, the ship riding at anchor, having in her eight Spaniards and three negroes; who, thinking us to have been Spaniards, and their friends, welcomed us with a drum, and made ready a *botija* of wine of Chile to drink to us. But as soon as we were entered, one of our company called Thomas Moone began to lay about him, and struck one of the Spaniards, and said unto him, *Abaxo, perro!* that is in English, 'Go down, dog!' One of these Spaniards, seeing persons of that quality in those seas, all to – crossed and blessed himself. But, to be short, we stowed them under hatches, all save one Spaniard, who suddenly and desperately leapt overboard into the sea, and swam ashore to the town of Santiago, to give them warning of our arrival.

They of the town, being not above nine households, presently fled away and abandoned the town. Our General manned his boat and the Spanish ship's boat, and went to the town; and, being come to it, we rifled it, and came to a small chapel, which we entered, and found therein a silver chalice, two cruets, and one altar-cloth, the spoil whereof our General gave to Master Fletcher, his minister. We found also in this town a warehouse stored with wine of Chile and many boards of cedar-wood; all which wine we brought away with us, and certain of the boards to burn for firewood. And so, being come aboard, we departed the haven, having first set all the Spaniards on land, saving one John Griego, a Greek born, whom our General carried with him as pilot to bring him into the haven of Lima.

* According to Nuño da Silva the Indians killed the ship's surgeon and one other man, and wounded nine or ten, including Drake himself, who was wounded by arrows in the face and head. With his usual luck he had a very narrow escape from sharing Magellan's fate.

When we were at sea our General rifled the ship, and found in her good store of the wine of Chile, and 25,000 pesos of very pure and fine gold of Valdivia, amounting in value to 37,000 ducats of Spanish money, and above. So, going on our course, we arrived next at a place called Coquimbo, where our General sent fourteen of his men on land to fetch water. But they were espied by the Spaniards, who came with 300 horsemen and 200 footmen, and slew one of our men with a piece. The rest came aboard in safety, and the Spaniards departed. We went on shore again and buried our man, and the Spaniards came down again with a flag of truce; but we set sail, and would not trust them.

From hence we went to a certain port called Tarapaca; where, being landed, we found by the sea side a Spaniard lying asleep, who had lying by him thirteen bars of silver, which weighed 4,000 ducats Spanish. We took the silver and left the man. Not far from hence, going on land for fresh water, we met with a Spaniard and an Indian boy driving eight llamas or sheep of Peru, which are as big as asses; every of which sheep had on his back two bags of leather, each bag containing 50 lb. weight of fine silver. So that, bringing both the sheep and their burthen to the ships, we found in all the bags eight hundred weight of silver.

Herehence we sailed to a place called *Arica*; and, being entered the port, we found there three small barks, which we rifled, and found in one of them fifty-seven wedges of silver, each of them weighing about 20 lb. weight, and every of these wedges were of the fashion and bigness of a brickbat. In all these three barks, we found not one person. For they, mistrusting no strangers, were all gone a-land to the town, which consisteth of about twenty houses; which we would have ransacked if our company had been better and more in number. But our General, contented with the spoil of the ships, left the town and put off again to sea, and set sail for Lima, and, by the way, met with a small bark, which he boarded, and found in her good store of linen cloth, whereof taking some quantity, he let her go.

To Lima we came the 13 day of February; and, being entered the haven, we found there about twelve sail of ships lying fast moored at an anchor, having all their sail carried on shore; for the masters and merchants were here most secure, having never been assaulted by enemies, and at this time feared the approach of none such as we were. Our General rifled these ships, and found in one of them a chest full of royals of plate, and good store of silks and linen cloth; and took the chest into his own ship, and good store of the silks and linen. In which ship he had news of another ship called the *Cacafuego*, which was gone towards Paita, and that the same ship was laden with treasure. Whereupon we stayed no longer here, but, cutting all the cables of the ships in the haven, we let them drive whither they would either to sea or to the shore; and with all speed we followed the *Cacafuego* toward Paita, thinking there to have found her.

But before we arrived there she was gone from thence towards Panama; whom our General still pursued, and by the way met with a bark laden with ropes and tackle for ships, which he boarded and searched, and found in her 80 lb. weight of gold, and a crucifix of gold with goodly great emeralds set in it, which he took, and some of the cordage also for his own ship. From hence we departed, still following the *Cacafuego*; and our General promised our company that whosoever should first descry her should have his chain of gold for his good news. It fortuned that John Drake, going up into the top, descried her about three of the clock. And about six of the clock we came to her and boarded her, and shot at her three pieces of ordnance, and strake down her mizen; and, being entered, we found in her great riches, as jewels and precious stones, thirteen chests full of royals of plate, fourscore pound weight of gold, and six-and-twenty ton of silver. The place where we took this prize was called Cape de San Francisco, about 150 leagues [south] from Panama. The pilot's name of this ship was Francisco; and amongst other plate that our General found in this ship he found two very fair gilt bowls of silver, which were the pilot's. To whom our General said, 'Señor Pilot, you have here two silver cups, but I must needs have one of them'; which the pilot, because he could not otherwise choose, yielded unto, and gave the other to the steward of our General's ships. When this pilot departed from us, his boy said thus unto our General; 'Captain, our ship shall be called no more the *Cacafuego*, but the *Cacaplata*, and your ship shall be called the *Cacafuego*.' Which pretty speech of the pilot's boy ministered matter of laughter to us, both then and long after. When our General had done what he would with this *Cacafuego*, he cast her off, and we went on our course still towards the west; and not long after met with a ship laden with linen cloth and fine China dishes of white earth, and great store of China silks, of all which things we took as we listed. The owner himself of this ship was in her, who was a Spanish gentleman [Don Francesco de Zarate] from whom our General took a falcon of gold, with a great emerald in the breast thereof; and the pilot of the ship he took also with him, and so cast the ship off.

This pilot brought us to the haven of Guatulco, the town whereof, as he told us, had but 17 Spaniards in it. As soon as we were entered this haven, we landed, and went presently to the town and to the town-house; where we found a judge sitting in judgment, being associate with three other officers, upon three negroes that had conspired the burning of the town. Both which judges and prisoners we took, and brought them a-shipboard, and caused the chief judge to write his letter to the town to command all the townsmen to avoid, that we might safely water there. Which being done, and they departed, we ransacked the town; and in one house we found a pot, of the quantity of a bushel, full of royals of plate, which we brought to our ship. And here one Thomas Moone, one of our company, took a Spanish gentleman as he was flying out of the town; and, searching him, he found a chain of gold about him, and other jewels, which he took, and so let him go. At this place our General, among other Spaniards, set ashore his Portugal pilot [Nuño da Silva] which he took at the islands of Cape Verde out of a ship of St Mary port, of Portugal. And having set them ashore we departed hence, and sailed to the island of Canno; where our General landed, and brought to shore his own ship, and discharged her, mended and graved her, and furnished our ship with water and wood sufficiently.

And while we were here we espied a ship and set sail after her, and took her, and found in her two pilots and a Spanish governor, going for the islands of the Philippines. We searched the ship, and took some of her merchandises, and so let her go. Our General at this place and time, thinking himself, both in respect of his private injuries received from the Spaniards, as also of their contempts and indignities offered to our country and prince in general, sufficiently satisfied and revenged; and supposing that her Majesty at his return would rest contented with this service, purposed to continue no longer upon the Spanish coasts, but began to consider and to consult of the best way for his country.

He thought it not good to return by the Straits, for two special causes; the one, lest the Spaniards should there wait and attend for him in great number and strength, whose hands, he, being left but one ship, could not possibly escape. The other cause was the dangerous situation of the mouth of the Straits in the South Sea; where continual storms reigning and blustering, as he found by experience, besides the shoals and sands upon the coast, he thought it not a good course to adventure that way. He resolved, therefore, to avoid these hazards, to go forward to the islands of the Moluccas, and therehence to sail the course of the Portugals by the Cape of Buena Esperanza. Upon this resolution he began to think of his best way to the Moluccas, and finding himself, where he now was, becalmed, he saw that of necessity he must be forced to take a Spanish course; namely, to sail somewhat northerly to get a wind. We therefore set sail, and sailed 600 leagues at the least for a good wind; and thus much we sailed from the 16 of April till the 3 of June.*

* Presumably Drake was looking for the Straits of Anian (Behring), the Pacific entrance to the North-west Passage. It was thought that this entrance might be as far south as California.

The 5 day of June, being in 43 degrees towards the pole Arctic, we found the air so cold, that our men being grievously pinched with the same, complained of the extremity thereof; and the further we went, the more the cold increased upon us. Whereupon we thought it best for that time to seek the land, and did so; finding it not mountainous, but low plain land, till we came within 38 degrees towards the line. In which height it pleased God to send us into a fair and good bay, with a good wind to enter the same. In this bay we anchored; and the people of the country, having their houses close by the water's side, shewed themselves unto us, and sent a present to our General. When they came unto us, they greatly wondered at the things that we brought. But our General, according to his natural and accustomed humanity, courteously intreated them, and liberally bestowed on them necessary things to cover their nakedness; whereupon they supposed us to be gods, and would not be persuaded to the contrary. The presents which they sent to our General, were feathers, and cauls of net-work.

Their houses are digged round about with earth, and have from the uttermost brims of the circle, clifts of wood set upon them, joining close together at the top like a spire steeple, which by reason of that closeness are very warm. Their bed is the ground with rushes strowed on it; and lying about the house, [they] have the fire in the midst. The men go naked; the women take bulrushes, and kemb [comb] them after the manner of hemp, and thereof make their loose garments, which being knit about their middles, hang down about their hips, having also about their shoulders a skin of deer, with the hair upon it. These women are very obedient and serviceable to their husbands.

After they were departed from us, they came and visited us the second time, and brought with them feathers and bags of tobacco for presents. And when they came to the top of the hill, at the bottom whereof we had pitched our tents, they stayed themselves; where one appointed for speaker wearied himself with making a long oration; which done, they left their bows upon the hill, and came down with their presents. In the meantime the women, remaining upon the hill, tormented themselves lamentably, tearing their flesh from their cheeks, whereby we perceived that they were about a sacrifice. In the meantime our General with his company went to prayer, and to reading of the Scriptures, at which exercise they were attentive, and seemed greatly to be affected with it; but when they were come unto us, they restored again unto us those things which before we bestowed upon them.

The news of our being there being spread through the country, the people that inhabited round about came down, and amongst them the king himself, a man of a goodly stature, and comely personage, with many other tall and warlike men; before whose coming were sent two ambassadors to our General, to signify that their king was coming, in doing of which message, their speech was continued about half an hour. This ended, they by signs requested our General to send something by their hand to their king, as a token that his coming might be in peace. Wherein our General having satisfied them, they returned with glad tidings to their king, who marched to us with a princely majesty, the people crying continually after their manner; and as they drew near unto us, so did they strive to behave themselves in their actions with comeliness.

In the fore-front was a man of a goodly personage, who bare the sceptre or mace before the king; whereupon hanged two crowns, a less and a bigger, with three chains of a marvellous length. The crowns were made of knit work, wrought artificially with feathers of divers colours. The chains were made of a bony substance, and few be the persons among them that are admitted to wear them; and of that number also the persons are stinted, as some ten, some twelve, &c. Next unto him which bare the sceptre, was the king himself, with his guard about his person, clad with coney skins, and other skins. After them followed the naked common sort of people, every one having his face painted, some with white, some with black, and other colours, and having in their hands one thing or another for a present, not so much as their children, but they also brought their presents.

In the meantime, our General gathered his men together, and marched within his fenced place, making, against their approaching, a very warlike show. They being trooped together in their order, and a general salutation being made, there was presently a general silence. Then he that bare the sceptre before the king, being informed by another, whom they assigned to that office, with a manly and lofty voice proclaimed that which the other spake to him in secret, continuing half an hour. Which ended, and a general Amen, as it were, given, the king with the whole number of men and women, the children excepted, came down without any weapon; who, descending to the foot of the hill, set themselves in order. In coming towards our bulwarks and tents, the sceptre-bearer began a song, observing his measures in a dance, and that with a stately countenance; whom the king with his guard, and every degree of persons, following, did in like manner sing and dance, saving only the women, which danced and kept silence.

The General permitted them to enter within our bulwark, where they continued their song and dance a reasonable time. When they had satisfied themselves, they made signs to our General to sit down; to whom the king and divers other made several orations, or rather supplications, that he would take their province and kingdom into his hand, and become their king, making signs that they would resign unto him their right and title of the whole land, and become his subjects. In which, to persuade us the better, the king and the rest, with one consent, and with great reverence, joyfully singing a song, did set the crown upon his head, enriched his neck with all their chains, and offered unto him many other things, honouring him by the name of *Hioh*, adding thereunto, as it seemed, a sign of triumph; which thing our General thought not meet to reject, because he knew not what honour and profit it might be to our country. Wherefore in the name, and to the use of her Majesty, he took the sceptre, crown, and dignity of the said country into his hands, wishing that the riches and treasure thereof might so conveniently be transported to the enriching of her kingdom at home, as it aboundeth in the same.

The common sort of people, leaving the king and his guard with our General, scattered themselves together with their sacrifices among our people, taking a diligent view of every person: and such as pleased their fancy (which were the youngest), they enclosing them about offered their sacrifices unto them with lamentable weeping, scratching and tearing their flesh from their faces with their nails, whereof issued abundance of blood. But we used signs to them of disliking this, and stayed their hands from force, and directed them upwards to the living God, whom only they ought to worship. They shewed unto us their wounds, and craved help of them at our hands; whereupon we gave them lotions, plaisters, and ointments agreeing to the state of their griefs, beseeching God to cure their diseases. Every third day they brought their sacrifices unto us, until they understood our meaning, that we had no pleasure in them; yet they could not be long absent from us, but daily frequented our company to the hour of our departure, which departure seemed so grievous unto them, that their joy was turned into sorrow. They entreated us, that being absent we would remember them, and by stealth provided a sacrifice, which we misliked.

Our necessary business being ended, our General with his company travelled up into the country to their villages, where we found herds of deer by a thousand in a company, being most large, and fat of body. We found the whole country to be a warren of a strange kind of coneys; their bodies in bigness as be the Barbary coneys, their heads as the heads of ours, the feet of a want [mole], and the tail of a rat, being of great length. Under her chin is on either side a bag, into the which she gathereth her meat, when she hath filled her belly abroad. The people eat their bodies, and make great account of their skins, for their king's coat was made of them.

Our General called this country Nova Albion, and that for two causes; the one in respect of the white banks and cliffs, which lie towards the sea, and the other, because it might have some affinity with our country in name, which sometime was so called. There is no part of earth here to be taken up, wherein there is not some probable show of gold or silver.

At our departure hence our General set up a monument of our being there, as also of her Majesty's right and title to the same; namely a plate, nailed upon a fair great post, whereupon was engraved her Majesty's name, the day and year of our arrival there, with the free giving up of the province and people into her Majesty's hands, together with her Highness' picture and arms, in a piece of six pence of current English money, under the plate, whereunder was also written the name of our General.★

It seemeth that the Spaniards hitherto had never been in this part of the country, neither did ever discover the land by many degrees to the southwards of this place.

After we had set sail from hence, we continued without sight of land till the 13 day of October following, which day in the morning we fell with certain islands eight degrees to the northward of the line, from which islands came a great number of *canoas*, having in some of them four, in some six, and in some also fourteen men, bringing with them cocos and other fruits. Their *canoas* were hollow within, and cut with great art and cunning, being very smooth within and without, and bearing a glass [gloss], as if it were a horn daintily burnished, having a prow and a stern of one sort, yielding inward circle-wise, being of a great height, and full of certain white shells for a bravery; and on each side of them lie out two pieces of timber about a yard and a half long, more or less, according to the smallness or bigness of the boat. These people have the nether part of their ears cut into a round circle, hanging down very low upon their cheeks, whereon they hang things of a reasonable weight. The nails of their hands are an inch long, their teeth are as black as pitch, and they renew them often, by eating of an

★ In 1936 a brass plate was found on the shore near San Francisco bearing this inscription: BEE IT KNOWNE VNTO ALL MEN BY THESE PRESENTS IVNE 17. 1579. BY THE GRACE OF GOD AND IN THE NAME OF HERR MAIESTY QVEEN ELIZABETH OF ENGLAND AND HERR SVCCESSORS FOREVER I TAKE POSSESSION OF THIS KINGDOME WHOSE KING AND PEOPLE FREELY RESIGNE THEIR RIGHT AND TITLE IN THE WHOLE LAND VNTO HERR MAIESTIES KEEPEING NOW NAMED BY ME AN TO BEE KNOWNE VNTO ALL MEN AS NOVA ALBION. G FRANCIS DRAKE. Below this is a hole which could have housed the sixpence. The authenticity of this plate has been challenged, but the metallurgical and circumstantial evidence are very favourable.

herb with a kind of powder, which they always carry about them in a cane for the same purpose.

Leaving this island the night after we fell with it, the 18 of October we lighted upon divers others, some whereof made a great show of inhabitants. We continued our course by the islands of Tagulandag, Zelon, and Zewarra, being friends to the Portugals, the first whereof hath growing in it great store of cinnamon. The 14 of November we fell in with the islands of Moluccas. Which day at night (having directed our course to run with Tidore) in coasting along the island of Motir, belonging to the king of Ternate, his deputy or vice-king seeing us at sea, came with his *canoa* to us without all fear, and came aboard; and after some conference with our General, willed him in any wise to run in with Ternate, and not with Tidore, assuring him that the king would be glad of his coming, and would be ready to do what he would require, for which purpose he himself would that night be with the king, and tell him the news. With whom if he once dealt, we should find that as he was a king, so his word should stand; adding further, that if he went to Tidore before he came to Ternate, the king would have nothing to do with us, because he held the Portugal as his enemy. Whereupon our General resolved to run with Ternate. Where the next morning early we came to anchor; at which time our General sent a messenger to the king, with a velvet cloak for a present and token of his coming to be in peace, and that he required nothing but traffic and exchange of merchandise, whereof he had good store, in such things as he wanted.

In the meantime the vice-king had been with the king according to his promise, signifying unto him what good things he might receive from us by traffic. Whereby the king was moved with great liking towards us, and sent to our General, with special message, that he should have what things he needed and would require, with peace and friendship; and moreover that he would yield himself and the right of his island to be at the pleasure and commandment of so famous a prince as we served. In token whereof he sent to our General a signet; and within short time after came in his own person, with boats and *canoas*, to our ship, to bring her into a better and safer road than she was in at present. In the meantime, our General's messenger, being come to the Court, was met by certain noble personages with great solemnity, and brought to the king, at whose hands he was most friendly and graciously entertained.

This king, purposing to come to our ship, sent before four great and large *canoas*, in every one whereof were certain of his greatest states that were about him, attired in white lawn of cloth of Calicut, having over their heads, from the one end of the *canoa* to the other, a covering of thin perfumed mats, borne up with a frame made of reeds for the same use; under which every one did sit in his order according to his dignity, to keep him from the heat of the sun; divers of whom being of good age and gravity, did make an ancient and fatherly show. There were also divers young and comely men attired in white, as were the others; the rest were soldiers, which stood in comely order round about on both sides. Without whom sat the rowers in certain galleries; which being three on a side all along the *canoas*, did lie off from the side thereof three or four yards, one being orderly builded lower than another, in every of which galleries were the number of fourscore rowers. These *canoas* were furnished with warlike munition, every man for the most part having his sword and target, with his dagger, beside other weapons, as lances, calivers, darts, bows and arrows; also every *canoa* had a small cast base mounted at the least one full yard upon a stock set upright.

Thus coming near our ship, in order, they rowed about us one after another, and passing by, did their homage with great solemnity; the great personages beginning with great gravity and fatherly countenances, signifying that the king had sent them to conduct our ship into a better road. Soon after the king himself repaired, accompanied with six grave and ancient persons, who did their obeisance with marvellous humility. The king was a man of tall stature, and seemed to be much delighted with the sound of our music; to whom, as also to his nobility, our General gave presents, wherewith they were passing well contented.

At length the king craved leave of our General to depart, promising the next day to come aboard, and in the meantime to send us such victuals as were necessary for our provision. So that the same night we received of them meal, which they call *sagu*, made of the tops of certain trees, tasting in the mouth like sour curds, but melteth like sugar, whereof they make certain cakes, which may be kept the space of ten years, and yet then good to be eaten. We had of them store of rice, hens, unperfect and liquid sugar, sugar-canes, and a fruit which they call *figu*, with store of cloves.

The king having promised to come aboard, brake his promise, but sent his brother to make his excuse, and to entreat our General to come on shore, offering himself pawn aboard for his safe return. Whereunto our General consented not, upon mislike conceived of the breach of his promise; the whole company also utterly refusing it. But to satisfy him, our General sent certain of his gentlemen to the Court, to accompany the king's brother, reserving the vice-king for their safe return. They were received of another brother of the king's, and other states, and were conducted with great honour to the castle. The place that they were brought unto was a large and fair house, where were at the least a thousand persons assembled.

The king being yet absent, there sat in their places 60 grave personages, all which were said to be of the king's council. There were besides four grave persons, apparelled all in red, down to the ground, and attired on their heads like the Turks; and these were said to be Romans* and ligiers there to keep continual traffic with the people of *Ternate*. There were also two Turks ligiers in this place, and one Italian. The king at last came in guarded with twelve lances, covered over with a rich canopy with embossed gold. Our men, accompanied with one of their captains called Moro, rising to meet him, he graciously did welcome and entertain them. He was attired after the manner of the country, but more sumptuously than the rest. From his waist down to the ground was all cloth of gold, and the same very rich; his legs were bare, but on his feet were a pair of shoes, made of Cordovan skin. In the attire of his head were finely wreathed hooped rings of gold, and about his neck he had a chain of perfect gold, the links whereof were great, and one fold double. On his fingers he had six very fair jewels; and sitting in his chair of estate, at his right hand stood a page with a fan in his hand, breathing and gathering the air to the king. The same was in length two foot, and in breadth one foot, set with eight sapphires richly embroidered, and knit to a staff three foot in length, by the which the page did hold and move it.

Our gentlemen having delivered their message and received order accordingly, were licensed to depart, being safely conducted back again by one of the king's council. This island is the chief of all the islands of Moluccas, and the king hereof is king of 70 islands besides. The king with his people are Moors in religion, observing certain new moons, with fastings; during which fasts they neither eat nor drink in the day, but in the night.

After that our gentlemen were returned, and that we had here by the favour of the king received all necessary things that the place could yield us; our General considering the great distance, and how far he was yet off from his country, thought it not best here to linger the time any longer, but weighing his anchors, set out of the island, and sailed to a certain little island to the southwards of Celebes, where we graved our ship, and continued there, in that and other businesses, 26 days. This island is throughly grown with wood of a large and high growth, very straight, and without boughs, save only in the head or top, whose leaves are not much differing from our broom in England. Amongst these trees night by night, through the whole land, did shew themselves an infinite swarm of fiery worms flying in the air, whose

* Probably Greeks; from the Arabic *rumi*.

bodies being no bigger than our common English flies, make such a show and light as if every twig or tree had been a burning candle. In this place breedeth also wonderful store of bats, as big as large hens. Of cray-fishes also here wanted no plenty, and they of exceeding bigness, one whereof was sufficient for four hungry stomachs at a dinner, being also very good and restoring meat, whereof we had experience: and they dig themselves holes in the earth like coneys.

When we had ended our business here we weighed, and set sail to run for the Moluccas. But having at that time a bad wind, and being amongst the islands, with much difficulty we recovered to the northward of the island of Celebes; where by reason of contrary winds, not able to continue our course to run westwards, we were enforced to alter the same to the southward again, finding that course also to be very hard and dangerous for us, by reason of infinite shoals which lie off and among the islands; whereof we had too much trial, to the hazard and danger of our ship and lives. For, of all other days, upon the 9 of January, in the year 1579* we ran suddenly upon a rock, where we stuck fast from eight of the clock at night till four of the clock in the afternoon the next day, being indeed out of all hope to escape the danger. But our General, as he had always hitherto shewed himself courageous, and of a good confidence in the mercy and protection of God, so now he continued in the same. And lest he should seem to perish wilfully, both he and we did our best endeavour to save ourselves; which it pleased God so to bless, that in the end we cleared ourselves most happily of the danger.

We lighted our ship upon the rocks of three ton of cloves, eight pieces of ordnance, and certain meal and beans; and then the wind, as it were in a moment by the special grace of God, changing from the starboard to the larboard of the ship, we hoised our sails, and the happy gale drove our ship off the rock into the sea again, to the no little comfort of all our hearts, for which we gave God such praise and thanks, as so great a benefit required.†

* 1580 by modern reckoning; the year then ended in March. The rock was probably the Mulapatia reef, to the east of Celebes.
† 'Drake excommunicated Fletcher [the chaplain] shortly after that they were come off the rock . . . He caused him to be made fast by one of the legs with a . . . staple knocked fast into the hatches in the forecastle . . . He called all the company together, and then put a lock about one of his legs and Drake sitting crosslegged on a chest, and a pair of pantofles in his hand, he said, "Francis Fletcher, I do here excommunicate thee out of the church of God and from all the benefits and graces thereof, and I denounce thee to the Devil and all his angels. . . ." And Drake caused a posy to be written and bound about Fletcher's arm with charge that if he took it off he should then be hanged. The posy was "Francis Fletcher, ye falsest knave that liveth".' – From an anonymous narrative of the voyage,

The 8 of February following, we fell with the fruitful island of Barateve, having in the mean time suffered many dangers by winds and shoals. The people of this island are comely in body and stature, and of a civil behaviour, just in dealing, and courteous to strangers; whereof we had the experience sundry ways, they being most glad of our presence, and very ready to relieve our wants in those things which their country did yield. The men go naked, saving their heads and privities, every man having something or other hanging at their ears. Their women are covered from the middle down to the foot, wearing a great number of bracelets upon their arms; for some had eight upon each arm, being made some of bone, some of horn, and some of brass, the lightest whereof, by our estimation, weighed two ounces apiece.

With this people linen-cloth is good merchandise, and of good request; whereof they make rolls for their heads, and girdles to wear about them. Their island is both rich and fruitful; rich in gold, silver, copper, and sulphur, wherein they seem skilful and expert, not only to try the same, but in working it also artificially into any form and fashion that pleaseth them. Their fruits be divers and plentiful; as nutmegs, ginger, long pepper, lemons, cucumbers, cocos, *figu*, *sagu*, with divers other sorts. And among all the rest we had one fruit, in bigness, form and husk, like a bay berry, hard of substance and pleasant of taste, which being sodden [boiled] becometh soft, and is a most good and wholesome victual; whereof we took reasonable store, as we did also of the other fruits and spices. So that to confess a truth, since the time that we first set out of our own country of England, we happened upon no place, Ternate only excepted, wherein we found more comforts and better means of refreshing.

At our departure from Barateve, we set our course for Java Major; where arriving, we found great courtesy, and honourable entertainment. This island is governed by five kings, whom they call Rajah; as Rajah Donaw, and Rajah Mang Bange, and Rajah Cabuccapollo, which live as having one spirit and one mind. Of these five we had four a-shipboard at once, and two or three often. They are wonderfully delighted in coloured clothes, as red and green; the upper part of their bodies are naked, save their heads, whereupon they wear a Turkish roll as do the Moluccans. From the middle downward they wear a *pintado* of silk, trailing upon the ground, in colour as they best like.

The Moluccans hate that their women should be seen of strangers; but these offer them of high courtesy, yea, the kings themselves. The

Harleian MS 280. It seems probable that when the company were facing what appeared to be certain death on the reef Fletcher said that they were being punished by God for Doughty's execution and their robberies on the South American coast.

people are of goodly stature and warlike, well provided of swords and targets, with daggers, all being of their own work, and most artificially done, both in tempering their metal, as also in the form; whereof we bought reasonable store.

They have an house in every village for their common assembly; every day they meet twice, men, women, and children, bringing with them such victuals as they think good, some fruits, some rice boiled, some hens roasted, some *sagu,* having a table made three foot from the ground, whereon they set their meat, that every person sitting at the table may eat, one rejoicing in the company of another.

They boil their rice in an earthen pot, made in form of a sugar loaf, being full of holes, as our pots which we water our gardens withal, and it is open at the great end, wherein they put their rice dry, without any moisture. In the mean time they have ready another great earthen pot, set fast in a furnace, boiling full of water, whereinto they put their pot with rice, by such measure, that they swelling become soft at the first, and by their swelling stopping the holes of the pot, admit no more water to enter, but the more they are boiled, the harder and more firm substance they become. So that in the end they are a firm and good bread, of the which with oil, butter, sugar, and other spices, they make divers sorts of meats very pleasant of taste, and nourishing to nature.

The French pox is here very common to all, and they help themselves, sitting naked from ten to two in the sun, whereby the venomous humour is drawn out.

Not long before our departure they told us that not far off there were such great ships as ours, wishing us to beware; upon this our captain would stay no longer. From Java Major we sailed for the Cape of Good Hope, which was the first land we fell withal; neither did we touch with it, or any other land, until we came to Sierra Leona, upon the coast of Guinea; notwithstanding we ran hard aboard the cape, finding the report of the Portugals to be most false, who affirm that it is the most dangerous cape of the world, never without intolerable storms and present danger to travellers which come near the same. This cape is a most stately thing, and the fairest cape we saw in the whole circumference of the earth, and we passed by it the 18 of June.

From thence we continued our course to Sierra Leona, on the coast of Guinea, where we arrived the 22 of July, and found necessary provisions, great store of elephants, oysters upon trees of one kind, spawning and increasing infinitely, the oyster suffering no bud to grow. We departed thence the four and twentieth day.

We arrived in England the third of November, 1580, being the third year of our departure.

This great feat of seamanship, navigation, leadership and piracy made Drake the most famous sea-captain in Europe and the New World, a legendary hero who, with a single ship, had shaken the vast prestige of Spain and shown that the super-power was not invulnerable. Drake had also won the Queen's favour, enriched himself for life and made himself a national hero. There were some dissident voices. The peace party, led by Burghley, and merchants engaged in Anglo-Spanish trade, strongly disapproved. The execution of Doughty was roundly condemned by some. Drake's arrogance and boasting alienated 'the better sort'. 'The commons nevertheless applauded him . . . swarming daily in the streets to behold him. . . . Books, pictures and ballads were published in his praise.' While the Spanish ambassador clamoured in vain for restitution, the Queen quietly took a large share of the plunder for herself, while the other shareholders probably received a net profit of 4,700 per cent. The Queen told Drake to bring the Golden Hind to Deptford, he gave her a magnificent banquet on board, and she knighted him, handing her sword to a French envoy to confer the accolade. It was an open defiance of Spain and one of the most dramatic moments in English history.

A TRIP TO JERUSALEM

Laurence Aldersey

Master Aldersey, who is known only by his travels, made a venturesome and interesting journey, but he was by no means the only Elizabethan to travel far. Many did so, and some of their exploits seem now almost incredible. Ralph Fitch took ship to the Levant in 1583, went down the Euphrates by caravan and boat, was imprisoned by the Portuguese in Ormuz and Goa, escaped, travelled through India, Burma and Siam and returned by way of the Middle East, reaching London in 1591. Between 1546 and 1572 Anthony Jenkinson visited almost every country in western Europe, all the larger Mediterranean islands, Greece, Turkey, Syria, Palestine, Norway, Lapland, Russia, Armenia, Persia and many other countries, 'not without great dangers and perils sundry times'. Laurence Aldersey wrote more entertainingly, however, than most travellers.

The first voyage or journey, made by Master Laurence Aldersey, merchant of London, to the cities of Jerusalem and Tripolis, etc., in the year 1581. Penned and set down by himself.

I DEPARTED from London the first day of April in the year of our Lord 1581, passing through the Netherland and up the river Rhine by Cologne, and other cities of Germany. And upon Thursday, the third day of May, I came to Augusta [Augsburg] where I delivered the letter I had to Master Jenise and Master Castler, whom I found very willing to pleasure me in anything that I could or would reasonably demand. He first furnished me with a horse to Venice, for my money, and then took me with him awalking to show me the city, for that I had a day to tarry there, for him that was to be my guide. He showed me first the State-house, which is very fair and beautiful. Then he brought me to the finest garden and orchard that ever I saw in my life; for there was in it a place for canary birds as large as a fair chamber, trimmed with wire both above and beneath, with fine little branches of trees for them to sit in, which was full of those canary birds. There was such another for turtle doves; also there were two pigeon houses joining to them, having in them store of turtle doves, and pigeons. In the same garden also were six or seven fishponds, all railed about and full of very good fish. Also seven or eight fine fountains, or water springs, of divers fashions. As for fruit, there wanted none of all sorts, as oranges, figs, raisins, walnuts, grapes, besides apples, pears, filberts, small nuts, and such other fruit as we have in England.

Then did he bring me to the water tower of the same city that by a sleight and device hath the water brought up as high as any Church in the town, and to tell you the strange devices of all it passeth my capacity. Then he brought me to another fair garden, called the Shooter's house, where are butts for the long bow, the cross-bow, the stone-bow, the long piece, and for divers other exercises more.

After this we walked about the walls of the city, where is a great, broad and deep ditch upon one side of the town, so full of fish as ever I saw any pond in my life, and it is reserved only for the States of the city. And upon the other side of the city is also a deep place, all green, wherein deer are kept, and when it pleaseth the States to hunt for their pleasure thither they resort, and have their courses with greyhounds which are kept for that purpose.

The fifth of May I departed from Augusta towards Venice, and came thither upon Whit Sunday, the thirteenth of the same month. It is needless to speak of the height of the mountains that I passed over and of the danger thereof, it is so well known already to the world: the height of them is marvellous, and I was the space of six days in passing them.

I came to Venice at the time of a Fair, which lasted fourteen days, wherein I saw very many and fair shows of wares. I came thither too short for the first passage, which went away from Venice about the seventh or eighth of May, and with them about three score pilgrims, which ship was cast away at a town called Estria, two miles from Venice, and all the men in her, saving thirty or thereabout, lost.

Within eight days after fell Corpus Christi day, which was a day amongst them of procession in which was showed the plate and treasure of Venice, which is esteemed to be worth two millions of pounds, but I do not account it worth half a quarter of that money except there be more than I saw. To speak of the sumptuousness of the copes and vestments of the Church I leave, but the truth is they be very sumptuous, many of them set all over with pearl and made of cloth of gold. And for the Jesuits, I think there be as many at Venice as there be in Cologne.

The number of Jews is there thought to be 1,000, who dwell in a certain place of the city, and have also a place to which they resort to pray which is called the Jews' Synagogue. They all and their offspring use to wear red caps (for so they are commanded) because they may thereby be known from other men. For my further knowledge of these people I went into their Synagogue upon a Saturday, which is their Sabbath day, and I found them in their service or prayers very devout: they receive the five books of Moses and honour them by carrying them about their Church, as the Papists do their Cross.

Their Synagogue is in form round and the people sit round about it, and in the midst there is a place for him that readeth to the rest. As for their apparel, all of them wear a large white lawn over their garments, which reacheth from their head down to the ground.

The Psalms they sing as we do, having no image nor using any manner of idolatry. Their error is that they believe not in Christ, nor yet receive the New Testament. This city of Venice is very fair and greatly to be commended, wherein is good order for all things: and also it is very strong and populous. It standeth upon the main Sea, and hath many islands about it that belong to it.

To tell you of the Duke of Venice, and of the Seigniory: there is one chosen that ever beareth the name of a Duke, but in truth he is but servant to the Seigniory, for of himself he can do little: it is no otherwise with him than with a priest that is at Mass upon a festival day which, putting on his golden garment, seemeth to be a great man, but if any man come unto him and crave some friendship at his hands he will say, 'You must go to the Masters of the Parish, for I cannot pleasure you otherwise than by preferring of your suit'. And so it is with the Duke of Venice. If any man, having a suit, come to him and make his complaint and deliver his supplication, it is not in him to help him, but he will tell him, 'You must come this day, or that day, and then I will prefer your suit to the Seigniory, and do you the best friendship that I may'. Furthermore, if any man bring a letter unto him he may not open it but in the presence of the Seigniory, and they are to see it first, which, being read, perhaps they will deliver it to him, perhaps not. Of the Seigniory there be about three hundred, and about forty of the Privy Council of Venice, who usually are arrayed in gowns of crimson satin, or crimson damask, when they sit in Council.

In the city of Venice no man may wear a weapon except he be a soldier for the Seigniory, or a scholar of Padua, or a gentleman of great countenance, and yet he may not do that without licence.

As for the women of Venice, they be rather monsters than women. Every shoemaker's or tailor's wife will have a gown of silk, and one to carry up her train, wearing their shoes very near half a yard high from the ground. If a stranger meet one of them he will surely think by the state that she goeth with that he meeteth a lady.

I departed from this city of Venice upon Midsummer Day, being the four and twentieth of June, and thinking that the ship would the next day depart I stayed and lay ashipboard all night, and we were made believe from time to time that we should this day and that day depart, but we tarried still till the fourteenth of July, and then, with scant wind, we set sail and sailed that day and that night not above fifty Italian miles. And upon the sixteenth day at night the wind turned flat contrary, so that the Master knew not what to do. And about the fifth hour of the night, which we reckon to be about one of the clock after midnight, the Pilot descried a sail, and at last perceived it to be a galley of the Turks, whereupon we were in great fear.

The Master, being a wise fellow and a good sailor, began to devise how to escape the danger and to lose little of our way. And while both he and all of us were in our dumps God sent us a merry gale of wind that we ran threescore and ten leagues before it was twelve o'clock the next day, and in six days after we were seven leagues past Zante. And upon Monday morning, being the three and twenty of the same month, we came in the sight of Candia, which day the wind came contrary, with great blasts and storms, until the eight and twenty of the same month. In which time the mariners cried out upon me, because I was an Englishman, and said I was no good Christian and wished that I were in the midst of the sea, saying that they and the ship were the worse for me. I answered, 'Truly it may well be, for I think myself the worst creature in the world, and consider you yourselves also, as I do myself, and then use your discretion'.

The Friar preached, and the sermon being done I was demanded whether I did understand him. I answered, 'Yea,' and told the Friar himself, 'Thus you said in your sermon that we were not all good Christians or else it were not possible for us to have such weather: to which I answered, be you well assured that we are not indeed all good Christians, for there are in the ship some that hold very unchristian opinions'. So for that time I satisfied him, although (they said) that I would not see when they said the procession, and honoured their images, and prayed to Our Lady and St Mark.

There was also a gentleman, an Italian, which was a passenger in the ship, and he told me what they said of me because I would not sing Salve Regina and Ave Maria as they did. I told them that they that prayed to so many, or sought help of any other than of God the Father, or of Jesus Christ His Only Son, go a wrong way to work, and robbed God of His honour, and wrought their own destructions.

All this was told the Friars, but I heard nothing of it in three days after. And then, at evening prayer, they sent the purser about with the image of Our Lady to every one to kiss, and I, perceiving it, went another way from him and would not see it. Yet at last he fetched his course about so that he came to me, and offered it to me as he did to others, but I refused it: whereupon there was a great stir. The patron and all the friars were told of it, and everyone said I was a Lutheran, and so called me: but two of the friars that were of greatest authority seemed to bear me better goodwill than the rest, and travelled to the patron in my behalf, and made all well again.

The second day of August we arrived in Cyprus, at a town called Missagh. The people there be very rude and like beasts, and no better; they eat their meat sitting upon the ground with their legs across like tailors; their beds for the most part be hard stones, but yet some of them have fair mattresses to lie upon.

Upon Thursday, the eight of August, we came to Joppa in a small barque which we hired betwixt Missagh and Salina, and could not be suffered to come on land till noon the next day, and then we were permitted by the great Basha, who sat upon the top of a hill to see us sent away. Being come on land we might not enter into any house for victuals, but were to content ourselves with our own provision, and that which we bought to carry with us was taken from us. I had a pair of stirrups which I bought at Venice to serve me in my journey, and [was] trying to make them fit for me, when the Basha saw me up before the rest of the company he sent one to dismount me and to strike me. Whereupon I turned me to the Basha and made a long leg, saying, 'Grand merci, Signor'. And after a while we were horsed upon little asses and sent away with about fifty light horsemen to be our conduct through the wilderness called Deserta Felix, who made us good sport by the way with their pikes, guns and falchions.

That day being St Laurence day, we came to Ramah, which is ten Italian miles from Joppa, and there we stayed that night, and paid to the captain of the castle every man a chekin, which is seven shillings and two pence sterling. So then we had a new guard of soldiers, and left the other.

The house we lodged in at Ramah had a door so low to enter into that I was fain to creep in as it were upon my knees, and within it are three rooms to lodge travellers that come that way. There are no beds, except a man buy a mat and lay it on the ground; that is all the provision, without stools or benches to sit upon. Our victuals were brought us out of the town, as hens, eggs, bread, great store of fruit as pomegranates, figs, grapes, oranges, and such like, and drink we drew out of the well. The town itself is so ruinated that I take it rather to be a heap of stones than a town.

Then the next morning we thought to have gone away, but we could not be permitted that day, so we stayed there till two of the clock the next morning, and then, with a fresh guard of soldiers, we departed toward Jerusalem. We had not ridden five English miles but we were encountered with a great number of the Arabians, who stayed us and would not suffer us to pass till they had somewhat, so it cost us for all our guard above twenty shillings a man betwixt Joppa and Jerusalem. These Arabians troubled us oftentimes. Our truchman that paid the money for us was striken down and had his head broken because he would not give them as much as they asked: and they that should have rescued both him and us stood still and durst do nothing, which was to our cost.

Being come within sight of Jerusalem, the manner is to kneel down and give God thanks that it hath pleased Him to bring us to that holy place, where He Himself had been. And there we leave our horses and go on foot to the town, and being come to the gates there they took our names and our fathers' names, and so we were permitted to go to our lodgings.

The governor of the house met us a mile out of the town, and very courteously bade us all welcome and brought us to the monastery. The gates of the city are all covered with iron. The entrance into the house of the Christians is a very low and narrow door, barred or plated with iron, and then come we into a very dark entry: the place is a monastery. There we lay and dieted of free cost; we fared reasonable well; the bread and wine was excellent good, the chambers clean, and all the meat well served in, with clean linen.

We lay at the monastery two days, Friday and Saturday, and then we went to Bethlehem with two or three of the friars of the house with us. In the way thither we saw many monuments, as: –

The mountain where the Angel took up Habakkuk by the hair and brought him to Daniel in the lions' den.

The fountain of the prophet Jeremiah.

The place where the wise men met that went to Bethlehem to worship Christ, where is a fountain of stone.

Being come to Bethlehem we saw the place where Christ was born, which is now a chapel with two altars whereupon they say Mass. The place is built with grey marble, and hath been beautiful but now it is partly decayed.

Near thereto is the sepulchre of the Innocents slain by Herod, the sepulchres of Paul, of Jerome, and of Eusebius.

Also a little from this monastery is a place under the ground where the Virgin Mary abode with Christ when Herod sought Him to destroy Him.

We stayed at Bethlehem that night, and the next day we went from thence to the mountains of Judea, which are about eight miles from Jerusalem, where are the ruins of an old monastery. In the mid-way from the monastery to Jerusalem is the place where John Baptist was born, being now an old monastery, and cattle kept in it. Also a mile from Jerusalem is a place called *Inventio Sanctae Crucis*, where the wood was found that made the Cross.

In the city of Jerusalem we saw the hall where Pilate sat in judgment when Christ was condemned, the stairs whereof are at Rome, as they told us. A little from thence is the house where the Virgin Mary was born.

There is also the piscina, or fish-pool, where the sick folks were healed, which is by the walls of Jerusalem. But the pool is now dry.

The Mount of Calvary is a great church, and within the door thereof, which is little and barred with iron, and five great holes in it to look in like the holes of tavern doors in London, they sit that are appointed to receive our money with a carpet under them upon a bank of stone and their legs across like tailors. Having paid our money we are permitted to go into the Church. Right against the Church door is the grave where Christ was buried, with a great long stone of white marble over it and railed about. The outside of the sepulchre is very foul, by means that every man scrapes his name and mark upon it, and is ill kept.

Within the sepulchre is a partition, and in the further part thereof is a place like an altar where they say Mass, and at the door thereof is the stone whereupon the Angel sat when he said to Mary, 'He is risen,' which stone was also rolled to the door of the sepulchre.

The altar stone within the sepulchre is of white marble; the place able to contain but four persons. Right over the sepulchre is a device or lantern for light, and over that a great louvre such as are in England in ancient houses. There is also the Chapel of the Sepulchre, and in the midst thereof is a canopy as it were of a bed, with a great sort of ostrich eggs hanging at it, with tassels of silk and lamps.

Behind the sepulchre is a little chapel for the Chaldeans and Syrians.

Upon the right hand coming into the Church is the tomb of Baldwin, King of France, and of His son: and in the same place the tomb of Melchizedek.

There is a chapel also in the same church erected to St Helen, through which we go up to the place where Christ was crucified. The stairs are fifty steps high; there are two altars in it. Before the High Altar is the place where the Cross stood, the hole whereof is trimmed about with silver, and the depth of it is half a man's arm deep. The rent also of the mountain is there to be seen in the crevice wherein a man may put his arm.

Upon the other side of the Mount of Calvary is the place where Abraham would have sacrificed his son, where also is a chapel, and the place paved with stones of divers colours.

There is also the house of Annas, the High Priest, and the olive tree whereunto Christ was bound when He was whipped: also the house of Caiaphas, and by it the prison where Christ was kept, which is but the room of one man and hath no light but the opening of the door.

Without Jerusalem in the valley of Jehosaphat is a church under the ground, like to the shrouds in Paul's, where the sepulchre of the Virgin Mary is: the stairs be very broad, and upon the stairs going down are two sepulchres; upon the left hand lieth Jehosaphat, and upon the right hand lieth Joachim and Anna, the father and mother of the Virgin Mary.

Going out of the valley of Jehosaphat we came to Mount Olivet, where Christ prayed unto His Father before His death: and there is to be seen (as they told me) the water and blood that fell from the eyes of Christ. A little higher upon the same Mount is the place where the Apostles slept, and watched not. At the foot of the Mount is the place where Christ was imprisoned.

Upon the mountain also is the place where Christ stood when He wept over Jerusalem, and where He ascended into heaven.

Now, having seen all these monuments, I with my company set from Jerusalem the 20 day of August, and came again to Joppa the 22 of the same month, where we took shipping presently for Tripolis, and in four days we came to Messina, the place where the ships lie that come for Tripolis.

The city of Tripolis is a mile and a half within the land, so that no ship can come further than Messina: so that night I came thither, where I lay nine days for passage, and at last we embarked ourselves in a good ship of Venice, called the new *Nave Ragasona*. We entered the ship the second of September, the fourth we set sail, the seventh we came to Salina, which is 140 miles from Tripolis. There we stayed four days to take in more lading, in which meantime I fell sick of an ague, but recovered again, I praise God.

Salina is a ruinated city, and was destroyed by the Turk ten years past: there are in it now but seventeen persons, women and children. A little from this city of Salina is a salt piece of ground where the water groweth salt that raineth upon it.

Thursday, the 21 of September, we came to Missagh, and there we stayed eight days for our lading. The 18 of September before we came to Missagh, and within ten miles of the town, as we lay at an anchor because the wind was contrary, there came a great boat full of men to board us; they made an excuse to seek for four men which (they said) our ship had taken from theirs about Tripolis, but our Captain would not suffer any of them to come in to us.

The next morning they came to us again with a great galley, manned with 500 men at the least, whereupon our Captain sent the boat to them with twelve men to know their pleasure. They said they sought for four men and therefore would talk with our master. So then the master's mate was sent them, and him they kept and went their way. The next morning they came again with him and with three other galleys, and then would needs speak with our Captain, who went to them in a gown of crimson damask and other very brave apparel, and five or six other gentlemen richly apparelled also. They, having the Turk's safe conduct, showed it to the Captain of the galleys and laid it upon his head, charging him to obey it. So, with much ado and with the gift of 100 pieces of gold we were quit of them, and had our man again.

That day, as aforesaid, we came to Missagh and there stayed eight days, and at last departed towards Candia with a scant wind.

The 11 day of October we were boarded with four galleys, manned with 1,200 men, which also made a sleeveless [fruitless] errant and troubled us very much, but our Captain's passport and the gift of 100 chickens discharged all.

The 27 of October we passed by Zante with a merry wind, the 29 by Corfu, and the third of November we arrived at Istria, and there we left our great ship and took small boats to bring us to Venice.

The 9 of November I arrived again at Venice in good health, where I stayed nine days, and the 25 of the same month I came to Augusta and stayed there but one day.

The 27 of November I set towards Nuremberg, where I came the 29, and there stayed till the 9 of December and was very well entertained of the English merchants there: & the governors of the town sent me and my company sixteen gallons of excellent good wine.

From thence I went to Frankfurt, from Frankfurt to Cologne, from Cologne to Arnhem, from Arnhem to Utrecht, from Utrecht to Dort, from Dort to Antwerp, from Antwerp to Flushing, from Flushing to London, where I arrived upon Twelfth Eve in safety and gave thanks to God, having finished my journey to Jerusalem and home again in the space of nine months and five days.

AN EMBASSY TO THE GREAT TURK

Anonymous

That famous merchant-traveller, Anthony Jenkinson, who journeyed extensively from Russia into the Middle East, secured trading privileges from the Sultan of Turkey, the 'Great Turk', and on a new attempt was made to revive the English seaborne trade to the Levant in 1575. In that year two wealthy London merchants, Edward Osborne (knighted later) and Richard Staper, 'seriously considering what benefit might grow to the commonwealth', sent envoys through Poland to Turkey and obtained a safe-conduct for their factor, William Harborne, from the Sultan, Murad III. How the Sultan honoured this will be seen from the following narrative.

The voyage of the *Susan* of London to Constantinople, wherein the Worshipful Master William Harborne was sent first Ambassador unto Sultan Murad Khan, the Great Turk, with whom he continued as Her Majesty's Ligier almost six years.

THE 14th of November, 1582, we departed from Blackwall bound for the city of Constantinople in the tall ship called the *Susan* of London: the Master whereof was Richard Parsons, a very excellent and skilful man in his faculty. But by occasion of contrary weather we spent two months before we could recover the Cowes in the Isle of Wight, where the 14th of January following we took in the Worshipful Master William Harborne, Her Majesty's Ambassador to the Turk, and his company, and sailed thence to Yarmouth in the foresaid Isle of Wight. The 19th we put from Wight. The 26th we did see Cabo de Sant Vincente. The same day we were thwart of Cabo Santa Maria. The 27th we passed by Tarifa and Gibraltar. The 28th in the morning we passed by Velez Malaga: and that night were thwart of Cabo de Gates. The 29th at night we had sight of Cabo de Palos. The 30th in the morning we did see the high land of Denia, in the kingdom of Valencia, and that night we had sight of the island Formentera. The 31st in the morning appeared the island of Cabrera.

The 1st of February we put into a port in Majorca, called Porto de Sant Pedro, where they would have evil intreated us for coming into the harbour: we thought we might have been as bold there as in other places of Christendom, but it proved far otherwise. The first man we met on land was a simple shepherd, of whom we demanded whether we might have a sheep or suchlike to refresh ourselves, who told us yea. And by such conference had with him at the last he came aboard once or twice, and had the best cheer that we could make him: and our Ambassador himself talked with him, and still he made us fair promises, but nothing at all meant to perform the same, as the end showed.

In the meantime came in a ship of Marseilles, the Master whereof did know our Ambassador very well, with whom our Ambassador had conference and with his merchants also. They came from Algier in Barbary, which is under the government of the Great Turk. They did present our Ambassador with an ape, wherefore he made very much of them and had them often aboard. By them, I suppose, he was bewrayed of his purpose as touching his message, but yet still we had fair words of the shepherd aforesaid, and others: so that upon their words our purser and another man went to a town which was three or four miles from the port, and there were well entertained and had of the people very fair speeches and such small things as could be gotten upon the sudden, and so returned to the ship that day. Then we were emboldened, and thought all had been well according to their talk.

The next day, being the 6th day of February, two of our gentlemen, with one of our merchants and the purser, and one of the Ambassador's men, went to the town aforesaid, thinking to do as the purser and the other had done before, but it proved contrary; for at their coming thither they had fair words a while, and had bread and wine and such necessaries for their money, until such time as they were beset with men, and the Majorcans never showed in their countenance any such matter, but as the manner of all the people in the dominions of Spain is, for the most part to be treacherous to us if they think they have any advantage. For upon the sudden they laid hands on them and put them in hold, as sure as might be in such a simple town.

Then were they well guarded with men both day and night, and still deluded with fair words, and they said to our men it was for no hurt but that the Viceroy of the island would come aboard to see the ship. But they presently sent the purser to the town of Majorca, where he was examined by the Viceroy very straightly, what their ship and Captain were, and what voyage they intended, but he confessed nothing at all. In the meantime they in the town were likewise straightly examined by a priest and other officers upon their oaths; who for their oaths' sake declared the whole estate of their voyage.

The Ambassador's man was a Frenchman and therefore was suffered to go to the ship on a message, but he could tell the Ambassador none other news but that the Viceroy would come aboard the ship and that our men should come with him, but they had another meaning. For the Marseillian merchants were stayed in like manner in the town, only to make a better show unto us. But in the meantime, being there three or four days, there came men unto us every day, more or less, but one day especially there came two men on horseback whom we took to be officers, being lusty men and very well horsed. These men desired to speak with our Captain (for all things that passed there were done in the name of our Captain, John Gray) for it was said by us there that he was Captain of one of Her Majesty's ships; wherefore all things passed in his name: and the Ambassador not seen in anything but rather concealed, and yet did all because of his tongue and good inditing in that language. For he himself went on land clothed in velvet, and talked with these men, and with him ten or twelve lusty fellows well weaponed, each one having a boarspear or a caliver, the Captain, John Gray, being one of them, and our boat lying by very warily kept and ready. For then we began to suspect, because the place was more frequented with men than it was wont. The men on horseback were in doubt to come near, because he came so well weaponed. But they bade him welcome, and gave him great salutations in words as their manner is: and demanded why he came so strong, for they said he needed not to fear any man in the island. Answer was made that it was the manner of English Captains to go with their guard in strange places.

Then they told our Ambassador (thinking him to be the Captain) that they were sent from the Viceroy to know what they did lack, for they promised him beef or mutton or anything that was in the island to be had, but their purpose was to have gotten more of our men if they could, and they said that we should have our men again the next day: with such pretty delusions they fed us still. Then our Ambassador did write a letter to the Viceroy in Her Majesty's name, and in our Captain, John Gray's name, and not in his own, and sent it by them, desiring him to send his men and not to trouble him in his voyage, for he had given him no such cause, nor any of his. So these men departed with great courtesy in words on both parts. And in all this time we did see men on horseback and on foot in the woods and trees more than they were accustomed to be, but we could perceive nothing thereby.

The next day, or the second, came either four or six of the best of them as we thought (the Viceroy excepted) and very many men besides in the fields, both on foot and on horse, but came not near the water side. And those in like order desired to speak with the Captain and that when he came on land the trumpets might sound.

But then the Ambassador, whom they thought to be Captain,

would not go, nor suffer the trumpets to be sounded (for that he thought it was a trap to take himself and more of his company), but did send one of the principal of the merchants to talk with them. And the Captain, John Gray, went also with him, not being known of the Spaniards, for he went as a soldier. Thus they received of those men the like words as they had of the other before mentioned, who said we should have our men again for they meant us no hurt. Then our Ambassador did write another letter and sent it by them to the Viceroy in like order as he did before, but he received no answer of any of them.

In all this time they had privily gathered together the principal men of the island and had laboured day and night to bring down ordnance, not making any show of their treachery towards us. But the same night following we saw very many lights pass in the woods among the trees. And in the morning, when the watch was broken up, being Saturday, the ninth of February, at fair daylight one of our men looked forth and saw standing on land the carriage of a piece.

Then was one commanded to go into the top, and there he did descry two or three pieces and also many men on the shore, with divers weapons that they brought. Then they suddenly took four or five brass pieces and placed them on either side of the harbour where we should go out, and hid them with stones and bushes that we should not see them. Now I think the harbour not to be above the eighth part of a mile over. Thus perceiving their meaning, which was most plain, we agreed to take up our anchor and go out, and leave our men there, having none other way to take.

Then our Ambassador entreated the Master of the Marseillian, his friend, to go on land with his boat and to know the truth; who satisfied his request. And at his return he told us that it was very true that they would lay hold of us if they could. Then we weighed our anchors; but having little wind we towed the ship forward with the boat. The Viceroy himself was at the waterside, with more than five hundred men on both sides of the harbour as we thought. And when we came out with our ship as far as their ordnance, our Ambassador and the Captain being in their armour, the Master commanding of the company and trimming of the sails, the pilot standing on the poop attending to his charge, with other very well furnished, and every man in order about their business very ready, they on land on the contrary part having a very fair piece mounted on the north side openly in all our sights, as the ship passed by they traversed that piece right with the mainmast or after-quarter of the ship, and a gunner standing by, with a lint-stock in his hand about fourteen or fifteen foot long, being (as we thought) ready to give fire. Our whole noise of trumpets were sounding on the poop, with drum and flute, and a minion of brass on the summer deck, with two or three other pieces, always by our gunners traversed mouth to mouth with theirs on land, still looking when they on land should shoot for to answer them again.

The pilot standing on the poop, seeing this readiness and the ship going very softly because of the calmness of the wind, he called to them on the south side, where the Viceroy was, and said unto him, 'Have you wars with us? If you have it is more than we know; but by your provision it seemeth so: if you have, shoot in God's name and spare not.'

But they held all fast and shot not. Then the Viceroy himself held up a paper and said he had a letter for our Captain, and desired us to stay for it. Then we answered and said we would not, but willed him to send it by the Marseillians' boat, and our men also. All this while our trumpets, drum and flute sounded, and so we passed out in the face of them all.

When they perceived that they could lay no hold on us they presently sent to the town for our men, whom within less than three hours after they sent aboard with the said letter, wherein he desired our Captain and his company not to take it in ill part, for he meant them no harm, but would have seen our ship. His letter did import these and suchlike fair speeches; for it altogether contained courteous salutations, saying that he might boldly come into any port within his island, and that he and his would show him what friendship they might; and that the injury that was offered was done at the request of the shepherds and poor people of the country, for the more safeguard of their flocks, and because it was not a thing usual to have any such ship to come into that port, with many other deceitful words in the said letter.

Then our Ambassador wrote unto him another letter to answer that, and gave him thanks for his men that he had sent him, and also for his goodwill, and sent him a present. This done, we shot off half a dozen pieces, hoisted our sails, and departed on our voyage. Then the purser and the rest of our men that had been in hold told us that they did see the Captain and other gentlemen of the island having their buskins and stockings torn from their legs with labouring in the bushes day and night to make that sudden provision.

The 12th of February we saw an island of Africa side called Galita, where they use to drag out of the sea much coral, and we saw likewise Sardinia, which is an island subject to Spain. The 13th in the morning we were hard by Sardinia. The 15th we did see an island near Sicilia, and an island on Africa side called Cysimbre. The same day likewise we saw an island called Pantellaria, and that night we were thwart the middle of Sicilia. The 16th at night we were as far as Capo Passaro, which is the south-east part of Sicilia. The 24th we were put into a port called Porto de Conte, in an island called Cephalonia: it is an out island in the dominions of Greece, and now at this present governed by the seigneury of Venice, as the rest of Greece is under the Turk for the most part.

The 27th we came from thence, and that day arrived at Zante [Zakinthos] which is also in Greece; for at this present we entered the parts of Greece. The second of March we came from Zante, and the same day were thwart of an island called Prodeno; and the 4th we were thwart of an island called Sapientia. There standeth a fair town and a castle on the main over against it, called Modon. The same day by reason of contrary winds we put back again to Prodeno, because we could not fetch Sapientia. The 9th we came from thence and were as far as Sapientia again. The 10th we were as far shot as Cabo Matapan [Akra Taimaron]; and that day we entered the Archipelago and passed through between Cerigo [Kithira] and Cabo Malio [Akra Maléa]. This Cerigo is an island where one, Menelaus, did sometimes reign, from whom was stolen by Paris fair Helena and carried to Troy, as ancient records do declare.

The same day we had sight of a little island called Bellapola, and did likewise see both the Milos, being islands in the Archipelago. The 11th in the morning we were hard by an island called Falconara and the island of Antemila. The 12th in the morning we were between Fermenia and Zea, being both islands. That night we were between Negroponte and Andri [Andros], being likewise islands. The 13th in the morning we were hard by Psara and Sarafo, being islands nine or ten miles from Chios, and could not fetch Chios. So we put room with a port in Metelin [Lésvos], called Sigra, and about nine of the clock at night we anchored there.

The 15th we came from thence, the 16th we put into Porto Delfi. The port is nine English miles to the northward of the city of Chios (and it may be twelve of their miles). This night we stayed in the said port, being in the island of Chios. Then went our merchant and one or two with him to the city of Chios. And when the Bey, who is the governor of the island (and is in their language a Duke), had communed with the merchant and those that were with him, and understood of our arrival within his dominion, the day following he armed his galleys and came to welcome our Ambassador, accompanied with the Ermine, that is, the King's Customer [Customs House officer], and also the French Consul, with divers of the Chief of the City, and offered him as much friendship as he could or would desire: for he did offer to attend upon us and tow us if need were to the Castles.

The 21st we departed from thence, and that day passed by port Sigra again. This island of Metelin is part of Asia, and is near to

Natolia. The 22nd we passed by a headland called Baberno, and is also in Asia. And that day at night we passed by the isle of Tenedos, part of Asia, and by another island called Maure. And the same day we passed through the Straits of Gallipoli, and by the Castles, and also by the town of Gallipoli itself, which standeth in Europa. And that night we were in sight of Marmora, which is near Natolia and part of Asia.

The 23rd in the morning we were thwart of Heracleia, and that night we anchored in Silauria. The 24th in the morning the merchant and the pilot were set on land to go to the city about the Ambassador's business, but there they could not land because we had the wind fair. That place of some is called Ponte Grande, and is four and twenty miles on this side of Constantinople, and because of the wind they followed in the skiff until they came to a place called Ponte Picola, and there is a little bridge, it standeth eight Turkish miles from Constantinople; there the merchant and the pilot landed. At this bridge is an house of the Great Turk's with a fair garden belonging unto it, near the which is a point called Ponta St Stephano, and there the ship anchored that day.

The 26th day the ship came to the seven towers, and the 27th we came nearer. The 29th there came three galleys to bring us up further; and when the ship came against the Great Turk's palace we shot off all our ordnance to the number of four and thirty pieces. Then landed our Ambassador, and then we discharged four and twenty pieces, who was received with more than fifty or threescore men on horseback. The 9th of April he presented the Great Bassa with six cloths, four cans of silver double gilt, and one piece of fine holland, and to three other Bassas, that is to say, the second Bassa, which is a gelded man and his name is Mahomet Bassa, to the third, who married the Great Turk's sister, and to the fourth, whom they call Abraham Bassa; to everyone of these he gave four cloths.

Now, before the Great Bassa, and Abraham Bassa, at their return from the Court (and as we think at other times, but at that time for a certain) there came a man in manner of a fool who gave a great shout three or four times, crying very hollowly. The place rebounded with the sound, and this man, say they, is a Prophet of Mahomet, his arms and legs naked, on his feet he did wear wooden pattens of two sorts, in his hand a flag or streamer set on a short spear painted; he carried a mat and bottles and other trumpery at his back, and sometimes under his arm; on his head he had a cap of white camel's hair, flat like an helmet, written about with letters, and about his head a linen roll.

Other serving-men there were with the said Bassas, with red attire on their heads, much like French hoods, but the long flap somewhat smaller towards the end, with scuffs or plates of metal, like unto the shape of an ancient arming sword, standing on their foreheads like other janissaries. These Bassas entertained us as followeth: First, they brought us into a hall, there to stand on one side, and our Ambassador and gentlemen on the other side, who sat them down on a bench covered with carpets, the Ambassador in the midst; on his left hand sat our gentlemen, and on his right hand the Turks, next to the door where their master goeth in and out: the common sort of Turks stayed in the courtyard, not suffered to come near us. When our Ambassador had sitten half an hour the Bassas (who sat by themselves in an inner small room) sent for him; to whom the Ambassador and his gentlemen went: they all kissed his hand, and presently returned (the Ambassador only excepted, who stayed there and a Turk's chaus with him). With the Ambassador and his gentlemen went in also so many of our men as there were presents to carry in, but these neither kissed his hand nor tarried.

After this I went to visit the church of Santa Sophia, which was the chief church when it was the Christians', and now is the chief see and church of primacy of this Turk present. Before I entered I was willed to put off my shoes, to the end I should not profane their church, I being a Christian. The pillars on both sides of the church are very costly and rich, their pulpits seemly and handsome, two are common to preach in, the third reserved only for their paschal. The ground is covered with mats, and the walls hanged with tapestry. They have also lamps in their churches, one in the middle of the church of exceeding greatness, and another in another part of the church of clean gold, or double gilded, full as big as a barrel. Round about the church there is a gallery builded upon rich and stately pillars.

That day I was in both the chapels, in one of the which lieth the Turk's father and five of his sons in tombs right costly, with their turbans very white and clean, shifted (as they say) every Friday; they be not on their heads but stand on moulds made for that purpose. At the ends over and about their tombs are belts, like girdles, beset with jewels. In the other chapel are four other of his sons and one daughter in like order. In the first chapel is a thing four foot high, covered with green, beset with mother-of-pearl very richly. This is a relic of Mahomet, and standeth on the left side of the head of the great Turk's tomb. These chapels have their floors covered, and their walls hanged with tapestry of great price: I could value the covering and hangings of one of the chapels at no less than five hundred pounds, besides their lamps hanging richly gilded. These chapels have their roofs curiously wrought with rich stone and gilded. And there lie the books of their Laws for every man to read.

The 11th day of April the ship came to the quay of the Custom

House. The 16th, the Ambassador and we, his men, went to the Captain Bassa, who is Admiral of the seas; his name is Uchali. He would not receive us into his house but into his galley, to deliver our present, which was as followeth: Four pieces of cloth, and two silver pots, gilt and graven. The poop or stern of his galley was gilded both within and without, and under his feet, and where he sat was all covered with very rich tapestry. Our Ambassador and his gentlemen kissed his hand, and then the gentlemen were commanded out, and our Ambassador sat down by him on his left hand and the chaus stood before him. Our men might walk in the galley fore and after, some of us tarried, and some went out again. The galley had seven pieces of brass in her prow, small and great, she had thirty banks or oars on either side, and at every bank or oar seven men to row.

The 18th day the ship went from the quay. And 21st the Admiral took his leave of the Great Turk, being bound to the sea with six and thirty galleys, very fairly beautified with gilding and painting, and beset with flags and streamers, all the which galleys discharged their ordnance: and we for his farewell gave him one and twenty pieces. Then he went to his house with his galleys, and the 22nd he went to the sea, and the castle that standeth in the water gave him fourteen or sixteen pieces: and when he came against the Turk's seraglio he shot off all his calivers and his great pieces, and so he went his way.

The 24th our Ambassador went to the Court, whose entertainment with the order thereof followeth. When we came first on land there was way made for us by two or three Bassas and divers chauses on horseback with their men on foot, to accompany our Ambassador to the Court. Also they brought horses for him and his gentlemen for to ride, which were very richly furnished: and by the way there met with us other chauses to accompany us to the Court. When we came there we passed through two gates; at the second gate there stood very many men with horses attending on their masters. When we came within that gate we were within a very fair courtyard, in compass twice so big as Paul's churchyard. On the right hand of the said court was a fair gallery like an alley, and within it were placed rails and such other provision. On the left side was the like, half the court over: it was divided into two parts, the innermost fairer than the other. The other part of that side is the place where the Council do usually sit, and at the inner end of that is a fair place to sit in, much like unto that place in Paul's churchyard where the Mayor and his brethren use to sit; thither was our Ambassador brought and set in that place. Within that said place is another like open room where he did eat.

As soon as we came in we were placed in the innermost alley of the second room, on the left side of the court, which was spread with carpets on the ground, fourscore or fourscore and ten foot long, with an hundred and fifty several dishes set thereon, that is to say, mutton boiled and roasted, rice diversely dressed, fritters of the finest fashion, and dishes daintily dight [decorated] with pretty paper, with infinite others, I know not how to express them. We had also roasted hens with sundry sorts of fowls to me unknown. The gentlemen and we sat down on the ground, for it is their manner so to feed. There were also Greeks and others set to furnish out the room. Our drink was made with rose water and sugar and spices brewed together. Those that did serve us with it had a great bag tied over their shoulders, with a broad belt like an arming belt full of plates of copper and gilt, with part of the said bag under his arm, and the mouth in his hand; then he had a device to let it out when he would into cups when we called for drink. The Ambassador when he had eaten passed by us, with the chauses aforesaid, and sat him down in an inner room.

This place where he sat was against the gate where we came in and hard by the Council Chamber end, somewhat on the left side of the court; this was at the east end of the court, for we came in at the west. All this time our presents stood by us until we had dined, and dinner once ended this was their order of taking up the dishes. Certain were called in, like those of the Black Guard in the Court of England, the Turks call them Moglans. These came in like rude and ravening mastiffs, without order or fashion, and made clean riddance; for he whose hungry eye one dish could not fill turned two one into the other, and thus even on the sudden was made a clean riddance of all. Then came certain chauses and brought our gentlemen to sit with the Ambassador. Immediately came officers and appointed janissaries to bear from us our presents, who carried them on the right side of the court, and set them hard by the door of the Privy Chamber, as we call it: there all things stood for the space of an hour.

Thus the Ambassador and his gentlemen sat still, and to the southward of them was a door whereas the Great Turk himself went in and out at, and on the south side of that door sat on a bench all his chief lords and gentlemen, and on the north side of the west gate stood his guard, in number as I guess them a thousand men. These men have on their heads round caps of metal like skulls, but sharp in the top; in this they have a bunch of ostrich feathers as big as a brush, with the corner or edge forward; at the lower end of these feathers was there a smaller feather, like those that are commonly worn here. Some of his guard had small staves, and most of them were weaponed with bows and arrows. Here they waited, during our abode at the Court, to guard their Lord.

After the Ambassador with his gentlemen had sitten an hour and more there came three or four chauses and brought them into the

Great Turk's presence. At the Privy Chamber door two noblemen took the Ambassador by each arm one, and put their fingers within his sleeves, and so brought him to the Great Turk where he sumptuously sat alone. He kissed his hand and stood by until all the gentlemen were brought before him in like manner, one by one, and led backwards again, his face towards the Turk; for they might neither tarry nor turn their backs, and in like manner returned the Ambassador. The salutation that the noblemen did was taking them by the hands. All this time they trod on cloth of gold; most of the noblemen that sat on the south side of the Privy Chamber sat likewise on cloth of gold. Many officers or janissaries there were with staves, who kept very good order for no Turk whatsoever might go any further than they willed him.

At our Ambassador's entering they followed that bare his presents, to say, twelve fine broad cloths, two pieces of fine holland, ten pieces of plate double gilt, one case of candlesticks, the case whereof was very large and three foot high and more, two very great cans or pots, and one lesser, one basin and ewer, two popinjays of silver, the one with two heads, they were to drink in; two bottles with chains, three fair mastiffs in coats of red cloth, three spaniels, two bloodhounds, one common hunting hound, two greyhounds, two little dogs in coats of silk; one clock valued at five hundred pounds sterling; over it was a forest with trees of silver, among the which were deer chased with dogs, and men on horseback following, men drawing of water, others carrying mine ore on barrows: on the top of the clock stood a castle, and on the castle a mill. All these were of silver. And the clock was round beset with jewels.

All the time that we stayed at the Council Chamber door they were telling or weighing of money to send into Persia for his soldiers' pay. There were carried out an hundred and three and thirty bags, and in every bag, as it was told us, one thousand ducats, which amounteth to three hundred and thirty thousand, and in sterling English money to fourscore and nineteen thousand pounds.

The Captain of the Guard in the meantime went to the Great Turk, and returned again; then they of the Court made obeisance to him, bowing down their heads and their hands on their breasts, and he in like order resaluted them; he was in cloth of silver; he went and came with two or three with him and no more. Then we went out at the first gate, and there we were commanded to stay until the Captain of the guard was passed by and all his guard with him, part before him and part behind him, some on horseback and some on foot, but the most part on foot carrying on their shoulders the money before mentioned, and so we passed home.

There was in the Court during our abode there for the most part a fool resembling the first, but not naked as was the other at the Bassas: but he turned him continually and cried 'Hough' very hollowly.

The 3rd of May I saw the Turk go to the church: he had more than two hundred and fifty horses before and behind him, but most before him. There were many empty horses that came in no order. Many of his nobility were in cloth of gold, but himself in white satin. There did ride behind him six or seven youths, one or two whereof carried water for him to drink as they said. There were many of his guard running before him and behind him, and when he alighted they cried 'Hough' very hollowly, as the aforesaid fools.

The 'Great Turk' granted various privileges to English merchants, who formed the joint-stock Turkey Company, which traded profitably with Turkey and through Turkey with Asiatic countries. This was possible because the Company built a fleet of merchant ships so heavily armed that they could deal with pirates in the Mediteranean and were the most powerful English naval force apart from the Royal Navy. In 1592 it amalgamated with the Venice Company to form the Levant Company, which continued to operate until the nineteenth century.

THE DISCOVERY OF VIRGINIA

Arthur Barlowe

For years Elizabethan geographers, politicians, sea-captains and merchants discussed the possibility of 'planting' an English colony somewhere in the western hemisphere – in the mythical Terra Australis Incognita, *in the Straits of Magellan, on the eastern or western coast of South America, or in the Caribbean.*

Then in the 1570s a more rational scheme was formulated: to plant a colony in North America. The coast-line from Florida north to Newfoundland was unknown but claimed by England in virtue of the Cabots' early discoveries, and it was thought that a colony in this congenial climate was practicable. It should help to solve the nation's great problems: to increase exports and reduce imports, creating a favourable balance of trade and reducing unemployment. In 1578 the Queen granted Sir Humphrey Gilbert a patent to plant such a colony. In 1583 he formally annexed Newfoundland and then sailed south, but he and all the would-be colonists were drowned at sea.

Sir Walter Raleigh, Gilbert's half-brother, then secured a patent, 'at all times and for ever hereafter to discover, search, find out and view such remote, heathen and barbarous lands . . . [as are] not actually possessed of any Christian prince . . . to have, hold, occupy and enjoy to him, his heirs and assigns for ever . . .' In the same year he 'set forth' this voyage, which discovered what is now North Carolina. He named it Virginia.

The first voyage made to the coasts of America, with two barks, wherein were captains Master Philip Amadas, and Master Arthur Barlowe, who discovered part of the country now called Virginia, anno 1584. Written by one of the said captains, and sent to Sir Walter Raleigh, Knight, at whose charge and direction the said voyage was set forth.

THE 27 day of April, in the year of our redemption 1584, we departed the west of England, with two barks well furnished with men and victuals, having received our last and perfect directions by your letters, confirming the former instructions and commandments delivered by yourself at our leaving the river of Thames. And I think it a matter both unnecessary, for the manifest discovery of the country, as also for tediousness' sake, to remember unto you the diurnal of our course, sailing thither and returning; only

I have presumed to present unto you this brief discourse, by which you may judge how profitable this land is likely to succeed, as well to yourself, by whose direction and charge, and by whose servants, this our discovery hath been performed, as also to her Highness and the commonwealth. In which we hope your wisdom will be satisfied, considering that as much by us hath been brought to light as by those small means and number of men we had could any way have been expected, or hoped for.

The tenth of May we arrived at the Canaries, and the tenth of June in this present year we were fallen with the islands of the West Indies, keeping a more south-easterly course than was needful, because we doubted that the current of the Bay of Mexico, disboguing between the Cape of Florida and Havana, had been of greater force than afterwards we found it to be. At which islands we found the air very unwholesome, and our men grew for the most part ill-disposed: so that having refreshed ourselves with sweet water and fresh victual, we departed the twelfth day of our arrival there. These islands, with the rest adjoining, are so well known to yourself, and to many others, as I will not trouble you with the remembrance of them.

The second of July we found shoal water, where we smelt so sweet and so strong a smell, as if we had been in the midst of some delicate garden, abounding with all kind of odoriferous flowers; by which we were assured that the land could not be far distant. And keeping good watch and bearing but slack sail, the fourth of the same month we arrived upon the coast, which we supposed to be a continent and firm land, and we sailed along the same 120 English miles before we could find any entrance, or river issuing into the sea.

The first that appeared unto us we entered, though not without some difficulty, and cast anchor three arquebus-shot within the haven's mouth, on the left hand of the same; and after thanks given to God for our safe arrival thither, we manned our boats, and went to view the land next adjoining, and to take possession of the same in the right of the Queen's most excellent Majesty, as rightful queen and princess of the same, and after delivered the same over to your use, according to her Majesty's grant and letters patents, under her Highness' great Seal. Which being performed, according to the ceremonies used in such enterprises, we viewed the land about us, being, where we first landed, very sandy and low towards the water's side, but so full of grapes as the very beating and surge of the sea overflowed them. Of which we found such plenty, as well there as in all places else, both on the sand and on the green soil on the hills, as in the plains, as well on every little shrub, as also climbing towards the tops of high cedars, that I think in all the world the like abundance is not to be found: and myself having seen those parts of Europe that most abound, find such difference as were incredible to be written.

We passed from the sea side towards the tops of those hills next adjoining, being but of mean height; and from thence we beheld the sea on both sides, to the north and to the south, finding no end any of both ways. This land lay stretching itself to the west, which after we found to be but an island of twenty miles long, and not above six miles broad. Under the bank or hill whereon we stood, we beheld the valleys replenished with goodly cedar trees, and having discharged our arquebus-shot, such a flock of cranes (the most part white) arose under us, with such a cry redoubled by many echoes, as if an army of men had shouted all together.

This island had many goodly woods full of deer, coneys, hares and fowl, even in the midst of summer, in incredible abundance. The woods are not such as you find in Bohemia, Moscovia, or Hercynia,★ barren and fruitless, but the highest and reddest cedars of the world, far bettering the cedars of the Azores, of the Indies, or Libanus [Lebanon]; pines, cypress, sassafras, the lentisk, or the tree that beareth the mastic; the tree that beareth the rind of black cinnamon, of which Master Winter brought from the Straits of Magellan; and many other of excellent smell and quality.

We remained by the side of this island two whole days before we saw any people of the country. The third day we espied one small boat rowing towards us, having in it three persons. This boat came to the island side, four arquebus-shot from our ships; and there two of the people remaining, the third came along the shore side towards us, and we being then all within board, he walked up and down upon the point of the land next to us. Then the master and the pilot of the Admiral, Simon Ferdinando, and the captain, Philip Amadas, myself, and others, rowed to the land; whose coming this fellow attended, never making any shew of fear or doubt. And after he had spoken of many things, not understood by us, we brought him, with his own good liking, aboard the ships, and gave him a shirt, a hat, and some other things, and made him taste of our wine and our meat, which he liked very well; and, after having viewed both barks, he departed, and went to his own boat again, which he had left in a little cove or creek adjoining. As soon as he was two bow-shot into the water he fell to fishing, and in less than half-an-hour he had laden his boat as deep as it could swim, with which he came again to the point of the land, and there he divided his fish into two parts, pointing one part to the ship and the other to the pinnace. Which, after he had, as much as he might, requited the former benefits received, departed out of our sight.

★ Hercynia, Hyrcania, the ancient name for a region south of the Caspian Sea.

The next day there came unto us divers boats, and in one of them the king's brother, accompanied with forty or fifty men, very handsome and goodly people, and in their behaviour as mannerly and civil as any of Europe. His name was Granganimeo, and the king is called Wingina; the country, Wingandacoa, and now, by her Majesty, Virginia. The manner of his coming was in this sort: he left his boats, altogether as the first man did, a little from the ships by the shore, and came along to the place over against the ships, followed with forty men. When he came to the place, his servants spread a long mat upon the ground, on which he sat down, and at the other end of the mat four others of his company did the like; the rest of his men stood round about him somewhat afar off. When we came to the shore to him, with our weapons, he never moved from his place, nor any of the other four, nor never mistrusted any harm to be offered from us; but, sitting still, he beckoned us to come and sit by him, which we performed; and, being set, he made all signs of joy and welcome, striking on his head and his breast and afterwards on ours, to shew we were all one, smiling and making shew the best he could of all love and familiarity. After he had made a long speech unto us we presented him with divers things, which he received very joyfully and thankfully. None of the company durst speak one word all the time; only the four which were at the other end spake one in the other's ear very softly.

The king is greatly obeyed, and his brothers and children reverenced. The king himself in person was at our being there sore wounded in a fight which he had with the king of the next country called Wingiana, and was shot in two places through the body, and once clean through the thigh, but yet he recovered; by reason whereof, and for that he lay at the chief town of the country, being six days' journey off, we saw him not at all.

After we had presented this his brother with such things as we thought he liked, we likewise gave somewhat to the other that sat with him on the mat. But presently he arose and took all from them and put it into his own basket, making signs and tokens that all things ought to be delivered unto him, and the rest were but his servants and followers. A day or two after this we fell to trading with them, exchanging some things that we had for chamois, buff, and deer skins. When we shewed him all our packet of merchandise, of all things that he saw a bright tin dish most pleased him, which he presently took up and clapt it before his breast, and after made a hole in the brim thereof and hung it about his neck, making signs that it would defend him against his enemies' arrows. For those people maintain a deadly and terrible war with the people and king adjoining. We exchanged our tin dish for twenty skins, worth twenty crowns or

The manner of their attire and painting themselues when they goe to their generall huntinges or at theire Solemne feasts.

A Native of Virginia: drawing by John White, *c.* 1585–90

twenty nobles; and a copper kettle for fifty skins, worth fifty crowns. They offered us good exchange for our hatchets and axes, and for knives, and would have given anything for swords; but we would not depart with any.

After two or three days the king's brother came aboard the ships and drank wine, and eat of our meat and of our bread, and liked exceedingly thereof. And after a few days overpassed, he brought his wife with him to the ships, his daughter, and two or three children. His wife was very well-favoured, of mean stature, and very bashful. She had on her back a long cloak of leather, with the fur side next to her body, and before her a piece of the same. About her forehead she had a band of white coral, and so had her husband many times. In her ears she had bracelets of pearls hanging down to her middle, whereof we delivered your worship a little bracelet, and those were of the bigness of good peas. The rest of her women of the better sort had pendants of copper hanging in either ear, and some of the children of the king's brother and other noblemen have five or six in either ear; he himself had upon his head a broad plate of gold, or copper; for, being unpolished, we knew not what metal it should be, neither would he by any means suffer us to take it off his head, but feeling it, it would bow very easily. His apparel was as his wife's, only the women wear their hair long on both sides, and the men but on one. They are of colour yellowish, and their hair black for the most part; and yet we saw children that had very fine auburn and chestnut-coloured hair.

After that these women had been there, there came down from all parts great store of people, bringing with them leather, coral, divers kinds of dyes very excellent, and exchanged with us. But when Granganimeo, the king's brother, was present, none durst trade but himself, except such as wear red pieces of copper on their heads like himself; for that is the difference between the noblemen and the governors of countries, and the meaner sort. And we both noted there, and you have understood since by these men which we brought home, that no people in the world carry more respect to their king, nobility, and governors than these do. The king's brother's wife, when she came to us (as she did many times), was followed with forty or fifty women always. And when she came into the ship she left them all on land, saving her two daughters, her nurse, and one or two more. The king's brother always kept this order: as many boats as he would come withal to the ships, so many fires would he make on the shore afar off, to the end we might understand with what strength and company he approached. Their boats are made of one tree, either of pine, or of pitch-trees; a wood not commonly known to our people, nor found growing in England. They have no edge-tools to make them withal; if they have any they are very few, and those, it seems, they had 20 years since, which, as those two men declared, was out of a wreck, which happened upon their coast, of some Christian ship, being beaten that way by some storm and outrageous weather, whereof none of the people were saved, but only the ship, or some part of her, being cast upon the sand, out of whose sides they drew the nails and the spikes, and with those they made their best instruments. The manner of making their boats is thus: they burn down some great tree, or take such as are wind-fallen, and, putting gum and resin upon one side thereof, they set fire into it, and when it hath burnt it hollow they cut out the coal with their shells, and ever where they would burn it deeper or wider they lay on gums, which burn away the timber, and by this means they fashion very fine boats, and such as will transport 20 men. Their oars are like scoops, and many times they set with long poles, as the depth serveth.

The king's brother had great liking of our armour, a sword, and divers other things which we had, and offered to lay a great box of pearl in gage for them; but we refused it for this time, because we would not make them know that we esteemed thereof, until we had understood in what places of the country the pearl grew, which now your worship doth very well understand. He was very just of his promise: for many times we delivered him merchandise upon his word, but ever he came within the day and performed his promise. He sent us every day a brace or two of fat bucks, coneys, hares, fish the best of the world. He sent us divers kinds of fruits, melons, walnuts, cucumbers, gourds, pease, and divers roots, and fruits very excellent good, and of their country corn, which is very white, fair, and well tasted, and groweth three times in five months: in May they sow, in July they reap; in June they sow, in August they reap; in July they sow, in September they reap. Only they cast the corn into the ground, breaking a little of the soft turf with a wooden mattock or pickaxe. Ourselves proved the soil, and put some of our peas in the ground, and in ten days they were of 14 inches high. They have also beans very fair, of divers colours, and wonderful plenty, some growing naturally and some in their gardens; and so have they both wheat and oats. The soil is the most plentiful, sweet, fruitful, and wholesome of all the world. There are above fourteen several sweet-smelling timber-trees, and the most part of their underwoods are bays and suchlike. They have those oaks that we have, but far greater and better.

After they had been divers times aboard our ships, myself with seven more went twenty mile into the river that runneth toward the city of Skicoak, which river they call Occam; and the evening following we came to an island which they call Roanoake, distant from the harbour by which we entered seven leagues; and at the north end thereof was a village of nine houses built of cedar and fortified round about with sharp trees to keep out their enemies, and the entrance into it made like a turnpike very artificially. When we came towards it, standing near unto the water's side, the wife of Granganimeo, the king's brother, came running out to meet us very cheerfully and friendly. Her husband was not then in the village. Some of her people she commanded to draw our boat on shore, for the beating of the billow. Others she appointed to carry us on their backs to the dry ground, and others to bring our oars into the house for fear of stealing. When we were come into the outer room (having five rooms in her house) she caused us to sit down by a great fire, and after took off our clothes and washed them and dried them again. Some of the women plucked off our stockings and washed them, some washed our feet in warm water, and she herself took great pains to see all things ordered in the best manner she could, making great haste to dress some meat for us to eat.

After we had thus dried ourselves, she brought us into the inner room, where she set on the board standing along the house some wheat like furmenty, sodden [boiled] venison, and roasted, fish sodden and roasted, melons raw and sodden, roots of divers kinds, and divers fruits. Their drink is commonly water, but while the grape lasteth they drink wine, and for want of casks to keep it, all the year after they drink water; but it is sodden with ginger in it, and black cinnamon, and sometimes sassafras, and divers other wholesome and medicinable herbs and trees. We were entertained with all love and kindness, and with as much bounty (after their manner) as they could possibly devise.

We found the people most gentle, loving, and faithful, void of all guile and treason, and such as live after the manner of the golden age. The people only care how to defend themselves from the cold in their short winter, and to feed themselves with such meat as the soil affordeth; their meat is very well sodden, and they make broth very sweet and savoury. Their vessels are earthen pots, very large, white, and sweet; their dishes are wooden platters of sweet timber. Within the place where they feed was their lodging, and within that their idol, which they worship, of whom they speak incredible things. While we were at meat, there came in at the gates two or three men with their bows and arrows from hunting, whom when we espied we began to look one towards another, and offered to reach our weapons: but as soon as she espied our mistrust, she was very much moved, and caused some of her men to run out, and take away their bows and arrows and break them, and withal beat the poor fellows out of the gate again. When we departed in the evening and would not tarry all night, she was very sorry, and gave us into our boat our supper half-dressed, pots and all, and brought us to our boat side, in which we lay all night, removing the same a pretty distance from the shore. She perceiving our jealousy, was much grieved, and sent divers men and thirty women to sit all night on the bank-side by us, and sent us into our boats fine mats to cover us from the rain, using very many words to entreat us to rest in their houses. But because we were few men, and if we had miscarried the voyage had been in very great danger, we durst not adventure anything, although there was no cause of doubt; for a more kind and loving people there cannot be found in the world, as far as we have hitherto had trial.

Beyond this island there is the mainland, and over against this island falleth into this spacious water the great river called Occam by the inhabitants, on which standeth a town called Pomeiock, and six days' journey from the same is situate their greatest city called Skicoak, which this people affirm to be very great; but the savages were never at it, only they speak of it by the report of their fathers and other men, whom they have heard affirm it to be above one hour's journey about. Into this river falleth another great river called Cipo, in which there is found great store of mussels in which there are pearls; likewise there descendeth into this Occam another river called Nomopana, on the one side whereof standeth a great town called Chawanook, and the lord of that town and country is called Pooneno. This Pooneno is not subject to the king of Wingandacoa, but is a free lord. Beyond this country is there another king, whom they call Menatonon, and these three kings are in league with each other. Towards the south-west, four days' journey, is situate a town called Secotan, which is the southernmost town of Wingandacoa, near unto which six-and-twenty years past there was a ship cast away, whereof some of the people were saved, and those were white people, whom the country people preserved. And after ten days remaining in an out island unhabited, called Wocokon, they, with the help of some of the dwellers of Secotan, fastened two boats of the country together, and made masts unto them, and sails of their shirts, and having taken into them such victuals as the country yielded, they departed after they had remained in this out island three weeks. But shortly after, it seemed, they were cast away, for the boats were found upon the coast, cast a-land in another island adjoining. Other than these, there was never any people apparelled, or white of colour, either seen or heard of amongst these people, and these aforesaid were seen only of the inhabitants of Secotan; which appeared to be very true, for they wondered marvellously when we were amongst them at the whiteness of our skins, ever coveting to touch our breasts, and to view the same.

Besides they had our ships in marvellous admiration, and all things else were so strange unto them, as it appeared that none of them had ever seen the like. When we discharged any piece, were it but an arquebus, they would tremble thereat for very fear, and for the strangeness of the same, for the weapons which themselves use are bows and arrows. The arrows are but of small canes, headed with a sharp shell or tooth of a fish sufficient enough to kill a naked man. Their swords be of wood hardened; likewise they use wooden breastplates for their defence. They have beside a kind of club, in the end whereof they fasten the sharp horns of a stag, or other beast. When they go to wars they carry about with them their idol, of whom they ask counsel, as the Romans were wont of the oracle of Apollo. They sing songs as they march towards the battle, instead of drums and trumpets. Their wars are very cruel and bloody, by reason whereof, and of their civil dissensions which have happened of late years amongst them, the people are marvellously wasted, and in some places the country left desolate.

Adjoining to this country aforesaid, called Secotan, beginneth a country called Pomovik, belonging to another king, whom they call Piemacum; and this king is in league with the next king adjoining towards the setting of the sun, and the country Newsiok, situate upon a goodly river called Neus. These kings have mortal war with Wingina, king of Wingandacoa; but about two years past there was a peace made between the king Piemacum and the lord of Secotan, as these men which we have brought with us to England have given us to understand; but there remaineth a mortal malice in the Secotans, for many injuries and slaughters done upon them by this Piemacum. They invited divers men, and thirty women of the best of his country, to their town to a feast, and when they were altogether merry, and praying before their idol (which is nothing else but a mere illusion of the devil) the captain or lord of the town came suddenly upon them, and slew them every one, reserving the women and children; and these two have oftentimes since persuaded us to surprise Piemacum his town, having promised and assured us that there will be found in it great store of commodities. But whether their persuasion be to the end they may be revenged of their enemies, or for the love they bear to us, we leave that to the trial hereafter.

Beyond this island called Roanoake are many islands, very plentiful of fruits and other natural increases, together with many towns and villages along the side of the continent, some bounding upon the islands, and some stretching up further into the land.

When we first had sight of this country, some thought the first land we saw to be the continent; but after we entered into the haven we saw before us another mighty long sea, for there lieth along the coast a tract of islands 200 miles in length, adjoining to the ocean sea, and between the islands two or three entrances. When you are entered between them, these islands being very narrow for the most part, as in some places six miles broad, in some places less, in few more, then there appeareth another great sea, containing in breadth in some places 40, in some 50, in some 20 miles over, before you come unto the continent; and in this enclosed sea there are above 100 islands of divers bignesses, whereof one is 16 miles long, at which we were, finding it a most pleasant and fertile ground, replenished with goodly cedars, and divers other sweet woods, full of currants, of flax, and many other notable commodities, which we at that time had no leisure to view. Besides this island there are many, as I have said, some of two, of three, of four, of five miles, some more, some less, most beautiful and pleasant to behold, replenished with deer, coneys, hares, and divers beasts, and about them the goodliest and best fish in the world, and in greatest abundance.

Thus, Sir, we have acquainted you with the particulars of our discovery made this present voyage, as far forth as the shortness of the time we there continued would afford us to take view of; and so contenting ourselves with this service at this time, which we hope hereafter to enlarge, as occasion and assistance shall be given, we resolved to leave the country, and to apply ourselves to return for England, which we did accordingly, and arrived safely in the west of England about the midst of September.

And whereas we have above certified you of the country taken in possession by us to her Majesty's use, and so to yours by her Majesty's grant, we thought good for the better assurance thereof, to record some of the particular gentlemen, and men of account, who then were present, as witnesses of the same, that thereby all occasion of cavil to the title of the country, in her Majesty's behalf, may be prevented, which otherwise such as like not the action may use and pretend. Whose names are, Master Philip Amadas, Master Arthur Barlowe, Captains; William Grenville, John Wood, James Bromewich, Henry Greene, Benjamin Wood, Simon Ferdinando, Nicholas Petman, John Hughes, of the company.

We brought home also two of the savages, being lusty men, whose names were Wanchese and Manteo.

THE ESCAPE OF THE *PRIMROSE*

Anonymous

There was a shortage of corn in Spain in 1585, and Philip II invited English merchants to send cargoes of corn, giving them a specific promise of safe-conduct. As soon as they entered the Spanish ports the ships and cargoes were confiscated and their crews thrown into prison, along with those from 'Holland, Zeeland, Easterland and Germany'. Only the Primrose *escaped, bringing home the King's instructions to the Corregidor, which stated that 'a great fleet' was being prepared. This made it clear that Philip had at last abandoned his peace policy and intended to conquer England. In the same year Francis Drake, with a powerful combined force, ravaged the Caribbean. Open war had become inevitable.*

The escape of the *Primrose*, a tall ship of London, from before the town of Bilbao in Biscay: which ship the Corregidor of the same province, accompanied with 97 Spaniards, offered violently to arrest, and was defeated of his purpose and brought prisoner into England.

IT is not unknown unto the world what danger our English ships have lately escaped, how sharply they have been intreated, and how hardly they have been assaulted: so that the valiancy of those that managed them is worthy remembrance. And therefore in respect of the courageous attempt and valiant enterprise of the ship called the *Primrose* of London, which hath obtained renown, I have taken in hand to publish the truth thereof, to the intent that it may be generally known to the rest of the English ships that, by the good example of this, the rest may in time of extremity adventure to do the like; to the honour of the realm and the perpetual remembrance of themselves. The manner whereof was as followeth.

Upon Wednesday, being the six and twentieth day of May, 1585, the ship called the *Primrose*, being of one hundred and fifty tons, lying without the Bay of Bilbao, having been there two days, there came a Spanish pinnace to them wherein was the Corregidor and six others with him. These came aboard the *Primrose*, seeming to be merchants of Biscay or such like, bringing cherries with them, and spake very friendly to the master of the ship, whose name was Foster, and he in courteous wise bade them welcome, making them the best cheer that he could with beer, beef and biscuit, wherewith that ship was well furnished. And while they were thus in banqueting with the master four of the seven departed in the said pinnace and went back again to Bilbao: the other three stayed and were very pleasant for the time. But Master Foster, misdoubting some danger, secretly gave speech that he was doubtful of these men, what their intent was; nevertheless he said nothing, nor seemed in any outward wise to mistrust them at all.

Forthwith there came a ship-boat wherein were seventy persons, being merchants and such like of Biscay: and besides this boat there came also the pinnace which before had brought the other three, in which pinnace there came four and twenty, as the Spaniards themselves since confessed. These made towards the *Primrose*, and being come thither there came aboard the Corregidor with three or four of his men: but Master Foster, seeing this great multitude, desired that there might no more come aboard but that the rest should stay in their boats, which was granted. Nevertheless they took small heed of these words, for on a sudden they came forth of the boat, entering the ship, every Spaniard taking him to his rapier which they brought in the boat with other weapons, and a drum wherewith to triumph over them.

Thus did the Spaniards enter the ship, plunging in fiercely upon them, some planting themselves under the deck, some entering the cabins, and a multitude attending their prey. Then the Corregidor, having an officer with him which bare a white wand in his hand, said to the master of the ship, 'Yield yourself, for you are the King's prisoner'. Whereat the Master said to his men, 'We are betrayed'. Then some of them set daggers to his breast and seemed in furious manner as though they would have slain him, meaning nothing less than to do any such act, for all that they sought was to bring him and his men safe alive to shore. Whereat the Master was amazed, and his men greatly discomfited to see themselves ready to be conveyed even to the slaughter: notwithstanding some of them, respecting the danger of the Master and seeing how with themselves there was no way but present death if they were once landed among the Spaniards, they resolved themselves either to defend the master and generally to shun that danger, or else to die and be buried in the midst of the sea, rather than to suffer themselves to come unto the tormentors' hands.

And therefore in very bold and manly sort some took them to their javelins, lances, boar-spears, and shot, which they had set in readiness before, and having five calivers ready charged, which was all the small shot they had, those that were under the hatches or the grate did shoot up at the Spaniards that were over their heads, which shot so amazed the Spaniards on the sudden as they could hardly tell which way to escape the danger, fearing this their small shot to be of greater number than it was. Others, in very manlike sort, dealt about among them, showing themselves of that courage with boar-spears and lances that they dismayed at every stroke two or three Spaniards. Then some of them desired the master to command his men to cease and hold their hands, but he answered that such was the courage of the English nation in defence of their own lives that they would slay them and him also: and therefore it lay not in him to do it.

Now did their blood run about the ship in great quantity, some of them being shot in between the legs, the bullets issuing forth at their breasts, some cut in the head, some thrust into the body, and many of them very sore wounded, so that they came not so fast in on the one side, but now they tumbled as fast overboard on both sides with their weapons in their hands, some falling into the sea, and some getting into their boats, making haste towards the city. And this is to be noted, that although they came very thick thither there returned but a small company of them, neither is it known as yet how many of them were slain or drowned. Only one Englishman was then slain, whose name was John Tristram, and six other hurt. It was great pity to behold how the Spaniards lay swimming in the sea and were not able to save their lives. Four of them, taking hold of the ship, were for pity's sake taken up again by Master Foster and his men, not knowing what they were. All the Spaniards' bosoms were stuffed with paper to defend them from shot, and these four, having some wounds, were dressed by the surgeon of the ship. One of them was the Corregidor himself, who is Governor of a hundred towns and cities in Spain, his living by his office being better than six hundred pound yearly. This skirmish happened in the evening about six of the clock, after they had laden twenty ton of goods and better out of the said ship; which goods were delivered by two of the same ship, whose names were John Burrell and John Brodbanke, who, being on shore, were apprehended and stayed.

After this valiant enterprise of eight and twenty Englishmen against 97 Spaniards they saw it was in vain for them to stay and therefore set up sails, and by God's providence avoided all danger, brought home the rest of their goods, and came thence with all expedition: and (God be thanked) arrived safely in England near London on Wednesday, being the 8th day of June, 1585. In which their return to England the Spaniards that they brought with them offered five hundred crowns to be set on shore in any place: which, seeing the master would not do, they were content to be ruled by him and his company and craved mercy at their hands. And after Master Foster demanded why they came in such sort to betray and destroy them, the Corregidor answered that it was not done only of themselves but by the commandment of the King himself; and calling for his hose, which were wet, did pluck forth the King's Commission, by which he was authorized to do all that he did.★

★ The translation of the Corregidor's commission is included in the original but is here omitted.

THREE VOYAGES TO THE NORTH-WEST

John Davis

The disastrous bursting of Frobisher's north sea bubble by no means ended the quest for the North-west Passage. In 1585 Adrian Gilbert, Sir Humphrey's brother, obtained a patent to continue the search, which gave him and his associates (Walsingham and Raleigh among them) the monopoly of any trade which might result. A London merchant, William Sanderson, put up most of the money and Davis was given command of the ships.

John Davis of Dartmouth is the least known of the great Elizabethan sea-captains; he had no flair for self-advertisement or for making money, no sensational career as a freebooter along the Spanish Main. But he was probably the most skilful English navigator of his time, with a disinterested scientific devotion to navigation and exploration which is shown in his writings as well as his achievements. Despite his inadequate resources he did more than any of his predecessors towards the accurate mapping of the Arctic north-west. The war with Spain cut short his explorations. Then he took part in ill-fated expeditions towards the east. He was killed by pirates near Singapore in 1605.

The search for the North-west Passage continued, sometimes tragically, and without success until the passage was made by the great Norwegian explorer, Roald Amundsen, in 1903–5, when his ship spent two winters frozen in the Arctic ice.

A report of Master John Davis of his three voyages made for the discovery of the North-west Passage, taken out of a treatise of his entitled, The World's Hydrographical Description.

Now there only resteth the north parts of America, upon which coast myself have had most experience of any in our age: for thrice I was that way employed for the discovery of this notable passage by the honourable care and some charge of Sir Francis Walsingham, knight, Principal Secretary to Her Majesty, with whom divers noble men and worshipful merchants of London joined in purse and willingness for the furtherance of that attempt, but when His Honour died the voyage was friendless, and men's minds alienated from adventuring therein.

In my first voyage [in 1585], not experienced of the nature of those climates and having no direction either by chart, globe, or other certain relation in what altitude that passage was to be searched, I shaped a northerly course and so sought the same toward the south, and in that my northerly course I fell upon the shore which in ancient time was called Greenland, five hundred leagues distant from the Durseys west north-west northerly, the land being very high and full of mighty mountains all covered with snow, no view of wood, grass or earth to be seen, and the shore two leagues off into the sea so full of ice as that no shipping could by any means come near the same. The loathsome view of the shore and irksome noise of the ice was such as that it bred strange conceits among us, so that we supposed the place to be waste

and void of any sensible or vegetable creatures, whereupon I called the same Desolation. So, coasting this shore towards the south in the latitude of sixty degrees I found it to trend towards the west; I still followed the leading thereof in the same height, and after fifty or sixty leagues it failed and lay directly north, which I still followed, and in thirty leagues sailing upon the west side of this coast, by me named Desolation, we were past all the ice and found many green and pleasant isles bordering upon the shore, but the hills of the main were still covered with great quantities of snow.

I brought my ship among those isles and there moored to refresh ourselves in our weary travel, in the latitude of sixty-four degrees or thereabout. The people of the country, having espied our ships, came down unto us in their canoes, and holding up their right hand to the sun and crying 'yliaout', would strike their breasts: we doing the like the people came aboard our ships, men of good stature, unbearded, small-eyed and of tractable conditions, by whom, as signs would permit, we understood that towards the north and west there was a great sea. And using the people with kindness in giving them nails and knives, which of all things they most desired, we departed, and finding the sea free from ice, supposing ourselves to be past all danger, we shaped our course west north-west thinking thereby to pass for China. But in the latitude of sixty-six degrees we fell with another shore, and there found another passage of twenty leagues broad directly west into the same which we supposed to be our hoped strait. We entered into the same thirty or forty leagues, finding it neither to widen nor straighten. Then considering that the year was spent (for this was the fine of August) not knowing the length of the strait and dangers thereof, we took it our best course to return with notice of our good success for this small time of search.

And so returning in a sharp fret of westerly winds, the 29th of September [1585] we arrived at Dartmouth. And acquainting Master Secretary Walsingham, with the rest of the honourable and worshipful Adventurers, of all our proceedings, I was appointed again the second year [1586] to search the bottom of this strait because by all likelihood it was the place and passage by us laboured for.

In this second attempt the merchants of Exeter and other places of the West became Adventurers in the action, so that being sufficiently furnished for six months, and having direction to search these straits until we found the same to fall into another sea upon the west side of this part of America, we should again return; for then it was not to be doubted but shipping with trade might safely be conveyed to China and the parts of Asia. We departed from Dartmouth, and arriving upon the south part of the coast of Desolation coasted the same upon his west shore to the latitude of sixty-six degrees, and there anchored among the isles bordering upon the same where we refreshed ourselves. The people of this place came likewise unto us, by whom I understood through their signs that towards the north the sea was large.

At this place the chief ship whereupon I trusted, called the *Mermaid of Dartmouth*, found many occasions of discontentment, and, being unwilling to proceed, she there forsook me. Then, considering how I had given my faith and most constant promise to my Worshipful good friend, Master William Sanderson, who of all men was the greatest adventurer in that action and took such care for the performance thereof that he hath to my knowledge at one time disbursed as much money as any five others whatsoever out of his own purse, when some of the company have been slack in giving in their adventure, and also knowing that I should lose the favour of Master Secretary Walsingham if I should shrink from his direction, in one small bark of 30 tons, whereof Master Sanderson was owner, alone without further company I proceeded on my voyage and, arriving at these straits, followed the same 80 leagues until I came among many islands, where the water did ebb and flow six fathoms upright, and where there had been great trade of people to make train. But by such things as there we found we knew that they were not Christians of Europe that had used that trade.

In fine, by searching with our boat we found small hope to pass any further that way, and therefore recovered the sea and coasted the shore towards the south, and in so doing (for it was too late to search towards the north) we found another great inlet near 40 leagues broad where the water entered in with violent swiftness. This we also thought might be a passage; for no doubt the north parts of America are all islands by aught that I could perceive therein. But because I was alone in a small bark of thirty tons, and the year spent, I entered not into the same for it was now the seventh of September [1586], but coasting the shore towards the south we saw an incredible number of birds.

Having divers fishermen aboard our bark they all concluded that there was a great school of fish. We, being unprovided of fishing furniture, with a long spike nail made a hook and fastened the same to one of our sounding lines. Before the bait was changed we took more than forty great cods, the fish swimming so abundantly thick about our bark as is incredible to be reported: of which, with a small portion of salt that we had, we preserved some thirty couple, or thereabouts, and so returned for England. And having reported to Master Secretary Walsingham the whole success of this attempt he commanded me to present unto the most honourable Lord High Treasurer of England some part of that fish: which when His Lordship saw and heard at large the relation of this second attempt I received favourable countenance from his honour, advising me to prosecute the action, of which his Lordship conceived a very good opinion.

The next year, although divers of the adventurers fell from the action, as all the western merchants and most of those in London, yet some of the adventurers, both honourable and worshipful, continued their willing favour and charge, so that by this means the next year two ships were appointed for the fishing and one pinnace for the discovery.

Departing from Dartmouth [in 1587], through God's merciful favour, I arrived at the place of fishing, and there according to my direction I left the two ships to follow that business, taking their faithful promise not to depart until my return unto them, which should be in the fine of August. And so in the bark I proceeded for the discovery. But after my departure in sixteen days the two ships had finished their voyage, and so presently departed for England without regard of their promise.

Myself, not distrusting any such hard measure, proceeded for the discovery, and followed my course in the free and open sea between north and north-west to the latitude of 67 degrees; and there I might see America west from me and Greenland, which I called Desolation, east. Then when I saw the land of both sides I began to distrust it would prove but a gulf. Notwithstanding, desirous to know the full certainty I proceeded, and in 68 degrees the passage enlarged so that I could not see the western shore. Thus I continued to the latitude of 73 degrees in a great sea, free from ice, coasting the western shore of Desolation.

The people came continually rowing out unto me in their canoes, twenty, forty, and one hundred at a time, and would give me fishes dried, salmon, salmon peal, cod, capelin, lump, stone-bass and such like, besides divers kinds of birds, as partridge, pheasant, gulls, sea birds and other kinds of flesh. I still laboured by signs to know from them what they knew of any sea toward the north; they still made signs of a great sea as we understood them.

Then I departed from that coast, thinking to discover the north parts of America; and after I had sailed towards the west 40 leagues I fell upon a great bank of ice: the wind being north and blew much, I was constrained to coast the same toward the south, not seeing any shore west from me, neither was there any ice towards the north, but a great sea, free, large, very salt and blue, and of an unsearchable depth. So coasting towards the south I came to the place where I left the ships to fish, but found them not. Then being forsaken and left in this distress, referring myself to the merciful providence of God, I shaped my course for England and, unhoped for of any, God alone relieving me, I arrived at Dartmouth.

By this last discovery it seemed most manifest that the passage was free and without impediment toward the north: but by reason of the Spanish fleet and unfortunate time of Master Secretary's death, the voyage was omitted and never sithens attempted. The cause why I use this particular relation of all my proceedings for this discovery is to stay this objection, why hath not Davis discovered this passage, being thrice that ways employed?

How far I proceeded and in what form this discovery lieth doth appear upon the globe which Master Sanderson to his very great charge hath published, for the which he deserveth great favour and commendations.

THE FOURTH VOYAGE TO VIRGINIA

Anonymous

On receiving such an encouraging report from Barlowe and Amadas, Raleigh sent an expedition to establish a colony, and as he could not go himself Sir Richard Grenville took command. He left the colonists on Roanoke island, and promised to return with supplies in the following year. But the Indians soon proved hostile to permanent settlers, and life was much more difficult than they had expected. When Drake visited Roanoke in 1586, on his return from his great raid on the Caribbean, the settlers persuaded him to take them back to England and Grenville arrived three weeks later to find them all gone. Next year Raleigh made the second attempt, which is described in the following narrative.

The fourth voyage made to Virginia with three ships, in the year 1587, wherein was transported the second colony.

IN the year of Our Lord 1587 Sir Walter Raleigh, intending to persevere in the planting of his country of Virginia, prepared a new colony of one hundred and fifty men to be sent thither, under the charge of John White, whom he appointed Governor, and also appointed unto him twelve assistants unto whom he gave a Charter and incorporated them by the name of Governor and Assistants of the City of Raleigh in Virginia.

April. Our fleet, being in number three sail, viz. the admiral, a ship of one hundred and twenty tons, a fly-boat, and a pinnace, departed the six and twentieth of April from Portsmouth, and the same day came to an anchor at the Cowes in the Isle of Wight, where we stayed eight days.

May. The fifth of May, at nine of the clock at night, we came to Plymouth, where we remained the space of two days.

The 8th we weighed anchor at Plymouth and departed thence for Virginia.

The 16th Simon Ferdinando, Master of our admiral, lewdly forsook our fly-boat, leaving her distressed in the Bay of Portugal.

June. The 19th we fell with Dominica, and the same evening we sailed between it and Guadaloupe: the 21st the fly-boat also fell with Dominica.

The 22nd we came to an anchor at an island called Santa Cruz, where all the planters were set on land, staying there till the 25th of the same month. At our first landing on this island some of our women and men, by eating a small fruit like green apples, were fearfully troubled with a sudden burning in their mouths, and swelling of their tongues so big that some of them could not speak. Also a child by sucking one of those women's breasts had at that instant his mouth set on such a burning that it was strange to see how the infant was tormented for the time: but after 24 hours it ware away of itself.

Also the first night of our being on this island we took five great tortoises, some of them of such bigness that sixteen of our strongest men were tired with carrying of one of them but from the seaside to our cabins. In this island we found no watering place but a standing pond, the water whereof was so evil that many of our company fell sick with drinking thereof; and as many as did but wash their faces with that water, in the morning before the sun had drawn away the corruption, their faces did so burn and swell that their eyes were shut up and could not see in five or six days, or longer.

The second day of our abode there we sent forth some of our men to search the island for fresh water, three one way and two another way. The Governor also, with six others, went up to the top of an high hill to view the island but could perceive no sign of any men, or beasts, nor any goodness, but parrots and trees of guiacum. Returning back to our cabins another way he found in the descent of a hill certain pot-sherds of savage making, made of the earth of that island; whereupon it was judged that this island was inhabited with savages, though Ferdinando had told us for certain the contrary. The same day at night the rest of our company very late returned to the Governor. The one company affirmed that they had seen in a valley eleven savages and divers houses half a mile distant from the steep or top of the hill where they stayed. The other company had found running out of a high rock a very fair spring of water, whereof they brought three bottles to the company, for before that time we drank the stinking water of the pond.

The same second day, at night, Captain Stafford, with the pinnace, departed from our fleet riding at Santa Cruz to an island, called Beak, lying near S. John, being so directed by Ferdinando, who assured him he should there find great plenty of sheep. The next day at night our planters left Santa Cruz and came all aboard, and the next morning after, being the 25th of June, we weighed anchor and departed from Santa Cruz.

The seven and twentieth we came to anchor at Cottea where we found the pinnace riding at our coming.

The 28th we weighed anchor at Cottea, and presently came to anchor at S. John's in Mosquitoes Bay, where we spent three days unprofitable in taking in fresh water, spending in the meantime more beer than the quantity of the water came unto.

July. The first day we weighed anchor at Mosquitoes Bay, where were left behind two Irishmen of our company, Darby Glaven and Denis Carrol, bearing along the coast of S. John's till evening, at which time we fell with Ross Bay. At this place Ferdinando had promised we should take in salt, and had caused us before to make and provide as many sacks for that purpose as we could. The Governor also, for that he understood there was a town in the bottom of the Bay not far from the salt hills, appointed thirty shot, ten pikes, and ten targets to man the pinnace, and to go aland for salt. Ferdinando, perceiving them in a readiness, sent to the Governor, using great persuasions with him not to take in salt there, saying that he knew not well whether the same were the place or not: also that if the pinnace went into the Bay she could not without great danger come back till the next day at night, and that if in the meantime any storm should rise the admiral were in danger to be cast away. Whilst he was thus persuading he caused the lead to be cast, and having craftily brought the ship in three fathoms and a half water he suddenly began to swear and tear God in pieces, dissembling great danger, crying to him at the helm, 'Bear up hard, bear up hard'. So we went off and were disappointed of our salt by his means.

The next day, sailing along the west end of S. John the Governor determined to go aland in S. German's Bay to gather young plants of oranges, pines, mammeas, and plantanos to set at Virginia, which we knew might easily be had for that they grow near the shore, and the places where they grew well known to the Governor and some of the planters. But our Simon denied it, saying he would come to an anchor at Hispaniola, and there land the Governor and some other of the assistants, with the pinnace, to see if he could speak with his friend, Alanson, of whom he hoped to be furnished both of cattle and all such things as we would have taken in at S. John; but he meant nothing less, as it plainly did appear to us afterwards.

The next day after, being the third of July, we saw Hispaniola and bare with the coast all that day, looking still when the pinnace should be prepared to go for the place where Ferdinando his friend, Alanson, was; but that day passed and we saw no preparation for landing in Hispaniola.

The fourth of July, sailing along the coast of Hispaniola until the next day at noon, and no preparation yet seen for the staying there, we having knowledge that we were past the place where Alanson dwelt and were come with Isabella. Hereupon Ferdinando was asked by the Governor whether he meant to speak with Alanson for the taking in of cattle and other things according to his promise, or not; but he answered that he was now past the place, and that Sir Walter Raleigh told him the French Ambassador certified him that the King of Spain had sent for Alanson into Spain; wherefore he thought him dead, and that it was to no purpose to touch there in any place at this voyage.

The next day we left sight of Hispaniola and haled off for Virginia, about four of the clock in the afternoon.

The sixth of July we came to the island Caicos, wherein Ferdinando said were two salt ponds, assuring us if they were dry we might find salt to shift with until the next supply. But it proved as true as finding of sheep at Baque. In this island, whilst Ferdinando solaced himself ashore with one of the company in part of the island, others spent the latter part of that day in other parts of the island, some to seek the salt ponds, some fowling, some hunting swans whereof we caught many. The next day early in the morning we weighed anchor, leaving Caicos with good hope that the first land that we saw next should be Virginia.

About the 16th of July we fell with the main of Virginia, which Simon Ferdinando took to be the island of Croatan, where we came to anchor and rode there two or three days; but finding himself deceived he weighed and bare along the coast, where in the night, had not Captain Stafford been more careful in looking out than our Simon Ferdinando, we had been all cast away upon the breach, called the Cape of Fear, for we were come within two cables' length upon it: such was the carelessness and ignorance of our Master.

The two and twentieth of July we arrived safe at Hatteras, where our ship and pinnace anchored. The Governor went aboard the pinnace, accompanied with forty of his best men, intending to pass up to Roanoke forthwith, hoping there to find those fifteen Englishmen which Sir Richard Grenville had left there the year before, with whom he meant to have conference concerning the state of the country and savages, meaning after he had so done to return again to the fleet and pass along the coast to the Bay of Chesapeake, where we intended to make our seat and fort, according to the charge given us among other directions in writing under the hand of Sir Walter Raleigh. But as soon as we were put with our pinnace from the ship a gentleman by the means of Ferdinando, who was appointed to return for England, called to the sailors in the pinnace, charging them not to bring any of the planters back again but to leave them in the island, except the Governor and two or three such as he approved, saying that the summer was far spent, wherefore he would land all the planters in no other place. Unto this were all the sailors, both in the pinnace and ship, persuaded by the Master, wherefore it booted not the Governor to contend with them, but passed to Roanoke, and the same night at sunset went aland on the island in the place where our fifteen men were left, but we found none of them nor any sign that they had been there, saving only we found the bones of one of those fifteen which the savages had slain long before.

The three and twentieth of July the Governor, with divers of his company, walked to the north end of the island where Master Ralph Lane had his fort, with sundry necessary and decent dwelling houses made by his men about it the year before, where we hoped to find some signs or certain knowledge of our fifteen men. When we came thither we found the fort razed down but all the houses standing unhurt, saving that the nether rooms of them and also of the fort were overgrown with melons of divers sorts, and deer within them feeding on those melons. So we returned to our company without hope of ever seeing any of the fifteen men living.

The same day, order was given that every man should be employed for the repairing of those houses which we found standing, and also to make other new cottages for such as should need.

The 25th our flyboat and the rest of our planters arrived all safe at Hatteras, to the great joy and comfort of the whole company. But the Master of our admiral, Ferdinando, grieved greatly at their safe coming; for he purposely left them in the Bay of Portugal and stole away from them in the night, hoping that the Master thereof, whose name was Edward Spicer, for that he never had been in Virginia would hardly find the place, or else being left in so dangerous a place as that was by means of so many men of war as at that time were abroad they should surely be taken, or slain: but God disappointed his wicked pretences.

The eight and twentieth, George Howe, one of our twelve Assistants, was slain by divers savages which were come over to Roanoke, either of purpose to espy our company and what number we were, or else to hunt deer whereof were many in the island. These savages being secretly hidden among high reeds, where oftentimes they find the deer asleep and so kill them, espied our man wading in the water alone, almost naked, without any weapon save only a small forked stick, catching crabs therewithal, and also being strayed two miles from his company, and shot at him in the water where they gave him sixteen wounds with their arrows. And after they had slain him with their wooden swords they beat his head in pieces and fled over the water to the main.

On the thirtieth of July Master Stafford and twenty of our men passed by water to the island of Croatan with Manteo, who had his mother and many of his kindred dwelling in that island, of whom we hoped to understand some news of our fifteen men, but especially to learn the disposition of the people of the country towards us and to renew our old friendship with them. At our first landing they seemed as though they would fight with us; but perceiving us begin to march with our shot towards them they turned their backs and fled. Then Manteo, their countryman, called to them in their own language, whom as soon as they heard they returned and threw away their bows and arrows, and some of them came unto us, embracing and entertaining us friendly, desiring us not to gather or spill any of their corn for that they had but little. We answered them that neither their corn nor any other thing of theirs should be diminished by any of us, and that our coming was only to renew the old love that was between us and them at the first, and to live with them as brethren and friends; which answer seemed to please them well, wherefore they requested us to walk up to their town, who there feasted us after their manner, and desired us earnestly that there might be some token or badge given them of us, whereby we might know them to be our friends when we met them anywhere out of the town or island. They told us further that for want of some such badge divers of them were hurt the year before, being found out of the island by Master Lane his company, whereof they showed us one which at that very instant lay lame, and had lieu of that hurt ever since; but they said they knew our men mistook them and hurt them instead of Wingino's men, wherefore they held us excused.

August. The next day we had conference further with them concerning the people of Secotan, Aquascogoc and Pomeiok, willing them of Croatan to certify the people of those towns that if they would accept our friendship we would willingly receive them again, and that all unfriendly dealings past on both parts should be utterly forgiven and forgotten. To this the chief men of Croatan answered that they would gladly do the best they could, and within seven days bring the Wiroances and Chief Governors of those towns with them to our Governor at Roanoke, or their answer. We also understood of the men of Croatan that our man, Master Howe, was slain by the remnant of Wingino's men dwelling then at Dasamonguepeuk, with whom Wanchese kept company. And also we understood by them of Croatan how that the fifteen Englishmen left at Roanoke the year before by Sir Richard Grenville were suddenly set upon by thirty of the men of Secota, Aquascogoc and Dasamonguepeuk in manner following.

They conveyed themselves secretly behind the trees near the houses where our men carelessly lived: and having perceived that of those fifteen they could see but eleven only, two of those savages appeared to the eleven Englishmen, calling to them by friendly signs that but two of their chiefest men should come unarmed to speak with those two savages, who seemed also to be unarmed. Wherefore two of the chiefest of our Englishmen went gladly to them; but whilst one of those savages traitorously embraced one of our men the other with his sword of wood, which he had secretly hidden under his mantle, struck him on the head and slew him, and presently the other eight and twenty savages showed themselves. The other Englishman, perceiving this, fled to his company, whom the savages pursued with their bows and arrows so fast that the Englishmen were forced to take the house wherein all their victual and weapons were: but the savages forthwith set the same on fire, by means whereof our men were forced to take up such weapons as came first to hand and without order to run forth among the savages, with whom they skirmished above an hour. In this skirmish another of our men was shot into the mouth with an arrow, where he died: and also one of the savages was shot into the side by one of our men with a wild fire arrow, whereof he died presently.

The place where they fought was of great advantage to the savages by means of the thick trees behind which the savages through their nimbleness defended themselves, and so offended our men with their arrows that our men, being some of them hurt, retired fighting to the water side where their boat lay, with which they fled towards Hatteras. By that time they had rowed but a quarter of a mile they espied their four fellows coming from a creek thereby, where they had been to fetch oysters. These four they received into their boat, leaving Roanoke, and landed on a little island on the right hand of our entrance into the harbour of Hatteras, where they remained awhile but afterward departed, whither as yet we know not.

Having now sufficiently despatched our business at Croatan the same day we departed friendly, taking our leave, and came aboard the fleet at Hatteras.

The eighth of August, the Governor having long expected the coming of the Wiroances of Pomeiok, Aquascogoc, Secota and Dasamonguepeuk, seeing that the seven days were past within which they promised to come in or to send their answers by the men of Croatan, and no tidings of them heard, being certainly also informed by those men of Croatan that the remnant of Wingina his men which were left alive, who dwelt at Dasamonquepeuk, were they which had slain George Howe and were also at the driving of our eleven Englishmen from Roanoke, he thought to defer the revenge thereof no longer. Wherefore the same night, about midnight, he passed over the water, accompanied with Captain Stafford and twenty-four men, whereof Manteo was one whom we took with us to be our guide to the place where those Savages dwelt, where he behaved himself toward us as a most faithful Englishman.

The next day, being the 9th of August, in the morning so early that it was yet dark, we landed near the dwelling place of our enemies and very secretly conveyed ourselves through the woods to that side where we had their houses between us and the water; and having espied their fire, and some sitting about it, we presently set on them. The miserable souls, herewith amazed, fled into a place of thick reeds, growing fast by, where our men perceiving them shot one of them through the body with a bullet, and therewith we entered the reeds, among which we hoped to acquit their evil doing towards us, but we were deceived, for those savages were our friends and were come from Croatan to gather the corn and fruit of that place, because they understood our enemies were fled immediately after they had slain George Howe, and for haste had left all their corn, tobacco and pompions standing in such sort that all had been devoured of the birds and deer if it had not been gathered in time. But they had like to have paid dearly for it; for it was so dark that they being naked, and their men and women apparelled all so like others, we knew not but that they were all men; and if that one of them which was a Wiroance's wife had not had a child at her back she had been slain instead of a man, and as hap was another savage knew Master Stafford and ran to him, calling him by his name, whereby he was saved. Finding ourselves thus disappointed of our purpose we gathered all the corn, peas, pompions and tobacco that we found ripe, leaving the rest unspoiled, and took Menatoan his wife, with the young child, and the other savages with us over the water to Roanoke. Although the mistaking of these savages somewhat grieved Manteo, yet he imputed their harm to their own folly, saying to them that if their Wiroances had kept their promise in coming to the Governor at the day appointed they had not known that mischance.

The 13th of August our savage, Manteo, by the commandment of Sir Walter Raleigh, was christened in Roanoke and called Lord thereof, and of Dasamonguepeuk, in reward of his faithful service.

The 18th Eleanor, daughter to the Governor and wife to Ananias Dare, one of the Assistants, was delivered of a daughter in Roanoke, and the same was christened there the Sunday following, and because this child was the first Christian born in Virginia she was named Virginia. By this time our ships had unladen the goods and victuals of the planters and began to take in wood and fresh water, and to new caulk and trim them for England. The planters also prepared their letters and tokens to send back into England.

Our two ships, the *Lion* and the *Flyboat*, almost ready to depart, the 21st of August there arose such a tempest at northeast that our admiral, then riding out of the harbour, was forced to cut his cables and put to sea, where he lay beating off and on six days before he could come to us again, so that we feared he had been cast away, and the rather for that at the time that the storm took them the most and best of their sailors were left aland.

At this time some controversies arose between the Governor and Assistants about choosing two out of the twelve Assistants which should go back as factors for the company into England, for every one of them refused, save only one, which all other thought not sufficient. But at length, by much persuading of the Governor, Christopher Cooper only agreed to go for England: but the next day, through the persuasion of divers of his familiar friends, he changed his mind, so that now the matter stood as at the first.

The next day, the 22nd of August, the whole company, both of the Assistants and planters, came to the Governor, and with one voice requested him to return himself into England for the better and sooner obtaining of supplies and other necessaries for them; but he refused it and alleged many sufficient causes why he would not. The one was that he could not so suddenly return back again without his great discredit, leaving the action and so many whom he partly had procured through his persuasions to leave their native country and undertake that voyage, and that some enemies to him and the action, at his return into England, would not spare to slander falsely both him and the action by saying he went to Virginia but politically, and to no other end but to lead so many into a country in which he never meant to stay himself and there to leave them behind him. Also he alleged that seeing they intended to remove 50 miles further up into the main presently, he being then absent, his stuff and goods might be both spoiled and most of them pilfered away in the carriage, so that at his return he should be either forced to provide himself of all such things again, or else at his coming again to Virginia find himself utterly unfurnished, whereof already he had found some proof, being but once from them but three days. Wherefore he concluded that he would not go himself.

The next day, not only the Assistants but divers others, as well women as men, began to renew their requests to the Governor again to take upon him to return into England for the supply and dispatch of all such things as there were to be done, promising to make him their bond under all their hands and seals for the safe preserving of all his goods for him at his return to Virginia, so that if any part thereof were spoiled or lost they would see it restored to him, or his assigns, whensoever the same should be missed and demanded: which bond, with a testimony under their hands and seals they forthwith made and delivered into his hands. The copy of the testimony I thought good to set down:

May it please you, her Majesty's subjects of England, we your friends and countrymen, the planters in Virginia, do by these presents let you and every of you to understand that for the present and speedy supply of certain our known and apparent lacks and needs, most requisite and necessary for the good and happy planting of us, or any other in this land of Virginia, we all of one mind and consent have most earnestly entreated and incessantly requested John White, Governor of the planters in Virginia, to pass into England for the better and more assured help, and setting forward of the foresaid supplies: and knowing assuredly that he both can best and will labour and take pains in that behalf for us all, and he not once but often refusing it, for our sakes and for the honour and maintenance of the action, hath at last, though much against his will, through our importunacy yielded to leave his government and all his goods among us, and himself in all our behalfs to pass into England, of whose knowledge and fidelity in handling this matter, as all others, we do assure ourselves by these presents, and will you to give all credit thereunto, the 25th of August, 1587.

The Governor, being at the last through their extreme entreating constrained to return into England, having then but half a day's respite to prepare himself for the same, departed from Roanoke the seven and twentieth of August in the morning, and the same day about midnight came aboard the flyboat, who already had weighed anchor, and rode without the bar, the admiral riding by them, who but the same morning was newly come thither again. The same day both the ships weighed anchor and set sail for England. At this weighing their anchors twelve of the men which were in the flyboat were thrown from the capstan, which by means of a bar and brake came so fast about upon them that the other two bars thereof struck and hurt most of them so sore that some of them never recovered it. Nevertheless they assayed presently again to weigh their anchor, but being so weakened with the first fling they were not able to weigh it but were thrown down and hurt the second time. Wherefore having in all but fifteen men aboard, and most of them by this unfortunate beginning so bruised and hurt, they were forced to cut their cable and leese their anchor. Nevertheless, they kept company with the admiral until the seventeenth of September, at which time we fell with Corvo, and saw Flores.

September. The eighteenth, perceiving of all our fifteen men in the flyboat there remained but five which by means of the former mischance were able to stand to their labour, and that the admiral meant not to make any haste for England but to linger about the island of Terceira for purchase, the flyboat departed for England with letters, where we hoped by the help of God to arrive shortly. But by that time we had continued our course homeward about twenty days, having had sometimes scarce and variable winds, our fresh water also by leaking almost consumed, there arose a storm at northeast, which for six days ceased not to blow so exceeding that we were driven further in those six than we could recover in thirteen days; in which time others of our sailors began to fall very sick and two of them died. The weather also continued so close that our Master sometimes in four days together could see neither sun nor star, and all the beverage we could make with stinking water, dregs of beer, and lees of wine which remained, was but three gallons, and therefore now we expected nothing but famine to perish at sea.

October. The 16th of October we made land but we knew not what land it was, bearing in with the same land at that day. About sunset we put into a harbour, where we found a hulk of Dublin, and a pinnace of Hampton riding, but we knew not as yet what place this was, neither had we any boat to go ashore until the pinnace sent off their boat to us with six or eight men, of whom we understood we were in Smerwick, in the west parts of Ireland. They also relieved us presently with fresh water, wine and other fresh meat.

The 18th the Governor and the Master rid to Dingenacush, five miles distant, to take order for the new victualling of our flyboat for England, and for relief of our sick and hurt men, but within four days after, the boatswain, the steward, and the boatswain's mate died aboard the flyboat, and the 28th the Master's mate and two of our chief sailors were brought sick to Dingen.

November. The first the Governor shipped himself in a ship called the *Monkey*, which at that time was ready to put to sea from Dingen for England, leaving the flyboat and all his company in Ireland. The same day we set sail, and on the third day we fell with the north side of the Land's End, and were shut up the Severn, but the next day we doubled the same for Mounts Bay.

The 5th the Governor landed in England at Martasew, near Saint Michael's Mount in Cornwall.

The 8th we arrived at Hampton, where we understood that our consort, the admiral, was come to Portsmouth and had been there three weeks before: and also that Ferdinando, the Master, with all his company, were not only come home without any purchase, but also in such weakness by sickness, and death of their chiefest men, that they were scarce able to bring their ship into harbour, but were forced to let fall anchor without, which they could not weigh again, but might all have perished there if a small bark, by great hap, had not come to them to help them. The names of the chief men that died are these;

Roger Large, John Matthew, Thomas Smith, and some other sailors whose names I knew not at the writing hereof.   An. Dom. 1587.

The Armada campaign prevented John White from returning to Virginia until 1591. The colonists had all vanished without trace, and their fate was never known. Raleigh made no further attempt, and Virginia was not permanently colonised until 1607.

DRAKE'S RAID ON CADIZ

Anonymous

Sir Francis Drake had already left behind him his brilliant career as a lone privateer, or pirate. On his devastating raid on the West Indies in 1585–6, and all his later voyages, he was a naval officer commanding powerful fleets. But, except in battle with the Armada, he was still expected to bring home a profit, for the expeditions, however official, were always financed by private subscribers. The Queen contributed by lending her ships, and she too expected a profit. For Cadiz, London privateering merchants supplied eight well-armed ships and two pinnaces, which they had fitted out to raid Spanish shipping, and they were a valuable addition to the fleet, but they were half-independent and left Drake as soon as it suited them knowing that they would get their share of all the plunder.

The ships which Philip was gathering were still scattered among various Spanish and Portuguese harbours. Drake's orders were to destroy as many as he could, to disrupt the preparations in general, and to take valuable prizes.

A brief relation of the notable service performed by Sir Francis Drake upon the Spanish Fleet prepared in the Road of Cadiz: and of his destroying of 100 sail of barks; passing from thence all along the coast to Cape Sacre, where also he took certain forts: and so to the mouth of the River of Lisbon, and thence crossing over to the isle of Saint Michael surprised a mighty carrack, called the *Saint Philip*, coming out of the East India, which was the first of that kind that ever was seen in England: performed in the year 1587.

HER MAJESTY, being informed of a mighty preparation by sea begun in Spain for the invasion of England, by good advice of her grave and prudent Council thought it expedient to prevent the same. Whereupon she caused a fleet of some 30 sails to be rigged and furnished with all things necessary. Over that fleet she appointed General Sir Francis Drake (of whose manifold former good services she had sufficient proof), to whom she caused four ships of her Navy Royal to be delivered, to wit, the *Bonaventure* wherein himself went as General, the *Lion*, under the conduct of Master William Borough,

Sir Francis Drake: engraving by Jodocus Hondius, *c.* 1583

Controller of the Navy, the *Dreadnought*, under the command of Master Thomas Fenner, and the *Rainbow*, Captain whereof was Master Henry Bellingham: unto which four ships two of her pinnaces were appointed as handmaids. There were also added unto this fleet certain tall ships of the City of London, of whose especial good service the General made particular mention in his private letters directed to Her Majesty. This fleet set sail from the Sound of Plymouth in the month of April towards the coast of Spain.

The 16th of the said month we met in the latitude of 40 degrees with two ships of Middlesbrough which came from Cadiz; by which we understood that there was great store of warlike provision at Cadiz and thereabout ready to come for Lisbon. Upon this information our General, with all speed possible, bending himself thither to cut off their said forces and provisions, upon the 19th of April entered with his fleet into the harbour of Cadiz; where at our first entering we were assailed over against the town by six galleys, which notwithstanding in short time retired under their fortress.*

There were in the road 60 ships and divers other small vessels under the fortress: there fled about 20 French ships to Porto Real, and some small Spanish vessels that might pass the shoals. At our first coming in we sunk with our shot a ship of Ragusa of a thousand tons, furnished with forty pieces of brass and very richly laden. There came two galleys more from St Maryport and two from Porto Real, which shot freely at us but altogether in vain: for they went away with the blows well beaten for their pains.

Before night we had taken thirty of the said ships and became masters of the road in despite of the galleys, which were glad to retire them under the Fort: in the number of which ships there was one new ship of an extraordinary hugeness in burden above 1,200 tons,† belonging to the Marquis of Santa Cruz, being at that instant High Admiral of Spain. Five of them were great ships of Biscay, whereof four we fired as they were taking in the King's provision of victuals for the furnishing of his fleet at Lisbon: the fifth, being a ship about 1,000 tons in burden, laden with iron spikes, nails, iron hoops, horse-shoes,

---

* This was an epoch-making engagement. For many centuries the galley had been, in quiet waters, the most deadly warship afloat, and the invention of gunpowder had made little difference so long as ships were armed only with small guns intended to kill enemy crews. But the English ocean-going warships were now being armed with big guns, to sink an enemy before she could board. The reign of the galley was coming to an end.

† At dawn on the second day Drake himself led his pinnaces into the inner harbour, where lay the only Spanish warship, belonging to Santa Cruz, and where many other ships had taken refuge. The pinnaces destroyed the warship and many of the others.

and other like necessaries bound for the West Indies, we fired in like manner. Also we took a ship of 250 tons laden with wines for the King's provision which we carried out to the sea with us and there discharged the said wines for our own store, and afterward set her on fire. Moreover we took three flyboats of 300 tons apiece laden with biscuit, whereof one was half unladen by us in the harbour and there fired, and the other two we took in our company to the sea. Likewise there were fired by us ten other ships which were laden with wine, raisins, figs, oils, wheat, and suchlike. To conclude, the whole number of ships and barks (as we suppose) then burnt, sunk, and brought away with us, amounted to thirty at the least, being (in our judgment) about 10,000 tons of shipping.

There were in sight of us at Porto Real about 40 ships besides those that fled from Cadiz.

We found little ease during our abode there by reason of their continual shooting from the galleys, the fortresses, and from the shore, where continually at places convenient they planted new ordnance to offend us with; besides the inconvenience which we suffered from their ships which, when they could defend no longer, they set on fire to come among us. Whereupon when the flood came we were not a little troubled to defend us from their terrible fire, which nevertheless was a pleasant sight for us to behold because we were thereby eased of a great labour, which lay upon us day and night, in discharging the victuals and other provisions of the enemy. Thus by the assistance of the Almighty, and the invincible courage and industry of our General, this strange and happy enterprise was achieved in one day and two nights, to the great astonishment of the King of Spain, which bred such a corrosive in the heart of the Marquis of Santa Cruz, High Admiral of Spain, that he never enjoyed good day after, but within few months (as may justly be supposed) died of extreme grief and sorrow.

Thus having performed this notable service we came out of the road of Cadiz on the Friday morning, the 21st of the said month of April, with very small loss, not worth the mentioning.

After our departure ten of the galleys that were in the road came out, as it were in disdain of us, to make some pastime with their ordnance, at which time the wind scanted upon us, whereupon we cast about again and stood in with the shore and came to anchor within a league of the town; where the said galleys, for all their former bragging, at length suffered us to ride quietly.

We now have had experience of galley-fight: wherein I can assure you that only these four of Her Majesty's ships will make no account of twenty galleys if they may be alone and not busied to guard others.

There were never galleys that had better place and fitter opportunity for their advantage to fight with ships; but they were still forced to retire, we riding in a narrow gut, the place yielding no better, and driven to maintain the same until we had discharged and fired the ships, which could not conveniently be done but upon the flood, at which time they might drive clear off us.

Thus being victualled with bread and wine at the enemy's cost for divers months (besides the provisions that we brought from home) our General despatched Captain Cross into England with his letters, giving him further in charge to declare unto Her Majesty all the particularities of this our first enterprise.

After whose departure we shaped our course toward Cape Sagres, and in the way thither we took at several times of ships, barks, and caravels, well near an hundred, laden with hoops, galley-oars, pipe-staves, and other provisions of the King of Spain for the furnishing of his forces intended against England, all which we burned, having dealt favourably with the men and sent them on shore. We also spoiled and consumed all the fisher-boats and nets thereabouts to their great hindrance, and (as we suppose) to the utter overthrow of the rich fishing of their tunnies for the same year.

At length we came to the aforesaid Cape Sagres where we went on land; and the better to enjoy the benefit of the place and to ride in harbour at our pleasure we assailed the same castle and three other strongholds, which we took, some by force and some by surrender.

Thence we came before the haven of Lisbon, anchoring near unto Cascaes where the Marquis of Santa Cruz was with his galleys, who, seeing us chase his ships ashore and take and carry away his barks and caravels, was content to suffer us there quietly to tarry, and likewise to depart, and never charged us with one cannon-shot. And when our General sent him word that he was there, ready to exchange certain bullets with him, the Marquis refused his challenge, sending him word that he was not then ready for him, nor had any such commission from his King.

Our General, thus refused by the Marquis, and seeing no more good to be done in this place, thought it convenient to spend no longer time upon this coast: and therefore with consent of the chief of his company he shaped his course toward the isles of the Azores, and passing towards the isle of Saint Michael, within 20 or 30 leagues thereof, it was his good fortune to meet with a Portugal carrack called *Saint Philip*, being the same ship which in the voyage outward had carried the three Princes of Japan, that were in Europe, into the [East] Indies. This carrack without any great resistance he took, bestowing the people thereof in certain vessels well furnished with victuals and sending them courteously home into their country. And this was the first carrack that ever was taken coming forth of the East Indies, which the Portugals took for an evil sign because the ship bare the King's own name.

The riches of this prize* seemed so great unto the whole company (as in truth it was) that they assured themselves every man to have a sufficient reward for his travel: and thereupon they all resolved to return home for England; which they happily did, and arrived in Plymouth the same summer with their whole fleet and this rich booty, to their own profit and due commendation and to the great admiration of the whole kingdom.

And here by the way it is to be noted that the taking of this carrack wrought two extraordinary effects in England. First, that it taught others that carracks were no such bugs but that they might be taken (as since indeed it hath fallen out in the taking of the *Madre de Dios* [in 1592], and firing and sinking of others), and secondly, in acquainting the English nation more generally with the particularities of the exceeding riches and wealth of the East Indies: whereby themselves and their neighbours of Holland have been encouraged, being men as skilful in navigation and of no less courage than the Portugals, to share with them in the East Indies, where their strength is nothing so great as theretofore hath been supposed.

This account passes over in discreet silence Drake's violent quarrel with William Borough, his second in command. Borough questioned Drake's unconventional (but highly successful) tactics, and Drake, arrogant as ever, could not bear to be offered advice. He put Borough under arrest on his own ship, the Golden Lion, *which soon afterwards left the fleet and returned to England. Drake thereupon court martialled him in his absence and sentenced him to death for mutiny and desertion. But Borough had powerful friends at home who saved him.*

Apart from this Drake's conduct of the expedition was brilliantly successful. He had singed the King of Spain's beard, as he said himself. He had shaken Spanish morale, destroyed many ships, seriously disrupted the collection of supplies, made it more difficult and expensive for Philip to borrow the money which he needed to finance his preparations, and delayed the Armada until 1588. England had one more year in which to prepare.

* The cargo was officially valued in England at £114,000.

The Fireship attack on the Armada: contemporary painting by unknown artist

THE INVINCIBLE ARMADA

Emanuel van Meteran

There are many contemporary documents concerning the 'Invincible Armada', as the Spaniards called it, but no adequate account of it had been written in English when Hakluyt was editing his Voyages. *Van Meteran's narrative was a satisfactory choice and presumably Hakluyt translated it from the Latin himself. Van Meteran was a Dutchman living in London, a leading member of the Dutch Church in Austin Friars and a friend of both the Hakluyts.*

The two fleets were fairly evenly matched. The Spaniards mustered about 65 galleons and large ships, 32 small ships, 4 galleasses, and 4 galleys, besides storeships or 'hulks' and hospital ships; the English about 62 galleons and large ships and 43 small ships. There were about 19,000 soldiers, 8,000 sailors and 2,000 rowers (slaves) in the Spanish fleet, and the English numbered about 1,500 soldiers and 14,000 sailors. The spearheads of both fleets were the monarchs' naval ships, but the large fighting merchantmen were powerful auxiliaries. The Spanish ships were not larger, but the English often looked smaller because they had lower forecastles and more slender lines, which made them more 'nimble' in manoeuvre and able to sail closer to the wind. The finest ships engaged were the score of new galleons which Hawkins had built, the most efficient warships afloat, planned for the kind of battle which the English were determined to fight, a battle of ships against ships and not of floating forts full of soldiers who would fight hand to hand. The English had some advantage in guns, gunnery and mobility, but not in bravery.

The miraculous victory achieved by the English fleet, under the discreet and happy conduct of the Right Honourable, right prudent and valiant lord, the Lord Charles Howard, Lord High Admiral of England, etc., upon the Spanish huge armada, sent in the year 1588 for the invasion of England, together with the woeful and miserable success of the said armada afterward upon the coasts of Norway, of the Scottish western isles, of Spain, of France and of England, etc. Recorded in Latin by Emanuel Van Meteran in the fifteenth book of his History of the Low Countries.

HAVING in part declared the strange and wonderful events of the year eighty-eight, which hath been so long time foretold by ancient prophesies, we will now make relation of the most notable and great enterprise of all others which were in the foresaid year achieved in order as it was done. Which exploit (although in very deed it was not performed in any part of the Low Countries) was intended for their ruin and destruction. And it was the expedition which the Spanish King [Philip II], having a long time determined the same in his mind, and having consulted thereabout with the Pope, set forth and undertook against England and the Low Countries, to the end that he might subdue the realm of England and reduce it unto his Catholic religion, and by that means might be sufficiently revenged for the disgrace, contempt and dishonour which he (having thirty-four years before enforced them to the Pope's obedience)* had endured of the English nation, and for divers other injuries which had taken deep impression on his thoughts. And also for that he deemed this to be the most ready and direct course whereby he might recover his hereditary possession of the Low Countries, having restrained the inhabitants from sailing upon the coast of England, which verily, upon most weighty arguments and evident reasons, was thought would undoubtedly have come to pass considering the great abundance and store of all things necessary wherewith those men were furnished, which had the managing of that action committed unto them. But now let us describe the matter more particularly.

The Spanish King, having with small fruit and commodity for above twenty years together waged war against the Netherlanders, after deliberation with his counsellors thereabout, thought it most convenient to assault them once again by sea, which had been attempted sundry times heretofore but not with forces sufficient. Unto the which expedition it stood him now in hand to join great puissance as having the English people his professed enemies; whose island is so situate that it may either greatly help or hinder all such as sail into those parts. For which cause he thought good first of all to invade England, being persuaded by his Secretary Escovedo, and by divers other well experienced Spaniards and Dutchmen, and by many English fugitives, that the conquest of that island was less difficult than the conquest of Holland and Zeeland. Moreover, the Spaniards were of opinion that it would be far more behoveful for their King to conquer England and the Low Countries all at once than to be constrained continually to maintain a warlike navy to defend his East and West Indie fleets from the English Drake, and from such like valiant enemies.

* As the husband of Queen Mary of England.

And for the same purpose the Catholic King had given command-ment long before in Italy and Spain that a great quantity of timber should be felled for the building of ships; and had besides made great preparation of things and furniture requisite for such an expedition; as namely, in founding of brazen ordnance, in storing up of corn and victuals, in training of men to use warlike weapons, in levying and mustering of soldiers: insomuch that about the beginning of the year 1588 he had finished such a mighty navy, and brought it into Lisbon haven, as never the like had before that time sailed upon the ocean sea.

A very large and particular description of this navy was put in print and published by the Spaniards; wherein were set down the number, names, and burdens of the ships, the number of mariners and soldiers throughout the whole fleet; likewise the quantity of their ordnance, of their armour, of bullets, of match, of gunpowder, of victuals, and of all their naval furniture was in the said description particularised. Unto all these were added the names of the governors, captains, noblemen and gentlemen voluntaries, of whom there was so great a multitude that scarce was there any family of account, or any one principal man throughout all Spain, that had not a brother, son or kinsman in that fleet: who all of them were in good hope to purchase unto themselves in that navy (as they termed it) invincible, endless glory and renown, and to possess themselves of great seigniories and riches in England and in the Low Countries. But because the said description was trans-lated and published out of Spanish into divers other languages, we will here only make an abridgment or brief rehearsal thereof.

Portugal furnished and set forth under the conduct of the Duke of Medina Sidonia,* General of the Fleet, ten galleons, two zabras,† 1,300 mariners, 3,300 soldiers, 300 great pieces, with all requisite furniture.

Biscay, under the conduct of John Martinez de Recalde, Admiral of the whole Fleet, set forth ten galleons, four patches,‡ 700 mariners, 2,000 soldiers, 250 great pieces, etc.

Guipuzco, under the conduct of Michael de Oquendo, ten galleons, four patches, 700 mariners, 2,000 soldiers, 310 great pieces.

* Don Alonso Perez de Guzman el Bueno, fifth Marquis of Sanlucar de Barra-mada, ninth Conde of Niebla and seventh Duke of Medina Sidonia was one of the noblest grandees of Spain and for this reason only, very much against his will, he was appointed by Philip to the supreme command. He had little experi-ence of war or of the sea; he was a gentle quiet man who wanted only to be left in peace among his orange groves. But he had some very able and experienced lieutenants.
† Small vessels used off the coasts of Spain and Portugal.
‡ Small boats used for communications between the vessels of a fleet.

Italy with the Levant Islands, under Martine de Vertendona, ten
   galleons, 800 mariners, 2,000 soldiers, 310 great pieces, etc.
Castile, under Diego Flores de Valdes, fourteen galleons, two patches,
   1,700 mariners, 2,400 soldiers, and 380 great pieces, etc.
Andalusia, under the conduct of Pedro de Valdes, ten galleons, one
   patache, 800 mariners, 2,400 soldiers, 280 great pieces, etc.
Item, under the conduct of John Lopez de Medina, twenty-three great
   Flemish hulks, with 700 mariners, 3,200 soldiers, and 400 great
   pieces.
Item, under Hugo de Moncada, four galleasses containing 1,200 galley-
   slaves, 460 mariners, 870 soldiers, 200 great pieces, etc.
Item, under Diego de Mandrana, four galleys of Portugal, with 888
   galley-slaves, 360 mariners, 20 great pieces, and other requisite
   furniture.
Item, under Anthony de Mendoza, 22 patches and zabras, with 574
   mariners, 488 soldiers, and 193 great pieces.

Besides the ships aforementioned there were 20 caravels rowed with
oars, being appointed to perform necessary services unto the greater
ships: insomuch that all the ships appertaining to this navy amounted
unto the sum of 150, each one being sufficiently provided of furniture
and victuals.

The number of mariners in the said fleet were above 8,000, of slaves
2,088, of soldiers 20,000 (besides noblemen and gentlemen voluntaries),
of great cast pieces 2,650. The foresaid ships were of an huge and incredible capacity and receipt, for the whole fleet was large enough to
contain the burden of sixty thousand tons.

The galleons were 64 in number, being of an huge bigness, and very
stately built, being of marvellous force also, and so high that they
resembled great castles, most fit to defend themselves and to withstand any assault, but in giving any other ships the encounter far
inferior unto the English and Dutch ships, which can with great
dexterity wield and turn themselves at all assays. The upperwork of
the said galleons was of thickness and strength sufficient to bear off
musket-shot. The lower work and the timbers thereof were out of
measure strong, being framed of planks and ribs four or five foot in
thickness, insomuch that no bullets could pierce them but such as
were discharged hard at hand: which afterward proved true, for a great
number of bullets were found to stick fast within the massy substance
of those thick planks. Great and well-pitched cables were twined
about the masts of their ships to strengthen them against the battery
of shot.

The galleasses were of such bigness that they contained within them chambers, chapels, turrets, pulpits, and other commodities of great houses. The galleasses were rowed with great oars, there being in each one of them 300 slaves for the same purpose, and were able to do great service with the force of their ordnance. All these, together with the residue aforenamed, were furnished and beautified with trumpets, streamers, banners, warlike ensigns, and other suchlike ornaments.

Their pieces of brazen ordnance were 1,600, and of iron a thousand. The bullets thereto belonging were 120,000.

Item of gun-powder 5,600 quintals. Of match 1,200 quintals.

Of muskets and calivers 7,000. Of halberds and partisans 10,000.

Moreover they had great store of cannons, double-cannons, culverins and field-pieces for land services.

Likewise they were provided of all instruments necessary on land to convey and transport their furniture from place to place; as namely of carts, wheels, wagons, etc. Also they had spades, mattocks and baskets to set pioneers on work. They had in like sort great store of mules and horses, and whatsoever else was requisite for a land-army. They were so well stored of biscuit that for the space of half a year they might allow each person in the whole fleet half a quintal every month; whereof the whole sum amounteth unto an hundred thousand quintals.

Likewise of wine they had 147,000 pipes, sufficient also for half a year's expedition. Of bacon 6,500 quintals. Of cheese 3,000 quintals, besides fish, rice, beans, peas, oil, vinegar, etc.

Moreover they had 12,000 pipes of fresh water and all other necessary provision, as namely candles, lanterns, lamps, sails, hemp, ox-hides, and lead to stop holes that should be made with the battery of gunshot. To be short, they brought all things expedient either for a fleet by sea, or for an army by land.

This navy (as Diego Pimentell afterward confessed) was esteemed by the King himself to contain 32,000 persons, and to cost him every day 30,000 ducats.

There were in the said navy five terzaes of Spaniards (which terzaes the Frenchmen call regiments), under the command of five Governors termed by the Spaniards Masters of the Field, and amongst the rest there were many old and expert soldiers chosen out of the garrisons of Sicily, Naples, and Tercera. Their Captains or Colonels were Diego Pimentell, Don Francisco de Toledo, Don Alonso de Lucon, Don Nicolas de Isla, Don Augustin de Mexia, who had each of them thirty-two companies under their conduct. Besides the which companies there were many bands also of Castilians and Portugals, every one of which had their peculiar Governors, captains, officers, colours and weapons.

It was not lawful for any man, under grievous penalty, to carry any women or harlots in the fleet; for which cause the women hired certain ships wherein they sailed after the navy: some of the which, being driven by tempest, arrived upon the coast of France.

The General of this mighty navy was Don Alonso Perez de Guzman, Duke of Medina Sidonia, Lord of St Lucar, and Knight of the Golden Fleece, by reason that the Marquis of Santa Cruz, appointed for the same dignity, deceased before the time.

John Martinez de Recalde was Admiral of the Fleet.

Francis Bovadilla was Chief Marshal; who all of them had their officers fit and requisite for the guiding and managing of such a multitude. Likewise Martin Alorcon was appointed Vicar General of the Inquisition, being accompanied with more than a hundred monks, to wit, Jesuits, Capuchins, and friars mendicant. Besides whom also there were physicians, chirurgeons, apothecaries, and whatsoever else pertained unto the hospital.

Over and besides the forenamed Governors and officers, being men of chief note, there were 124 very noble and worthy gentlemen, which went voluntarily of their own costs and charges to the end they might see fashions, learn experience, and attain unto glory; amongst whom was the Prince of Ascoli, Alonzo de Leiva, the Marquis de Pennafiel, the Marquis de Ganes, the Marquis de Barlango, Count de Paredes, Count de Yelvas, and divers other Marquises and Earls of the honourable families of Mendoza, of Toledo, of Pachieco, of Cordova, of Guzman, of Manricques, and a great number of others.

While the Spaniards were furnishing this their navy, the Duke of Parma, at the direction of King Philip, made great preparation in the Low Countries to give aid and assistance unto the Spaniards, building ships for the same purpose and sending for pilots and shipwrights out of Italy.

In Flanders he caused certain deep channels to be made, and among the rest the channel of Ypres, commonly called Yper-lee, employing some thousands of workmen about that service, to the end that by the said channel he might transport ships from Antwerp and Ghent to Bruges, where he had assembled above a hundred small ships, called hoys, being well stored with victuals, which hoys he was determined to have brought into the sea by the way of Sluys, or else to have conveyed them by the said Yper-lee, being now of greater depth, into any port of Flanders whatsoever.

In the river of Waten he caused seventy ships with flat bottoms to be built, every one of which should serve to carry thirty horses, having each of them bridges likewise for the horses to come on board or to go forth on land. Of the same fashion he had provided two hundred other vessels at Nieuport but not so great. And at Dunkirk he procured twenty-eight ships of war, such as were there to be had, and caused a sufficient number of mariners to be levied at Hamburg, Bremen, Emden, and at other places. He put in the ballast of the said ships great store of beams of thick planks, being hollow and beset with iron spikes beneath but on each side full of clasps and hooks to join them together.

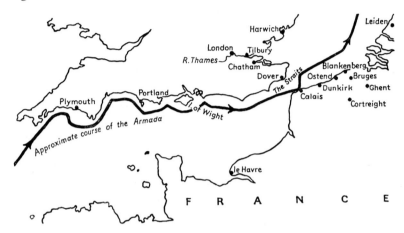

He had likewise at Gravelines provided twenty thousand of casks, which in a short space might be compact and joined together with nails and cords and reduced into the form of a bridge. To be short, whatsoever things were requisite for the making of bridges and for the barring and stopping up of havens' mouths with stakes, posts, and other means, he commanded to be made ready. Moreover, not far from Nieuport haven he had caused a great pile of wooden faggots to be laid, and other furniture to be brought for the rearing up of a mount.* The most part of his ships contained two ovens apiece to bake bread in, with a great number of saddles, bridles, and such other like apparel for horses. They had horses likewise which after their landing should serve to convey and draw engines, field-pieces, and other warlike provisions.

Near unto Nieuport he had assembled an army, over the which he had ordained Camillo de Monte to be Camp-master. This army consisted of thirty bands or ensigns of Italians, of ten bands of Walloons, eight of Scots, and eight of Burgundians, all which together amount unto fifty-six bands, every band containing a hundred persons. Near unto Dixmude there were mustered eighty bands of Dutchmen, sixty

* Presumably, making a pile on which soldiers could climb when storming a wall.

of Spaniards, six of high Germans, and seven bands of English fugitives under the conduct of Sir William Stanley, an English knight.*

In the suburbs of Cortreight there were 4,000 horsemen together with their horses in a readiness; and at Waten 900 horses, with the troop of the Marquis del Gwasto, Captain General of the horsemen.

Unto this famous expedition and presupposed victory many potentates, princes, and honourable personages hied themselves: out of Spain the Prince of Melito, called the Duke of Pastrana, and taken to be the son of one Ruygomes de Silva but in very deed accompted among the number of King Philip's base sons: also the Marquis of Burgrave, one of the sons of Archduke Ferdinand and Philippa Welsera: Vespasian Gonsaga of the family of Mantua, being for chivalry a man of great renown and heretofore Viceroy in Spain: item John Medici, base son unto the Duke of Florence, and Amadas of Savoy, the Duke of Savoy his base son, with many others of inferior degrees.

Likewise Pope Sixtus Quintus for the setting forth of the foresaid expedition, as they used to do against Turks and infidels, published a Cruzado with most ample indulgences which were printed in great numbers. These vain bulls the English and Dutchmen, deriding, said that the devil at all passages lay in ambush like a thief, no whit regarding such letters of safe conduct. Some there be which affirm that the Pope had bestowed the realm of England, with the title of Defensor Fidei, upon the King of Spain, giving him charge to invade it upon this condition, that he should enjoy the conquered realm as a vassal and tributary, in that regard, unto the See of Rome. To this purpose the said Pope proffered a million of gold, the one half thereof to be paid in ready money, and the other half when the realm of England or any famous port thereof were subdued. And for the greater furtherance of the whole business he dispatched one Dr [William] Allen, an Englishman (whom he had made Cardinal for the same end and purpose) into the Low Countries, unto whom he committed the administration of all matters ecclesiastical throughout England. This Allen, being enraged against his own native country, caused the Pope's bull to be translated into English, meaning upon the arrival of the Spanish fleet to have it so published in England; by which bull the excommunications of the two former Popes were confirmed, and the Queen's most sacred Majesty was by them most unjustly deprived of all princely titles and dignities, her subjects being enjoined to perform obedience unto the Duke of Parma and unto the Pope's Legate.

But that all matters might be performed with greater secrecy, and

---

* Sir William Stanley (1548–1630) was an Elizabethan adventurer in the Netherlands who went over to the Spaniards and led English and Irish Catholic volunteers who were fighting with them.

that the whole expedition might seem rather to be intended against the Low Countries than against England, and that the English people might be persuaded that all was but bare words and threatenings and that nought would come to effect, there was a solemn meeting appointed at Borborch in Flanders for a treaty of peace between Her Majesty and the Spanish King: against which treaty the United Provinces, making open protestation, used all means possible to hinder it, alleging that it was more requisite to consult how the enemy now pressing upon them might be repelled from off their frontiers. Howbeit, some there were in England that greatly urged and prosecuted this league, saying that it would be very commodious unto the state of the realm, as well in regard of traffic and navigation as for the avoiding of great expenses to maintain the wars, affirming also that at the same time peace might easily and upon reasonable conditions be obtained of the Spaniard. Others thought by this means to divert some other way, or to keep back, the navy now coming upon them, and so to escape the danger of that tempest. Howsoever it was, the Duke of Parma by these wiles enchanted and dazzled the eyes of many English and Dutchmen that were desirous of peace. Whereupon it came to pass that England and the United Provinces prepared indeed some defence to withstand that dreadful expedition and huge Armada, but nothing in comparison of the great danger which was to be feared, albeit the constant report of the whole expedition had continued rife among them for a long time before. Howbeit they gave ear unto the relation of certain that said that this navy was provided to conduct and waft over the Indian fleets: which seemed the more probable because the Spaniards were deemed not to be men of so small discretion as to adventure those huge and monstrous ships upon the shallow and dangerous Channel of England.

At length, whenas the French King, about the end of May, signified unto Her Majesty in plain terms that she should stand upon her guard, because he was now most certainly informed that there was so dangerous an invasion imminent upon her realm that he feared much lest all her land and sea forces would be sufficient to withstand it, etc., then began the Queen's Majesty more carefully to gather her forces together, and to furnish her own ships of war and the principal ships of her subjects with soldiers, weapons, and other necessary provision.

The greatest and strongest ships of the whole navy she sent unto Plymouth under the conduct of the Right Honourable Lord Charles Howard, Lord High Admiral of England, etc., under whom the renowned knight, Sir Francis Drake, was appointed Vice-Admiral. The number of these ships was about an hundred. The lesser ships, being thirty or forty in number and under the conduct of the Lord Henry Seymour, were commanded to lie between Dover and Calais.

On land likewise, throughout the whole realm, soldiers were mustered and trained in all places, and were committed unto the most resolute and faithful captains. And whereas it was commonly given out that the Spaniard, having once united himself unto the Duke of Parma, meant to invade by the river of Thames, there was at Tilbury in Essex, over against Gravesend, a mighty army encamped,* and on both sides of the river fortifications were erected according to the pre-scription of Frederigo Giambelli, an Italian engineer. Likewise there were certain ships brought to make a bridge, though it were very late first.† Unto the said army came in proper person the Queen's Most Royal Majesty, representing Thomyris, that Scythian warlike princess, or rather divine Pallas herself. Also there were other such armies levied in England.

The principal Catholic recusants (lest they should stir up any tumult in the time of the Spanish invasion) were sent to remain at certain convenient places, as namely in the Isle of Ely and at Wisbech. And some of them were sent unto other places, to wit, unto sundry bishops and noblemen, where they were kept from endangering the state of the commonwealth and of her sacred Majesty, who of her most gracious clemency gave express commandment that they should be entreated with all humanity and friendship.

The provinces of Holland and Zeeland, etc., giving credit unto their intelligence out of Spain, made preparation to defend themselves: but because the Spanish ships were described unto them to be so huge they relied partly upon the shallow and dangerous seas all along their coasts. Wherefore they stood most in doubt of the Duke of Parma his small and flat-bottomed ships. Howbeit they had all their ships of war to the number of ninety and above in a readiness for all assays; the greater part whereof were of a small burden as being more meet to sail upon their rivers and shallow seas: and with these ships they besieged all the havens in Flanders, beginning at the mouth of Scheldt, or from the town of Lillo, and holding on to Gravelines and almost unto Calais, and fortified all their sea-towns with strong garrisons.

Against the Spanish fleet's arrival they had provided twenty-five or thirty good ships, committing the government of them unto Admiral Lonck, whom they commanded to join himself unto the Lord Henry Seymour, lying between Dover and Calais. And whenas the foresaid ships (whereof the greater part besieged the haven of Dunkirk) were driven by tempest into Zeeland, Justin of Nassau, the Admiral of

* It was in fact only a few thousand men ill-organised under the Earl of Leicester.
† It was intended to make a pontoon bridge across the Thames.

Zeeland, supplied that squadron with thirty-five ships, being of no great burden but excellently furnished with guns, mariners and soldiers in great abundance, and especially with 1,200 brave musketeers, having been accustomed unto sea-fights, and being chosen out of all their companies for the same purpose. And so the said Justin of Nassau kept such diligent ward in that station that the Duke of Parma could not issue forth with his navy into the sea out of any part of Flanders.

In the meanwhile the Spanish Armada set sail out of the haven of Lisbon upon the 19th of May,★ An. Dom. 1588, under the conduct of the Duke of Medina Sidonia, directing their course for the Bay of Corunna, alias the Groyne of Galicia, where they took in soldiers and warlike provision, this port being in Spain the nearest unto England.

As they were sailing along there arose such a mighty tempest that the whole fleet was dispersed, so that when the Duke was returned unto his company he could not escry above eighty ships in all, whereunto the residue by little and little joined themselves, except eight which had their masts blown overboard. One of the four galleys of Portugal escaped very hardly, retiring herself into the haven. The other three were, upon the coast of Bayonne in France, by the assistance and courage of one David Gwyn, an English captive (whom the French and Turkish slaves aided in the same enterprise), utterly disabled and vanquished; one of the three being first overcome, which conquered the two other with the slaughter of their governors and soldiers and, among the rest, of Don Diego de Mandrana with sundry others. And so those slaves, arriving in France with the three galleys, set themselves at liberty.

The navy, having refreshed themselves at the Groyne and receiving daily commandment from the King to hasten their journey, hoisted up sails the 11th day of July, and so, holding on their course till the 19th of the same month, they came then unto the mouth of the narrow seas or English Channel, from whence (striking their sails in the mean season) they dispatched certain of their small ships unto the Duke of Parma. At the same time the Spanish fleet was escried by an English pinnace, Captain whereof was Master Thomas Fleming, after they had been advertised of the Spaniards' expedition by their scouts and spies, which having ranged along the coast of Spain were lately returned home into Plymouth for a new supply of victuals and other necessaries, who, considering the foresaid tempest, were of opinion that the navy, being of late dispersed and tossed up and down the main ocean, was by no means able to perform their intended voyage.

★ May 19th, New Style, by the Gregorian calendar used by the Spaniards; May 9th, Old Style, by the inaccurate Julian calendar which was still used by the English.

Moreover, the Lord Charles Howard, Lord High Admiral of England, had received letters from the Court signifying unto him that Her Majesty was advertised that the Spanish fleet would not come forth nor was to be any longer expected for, and therefore that upon Her Majesty's commandment he must send back four of her tallest and strongest ships unto Chatham.

The Lord High Admiral of England being thus on the sudden, namely upon the 19th of July about four of the clock in the afternoon, informed by the pinnace of Captain Fleming aforesaid of the Spaniards' approach, with all speed and diligence possible he warped his ships and caused his mariners and soldiers (the greater part of whom was absent for the cause aforesaid) to come on board, and that with great trouble and difficulty,* insomuch that the Lord Admiral himself was fain to lie without in the road with six ships only all that night, after the which many others came forth of the haven. The very next day, being the 20th of July, about high noon, was the Spanish fleet escried by the English, which with a southwest wind came sailing along and passed by Plymouth: in which regard (according to the judgment of many skilful navigators) they greatly overshot themselves, whereas it had been more commodious for them to have stayed themselves there considering that the Englishmen, being as yet unprovided, greatly relied upon their own forces and knew not the estate of the Spanish navy. Moreover, this was the most convenient port of all others where they might with greater security have been advertised of the English forces and how the commons of the land stood affected, and might have stirred up some mutiny, so that hither they should have bent all their puissance and from hence the Duke of Parma might more easily have conveyed his ships.

But this they were prohibited to do by the King and his Council, and were expressly commanded to unite themselves unto the soldiers and ships of the said Duke of Parma and so to bring their purpose to effect: which was thought to be the most easy and direct course for that they imagined that the English and Dutch men would be utterly daunted and dismayed thereat, and would each man of them retire unto his own province and port for the defence thereof, and transporting the army of the Duke under the protection of their huge navy they might invade England.

It is reported that the chief commanders in the navy and those which were more skilful in navigation, to wit, John Martinez de Recalde, Diego Flores de Valdez, and divers others, found fault that they were bound unto so strict directions and instructions because that in such

* Provisions were so bad that hundreds of seamen had already died of food poisoning and had been hastily replaced as far as possible.

a case many particular accidents ought to concur and to be respected at one and the same instant, that is to say, the opportunity of the wind, weather, time, tide, and ebb, wherein they might sail from Flanders to England. Oftentimes also the darkness and light, the situation of places, the depths and shoals were to be considered: all which especially depended upon the convenience of the winds and were by so much the more dangerous.

But it seemeth that they were enjoined by their commission to anchor near unto or about Calais, whither the Duke of Parma with his ships and all his warlike provision was to resort, and, while the English and Spanish great ships were in the midst of their conflict, to pass by and to land his soldiers upon the Downs.

The Spanish captives reported that they were determined first to have entered the River of Thames, and thereupon to have passed with small ships up to London, supposing that they might easily win that rich and flourishing city, being but meanly fortified and inhabited with citizens not accustomed to the wars, who durst not withstand their first encounter; hoping, moreover, to find many rebels against Her Majesty and Popish Catholics or some favourers of the Scottish Queen (which was not long before most justly beheaded)* who might be instruments of sedition.

Thus often advertising the Duke of Parma of their approach, the 20th of July they passed by Plymouth, which the English ships pursuing and getting the wind of them gave them the chase and the encounter, and so both fleets frankly exchanged their bullets.

The day following, which was the 21st of July, the English ships approached within musket shot of the Spanish; at what time the Lord Charles Howard most hotly and valiantly discharged his ordnance upon the Spanish vice-admiral. The Spaniards, then well perceiving the nimbleness of the English ships in discharging upon the enemy on all sides, gathered themselves close into the form of an half moon, and slackened their sails lest they should outgo any of their company. And while they were proceeding on in this manner one of their great galleasses was so furiously battered with shot that the whole navy was fain to come up rounder together for the safeguard thereof: whereby it came to pass that the principal galleon of Seville (wherein Don Pedro de Valdes, Vasques de Silva, Alonzo de Sayas, and other noble men were embarked), falling foul of another ship, had her foremast broken and by that means was not able to keep way with the Spanish fleet, neither would the said fleet stay to succour it but left the distressed galleon

* Mary, Queen of Scots, was executed in 1587, after nineteen years' imprisonment in England, during which, as Catholic heir to the throne, she was implicated in plots to assassinate Elizabeth.

behind. The Lord Admiral of England, when he saw this ship of Valdes and thought she had been void of mariners and soldiers, taking with him as many ships as he could, passed by it that he might not lose sight of the Spanish fleet that night. For Sir Francis Drake (who was not-withstanding appointed to bear out his lantern that night)* was giving of chase unto five great hulks which had separated themselves from the Spanish fleet; but finding them to be Easterlings† he dismissed them. The Lord Admiral all that night following the Spanish lantern instead of the English found himself in the morning to be in the midst of his enemy's fleet, but when he perceived it he cleanly conveyed himself out of that great danger.

The day following, which was the two and twentieth of July, Sir Francis Drake espied Valdes his ship whereunto he sent forth his pinnace, and being advertised that Valdes himself was there and 450 persons with him he sent him word that he should yield himself. Valdes, for his honour's sake, caused certain conditions to be pro-pounded unto Drake, who answered Valdes that he was not now at leisure to make any long parle but if he would yield himself he should find him friendly and tractable; howbeit, if he had resolved to die in fight he should prove Drake to be no dastard.

Upon which answer Valdes and his company understanding that they were fallen into the hands of fortunate Drake, being moved with the renown and celebrity of his name, with one consent yielded them-selves and found him very favourable unto them. Then Valdes with forty or fifty noblemen and gentlemen pertaining unto him came on board Sir Francis Drake's ship. The residue of his company were carried unto Plymouth, where they were detained a year and a half for their ransom.

Valdes coming unto Drake, and humbly kissing his hand, protested unto him that he and his had resolved to die in battle had they not by good fortune fallen into his power, whom they knew to be right cour-teous and gentle, and whom they had heard by general report to be most favourable unto his vanquished foe; insomuch that he said it was to be doubted whether his enemies had more cause to admire and love him for his great, valiant, and prosperous exploits, or to dread him for his singular felicity and wisdom which ever attended upon him in the wars and by the which he had attained unto so great honour. With that

---

* To show a light which the rest of the fleet could follow.
† 'Easterlings' was the English name for merchants of the Hanseatic League, a federation of north German cities. This desertion of his post at the head of the fleet was plain dereliction of duty on Drake's part. Apparently no one commented, and certainly no one would be surprised that it was Drake who captured the most profitable prize taken during the battle.

Drake embraced him and gave him very honourable entertainment, feeding him at his own table and lodging him in his cabin.

Here Valdes began to recount unto Drake the forces of all the Spanish fleet, and how four mighty galleys were separated by tempest from them; and also how they were determined first to have put into Plymouth haven, not expecting to be repelled thence by the English ships which they thought could by no means withstand their impregnable forces, persuading themselves that by means of their huge fleet they were become lords and commanders of the main ocean. For which cause they marvelled much how the English men in their small ships durst approach within musket shot of the Spaniards' mighty wooden castles, gathering the wind of them with many other such like attempts.

Immediately after Valdes and his company, being a man of principal authority in the Spanish fleet and being descended of one and the same family with that Valdes which in the year 1574 besieged Leiden in Holland, were sent captives into England. There were in the said ship fifty-five thousand ducats in ready money of the Spanish King's gold, which the soldiers merrily shared among themselves.

The same day was set on fire one of their greatest ships, being admiral of the squadron of Guipusco, and being the ship of Michael de Oquendo, Vice-Admiral of the whole fleet, which contained great store of gunpowder and other warlike provision. The upper part only of this ship was burnt and all the persons therein contained (except a very few) were consumed with fire. And thereupon it was taken by the English and brought into England with a number of miserable burnt and scorched Spaniards. Howbeit the gunpowder (to the great admiration of all men) remained whole and unconsumed.

In the mean season the Lord Admiral of England, in his ship called the *Ark Royal*, all that night pursued the Spaniards so near that in the morning he was almost left alone in the enemy's fleet, and it was four of the clock at afternoon before the residue of the English fleet could overtake him.

At the same time Hugo de Moncada, Governor of the four galleasses, made humble suit unto the Duke of Medina that he might be licensed to encounter the Admiral of England, which liberty the Duke thought not good to permit unto him because he was loth to exceed the limits of his commission and charge.

Upon Tuesday, which was the three and twentieth of July, the navy being come over against Portland, the wind began to turn northerly insomuch that the Spaniards had a fortunate and fit gale to invade the English. But the Englishmen having lesser and nimbler ships recovered again the vantage of the wind from the Spaniards, whereat the Spaniards seemed to be more incensed to fight than before. But when the

English fleet had continually and without intermission from morning to night beaten and battered them with all their shot, both great and small, the Spaniards, uniting themselves, gathered their whole fleet close together into a roundel so that it was apparent that they meant not as yet to invade others but only to defend themselves and to make haste unto the place prescribed unto them, which was near unto Dunkirk, that they might join forces with the Duke of Parma, who was determined to have proceeded secretly with his small ships under the shadow and protection of the great ones and so had intended circumspectly to perform the whole expedition.

This was the most furious and bloody skirmish of all in which the Lord Admiral of England continued fighting amidst his enemy's fleet, and seeing one of his Captains afar off he spake unto him in these words: 'Oh, George, what doest thou? Wilt thou now frustrate my hope and opinion conceived of thee? Wilt thou forsake me now?' With which words he being inflamed approached forthwith, encountered the enemy and did the part of a most valiant Captain. His name was George Fenner, a man that had been conversant in many sea-fights.

In this conflict there was a certain great Venetian ship with other small ships surprised and taken by the English.

The English navy in the meanwhile increased, whereunto out of all havens of the realm resorted ships and men; for they all with one accord came flocking thither as unto a set field where immortal fame and glory was to be attained, and faithful service to be performed unto their prince and country. In which number there were many great and honourable personages, as namely, the Earls of Oxford, of Northumberland, of Cumberland, etc., with many knights and gentlemen, to wit, Sir Thomas Cecil, Sir Robert Cecil, Sir Walter Raleigh, Sir William Hatton, Sir Horatio Pallavincino, Sir Henry Brook, Sir Robert Carew, Sir Charles Blunt, Master Ambrose Willoughby, Master Henry Noel, Master Thomas Gerard, Master Henry Dudley, Master Edward Darcy, Master Arthur George, Master Thomas Woodhouse, Master William Harvey, etc.

And so it came to pass that the number of the English ships amounted unto an hundred; which, when they were come before Dover, were increased to an hundred and thirty, being notwithstanding of no proportionable bigness to encounter with the Spaniards, except two or three and twenty of the Queen's greater ships which only, by reason of their presence, bred an opinion in the Spaniards' minds concerning the power of the English fleet; the mariners and soldiers whereof were esteemed to be twelve thousand.

The four and twentieth of July whenas the sea was calm and no wind stirring the fight was only between the four great galleasses and the

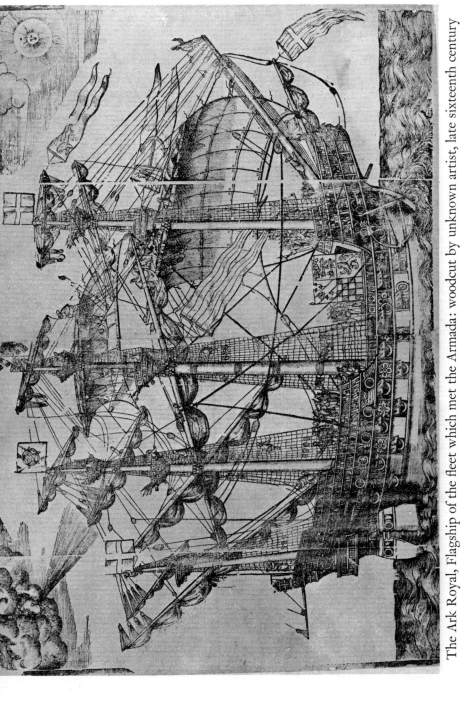

The Ark Royal, Flagship of the fleet which met the Armada: woodcut by unknown artist, late sixteenth century

English ships, which, being rowed with oars, had great vantage of the said English ships, which notwithstanding for all that would not be forced to yield but discharged their chain-shot to cut asunder their cables and cordage of the galleasses, with many other such stratagems. They were now constrained to send their men on land for a new supply of gunpowder, whereof they were in great scarcity by reason they had so frankly spent the greater part in the former conflicts.

The same day, a council being assembled, it was decreed that the English fleet should be divided into four squadrons; the principal whereof was committed unto the Lord Admiral; the second, to Sir Francis Drake; the third, to Captain Hawkins; the fourth, to Captain Frobisher.

The Spaniards in their sailing observed very diligent and good order, sailing three and four and sometimes more ships in a rank, and following close up one after another and the stronger and greater ships protecting the lesser.

The five and twentieth of July when the Spaniards were come over against the Isle of Wight the Lord Admiral of England, being accompanied with his best ships, (namely, the *Lion*, Captain whereof was the Lord Thomas Howard: the *Elizabeth Jonas*, under the commandment of Sir Robert Southwell, son-in-law unto the Lord Admiral: the *Bear*, under the Lord Sheffield, nephew unto the Lord Admiral: the *Victory*, under Captain Barker, and the *Galleon Leicester*, under the forenamed Captain George Fenner) with great valour and dreadful thundering of shot encountered the Spanish Admiral, being in the very midst of all his fleet. Which when the Spaniard perceived, being assisted with his strongest ships, he came forth and entered a terrible combat with the English, for they bestowed each on other the broadsides and mutually discharged all their ordnance, being within one hundred or an hundred and twenty yards one of another.

At length the Spaniards hoisted up their sails and again gathered themselves up close into the form of a roundel. In the meanwhile Captain Frobisher had engaged himself into a most dangerous conflict. Whereupon the Lord Admiral, coming to succour him, found that he had valiantly and discreetly behaved himself, and that he had wisely and in good time given over the fight because that after so great a battery he had sustained no damage. For which cause the day following, being the six and twentieth of July, the Lord Admiral rewarded him with the order of Knighthood, together with the Lord Thomas Howard, the Lord Sheffield, Master John Hawkins, and others.

The same day the Lord Admiral received intelligence from Newhaven [Le Havre] in France, by certain of his pinnaces, that all things were quiet in France and that there was no preparation of sending aid unto the Spaniards, which was greatly feared from the Guisian faction and from the Leaguers;* but there was a false rumour spread all about that the Spaniards had conquered England.

The seven and twentieth of July the Spaniards about the sunsetting were come over against Dover, and rode at anchor within the sight of Calais intending to hold on for Dunkirk, expecting there to join with the Duke of Parma's forces, without which they were able to do little or nothing.

Likewise the English fleet, following up hard upon them, anchored just by them within culverin-shot. And here the Lord Henry Seymour united himself unto the Lord Admiral with his fleet of thirty ships which rode before the mouth of Thames.

As the Spanish navy therefore lay at anchor, the Duke of Medina sent certain messengers unto the Duke of Parma, with whom upon that occasion many noblemen and gentlemen went to refresh themselves on land: and amongst the rest the Prince of Ascoli, being accounted the King's base son, and a very proper and towardly young gentleman, to his great good went on shore, who was by so much the more fortunate in that he had not opportunity to return on board the same ship out of which he was departed, because that in returning home it was cast away upon the Irish coast with all the persons contained therein.

The Duke of Parma, being advertised of the Spanish fleet's arrival upon the coast of England, made all the haste he could to be present himself in this expedition for the performance of his charge, vainly persuading himself that now by the means of Cardinal Allen he should be crowned King of England, and for that cause he had resigned the government of the Low Countries unto Count Mansfeld the Elder. And having made his vows unto St Mary of Hall in Hainault (whom he went to visit for his blind devotion's sake) he returned toward Bruges the twenty-eighth of July.

The next day, travelling to Dunkirk, he heard the thundering ordnance of either fleet; and the same evening being come to Dixmude he was given to understand the hard success of the Spanish fleet.

Upon Tuesday, which was the thirtieth of July, about high noon he came to Dunkirk whenas all the Spanish fleet was now passed by; neither durst any of his ships in the mean space come forth to assist the said Spanish fleet for fear of five and thirty warlike ships of Holland and Zeeland, which there kept watch and ward under the conduct of the Admiral Justin of Nassau.

The foresaid five and thirty ships were furnished with most cunning mariners and old expert soldiers, amongst the which were twelve hundred musketeers whom the States had chosen out of all their gar-

* The anti-Protestant parties in France.

risons, and whom they knew to have been heretofore experienced in sea-fights.

This navy was given especially in charge not to suffer any ship to come out of the haven, nor to permit any zabras, patches or other small vessels of the Spanish fleet (which were more likely to aid the Dunkirkers) to enter thereinto, for the greater ships were not to be feared by reason of the shallow sea in that place. Howbeit, the Prince of Parma, his forces being as yet unready, were not come on board his ships, only the English fugitives, being seven hundred in number, under the conduct of Sir William Stanley, came in fit time to have been embarked because they hoped to give the first assault against England. The residue showed themselves unwilling and loth to depart because they saw but a few mariners, who were by constraint drawn into this expedition, and also because they had very bare provision of bread, drink, and other necessary victuals.

Moreover, the ships of Holland and Zeeland stood continually in their sight, threatening shot and powder and many inconveniences unto them: for fear of which ships the mariners and seamen secretly withdrew themselves both day and night, lest that the Duke of Parma's soldiers should compel them by main force to go on board and to break through the Hollanders' fleet, which all of them judged to be impossible by reason of the straitness of the haven.

But it seemeth that the Duke of Parma and the Spaniards grounded upon a vain and presumptuous expectation that all the ships of England and of the Low Countries would at the first sight of the Spanish and Dunkirk navy have betaken themselves to flight, yielding them sea room, and endeavouring only to defend themselves, their havens and sea coasts from invasion. Wherefore their intent and purpose was that the Duke of Parma, in his small and flat-bottomed ships, should as it were under the shadow and wings of the Spanish fleet convey over all his troops, armour, and warlike provision, and with their forces so united should invade England; or, while the English fleet were busied in fight against the Spanish, should enter upon any part of the coast which he thought to be most convenient. Which invasion (as the captives afterward confessed) the Duke of Parma thought first to have attempted by the river of Thames, upon the banks whereof, having at his first arrival landed twenty or thirty thousand of his principal soldiers, he supposed that he might easily have won the City of London, both because his small ships should have followed and assisted his land-forces, and also for that the City itself was but meanly fortified and easy to overcome by reason of the citizens' delicacy and discontinuance from the wars, who with continual and constant labour might be vanquished if they yielded not at the first assault. They were in good hope also to have met with some rebels against Her Majesty and such as were discontented with the present state, as Papists, and others. Likewise they looked for aid from the favourers of the Scottish Queen, who was not long before put to death; all which they thought would have stirred up seditions and factions.

Whenas therefore the Spanish fleet rode at anchor before Calais to the end they might consult with the Duke of Parma what was best to be done, according to the King's commandment and the present estate of their affairs, and had now (as we will afterward declare) purposed upon the second of August, being Friday, with one power and consent to have put their intended business in practice; the Lord Admiral of England, being admonished by Her Majesty's letters from the Court, thought it most expedient either to drive the Spanish fleet from that place or at leastwise to give them the encounter. And for that cause (according to Her Majesty's prescription) he took forthwith eight of his worst and basest ships which came next to hand, and disburdening them of all things which seemed to be of any value filled them with gunpowder, pitch, brimstone, and with other combustible and fiery matter: and charging all their ordnance with powder, bullets and stones, he sent the said ships upon the twenty-eighth of July, being Sunday, about two of the clock after midnight, with the wind and tide against the Spanish fleet: which when they had proceeded a good space, being forsaken of the pilots and set on fire, were directly carried upon the King of Spain's navy; which fire in the dead of the night put the Spaniards into such a perplexity and horror (for they feared lest they were like unto those terrible ships which Frederigo Giambelli three years before, at the siege of Antwerp, had furnished with gunpowder, stones and dreadful engines for the dissolution of the Duke of Parma's bridge, built upon the River of Scheldt) that cutting their cables, whereon their anchors were fastened, and hoisting up their sails they betook themselves very confusedly unto the main sea.

In this sudden confusion the principal and greatest of the four galleasses, falling foul of another ship, lost her rudder; for which cause, when she could not be guided any longer, she was by the force of the tide cast into a certain shoal upon the shore of Calais, where she was immediately assaulted by divers English pinnaces, hoys and drumblers.★

And as they lay battering of her with their ordnance and durst not board her, the Lord Admiral sent thither his long boat with an hundred choice soldiers under the command of Captain Amyas Preston. Upon whose approach, their fellows being more emboldened did offer to board the galleas; against whom the Governor thereof and Captain

★ Small, fast vessels used as transports or fighting ships.

of all the four galleasses, Hugo de Moncada, stoutly opposed himself, fighting by so much the more valiantly in that he hoped presently to be succoured by the Duke of Parma. In the mean season Moncada, after he had endured the conflict a good while, being hit on the head with a bullet fell down stark dead, and a great number of Spaniards also were slain in his company. The greater part of the residue, leaping overboard into the sea to save themselves by swimming, were most of them drowned. Howbeit there escaped among others Don Antonio de Manriques, a principal officer in the Spanish fleet (called by them their Veador General), together with a few Spaniards besides; which Antonio was the first man that carried certain news of the success of the fleet into Spain.

This huge and monstrous galleas, wherein were contained three hundred slaves to lug at the oars and four hundred soldiers, was in the space of three hours rifled in the same place; and there were found amongst divers other commodities 50,000 ducats of the Spanish King's treasure. At length when the slaves were released out of their fetters the Englishmen would have set the said ship on fire, which Monsieur Gourdon, the Governor of Calais, for fear of the damage which might thereupon ensue to the town and haven, would not permit them to do but drave them from thence with his great ordnance.

Upon the 29th of July in the morning the Spanish fleet after the foresaid tumult having arranged themselves again into order were, within sight of Gravelines, most bravely and furiously encountered by the English, where they once again got the wind of the Spaniards; who suffered themselves to be deprived of the commodity of the place in Calais road and of the advantage of the wind near unto Dunkirk, rather than they would change their array or separate their forces now conjoined and united together, standing only upon their defence.

And albeit there were many excellent and warlike ships in the English fleet, yet scarce were there twenty-two or twenty-three among them all which matched ninety of the Spanish ships in bigness, or could conveniently assault them. Wherefore the English ships, using their prerogative of nimble steerage, whereby they could turn and wield themselves with the wind which way they listed, came oftentimes very near upon the Spaniards, and charged them so sore that now and then they were but a pike's length asunder; and so continually giving them one broadside after another they discharged all their shot both great and small upon them, spending one whole day from morning till night in that violent kind of conflict until such time as powder and bullets failed them. In regard of which want they thought it convenient not to pursue the Spaniards any longer, because they had many great vantages of the English, namely, for the extraordinary bigness of their ships, and also for that they were so nearly conjoined and kept together in so good array that they could by no means be fought withal one to one. The English thought, therefore, that they had right well acquitted themselves in chasing the Spaniards first from Calais and then from Dunkirk, and by that means to have hindered them from joining with the Duke of Parma's forces, and getting the wind of them to have driven them from their own coasts.

The Spaniards that day sustained great loss and damage having many of their ships shot through and through, and they discharged likewise great store of ordnance against the English; who indeed sustained some hindrance but not comparable to the Spaniards' loss, for they lost not any one ship or person of account. For very diligent inquisition being made, the Englishmen all that time wherein the Spanish navy sailed upon their seas are not found to have wanted above one hundred of their people: albeit Sir Francis Drake's ship was pierced with shot above forty times, and his very cabin was twice shot through, and about the conclusion of the fight the bed of a certain gentleman, lying weary thereupon, was taken quite from under him with the force of a bullet. Likewise, as the Earl of Northumberland and Sir Charles Blunt were at dinner upon a time, the bullet of a demi-culverin brake through the midst of their cabin, touched their feet, and struck down two of the standers-by, with many such accidents befalling the English ships which it were tedious to rehearse. Whereupon it is most apparent that God miraculously preserved the English nation; for the Lord Admiral wrote unto Her Majesty that in all human reason, and according to the judgment of all men (every circumstance being duly considered) the Englishmen were not of any such force whereby they might, without a miracle, dare once to approach within sight of the Spanish fleet; insomuch that they freely ascribed all the honour of their victory unto God, who had confounded the enemy and had brought his counsels to none effect.

The same day the Spanish ships were so battered with English shot that that very night and the day following two or three of them sunk right down; and among the rest a certain great ship of Biscay, which Captain Crosse assaulted, which perished even in the time of the conflict, so that very few therein escaped drowning; who reported that the governors of the same ship slew one another upon the occasion following; one of them which would have yielded the ship was suddenly slain; the brother of the slain party, in revenge of his death, slew the murderer, and in the meanwhile the ship sunk.

The same night two Portugal galleons of the burden of seven or eight hundred tons apiece, to wit, the *Saint Philip* and the *Saint Matthew*, were forsaken of the Spanish fleet for they were so torn with shot that the water entered into them on all sides. In the galleon of *Saint Philip* was Francis de Toledo, brother unto the Count de Orgas, being Colonel over two and thirty bands, besides other gentlemen; who seeing their mast broken with shot they shaped their course as well as they could for the coast of Flanders; whither, when they could not attain, the principal men in the ship, committing themselves to their skiff, arrived at the next town, which was Ostend; and the ship itself, being left behind with the residue of their company, was taken by the Ulishingers.*

In the other galleon, called the *Saint Matthew*, was embarked Don Diego Pimentel, another Camp-master and Colonel of 32 bands, being brother unto the Marquis of Tamnares, with many other gentlemen and captains. Their ship was not very great but exceeding strong, for of a great number of bullets which had battered her there were scarce twenty wherewith she was pierced or hurt; her upper work was of force sufficient to bear off a musket shot: this ship was shot through and pierced in the fight before Gravelines, insomuch that the leakage of the water could not be stopped. Whereupon the Duke of Medina sent his great skiff unto the Governor thereof that he might save himself and the principal persons that were in his ship; which he, upon a haut courage, refused to do. Wherefore the Duke charged him to sail next unto himself; which the night following he could not perform by reason of the great abundance of water which entered his ship on all sides; for the avoiding whereof, and to save his ship from sinking, he caused fifty men continually to labour at the pump, though it were to small purpose. And seeing himself thus forsaken and separated from his Admiral he endeavoured what he could to attain unto the coast of Flanders, where, being espied by four or five men of war, which had their station assigned them upon the same coast, he was admonished to yield himself unto them. Which he refusing to do was strongly assaulted by them all together, and his ship being pierced with many bullets, was brought into far worse case than before, and forty of his soldiers were slain. By which extremity he was enforced at length to yield himself unto Peter Banderduess and other Captains, which brought him and his ship into Zeeland; and that other ship also last before mentioned, which both of them, immediately after the greater and better part of their goods were unladen, sunk right down.

For the memory of this exploit the foresaid Captain Banderduess caused the banner of one of these ships to be set up in the great Church of Leiden in Holland, which is of so great a length that being fastened to the very roof it reached down to the ground.

About the same time another small ship, being by necessity driven upon the coast of Flanders, about Blankenberg, was cast away upon the

* The men of Flushing.

sands, the people therein being saved. Thus Almighty God would have the Spaniards' huge ships to be presented, not only to the view of the English but also of the Zeelanders; that at the sight of them they might acknowledge of what small ability they had been to resist such impregnable forces had not God endued them with courage, providence and fortitude, yea, and fought for them in many places with His own arm.

The 29th of July the Spanish fleet being encountered by the English (as is aforesaid) and lying close together under their fighting sails, with a south-west wind sailed past Dunkirk, the English ships still following the chase. Of whom the day following, when the Spaniards had got sea room, they cut their mainsails; whereby they sufficiently declared that they meant no longer to fight but to fly. For which cause the Lord Admiral of England dispatched the Lord Henry Seymour with his squadron of small ships unto the coast of Flanders, where, with the help of the Dutch ships, he might stop the Prince of Parma his passage if perhaps he should attempt to issue forth with his army. And he himself in the mean space pursued the Spanish fleet until the second of August because he thought they had set sail for Scotland. And albeit he followed them very near, yet did he not assault them any more for want of powder and bullets. But upon the fourth of August, the wind arising, when as the Spaniards had spread all their sails, betaking themselves wholly to flight, and leaving Scotland on the left hand trended toward Norway (whereby they sufficiently declared that their whole intent was to save themselves by flight, attempting for that purpose, with their battered and crazed ships, the most dangerous navigation of the Northern seas). The English, seeing that they were now proceeded unto the latitude of 57 degrees, and being unwilling to participate that danger whereinto the Spaniards plunged themselves, and because they wanted things necessary and especially powder and shot, returned back for England, leaving behind them certain pinnaces only, which they enjoined to follow the Spaniards aloof and to observe their course. And so it came to pass that the fourth of August, with great danger and industry, the English arrived at Harwich: for they had been tossed up and down with a mighty tempest for the space of two or three days together, which it is likely did great hurt unto the Spanish fleet, being (as I said before) so maimed and battered. The English now going on shore, provided themselves forthwith of victuals, gunpowder, and other things expedient, that they might be ready at all assays to entertain the Spanish fleet if it chanced any more to return. But being afterward more certainly informed of the Spaniards' course they thought it best to leave them unto those boisterous and uncouth northern seas, and not there to hunt after them.

The Spaniards, seeing now that they wanted four or five thousand of their people and having divers maimed and sick persons, and likewise having lost ten or twelve of their principal ships, they consulted among themselves what they were best to do, being now escaped out of the hands of the English, because their victuals failed them in like sort and they began also to want cables, cordage, anchors, masts, sails and other naval furniture, and utterly despaired of the Duke of Parma's assistance (who, verily hoping and undoubtedly expecting the return of the Spanish fleet, was continually occupied about his great preparation, commanding abundance of anchors to be made and other necessary furniture for a navy to be provided), they thought it good at length, so soon as the wind should serve them, to fetch a compass about Scotland and Ireland and so to return for Spain.

For they well understood that commandment was given throughout all Scotland that they should not have any succour or assistance there. Neither yet could they in Norway supply their wants. Wherefore having taken certain Scottish and other fisherboats they brought the men on board their own ships to the end they might be their guides and pilots. Fearing also lest their fresh water should fail them they cast all their horses and mules overboard. And so, touching nowhere upon the coast of Scotland but being carried with a fresh gale between the Orcades [Orkneys] and Fair Isles, they proceeded far north, even unto 61 degrees of latitude, being distant from any land at the least 40 leagues. Here the Duke of Medina, General of the Fleet, commanded all his followers to shape their course for Biscay: and he himself with twenty or five and twenty of his ships, which were best provided of fresh water and other necessaries, holding on his course over the main ocean, returned safely home. The residue of his ships, being about forty in number and committed unto his Vice-Admiral, fell nearer with the coast of Ireland, intending their course for Cape Clear because they hoped there to get fresh water and to refresh themselves on land. But after they were driven with many contrary winds, at length, upon the second of September, they were cast by a tempest arising from the south-west upon divers parts of Ireland, where many of their ships perished. And amongst others, the ship of Michael de Oquendo, which was one of the great galleasses; and two great ships of Venice also, namely, *La Ratta* and *Belanzara*, with other thirty-six or thirty-eight ships more, which perished in sundry tempests, together with most of the persons contained in them.

Likewise, some of the Spanish ships were the second time carried with a strong west wind into the Channel of England, whereof some were taken by the English upon their coast and others by the men of Rochelle upon the coast of France.

Moreover, there arrived at Newhaven [Le Havre] in Normandy, being by tempest enforced so to do, one of the four great galleasses, where they found the ships with the Spanish women which followed the fleet at their setting forth. Two ships also were cast away upon the coast of Norway, one of them being of a great burden; howbeit all the persons in the said great ship were saved: insomuch that of 134 ships which set sail out of Portugal there returned home 53 only, small and great; namely, of the four galleasses but one, and but one of the four galleys. Of the 91 great galleons and hulks there were missing 58, and 33 returned: of the pataches and zabras 17 were missing and 18 returned home. In brief, there were missing 81 ships, in which number were galleasses, galleys, galleons and other vessels, both great and small. And amongst the 53 ships remaining, those also are reckoned which returned home before they came into the English Channel.★ Two galleons of those which were returned were by misfortune burnt as they rode in the haven; and suchlike mishaps did many others undergo. Of 30,000 persons which went in this expedition there perished (according to the number and proportion of the ships) the greater and better part; and many of them which came home, by reason of the toils and inconveniences which they sustained in this voyage, died not long after their arrival. The Duke of Medina immediately upon his return was deposed from his authority, commanded to his private house, and forbidden to repair unto the Court; where he could hardly satisfy or yield a reason unto his malicious enemies and backbiters. Many honourable personages and men of great renown deceased soon after their return; as namely, John Martinez de Recalde, with divers others. A great part also of the Spanish nobility and gentry employed in this expedition perished either by fight, diseases, or drowning before their arrival; and among the rest Thomas Perenot of Granduell, a Dutchman, being Earl of Cantebroi, and son unto Cardinal Granduell's brother.

Upon the coast of Zeeland Don Diego de Pimentel, brother unto the Marquis de Tamnares and kinsman unto the Earl of Beneventum and Calva, and Colonel over 32 bands, with many other in the same ship, was taken and detained as prisoner in Zeeland.

Into England (as we said before) Don Pedro de Valdes, a man of singular experience and greatly honoured in his country, was led captive, being accompanied with Don Vasquez de Silva, Don Alonzo de Sayas, and others.

Likewise upon the Scottish Western Isles of Lewis, and Islay, and about Cape Kintyre upon the mainland, there were cast away certain

★ The figures are difficult to establish, but probably more than half the Armada ships returned. Many were badly battered.

Spanish ships out of which were saved divers captains and gentlemen, and almost four hundred soldiers, who for the most part, after their shipwreck, were brought unto Edinburgh in Scotland, and being miserably needy and naked were there clothed at the liberality of the King and the merchants, and afterwards were secretly shipped for Spain: but the Scottish fleet wherein they passed, touching at Yarmouth on the coast of Norfolk, were there stayed for a time until the Council's pleasure was known; who, in regard of their manifold miseries, though they were enemies winked at their passage.

Upon the Irish coast many of their noblemen and gentlemen were drowned, and divers slain by the barbarous and wild Irish. Howbeit there was brought prisoner out of Ireland Don Alonso de Lucon, Colonel of two and thirty bands, commonly called a tertia of Naples, together with Roderigo de Lasso, and two others of the family of Cordova, who were committed unto the custody of Sir Horatio Pallavincino, that Monsieur de Teligny, the son of Monsieur de la Noue (who being taken in fight near Antwerp was detained prisoner in Castle of Tournai) might be ransomed for them by way of exchange. To conclude, there was no famous nor worthy family in all Spain which in this expedition lost not a son, a brother, or a kinsman.★

For the perpetual memory of this matter the Zeelanders caused new coin of silver and brass to be stamped: which on the one side contained the arms of Zeeland, with this inscription: GLORY TO GOD ONLY: and on the other side the pictures of certain great ships, with these words: THE SPANISH FLEET: and in the circumference about the ships: IT CAME, WENT, AND WAS, Anno 1588. That is to say, the Spanish fleet came, went, and was vanquished this year; for which, Glory be given to God only.

★ 'In the Channel fighting the English had lost about a hundred men and not one ship. But afterwards came the reckoning exacted by filthy food and neglect of hygiene in almost every fleet in those days. Sickness had been rife from the beginning, and as the fleet turned back southwards to the Narrow Seas it grew into a terrible epidemic. Thousands died, some in the ships, some in the ports, where the sufferers were set ashore in such numbers that there were not roofs to cover them and they lay littered about the streets. As soon as it was known that the Armada would not return, a great effort was made to pay off and send the men home. Hawkins toiled manfully at the task, and the Lord Admiral, although summoned to court, was soon back among his men, bent on mitigating the tragedy so far as it was in his power. The Queen and Burghley were at their wits' end to find the money, for the costs of victory had well-nigh broken their finances. In public all was jubilation, with bonfires, processions and triumphant thanksgiving to God. But the mood of all those who knew what had taken place was of humble thankfulness for escape from a dreadful peril. "All the world," wrote Howard, "never saw such a force as theirs was."' – James A. Williamson: *The Age of Drake*.

Likewise they coined another kind of money; upon the one side whereof was represented a ship fleeing, and a ship sinking: on the other side four men making prayers and giving thanks unto God upon their knees; with this sentence: MAN PURPOSETH; GOD DIS-POSETH. 1588. Also, for the lasting memory of the same matter, they have stamped in Holland divers such like coins, according to the custom of the ancient Romans.

While this wonderful and puissant navy was sailing along the English coasts and all men did now plainly see and hear that which before they would not be persuaded of, all people throughout England prostrated themselves with humble prayers and supplications unto God: but especially the outlandish Churches (who had greatest cause to fear, and against whom by name the Spaniards had threatened most grievous torments) enjoined to their people continual fastings and supplications that they might turn away God's wrath and fury now imminent upon them for their sins; knowing right well that prayer was the only refuge against all enemies, calamities and necessities, and that it was the only solace and relief for mankind, being visited with affliction and misery. Likewise such solemn days of supplication were observed throughout the United Provinces.

Also a while after the Spanish fleet was departed there was in England, by the commandment of Her Majesty, and in the United Provinces by the direction of the States, a solemn festival day publicly appointed wherein all persons were enjoined to resort unto the Church and there to render thanks and praises unto God: and the preachers were commanded to exhort the people thereunto. The foresaid solemnity was observed upon the 29th of November; which day was wholly spent in fasting, prayer and giving of thanks.

Likewise, the Queen's Majesty herself, imitating the ancient Romans, rode into London in triumph in regard to her own and her subjects glorious deliverance. For being attended upon very solemnly by all the principal estates and officers of her realm she was carried through her said City of London in a triumphant chariot, and in robes of triumph, from her Palace unto the Cathedral Church of Saint Paul, out of the which the ensigns and colours of the vanquished Spaniards hung displayed. And all the citizens of London in their Liveries stood on either side the street, by their several companies, with their ensigns and banners: and the streets were hanged on both sides with blue cloth, which, together with the foresaid banners, yielded a very stately and gallant prospect. Her Majesty, being entered into the church, together with her clergy and nobles, gave thanks unto God, and caused a public sermon to be preached before her at Paul's cross; wherein none other argument was handled but that praise, honour and glory might be rendered unto God, and that God's Name might be extolled by thanksgiving. And with her own princely voice she most Christianly exhorted the people to do the same: whereupon the people with a loud acclamation wished her a most long and happy life, to the confusion of her foes.

Thus the magnificent, huge and mighty fleet of the Spaniards (which themselves termed in all places invincible) such as sailed not upon the ocean sea many hundred years before, in the year 1588 vanished into smoke; to the great confusion and discouragement of the authors thereof. In regard of which Her Majesty's happy success all her neighbours and friends congratulated with her, and many verses were penned to the honour of Her Majesty by learned men, whereof some which came to our hands we will here annex.

AD SERENISSIMAM ELIZABETHAM ANGLIAE REGINAM: THEODOR. BEZA.

The Spanish fleet did float in narrow seas,★
And bend her ships against the English shore,
With so great rage as nothing could appease,
And with such strength as never seen before:
    And all to join the kingdom of that land
    Unto the kingdoms that he had in hand.
Now if you ask what set this King on fire,
To practise war when he of peace did treat,
It was his pride, and never quenched desire
To spoil that Island's wealth, by peace made great:
    His pride which far above the heavens did swell,
    And his desire as unsufficed as hell.
But well have winds his proud blasts overblown,
And swelling waves allayed his swelling heart,
Well hath the sea with greedy gulfs unknown,
Devoured the devourer to his smart:
    And made his ships a prey unto the sand,
    That meant to prey upon another's land.
And now, O Queen, above all others blest,
For whom both winds and waves are pressed to fight,
So rule your own, so succour friends opprest,
(As far from pride, as ready to do right)
    That England you, you England long enjoy,
    No less your friends' delight than foes' annoy.

★ The original Latin is here omitted. The translation is presumably Hakluyt's.

A VOYAGE TO BENIN

Anthony Ingram

This voyage must have been typical of many. Apparently nothing could damp Elizabethan enterprise.

The voyage set forth by Master John Newton and Master John Bird, merchants of London, to the Kingdom and City of Benin in Africa, with a ship called the *Richard of Arundel* and a pinnace, in the year 1588, briefly set down in this letter following, written by the Chief Factor in the voyage to the foresaid merchants at the time of the ship's first arrival at Plymouth.

WORSHIPFUL Sirs, the discourse of our whole proceeding in this voyage will ask more time and a person in better health that I am at this present, so that I trust you will pardon me till my coming up to you. In the meantime let this suffice.

Whereas we departed in the month of December from the coast of England with your good ship, the *Richard of Arundel*, and the pinnace, we held on our direct course towards our appointed port, and the 14th day of February following we arrived in the haven of Benin, where we found not water enough to carry the ship over the bar, so that we left her without in the road, and with the pinnace and ship boat, into which we had put the chiefest of our merchandise, we went up the river to a place called Goto, where we arrived the 20th of February, the foresaid Goto being the nearest place that we could come to by water to go for Benin. From thence we presently sent negroes to the King to certify him of our arrival and of the cause of our coming thither: who returned to us again the 22nd day with a nobleman in their company to bring us up to the city, and with 200 negroes to carry our commodities. Hereupon the 23rd day we delivered our merchandise to the King's factor, and the 25th day we came to the great city of Benin, where we were well entertained. The six and twentieth day we went to the Court to have spoken with the King, which (by reason of a solemn feast then kept amongst them) we could not do: but yet we spake with his veadore, or chief man, that hath the dealing with the

Christians: and we conferred with him concerning our trading, who answered us that we should have all things to our desire, both in pepper and elephants' teeth.

The first of March we were admitted to the King's presence, and he made us the like courteous answer for our traffic. The next day we went again to the Court, where the foresaid veadore showed us one basket of green pepper and another of dry in the stalks: we desired to have it plucked from the stalks and made clean, who answered that it would ask time but yet it should be done; and that against another year it should be in better readiness, and the reason why we found it so unprepared was because in this King's time no Christians had ever resorted thither to lade pepper. The next day there were sent us 12 baskets, and so a little every day until the 9th of March, at which time we had made upon 64 serons of pepper and 28 elephants' teeth.

In this time of our being at Benin (our natures at this first time not so well acquainted with that climate) we fell all of us into the disease of the fever, whereupon the Captain sent me down, with those goods which we already had received, to the rest of our men at Goto; where, being arrived, I found all the men of our pinnace sick also, and by reason of their weakness not able to convey the pinnace and goods down to the place where our ship rode: but by good hap within two hours after my coming to Goto the boat came up from the ship, to see how all things stood with us, so that I put the goods into the boat and went down towards the ship. But by that time I was come aboard many of our men died; namely, Master Benson, the cooper, the carpenter, and three or four more, and myself was also in such a weak state that I was not able to return again to Benin. Whereupon I sent up Samuel Dunn and the chirurgeon with him to our men that were about to let them blood if it were thought needful; who at their coming to Benin found the Captain and your son, William Bird, dead, and Thomas Hempsteed very weak, who also died within two days after their coming thither. This sorrowful accident caused them, with such pepper and teeth [tusks] as they could then find, speedily to return to the ship, as by the cargason will appear. At their coming away the veadore told them that if they could or would stay any longer time he would use all possible expedition to bring in more commodities; but the common sickness so increased and continued amongst us all that by the time our men which remained were come aboard we had so many sick and dead of our company that we looked all for the same hap, and so thought to lose both our ship, life, country and all.

Very hardly and with much ado could we get up our anchors, but yet at the last by the mercy of God having gotten them up, but leaving our pinnace behind us, we got to sea and set sail, which was upon the 13th of April. After which by little and little our men began to gather up their crumbs and to recover some better strength. And so sailing betwixt the Islands of Cape Verde and the main we came to the Islands of the Azores upon the 25th of July, where our men began afresh to grow ill, and divers died, among whom Samuel Dunn was one, and as many as remained living were in a hard case. But in the midst of our distress it fell so well out, by God's good providence, that we met with your ship, the bark *Burre*, on this side the North Cape, which did not only keep us good company but also sent us six fresh men aboard, without whose help we should surely have tasted of many inconveniences. But by this good means we are now at the last arrived in Plymouth, this 9th day of September. And for want of better health at this time I refer the further knowledge of more particularities till my coming to London.

Yours to command,

Anthony Ingram

IN THE STRAITS OF MAGELLAN
William Magoths

To the sixteenth-century seamen the Straits of Magellan were probably the most dangerous sea-passage in the world. The broken channel, three hundred and sixty miles long, lay between mountainous cliffs and rocky inlets and islands, with sudden fierce storms, treacherous currents, hidden reefs, hostile Indians and often bitter cold to add to its terrors. In the last reach, from Cape Froward to the Pacific, unrelenting head-winds often drove a ship back again and again to the middle of the Straits. Magellan, the first to make the passage, had to chart his way and took 37 days. The first Englishman, Francis Drake, had copies of Magellan's charts, looted no doubt from a Spanish or Portuguese ship, and with his usual combination of genius and good luck he made a record passage in 16 days. The second English circumnavigator, Thomas Cavendish, took 49 days.

The Straits were long the only known way into the Pacific, for it was believed that the land to the south, Tierra del Fuego, was part of the hypothetical southern continent, Terra Australis Incognita, and even when the route round Cape Horn was known most ships preferred not to use it. On long voyages crews often faced the threat of starvation and the Straits offered fresh water, fresh food (penguins, seals and shell-fish) and wood for the cooks' galley-fires.

A brief relation of a voyage of the *Delight*, a ship of Bristol, one of the consorts of Master John Chidley, Esquire, and Master Paul Wheele, made unto the Strait of Magellan: with divers accidents that happened unto the company during their six weeks abode there. Begun in the year 1589. Written by William Magoths.

THE fifth of August, 1589, the worshipful Master John Chidley of Chidley, in the county of Devon, Esquire, with Master Paul Wheele and Captain Andrew Merick, set forth from Plymouth with three tall ships, the one called *The Wild Man*, of three hundred tons, wherein went for General the aforesaid Master John Chidley and Benjamin Wood as Master, the other called *The White Lion*, whereof Master Paul Wheele was Captain and John Ellis Master, of the burden of 340 tons; the third, *The Delight of Bristol*, wherein went Master Andrew Merick as Captain and Robert Burnet Master, with two pinnaces of 14 or 15 tons apiece. The General in his ship had 180 persons; Master Paul Wheele had 140; in our own ship we were 91 men and boys.

Our voyage was intended by the Strait of Magellan for the South Sea, and chiefly for the famous province of Arauco on the coast of Chile. We kept company together to the Isles of the Canaries, and so forward to Cape Blanco, standing near the northerly latitude of 20 degrees on the coast of Barbary, where some of our people went on shore, finding nothing to their content. Within twelve days after our departure from this place *The Delight*, wherein I, William Magoths, was, lost the company of the other two great ships and the two small pinnaces. Howbeit, we constantly kept our course according to our directions along the coast of Brazil, and by the River of Plate, without touching anywhere on land until we came to Port Desire in the latitude of 48 degrees to the southward of the Equinoctial.

Before we arrived at this place there died of our company by God's visitation of sundry diseases sixteen persons. We stayed in this harbour seventeen days to grave our ship and refresh our wearied people, hoping here to have met with our consorts; which fell out contrary to our expectations. During our abode in this place we found two little springs of fresh water, which were upon the north-westerly part of the land, and lighted upon good store of seals, both old and young. From hence we sailed toward the Strait of Magellan, and entered the same about the first of January. And coming to Penguin Island within the Strait we took and salted certain hogsheads of penguins, which must be eaten with speed, for we found them to be of no long continuance; we also furnished ourselves with fresh water. And here at the last sending off our boat to the island for the rest of our provision we lost her and 15 men in her by force of foul weather; but what became of them we could not tell. Here also in this storm we lost two anchors.

From hence we passed farther into the Strait, and by Port Famine we spake with a Spaniard, who told us that he had lived in those parts six years, and that he was one of the 400 men that were sent thither by the King of Spain in the year 1582 to fortify and inhabit there, to hinder the passage of all strangers that way into the South Sea. But that and the other Spanish colony, being both destroyed by famine, he said he had lived in an house by himself a long time, and relieved himself with his caliver until our coming thither.

Here we made a boat of the boards of our chests; which, being finished, we sent seven armed men in the same on land on the north shore, being wafted on land by the savages with certain white skins; who as soon as they came on shore were presently killed by an hundred of the wild people in the sight of two of our men which rowed them on shore, which two only escaped back again to us with the boat.

After this traitorous slaughter of our men we fell back again with our ship to the north-eastward of Port Famine to a certain road, where we refreshed ourselves with mussels, and took in water and wood. At this time we took in the Spaniard aforesaid, and so sailed forward again into the Strait. We passed seven or eight times ten leagues westward beyond Cape Froward, being still encountered with mighty north-west winds. These winds and the current were so vehement against us that they forced us back as much in two hours as we were getting up in eight hours.

Thus after we had spent six weeks in the Strait striving against the fury of the elements, and having at sundry times, partly by casualty and partly by sickness, lost 38 of our best men and three anchors, and now having but one anchor left us and small store of victuals, and, which was not the least mischief, divers of our company raising dangerous mutinies: we consulted, though somewhat with the latest, for the safeguard of our lives, to return while there was some small hope remaining; and so set sail out of the Strait homeward about the 14th of February, 1590.

We returned back again by the River of Plate. And sailing near the coast of Brazil we met with a Portugal ship of 80 tons, which rode at an anchor upon the coast, who as soon as she descried us to chase her incontinently weighed and ran herself on ground between the island of St Sebastian and the mainland. But we, for want of a good boat and by reason of the foul weather, were neither able to board her nor to go on shore. Thence in extreme misery we shaped our course for the isles of

Cape Verde, and so passing to the isles of the Azores, the Canaries being something out of our course.

The first land that we met withal in our narrow sea was the Isle of Alderney. And having now but six men of all our company left alive, the Master and his two mates and chief mariners being dead, we ran in with Monville de Hague, eight miles to the west of Cherbourg in Normandy, where the next day after our coming to an anchor, having but one in all left, being the last of August, 1590, by the foul weather that rose the anchor came home and our ship drave on the rocks. And the Normans, which were commanded by the Governor of Cherbourg (who came down to us that night) to have laid out another anchor for her, neglecting his commandment, suffered her miserably to be splitted, with desire to enrich themselves by her wrack.

Within few days after this last mischance four of us, being Englishmen, departed from Cherbourg, and passed home for England in a bark of Weymouth, leaving the two strangers there behind us.

The names of us six that returned of all our company were these: 1, William Magoths of Bristol; 2, Richard Bush; 3, John Read; 4, Richard Hodgkins of Westbury near Bristol: The two strangers: 5, Gabriel Valerosa, a Portugal; 6, Peter, a Breton.

A FIGHT WITH GALLEYS

Anonymous

This tale may well have been improved upon in the telling, but it shows clearly enough the dangers which English merchant ships had to face in the Mediterranean.

The valiant fight performed in the Straits of Gibraltar by the *Centurion* of London against five Spanish galleys, in the month of April, 1591.

IN the month of November, 1590, there were sundry ships appertaining to several merchants of London which were rigged and fraught forth with merchandise for sundry places within the Strait of Gibraltar; who, together having wind and weather, which ofttime fell out very uncertain, arrived safely in short space at such places as they desired: among whom was the *Centurion* of London, a very tall ship of burden, yet but weakly manned, as appeareth by this discourse following.

This aforesaid ship, called the *Centurion*, safely arrived at Marseilles, where after they had delivered their goods they stayed about the space of five weeks, and better, and then took in lading intending to return to England.

Now when the *Centurion* was ready to come away from Marseilles there were sundry other ships, of smaller burden, which entreated the Master thereof (whose name is Robert Bradshaw, dwelling at Limehouse), to stay a day or two for them until they were in a readiness to depart with them, thereby persuading them that it would be far better for them to stay and go together in respect of their assistance than to depart of themselves without company and so haply for want of aid fall into the hands of their enemies in the Spanish galleys. Upon which reasonable persuasion, notwithstanding that this ship was of such sufficiency as they might hazard her in the danger of the sea, yet they stayed for those little ships according to their request, who together did put to sea from Marseilles and vowed in general not to fly one from another if they should happen to meet with any Spanish galleys.

These small ships, accompanied with the *Centurion*, sailing along the coast of Spain were upon Easter Day in the Strait of Gibraltar suddenly becalmed, where immediately they saw sundry galleys make towards them in very valiant and courageous sort: the chief leaders and soldiers in those galleys, bravely apparelled in silk coats, with their silver whistles about their necks and great plumes of feathers in their hats, who with their calivers shot at the *Centurion* so fast as they might, so that by ten of the clock, and somewhat before, they had boarded the *Centurion*, who before their coming had prepared for them and intended to give them so sour a welcome as they might. And thereupon, having prepared their close fights and all things in a readiness, they called upon God, on whom only they trusted: and having made their prayers and cheered up one another to fight so long as life endured they began to discharge their great ordnance upon the galleys, but the little ships durst not come forward but lay aloof while five galleys had boarded them, yea, and with their grappling irons made their galleys fast to the said ship called the *Centurion*.

The galleys were grappled to the *Centurion* in this manner; two lay on one side, and two on another, and the admiral lay full in the stern, which galled and battered the *Centurion* so sore that her mainmast was greatly weakened, her sails filled with many holes, and the mizen and stern made almost unserviceable.

During which time there was a sore and deadly fight on both sides, in which the trumpet of the *Centurion* sounded forth the deadly points of war and encouraged them to fight manfully against their adversaries. On the contrary part, there was no warlike music in the Spanish galleys, but only their whistles of silver which they sounded forth to their own contentment; in which fight many a Spaniard was turned into the sea, and they in multitudes came crawling and hung upon the side of the ship, intending to have entered into the same, but such was the courage of the Englishmen that so fast as the Spaniards did come to enter they gave them such entertainment that some of them were glad to tumble alive into the sea, being remediless for ever to get up alive. In the *Centurion* there were in all, of men and boys, forty and eight, who together fought most valiantly, and so galled the enemy that many a brave and lusty Spaniard lost his life in that place.

The *Centurion* was fired five several times with wild fire and other provision, which the Spaniards threw in for that purpose: yet, God be thanked, by the great and diligent foresight of the Master it did no harm at all.

In every of the galleys there were about 200 soldiers; who, together with the shot, spoiled, rent and battered the *Centurion* very sore, shot through her mainmast, and slew four of the men in the said ship, the one of them being the Master's mate.

Ten other persons were hurt by means of splinters which the

Spaniards shot: yea, in the end when their provision was almost spent they were constrained to shoot at them hammers and the chains from their slaves, and yet, God be thanked, they received no more damage; but by spoiling and over-wearying of the Spaniards the Englishmen constrained them to ungrapple themselves, and get them going: and sure, if there had been any other fresh ship or succour to have relieved and assisted the *Centurion* they had slain, sunk, or taken all those galleys and their soldiers.

The *Dolphin* lay aloof off and durst not come near, while the other two small ships fled away, so that one of the galleys went from the *Centurion* and set upon the *Dolphin*, which ship immediately was set on fire with their own powder, whereby both men and ship perished: but whether it was with their goodwills or no, that was not known unto the *Centurion*, but sure, if it had come forward and been an aid unto the *Centurion* it is to be supposed that it had not perished.

Five hours and a half this fight continued, in which time both were glad to depart only to breath themselves, but when the Spaniards were gone they never durst return to fight: yet the next day six other galleys came and looked at them, but durst not at any hand meddle with them.

Thus God delivered them from the hands of their enemies and gave them the victory; for which they heartily praised Him, and not long after safely arrived in London.

There were present at this fight Master John Hawes, merchant, and sundry other of good accompt.

LANCASTER'S VOYAGE TO THE EAST INDIES

Richard Hakluyt

In 1589 a group of London merchants applied for authority to trade with the East Indies by the sea-route round the Cape of Good Hope which was used by the Portuguese. They were probably members of the Turkey Company (later the Levant Company), and they proposed to use ships belonging to the Company which were well armed to cope with Mediterranean pirates. The ultimate result of this was the expedition recorded below. It was expected to pay its way by looting Portuguese shipping in the east.

A voyage with three tall ships, the *Penelope*, admiral, the *Merchant Royal*, vice-admiral, and the *Edward Bonaventure*, rear-admiral, to the East Indies by the Cape of Buona Speranza, to Quitangone near Mozambique, to the isles of Comoro and Zanzibar on the backside of Africa, and beyond Cape Comorin in India to the isles of Nicobar and of Gomes Polo within two leagues of Sumatra, to the islands of Pulo Pinaom, and thence to the mainland of Malacca, begun by Master George Raymond in the year 1591, and performed by Master James Lancaster, and written from the mouth of Edmund Barker of Ipswich, his lieutenant in the said voyage, by Master Richard Hakluyt.

OUR fleet of the three tall ships above-named departed from Plymouth the 10th of April, 1591, and arrived at the Canary Islands the 25th of the same, from whence we departed the 29th of April. The 2nd of May we were in the height of Cape Blanco. The 5th we passed the Tropic of Cancer. The 8th we were in the height of Cape Verde. All this time we went with a fair wind at north-east, always before the wind until the 13th of the same month when we came within 8 degrees of the Equinoctial line where we met with a contrary wind. Here we lay off and on in the sea until the 6th of June, on which day we passed the said line. While we lay thus off and on we took a Portugal caravel laden by merchants of Lisbon for Brazil, in which caravel we had some 60 tons of wine, 1,200 jars of oil, about 100 jars of olives, certain barrels of capers, three fats of peason, with divers other necessaries fit for our voyage: which wine, oil, olives* and capers were better to us than gold.

We had two men died before we passed the Line, and divers sick which took their sickness in those hot climates; for they be wonderful unwholesome from 8 degrees of northerly latitude unto the Line at that time of the year: for we had nothing but tornadoes, with such thunder, lightning and rain that we could not keep our men dry three hours together, which was an occasion of the infection among them, and their eating of salt victuals, with lack of clothes to shift them. After we passed the Line we had the wind still at east-south-east which carried us along the coast of Brazil one hundred leagues from the main till we came in 26 degrees to the southward of the Line, where the wind came up to the north, at which time we did account that the Cape of Buona Esperanza did bear off us east and by south betwixt 900 and 1000 leagues. Passing this gulf from the coast of Brazil unto the Cape we had the wind often variable, as it is upon our coast, but for the most part so that we might lie our course. The 28th of July we had sight of the foresaid Cape of Buona Esperanza: until the 31st we lay off and on with the wind contrary to double the Cape, hoping to double it and so to have gone seventy leagues further to a place called Agoada de St Bras before we would have sought to have put into any harbour. But our men being weak and sick in all our ships we thought good to seek some place to refresh them. With which consent we bare up with the land to the northward of the Cape, and going along the shore we espied a goodly bay with an island lying to seawards of it, into which we did bear and found it very commodious for our ships to ride in. This bay is called Agoada de Saldanha, lying fifteen leagues northward on the hither side of the Cape.

The 1st of August, being Sunday, we came to an anchor in the bay, sending our men on land, and there came unto them certain black savages, very brutish, which would not stay but retired from them. For the space of fifteen or twenty days we could find no relief but only fowls which we killed with our pieces, which were cranes and geese; there was no fish but mussels and other shellfish which we gathered on the rocks.

After fifteen or twenty days being here our Admiral went with his pinnace unto the island which lieth off this bay, where he found great

* Oil and olives are often mentioned as valuable booty because there was a great demand for olive oil in England. It was essential in the making of woollen cloth, the country's most valuable export.

store of penguins and seals, whereof he brought good plenty with him. And twice after that we sent certain of our men which at both times brought their boats lading unto our ships. After we had been here some time we got here a negro, whom we compelled to march into the country with us making signs to bring us some cattle; but at this time we could come to the sight of none, so we let the negro go, with some trifles. Within eight days after he, with thirty or forty other negroes, brought us down some forty bullocks and oxen, with as many sheep; at which time we bought but few of them. But within eight days after they came down with as many more, and then we bought some twenty-four oxen with as many sheep. We bought an ox for two knives, a stirk [young bullock] for a knife, and a sheep for a knife, and some we bought for less value than a knife. The oxen be very large and well fleshed but not fat. The sheep are very big and very good meat; they have no wool on their backs but hair, and have great tails like the sheep in Syria.

There be divers sorts of wild beasts, as the antelope (whereof Master Lancaster killed one of the bigness of a young colt), the red and fallow deer, with other great beasts unknown unto us. Here are also great store of overgrown monkeys.

As touching our proceeding upon our voyage, it was thought good rather to proceed with two ships well manned than with three evil manned: for here we had of sound and whole men but 198, of which there went in the *Penelope* with the Admiral 101, and in the *Edward* with the worshipful Master Captain Lancaster 97. We left behind 50 men with the *Royal Merchant*, whereof there were many pretty well recovered, of which ship was Master and Governor Abraham Kendal, which for many reasons we thought good to send home. The disease that hath consumed our men hath been the scurvy. Our soldiers which have not been used to the sea have best held out, but our mariners dropped away, which (in my judgment) proceedeth of their evil diet at home.

Six days after our sending back for England of the *Merchant Royal* from Agoada de Saldanha our Admiral, Master Captain Raymond in the *Penelope*, and Master James Lancaster in the *Edward Bonaventure*, set forward to double the Cape of Good Hope, which they did very speedily. But being past as far as Cape dos Corrientes, the 14th of September, we were encountered with a mighty storm and extreme gusts of wind, wherein we lost our General's company, and could never hear of him nor his ship any more, though we did our best endeavour to seek him up and down a long while, and stayed for him certain days at the island of Comoro where we appointed to stay one for another.

Four days after this uncomfortable separation, in the morning toward ten of the clock, we had a terrible clap of thunder which slew four of our men outright, their necks being wrung in sunder without speaking any word, and of 94 men there was not one untouched, whereof some were stricken blind, others were bruised in their legs and arms, and others in their breasts so that they vomited blood two days after. Others were drawn out at length as though they had been racked. But (God be thanked) they all recovered saving only the four which were slain outright. Also with the same thunder our mainmast was torn very grievously from the head to the deck, and some of the spikes that were ten inches into the timber were melted with the extreme heat thereof. From thence we shaped our course to the north-east, and not long after we fell upon the north-west end of the mighty Island of St Laurence [Madagascar], which one of our men espied by God's good blessing late in the evening by moonlight, who, seeing afar off the breaking of the sea and calling to certain of his fellows, asked them what it was: which eftsoons told him that it was the breaking of the sea upon the shoals. Whereupon in very good time we cast about to avoid the danger which we were like to have incurred.

Thus passing on forward it was our luck to overshoot Mozambique and to fall with a place called Quitangone, two leagues to the northward of it, and we took three or four barks of Moors, which barks in their language they call pangaias, laden with millio, hens and ducks, with one Portugal boy, going for the provision of Mozambique.

Within few days following we came to an island an hundred leagues to the north-east of Mozambique, called Comoro, which we found exceeding full of people, which are Moors of tawny colour and good stature, but they be very treacherous and diligently to be taken heed of. Here we desired to store ourselves with water, whereof we stood in great need, and sent sixteen of our men well armed on shore in our boat; whom the people suffered quietly to land and water, and divers of them with their King came aboard our ship in a gown of crimson satin pinked after the Moorish fashion down to the knee, whom we entertained in the best manner, and had some conference with him of the state of the place and merchandises, using our Portugal boy which we had taken before for our interpreter, and in the end licensed the King and his company to depart, and sent out men again for more water, who then also dispatched their business and returned quietly. The third time likewise we sent them for more, which also returned without any harm. And though we thought ourselves furnished yet our Master, William Mace of Radcliffe, pretending that it might be long before we should find any good watering place, would needs go himself on shore with thirty men much against the will of our Captain, and he and sixteen of his company, together with one boat which was all that we had, and sixteen others that were awashing over against our ship, were betrayed of the perfidious Moors and in our sight for the most part slain, we being not able for want of a boat to yield them any succour.

From hence with heavy hearts we shaped our course for Zanzibar the 7th of November, where shortly after we arrived and made us a new boat of such boards as we had within board, and rid in the road until the 15th of February, where during our abode we saw divers pangaias or boats, which are pinned with wooden pins and sewed together with palmetto cords and caulked with the husks of cocos shells beaten, whereof they make oakum.

At length a Portugal pangaia, coming out of the harbour of Zanzibar, where they have a small factory, sent a canoe with a Moor which had been christened, who brought us a letter wherein they desired to know what we were and what we sought. We sent them word we were Englishmen come from Don Antonio upon business to his friends in the Indies: with which answer they returned, and would not any more come at us. Whereupon not long after we manned out our boat and took a pangaia of the Moors which had a priest of theirs in it, which in their language they call a sherif, whom we used very courteously: which the King took in very good part, having his priests in great estimation, and for his deliverance furnished us with two months' victuals, during all which time we detained him with us. These Moors informed us of the false and spiteful dealing of the Portugals towards us which made them believe that we were cruel people and men-eaters, and willed them if they loved their safety in no case to come near us. Which they did only to cut us off from all knowledge of the state and traffic of the country.

While we rode from the end of November until the middle of February in this harbour, which is sufficient for a ship of 500 tons to ride in, we set upon a Portugal pangaia with our boat, but because it was very little and our men not able to stir in it, we were not able to take the said pangaia, which was armed with ten good shot like our long fowling-pieces. This place, for the goodness of the harbour and watering and plentiful refreshing with fish, whereof we took great store with our nets, and for sundry sorts of fruits of the country, as cocos and others, which were brought us by the Moors, as also for oxen and hens, is carefully to be sought for by such of our ships as shall hereafter pass that way. But our men had need to take good heed of the Portugals; for while we lay here the Portugal Admiral of the coast from Melinde to Mozambique came to view and to betray our boat, if he could have taken at any time advantage, in a galley frigate of ten tons with eight or nine oars on a side. Of the strength of which frigate and their treacherous meaning we were advertised by an Arabian Moor which came from the King of Zanzibar divers times unto us about the delivery of the priest aforesaid, and afterward by another which we carried thence along with us: for wheresoever we came our care was to get into our hands some one or two of the countries, to learn the languages and states of those parts where we touched.

Moreover, here again we had another clap of thunder which did shake our foremast very much, which we fished and repaired with timber from the shore, whereof there is good store thereabout of a kind of trees some forty foot high, which is a red and tough wood, and, as I suppose, a kind of cedar. Here our surgeon, Arnold, negligently catching a great heat in his head, being on land with the Master to seek oxen, fell sick and shortly died, which might have been cured by letting of blood before it had been settled.

Before our departure we had in this place some thousand weight of pitch, or rather a kind of grey and white gum like unto frankincense, as clammy as turpentine, which in melting groweth as black as pitch and is very brittle of itself, but we mingled it with oil whereof we had 300 jars in the prize which we took to the northward of the Equinoctial, not far from Guinea, bound for Brazil.

Six days before we departed hence the Cape merchant of the factory wrote a letter unto our Captain in the way of friendship, as he pretended, requesting a jar of wine and a jar of oil and two or three pounds of gunpowder, which letter he sent by a negro, his man, and Moor in a canoe. We sent him his demands by the Moor, but took the negro along with us because we understood he had been in the East

Indies and knew somewhat of the country. By this negro we were advertised of a small bark of some thirty tons (which the Moors call a junco) which was come from Goa thither laden with pepper for the factory and service of that kingdom.

Thus, having trimmed our ship as we lay in this road in the end we set forward for the coast of the East India, the 15th of February aforesaid, intending if we could to have reached to Cape Comorin, which is the headland or promontory of the main of Malabar, and there to have lien off and on for such ships as should have passed from Zeilan, Sant Tome, Bengal, Pegu, Malacca, the Moluccas, the coast of China and the isle of Japan, which ships are of exceeding wealth and riches. But in our course we were very much deceived by the currents that set into the Gulf of the Red Sea along the coast of Melinde. And the winds, shortening upon us to the north-east and easterly, kept us that we could not get off and so with the putting in of the currents from the westward set us in further unto the northward within fourscore leagues of the isle of Socotra, far from our determined course and expectation. But here we never wanted abundance of dolphins, bonitos and flying fishes.

Now while we found ourselves thus far to the northward and the time being so far spent, we determined to go for the Red Sea, or for the island of Socotra, both to refresh ourselves and also for some purchase. But while we were in this consultation the wind very luckily came about to the north-west and carried us directly toward Cape Comorin. Before we should have doubled this Cape we were determined to touch at the islands of Mamale, of which we had advertisement that one had victuals, standing in the northerly latitude of twelve degrees. Howbeit, it was not our good luck to find it, which fell out partly by the obstinacy of our Master: for the day before we fell with part of the islands the wind came about to the south-west, and then shifting our course we missed it. So the wind increasing southerly we feared we should not have been able to have doubled the Cape, which would have greatly hazarded our casting away upon the coast of India, the winter season and western monsoons already being come in, which monsoons continue on that coast until August. Nevertheless it pleased God to bring the wind more westerly, and so in the month of May, 1592, we happily doubled Cape Comorin without sight of the coast of India.

From hence, thus having doubled this Cape, we directed our course for the islands of Nicobar, which lie north and south with the western part of Sumatra and in the latitude of 7 degrees to the northward of the Equinoctial: from which Cape of Comorin unto the aforesaid islands we ran in six days with a very large wind though the weather were foul with extreme rain and gusts of winds. These islands were missed through our Master's default for want of due observation of the South star. And we fell to the southward of them within the sight of the islands of Gomes Pulo, which lie hard upon the great island of Sumatra, the first of June, and at the north-east side of them we lay two or three days becalmed, hoping to have had a pilot from Sumatra within two leagues whereof we lay off and on.

Now the winter coming upon us with much contagious weather, we directed our course from hence with the islands of Pulo Pinaou (where by the way is to be noted that Pulo in the Malayan tongue signifieth an island), at which islands we arrived about the beginning of June, where we came to an anchor in a very good harbour between three islands: at which time our men were very sick and many fallen.

Here we determined to stay until the winter were overpast. This place is in 6 degrees and a half to the northward and some five leagues from the main between Malacca and Pegu. Here we continued until the end of August. Our refreshing in this place was very small, only of oysters growing on rocks, great whelks, and some few fish which we took with our hooks. Here we landed our sick men on these uninhabited islands for their health; nevertheless twenty-six of them died in this place, whereof John Hall, our Master, was one, and Master Reynold Golding another, a merchant of great honesty and much discretion. In these islands are abundance of trees of white wood, so right and tall that a man may make masts of them being an hundred foot long.

The winter passed, and having watered our ship and fitted her to go to sea we had left us but 33 men and one boy, of which not past 22 were sound for labour and help, and of them not past a third part sailors. Thence we made sail to seek some place of refreshing and went over to the main of Malacca. The next day we came to an anchor in a bay in six fathoms water some two leagues from the shore. Then Master James Lancaster, our Captain, and Master Edmund Barker, his Lieutenant, and other of the company manning the boat, went on shore to see what inhabitants might be found. And coming on land we found the tracking of some barefooted people which were departed thence not long before, for we saw their fire still burning but people we saw none, nor any other living creature save a certain kind of fowl called oxbirds, which are a grey kind of seafowl, like a snipe in colour but not in beak. Of these we killed some eight dozen with hail-shot being very tame, and spending the day in search returned toward night aboard.

The next day, about two of the clock in the afternoon, we espied a canoe which came near unto us but would not come aboard us, having in it some sixteen naked Indians, with whom nevertheless going afterward on land we had friendly conference and promise of victuals. The next day in the morning we espied three ships, being all of burden 60 or 70 tons, one of which we made to strike with our very boat: and understanding that they were of the town of Martaban, which is the chief haven town for the great city of Pegu, and the goods belonging to certain Portugal Jesuits and a biscuit baker, a Portugal, we took that ship and did not force the other two because they were laden for merchants of Pegu, but having this one at our command we came together to an anchor. The night following all the men except twelve, which we took into our ship being most of them born in Pegu, fled away in their boat, leaving their ship and goods with us. The next day we weighed our anchor and went to the leeward of an island hard by and took in her lading, being pepper, which she and the other two had laden at Pera, which is a place on the main 30 leagues to the south. Besides the aforesaid three ships we took another ship of Pegu laden with pepper, and perceiving her to be laden with merchants' goods of Pegu only we dismissed her without touching anything.

Thus having stayed here ten days and discharged her goods into the *Edward*, which was about the beginning of September, our sick men being somewhat refreshed and lusty with such relief as we had found in this ship, we weighed anchor, determining to run into the Straits of Malacca, to the islands called Pulo Sambilam which are some five and forty leagues northward of the city of Malacca, to which islands the Portugals must needs come from Goa or Saint Thome for the Moluccas, China and Japan. And when we were there arrived we lay to and again for such shipping as should come that way. Thus having spent some five days, upon a Sunday we espied a sail which was a Portugal ship that came from Negapatam, a town on the main of India over against the north-east part of the isle of Zeilan [Ceylon]; and that night we took her, being of 250 tons: she was laden with rice for Malacca. Captain Lancaster commanded their Captain and Master aboard our ship, and sent Edmund Barker, his lieutenant, and seven more to keep this prize, who being aboard the same came to an anchor in thirty fathoms water: for in that channel three or four leagues from the shore you shall find good anchorage.

Being thus at an anchor and keeping out a light for the *Edward*, another Portugal ship of Saint Thome of four hundred tons came and anchored hard by us. The *Edward*, being put to leeward for lack of help of men to handle her sails, was not able the next morning to fetch her up until we which were in the prize with our boat went to help to man our ship. Then coming aboard we went toward the ship of Saint Thome, but our ship was so foul that she escaped us. After we had taken out of our Portugal prize what we thought good we turned her and all her men away except a pilot and four Moors.

We continued here until the sixth of October, at which time we met with the ship of the Captain of Malacca of seven hundred tons which came from Goa: we shot at her many shot, and at last shooting her mainyard through she came to an anchor and yielded. We commanded her Captain, Master, Pilot and Purser to come aboard us. But the Captain, accompanied with one soldier only came, and after certain conference with him he made excuse to fetch the Master and purser, which he said would not come unless he went for them: but being gotten from us in the edge of the evening he, with all the people which were to the number of about three hundred men, women and children, got ashore with two great boats and quite abandoned the ship. At our coming aboard we found in her sixteen pieces of brass and three hundred butts of Canary wine, and nipa wine, which is made of the palm trees, and raisin wine which is also very strong; as also all kind of haberdasher wares, as hats, red caps knit of Spanish wool, worsted stockings knit, shoes, velvets, taffetas, chamlets and silks, abundance of suckets, rice, Venice glasses, certain papers full of false and counterfeit stones which an Italian brought from Venice to deceive the rude Indians withal, abundance of playing cards, two or three packs of French paper. Whatsoever became of the treasure, which usually is brought in royals of plate in this galleon, we could not find it. After that the mariners had disorderly pilled this rich ship the Captain, because they would not follow his commandment to unlade those excellent wines into the *Edward*, abandoned her and let her drive at sea, taking out of her the choicest things that she had.

And doubting the forces of Malacca we departed thence to a bay in the kingdom of Junkseylon, which is between Malacca and Pegu eight degrees to the northward, to seek for pitch to trim our ship. Here we sent our soldier, which the Captain of the aforesaid galleon had left behind him with us because he had the Malayan language, to deal with the people for pitch, which he did faithfully and procured us some two or three quintals with promise of more, and certain of the people came unto us. We sent commodities to their king to barter for ambergris and for the horns of abath [?rhinoceros], whereof the king only hath the traffic in his hands. Now this abath is a beast which hath one horn only in her forehead, and is thought to be the female unicorn, and is highly esteemed of all the Moors in those parts as a most sovereign remedy against poison. We had only two or three of these horns, which are of the colour of a brown grey, and some reasonable quantity of ambergris. At last the king went about to betray our Portugal with our merchandise; but he, to get aboard us, told him that we had gilt armour, shirts of mail and halberds, which things they greatly desire, for hope whereof he let him return aboard and so he escaped the danger.

Thus we left this coast and went back again in sight of Sumatra, and thence to the islands of Nicobar, where we arrived and found them inhabited with Moors, and after we came to an anchor the people daily came aboard us in their canoes with hens, cocos, plantains and other fruits: and within two days they brought unto us royals of plate, giving us them for calico cloth, which royals they find by diving for them in the sea which were lost not long before in two Portugal ships which were bound for China and were cast away there. They call in their language the coco *calambe*, the plantain *pison*, a hen *jam*, a fish *iccan*, a hog *babee*.

From thence we returned the 21st of November to go for the island of Zeilan, and arrived there about the 3rd of December, 1592, and anchored upon the south side in six fathoms water, where we lost our anchor, the place being rocky and foul ground. Then we ran along the south-west part of the said island to a place called Punta del Galle, where we anchored, determining there to have remained until the coming of the Bengal fleet of seven or eight ships, and the fleet of Pegu of two or three sails, and the Portugal ships of Tenasserim, being a great bay to the southward of Martaban in the Kingdom of Siam: which ships, by divers intelligences which we had, were to come that way within fourteen days to bring commodities to serve the carracks which commonly depart from Cochin for Portugal by the midst of January. The commodities of the ships which come from Bengal be fine pavilions for beds, wrought quilts, fine calico cloth, pintados and other fine works, and rice, and they make this voyage twice in the year. Those of Pegu bring the chiefest stones, as rubies and diamonds, but their chief freight is rice and certain cloth. Those of Tenasserim are chiefly freighted with rice and nipa wine, which is very strong and in colour like unto rock water somewhat whitish, and very hot in taste like unto *aqua vitae*.

Being shot up to the place aforesaid, called Punta del Galle, we came to an anchor in foul ground and lost the same, and lay all that night adrift because we had now but two anchors left us which were unstocked and in hold. Whereupon our men took occasion to come home, our Captain at that time lying very sick, more like to die than to live. In the morning we set our foresail, determining to lie up to the northward and there to keep ourselves to and again out of the current, which otherwise would have set us off to the southward from all known land. Thus having set our foresail, and in hand to set all our other sails, to accomplish our aforesaid determination, our men made answer that they would take their direct course for England and would stay there no longer. Now seeing they could not be persuaded by any means possible the Captain was constrained to give his consent to return, leaving all hope of so great possibilities.

Thus the eighth of December, 1592, we set sail for the Cape of *Buona Speranza*, passing by the islands of Maldiva, and leaving the mighty island of St Laurence [Madagascar] on the starboard or northward in the latitude of 26 degrees to the south. In our passage over from St Laurence to the main we had exceeding great store of bonitos and albacores, which are a greater kind of fish, of which our Captain, being now recovered of his sickness, took with an hook as many in two or three hours as would serve forty persons a whole day. And this school of fish continued with our ship for the space of five or six weeks, all which while we took to the quantity aforesaid, which was no small refreshing to us.

In February, 1593, we fell with the eastermost land of Africa, at a place called Baia de Agoa, some 100 leagues to the northeast of the Cape of Good Hope: and finding the winds contrary we spent a month or five weeks before we could double the Cape. After we had doubled it in March following we directed our course for the island of Saint Helena, and arrived there the third day of April, where we stayed to our great comfort nineteen days: in which mean space some one man of us took thirty goodly congers in one day, and other rocky fish, and some bonitos.

After our arrival at Saint Helena I, Edmund Barker, went on shore with four or five Peguins, or men of Pegu, which we had taken, and our surgeon, where in an house by the chapel I found an Englishman, one John Segar of Bury in Suffolk, who was left there eighteen months before by Abraham Kendall, who put in there with the *Royal Merchant* and left him there to refresh him on the island, being otherwise like to have perished on shipboard: and at our coming we found him as fresh in colour and in as good plight of body to our seeming as might be, but crazed in mind and half out of his wits as afterward we perceived: for whether he were put in fright of us, not knowing at first what we were, whether friends or foes, or of sudden joy when he understood we were his old consorts and countrymen, he became idle-headed, and for eight days' space neither night nor day took any natural rest and so at length died for lack of sleep.

Here two of our men, whereof the one was diseased with the scurvy and the other had been nine months sick of the flux, in short time while they were on the island recovered their perfect health. We found in this place great store of very wholesome and excellent good green figs, oranges, and lemons very fair, abundance of goats and hogs and great plenty of partridges, guinea cocks, and other wild fowls.

Our mariners, somewhat discontented, being now watered and having some provision of fish, contrary to the will of the Captain would straight home. The Captain, because he was desirous to go for

Pernambuco in Brazil, granted their request. And about the 12th of April, 1593, we departed from St Helena and directed our course for the place aforesaid. The next day our Captain, calling upon the sailors to finish a foresail which they had in hand, some of them answered that unless they might go directly home they would lay their hands to nothing; whereupon he was constrained to follow their humour.

And from thenceforth we directed our course for our country, which we kept until we came 8 degrees to the northward of the Equinoctial, between which 8 degrees and the line we spent some six weeks, with many calm and contrary winds at north, and sometimes to the eastward, and sometimes to the westward: which loss of time and expense of our victuals, whereof we had very small store, made us doubt to keep our course. And some of our men, growing into a mutiny, threatened to break up other men's chests, to the overthrow of our victuals and all our selves, for every man had his share of his victuals before in his own custody that they might be sure what to trust to and husband it more thriftily. Our Captain, seeking to prevent this mischief, being advertised by one of our company which had been at the isle of Trinidad in Master Chidley's voyage that there we should be sure to have refreshing, hereupon directed his course to that island, and not knowing the currents we were put past it in the night into the Gulf of Paria in the beginning of June, wherein we were eight days, finding the current continually setting in, and oftentimes we were in three fathoms water and could find no going out until the current had put us over to the western side under the mainland, where we found no current at all and more deep water. And so keeping by the shore, the wind off the shore every night did help us out to the northward.

Being clear, within four or five days after we fell with the isle of Mona where we anchored and rode some eighteen days: in which time the Indians of Mona gave us some refreshing. And in the mean space there arrived a French ship of Caen in which was Captain one Monsieur de Barbaterre, of whom we bought some two butts of wine and bread and other victuals. Then we watered and fitted our ship, and stopped a great leak which broke on us as we were beating out of the Gulf of Paria. And having thus made ready our ship to go to sea, we determined to go directly for Newfoundland. But before we departed there arose a storm, the wind being northerly, which put us from an anchor and forced us to the southward of Santo Domingo. This night we were in danger of shipwreck upon an island called Savona, which is environed with flats lying four or five miles off: yet it pleased God to clear us of them, and so we directed our course westward along the Island of Santo Domingo and doubled Cape Tiburon, and passed through the old channel between Santo Domingo and Cuba for the Cape of Florida.

And here we met again with the French ship of Caen, whose Captain could spare us no more victuals, as he said, but only hides which he had taken by traffic upon those islands, wherewith we were content and gave him for them to his good satisfaction.

After this, passing the Cape of Florida and clear of the channel of Bahama, we directed our course for the bank of Newfoundland. Thus running, to the height of 36 degrees and as far to the east as the isle of Bermuda, the 17th of September, finding the winds there very variable, contrary to our expectation and all men's writings, we lay there a day or two, the wind being northerly and increasing continually more and more it grew to be a storm and a great fret of wind, which continued with us some 24 hours with such extremity as it carried not only our sails away, being furled, but also made much water in our ship, so that we had six foot water in hold; and having freed our ship thereof with baling the wind shifted to the northwest and became dulled: but presently upon it the extremity of the storm was such that with the labouring of the ship we lost our foremast, and our ship grew as full of water as before.

The storm once ceased and the wind contrary to go our course we fell to consultation which might be our best way to save our lives. Our victuals now being utterly spent, and having eaten hides six or seven days, we thought it best to bear back again for Dominica and the islands adjoining, knowing that there we might have some relief, whereupon we turned back for the said islands. But before we could get thither the wind scanted upon us, which did greatly endanger us for lack of fresh water and victuals, so that we were constrained to bear up to the westward to certain other islands called the Nueblas or Cloudy Islands, towards the Isle of St Juan de Porto Rico, where at our arrival we found land-crabs and fresh water, and tortoises which came most on land about the full of the moon. Here having refreshed ourselves some 17 or 18 days and having gotten some small store of victuals into our ship, we resolved to return again for Mona: upon which our determination five of our men left us, remaining still on the isles of Nueblas for all persuasions that we could use to the contrary, which afterward came home in an English ship.

From these isles we departed and arrived at Mona about the twentieth of November, 1593; and there coming to an anchor toward two or three of the clock in the morning, the Captain and Edmund Barker, his Lieutenant, with some few others went on land to the houses of the old Indian and his three sons thinking to have gotten some food, our victuals being all spent and we not able to proceed any further until we had obtained some new supply. We spent two or three days in seeking provision to carry aboard to relieve the whole company.

And coming down to go aboard, the wind then being northerly and the sea somewhat grown, they could not come on shore with the boat, which was a thing of small succour and not able to row in any rough sea, whereupon we stayed until the next morning, thinking to have had less wind and safer passage. But in the night, about twelve of the clock, our ship did drive away with five men and a boy only in it, our carpenter secretly cut their own cable, leaving nineteen of us on land without boat or anything, to our great discomfort.

In the midst of these miseries, reposing our trust in the goodness of God, which many times before had succoured us in our greatest extremities, we contented ourselves with our poor estate and sought means to preserve our lives. And because one place was not able to sustain us we took our leaves one of another, dividing ourselves into several companies. The greatest relief that we six which were with the Captain could find for the space of nine and twenty days was the stalks of purslane boiled in water, and now and then a pompion which we found in the garden of the old Indian, who upon this our second arrival with his three sons stole from us and kept himself continually aloft in the mountains.

After the end of nine and twenty days we espied a French ship, which afterward we understood to be of Dieppe, called the *Luisa*, whose Captain was one Monsieur Felix, unto whom we made a fire, at sight whereof he took in his topsails, bare in with the land and showed us his flag, whereby we judged him French: so coming along to the western end of the island there he anchored, we making down with all speed unto him. At this time the Indian and his three sons came down to our Captain, Master James Lancaster, and went along with him to the ship. This night he went aboard the Frenchman, who gave him good entertainment, and the next day fetched eleven more of us aboard entreating us all very courteously.

This day came another French ship of the same town of Dieppe which remained there until night expecting our other seven men's coming down; who, albeit we caused certain pieces of ordnance to be shot off to call them, yet came not down. Whereupon we departed thence, being divided six into one ship and six into another, and leaving this island departed for the north side of Santo Domingo, where we remained until April following, 1594, and spent some two months in traffic with the inhabitants by permission for hides and other merchandises of the country.

In this meanwhile there came a ship of Newhaven to the place where we were, whereby we had intelligence of our seven men which we left behind us at the isle of Mona: which was that two of them brake their necks with venturing to take fowls upon the cliffs, other three were slain by the Spaniards which came from Santo Domingo upon knowledge given by our men which went away in the *Edward*, the other two this man of Newhaven had with him in his ship, which escaped the Spaniards' bloody hands.

From this place Captain Lancaster and his Lieutenant, Master Edmund Barker, shipped themselves in another ship of Dieppe, the captain whereof was one John La Noe, which was ready first to come away, and leaving the rest of their company in other ships, where they were well intreated, to come after him, on Sunday, the seventh of April, 1594, they set homeward, and disbocking through the Caicos from thence arrived safely in Dieppe within two and forty days after, on the 19th of May, where, after we had stayed two days to refresh ourselves, and given humble thanks unto God and unto our friendly neighbours, we took passage for Rye and landed there on Friday, the 24th of May, 1594, having spent in this voyage three years, six weeks and two days, which the Portugals perform in half the time, chiefly because we lost our fit time and season to set forth in the beginning of our voyage.

We understood in the East Indies, by certain Portugals which we took, that they have lately discovered the coast of China to the latitude of nine and fifty degrees, finding the sea still open to the northward; giving great hope of the North-east or North-west passage. Witness, Master James Lancaster.

About four-fifths of the men of this expedition died at sea, and the capital 'adventured' in it was entirely lost, but this was not the end of trade with the East Indies. Members of the Levant Company, with their heavily armed merchant-ships, took up the trade and on December 31st, 1600 Elizabeth granted a charter for the formation of the East India Company, which was destined to create the great Indian Empire and to administer it until 1858.

THE LAST FIGHT OF THE *REVENGE*

Sir Walter Raleigh

Sir Richard Grenville's lifetime of public service in the House of Commons and in Cornwall, his adventures at sea (piracy included) and his part in colonising Virginia have all been forgotten. He lives only in his death, which has been inscribed on the national memory by the eloquence first of Raleigh and then of Tennyson. He died as he had lived, a proud, harsh, high-tempered, reckless man.

He had the right ship for his last action. The Revenge *had been chosen by Drake as his flagship against the Armada because she was one of the most efficient warships afloat, a middle-weight ocean-going galleon, rated at 500 tons, long in proportion to her beam (92 feet: 32 feet) with low castles and a heavy armament of some forty guns. She should have escaped, as her master suggested. Grenville was free to choose. He may have believed that he could fight his way through the enemy fleet, but he must have known that he was choosing almost certain death for his ship, his crew and himself. C'était magnifique mais ce n'était pas la guerre. Howard chose the wiser, more patriotic course. But it is Grenville who is remembered.*

A report of the truth of the fight about the isles of Azores, the last of August, 1591, betwixt the *Revenge*, one of Her Majesty's ships, and an armada of the King of Spain. Penned by the Honourable Sir Walter Raleigh, Knight.

BECAUSE the rumours are diversely spread, as well in England as in the Low Countries and elsewhere, of this late encounter between Her Majesty's ships and the Armada of Spain: and that the Spaniards, according to their usual manner, fill the world with their vain-glorious vaunts, making great appearance of victories when, on the contrary, themselves are most commonly and shamefully beaten and dishonoured; thereby hoping to possess the ignorant multitude by anticipating and forerunning false reports; it is agreeable with all good reason, for manifestation of the truth, to overcome falsehood and untruth; that the beginning, continuance and success of this late honourable encounter of Sir Richard Grenville and other Her Majesty's Captains with the Armada of Spain should be truly set down and published without partiality or false imaginations.

And it is no marvel that the Spaniard should seek by false and slanderous pamphlets, advisos and letters to cover their own loss, and to derogate from others their due honours, especially in this fight being performed far off; seeing they were not ashamed in the year 1588, when they purposed the invasion of this land, to publish in sundry languages, in print, great victories in words, which they pleaded to have obtained against this Realm; and spread the same in a most false sort over all parts of France, Italy, and elsewhere. When shortly after it was happily manifested in very deed to all nations how their navy, which they termed invincible, consisting of 140 sail of ships, not only of their own kingdom but strengthened with the greatest argosies, Portugal carracks, Florentines, and huge hulks of other countries, were by 30 of Her Majesty's own ships of war and a few of our own merchants by the wise, valiant, and advantageous conduct of the Lord Charles Howard, High Admiral of England, beaten and shuffled together, even from the Lizard in Cornwall first to Portland, where they shamefully left Don Pedro de Valdes with his mighty ship; from Portland to Calais, where they lost Hugo de Moncado, with the galleass of which he was Captain; and from Calais, driven with squibs from their anchors, were chased out of the sight of England, round about Scotland and Ireland, where, for the sympathy of their barbarous religion hoping to find succour and assistance, a great part of them were crushed against the rocks, and those other that landed, being very many in number, were notwithstanding broken, slain and taken, and so sent from village to village coupled in halters, to be shipped into England. Where Her Majesty, of her princely and invincible disposition, disdaining to put them to death, and scorning either to retain or entertain them, they were all sent back again to their countries, to witness and recount the worthy achievements of their invincible and dreadful navy: of which the number of soldiers, the fearful burden of their ships, the commanders' names of every squadron, with all other their magazines of provisions, were put in print as an army and navy unresistable, and disdaining prevention. With all which so great and terrible an ostentation they did not in all their sailing round about England so much as sink or take one ship, bark, pinnace, or cock-boat of ours, or ever burnt so much as one sheepcote of this land. Whenas on the contrary, Sir Francis Drake, with only 800 soldiers, not long before landed in their Indies, and forced Santiago, Santo Domingo, Cartagena, and the forts of Florida.

And after that, Sir John Norris marched from Peniche in Portugal, with a handful of soldiers, to the gates of Lisbon, being above 40 English miles, where the Earl of Essex himself and other valiant gentlemen braved the city of Lisbon, encamped at the very gates; from whence, after many days abode, finding neither promised party nor provision to batter, they made retreat by land, in despite of all their garrisons, both of horse and foot.

In this sort I have a little digressed from my first purpose, only by the necessary comparison of theirs and our actions: the one covetous of honour without vaunt of ostentation: the other so greedy to purchase the opinion of their own affairs, and by false rumours to resist the blasts of their own dishonours as they will not only not blush to spread all manner of untruths, but even for the least advantage, be it but for the taking of one poor adventurer of the English, will celebrate the victory with bonfires in every town, always spending more in faggots than the purchase was worth they obtained: when as we never thought it worth the consumption of two billets when we have taken eight or ten of their Indian ships at one time, and twenty of the Brazil fleet. Such is the difference between true valour and ostentation; and between honourable actions and frivolous, vainglorious vaunts. But now to return to my purpose.

The Lord Thomas Howard, with six of Her Majesty's ships, six victuallers of London, the bark *Raleigh*, and two or three other pinnaces riding at anchor near unto Flores, one of the westerly islands of the Azores, the last of August [1591] in the afternoon, had intelligence by one, Captain Middleton, of the approach of the Spanish Armada. Which Middleton, being in a very good sailor, had kept them company three days before, of good purpose, both to discover their forces the more as also to give advice to my Lord Thomas of their approach. He had no sooner delivered the news but the fleet was in sight.

Many of our ship's companies were on shore in the island, some providing ballast for their ships, other filling of water and refreshing themselves from the land with such things as they could either for money or by force recover. By reason whereof our ships, being all pestered and rummaging everything out of order, very light for want of ballast and, that which was most to our disadvantage, the one half part of the men of every ship sick and utterly unserviceable: for in the *Revenge* there were ninety diseased; in the *Bonaventure* not so many in health as could handle her mainsail. For had not twenty men been taken out of a bark of Sir George Carey's, his being commanded to be sunk, and those appointed to her, she had hardly ever recovered England. The rest, for the most part, were in little better state. The names of Her Majesty's ships were these as followeth: the *Defiance*, which was admiral, the *Revenge* vice-admiral, the *Bonaventure*, commanded by Captain Cross, the *Lion* by George Fenner, the *Foresight* by Master Thomas Vavasour, and the *Crane* by Duffield; the *Foresight* and the *Crane* being but small ships, only the other were of the middle size: the rest, besides the bark *Raleigh*, commanded by Captain Thynne were victuallers and of small force or none.

The Spanish fleet, having shrouded their approach by reason of the Island, were now so soon at hand as our ships had scarce time to weigh their anchors, but some of them were driven to let slip their cables and set sail. Sir Richard Grenville was the last that weighed, to recover the men that were upon the island, which otherwise had been lost. The Lord Thomas, with the rest, very hardly recovered the wind, which Sir Richard Grenville, not being able to do, was persuaded by the Master and others to cut his mainsail and cast about, and to trust to the sailing of the ship; for the squadron of Seville were on his weather bow. But Sir Richard utterly refused to turn from the enemy, alleging that he would rather choose to die than to dishonour himself, his country, and Her Majesty's ship, persuading his company that he would pass through the two squadrons in despite of them, and enforce those of Seville to give him way. Which he performed upon divers of the foremost, who, as the mariners term it, sprang their luff and fell under the lee of the *Revenge*. But the other course had been the better, and might right well have been answered in so great an impossibility of prevailing. Notwithstanding, out of the greatness of his mind he could not be persuaded.

In the meanwhile as he attended those which were nearest him, the great *San Philip*, being in the wind of him and coming towards him, becalmed his sails in such sort as the ship could neither make way nor feel the helm; so huge and high charged was the Spanish ship, being of a thousand and five hundred tons: who after laid the *Revenge* aboard. When he was thus bereft of his sails, the ships that were under his lee, luffing up, also laid him aboard; of which the next was the admiral of the Biscayans very mighty and puissant ship commanded by Bertendona. The said *Philip* carried three tier of ordnance on a side, and eleven pieces in every tier. She shot eight forth right out of her chase, besides those of her stern ports.

After the *Revenge* was entangled with this *Philip* four other boarded her, two on her larboard and two on her starboard. The fight thus beginning at three of the clock in the afternoon continued very terrible all that evening. But the great *San Philip*, having received the lower tier of the *Revenge* discharged with crossbar shot, shifted herself with all diligence from her sides, utterly misliking her first entertainment. Some say that the ship foundered, but we cannot report it for truth unless we were assured. The Spanish ships were filled with companies of soldiers, in some two hundred besides the mariners, in some five, in others eight hundred. In ours there were none at all beside the mariners but the servants of the commanders and some few voluntary gentlemen only.

After many interchanged volleys of great ordnance and small shot the Spaniards deliberated to enter the *Revenge*, and made divers attempts, hoping to force her by the multitudes of their armed soldiers and musketeers, but were still repulsed again and again, and at all times beaten back into their own ships or into the seas. In the beginning of the fight the *George Noble* of London, having received some shot through her by the armadas, fell under the lee of the *Revenge* and asked Sir Richard what he would command him, being but one of the victuallers and of small force. Sir Richard bid him save himself and leave him to his fortune.

After the fight had thus, without intermission, continued while the day lasted and some hours of the night, many of our men were slain and hurt, and one of the great galleons of the armada and the admiral of the hulks both sunk, and in many other of the Spanish ships great slaughter was made. Some write that Sir Richard was very dangerously hurt almost in the beginning of the fight, and lay speechless for a time ere he recovered. But two of the *Revenge*'s own company, brought home in a ship of lime from the islands, examined by some of the Lords and others, affirmed that he was never so wounded as that he forsook the upper deck till an hour before midnight. And then, being shot into the body with a musket as he was a-dressing, was again shot into the head, and withal his chirurgeon wounded to death. This agreeth also with an examination taken by Sir Francis Godolphin of four other mariners of the same ship, being returned, which examination the said Sir Francis sent unto Master William Killegrue, of Her Majesty's Privy Chamber.

But to return to the fight. The Spanish ships which attempted to board the *Revenge*, as they were wounded and beaten off, so always others came in their places, she having never less than two mighty galleons by her sides and aboard her. So that ere the morning, from three of the clock the day before, there had fifteen several armadas assailed her: and all so ill approved their entertainment as they were by the break of day far more willing to hearken to a composition than hastily to make any more assaults or entries. But as the day increased, so our men decreased: and as the light grew more and more, by so much more grew our discomforts. For none appeared in sight but enemies, saving one small ship called the *Pilgrim*, commanded by Jacob Whiddon, who hovered all night to see the success; but in the morning, bearing with the *Revenge*, was hunted like a hare amongst many ravenous hounds, but escaped.

All the powder of the *Revenge* to the last barrel was now spent, all her pikes broken, forty of her best men slain, and the most part of the

Sir Richard Grenville: engraving by unknown artist
in *Heröologia Anglica* by Henry Holland, 1620

rest hurt. In the beginning of the fight she had but one hundred free from sickness, and fourscore and ten sick laid in hold upon the ballast. A small troup to man such a ship, and a weak garrison to resist so mighty an army. By those hundred all was sustained, the volleys, boardings, and enterings of fifteen ships of war, besides those which beat her at large.

On the contrary, the Spanish were always supplied with soldiers brought from every squadron; all manner of arms and powder at will. Unto ours there remained no comfort at all, no hope, no supply either of ships, men, or weapons; the masts all beaten overboard, all her tackle cut asunder, her upper work altogether razed, and in effect evened she was with the water, but the very foundation or bottom of a ship, nothing being left overhead either for flight or defence. Sir Richard, finding himself in this distress and unable any longer to make resistance, having endured in this fifteen hours' fight the assault of fifteen several armadas, all by turns aboard him, and by estimation eight hundred shot of great artillery, besides many assaults and entries, and that himself and the ship must needs be possessed by the enemy, who were now all cast in a ring round about him (the *Revenge* not able to move one way or other but as she was moved with the waves and billow of the sea), commanded the master gunner, whom he knew to be a most resolute man, to split and sink the ship, that thereby nothing might remain of glory or victory to the Spaniards; seeing in so many hours' fight and with so great a navy they were not able to take her, having had fifteen hours time, above ten thousand men, and fifty and three sail of men of war to perform it withal: and persuaded the company, or as many as he could induce, to yield themselves unto God and to the mercy of none else; but as they had, like valiant, resolute men, repulsed so many enemies, they should not now shorten the honour of their nation by prolonging their own lives for a few hours or a few days.

The master gunner readily condescended, and divers others. But the Captain and the Master were of another opinion, and besought Sir Richard to have care of them, alleging that the Spaniard would be as ready to entertain a composition as they were willing to offer the same: and that there being divers sufficient and valiant men yet living, and whose wounds were not mortal, they might do their country and Prince acceptable service hereafter. And whereas Sir Richard had alleged that the Spaniards should never glory to have taken one ship of Her Majesty, seeing they had so long and so notably defended themselves, they answered that the ship had six foot water in hold, three shot under water which were so weakly stopped as with the first working of the sea she must needs sink, and was besides so crushed and bruised as she could never be removed out of the place.

And as the matter was thus in dispute, and Sir Richard refusing to hearken to any of those reasons, the Master of the *Revenge* (while the Captain won unto him the greater party) was conveyed aboard the General, Don Alfonso Baçan [Alonso Bazan]. Who (finding none over hasty to enter the *Revenge* again, doubting lest Sir Richard would have blown them up, and himself, and perceiving by the report of the Master of the *Revenge* his dangerous disposition) yielded that all their lives should be saved, the company sent for England, and the better sort to pay such reasonable ransom as their estate would bear, and in the mean season to be free from galley or imprisonment. To this he so much the rather condescended as well, as I have said, for fear of further loss and mischief to themselves as also for the desire he had to recover Sir Richard Grenville, whom for his notable valour he seemed greatly to honour and admire.

When this answer was returned and that safety of life was promised, the common sort being now at the end of their peril, the most drew back from Sir Richard and the master gunner, being no hard matter to dissuade men from death to life. The master gunner, finding himself and Sir Richard thus prevented and mastered by the greater number, would have slain himself with a sword had he not been by force withheld and locked into his cabin. Then the General sent many boats aboard the *Revenge*, and divers of our men, fearing Sir Richard's disposition, stole away aboard the General and other ships. Sir Richard, thus over-matched, was sent unto by Alfonso Baçan to remove out of the *Revenge*, the ship being marvellous unsavoury, filled with blood and bodies of dead and wounded men like a slaughter house. Sir Richard answered that he might do with his body what he list, for he esteemed it not, and as he was carried out of the ship he swooned, and, reviving again, desired the company to pray for him. The General used Sir Richard with all humanity and left nothing unattempted that tended to his recovery, highly commending his valour and worthiness, and greatly bewailing the danger wherein he was, being unto them a rare spectacle and a resolution seldom approved, to see one ship turn toward so many enemies, to endure the charge and boarding of so many huge armadas, and to resist and repel the assaults and entries of so many soldiers. All which and more is confirmed by a Spanish Captain of the same armada, and a present actor in the fight, who, being severed from the rest in a storm, was by the *Lion* of London, a small ship taken, and is now prisoner in London.

The General Commander of the armada was Don Alphonso Baçan, brother to the Marquess of Santa Cruz. The Admiral of the Biscayan squadron was Brittandona; of the squadron of Seville the Marquess of Arumburch. The hulks and flyboats were commanded by Luis Coutinho. There were slain and drowned in this fight well near one thousand of the enemies, and two special Commanders, Don Luis de Sant John [San Juan], and Don George de Prunaria [?] de Malaga, as the Spanish Captain confesseth, besides divers other of special account whereof as yet report is not made.

The admiral of the hulks and the *Ascension* of Seville were both sunk by the side of the *Revenge*; one other recovered the road of Saint Michael and sunk also there; a fourth ran herself with the shore to save her men. Sir Richard died, as it is said, the second or third day aboard the General, and was by them greatly bewailed. What became of his body, whether it were buried in the sea or on the land we know not. The comfort that remaineth to his friends is that he hath ended his life honourably in respect of the reputation won to his nation and country, and of the same to his posterity, and that, being dead, he hath not outlived his own honour.

For the rest of Her Majesty's ships that entered not so far into the fight as the *Revenge* the reasons and causes were these. There were of them but six in all, whereof two but small ships; the *Revenge* engaged past recovery. The island of Flores was on the one side, 53 sail of the Spanish, divided into squadrons, on the other, all as full filled with soldiers as they could contain. Almost the one half of our men sick and not able to serve; the ships grown foul, unrummaged, and scarcely able to bear any sail for want of ballast, having been six months at the sea before. If all the rest had entered all had been lost; for the very hugeness of the Spanish fleet, if no other violence had been offered, would have crushed them between them into shivers. Of which the dishonour and loss to the Queen had been far greater than the spoil or harm that the enemy could any way have received.

Not withstanding it is very true that the Lord Thomas would have entered between the squadrons, but the rest would not condescend: and the Master of his own ship offered to leap into the sea rather than to conduct that Her Majesty's ship and the rest to be a prey to the enemy, where there was no hope nor possibility either of defence or victory. Which also in my opinion had ill sorted or answered the discretion and trust of a General, to commit himself and his charge to an assured destruction without hope or any likelihood of prevailing, thereby to diminish the strength of Her Majesty's Navy, and to enrich the pride and glory of the enemy.

The *Foresight* of the Queen's, commanded by Master Thomas Vavasour, performed a very great fight and stayed two hours as near the *Revenge* as the weather would permit him, not forsaking the fight till he was like to be encompassed by the squadrons, and with great difficulty cleared himself. The rest gave divers volleys of shot, and entered as far as the place permitted, and their own necessities to keep the weather-gauge of the enemy, until they were parted by night.

A few days after the fight was ended and the English prisoners dispersed into the Spanish and Indies ships, there arose so great a storm from the west and northwest that all the fleet was dispersed, as well the Indian fleet, which were then come unto them, as the rest of the armada that attended their arrival, of which 14 sail together with the *Revenge*, and in her 200 Spaniards, were cast away upon the Isle of St Michael. So it pleased them to honour the burial of that renowned ship, the *Revenge*, not suffering her to perish alone, for the great honour she achieved in her lifetime. On the rest of the islands there were cast away in this storm 15 or 16 more of the ships of war. And of an hundred and odd sail of the Indies fleet expected this year in Spain, what in this tempest, and what before in the Bay of Mexico, and about the Bermudas, there were 70 and odd consumed and lost, with those taken by our ships of London, besides one very rich Indies ship which set herself on fire, being boarded by the *Pilgrim*, and five other taken by Master Watts his ships of London, between the Havana and Cape St Antonio.

The fourth of this month of November we received letters from the Tercera affirming that there are 3,000 bodies of men remaining in that island, saved out of the perished ships: and that by the Spaniards' own confession there are 10,000 cast away in this storm, besides those that are perished between the islands and the main. Thus it hath pleased God to fight for us, and to defend the justice of our cause against the ambitious and bloody pretences of the Spaniard who, seeking to devour all nations, are themselves devoured. A manifest testimony how unjust and displeasing their attempts are in the sight of God, who hath pleased to witness by the success of their affairs His mislike of their bloody and injurious designs, purposed and practised against all Christian princes, over whom they seek unlawful and ungodly rule and empery.

One day or two before this wrack happened to the Spanish fleet, whenas some of our prisoners desired to be set on shore upon the islands, hoping to be from thence transported into England, which liberty was formerly by the General promised, one, Morice Fitzjohn, son of old John of Desmond, a notable traitor, cousin germane to the late Earl of Desmond, was sent to the English from ship to ship to persuade them to serve the King of Spain. The arguments he used to induce them were these: the increase of pay, which he promised to be trebled; advancement to the better sort; and the exercise of the true Catholic religion and safety of their souls to all. For the first,* even the beggarly

* This piece of propaganda was no doubt aimed at the English Catholics.

and unnatural behaviour of those English and Irish rebels that served the King in that present action was sufficient to answer that first argument of rich pay; for so poor and beggarly they were as for want of apparel they stripped their poor countrymen prisoners out of their ragged garments, worn to nothing by six months' service, and spared not to despoil them even of their bloody shirts from their wounded bodies, and the very shoes from their feet: a notable testimony of their rich entertainment and great wages.

The second reason was hope of advancement if they served well and would continue faithful to the King. But what man can be so blockishly ignorant ever to expect place or honour from a foreign King, having no other argument or persuasion than his own disloyalty: to be unnatural to his own country that bred him; to his parents that begat him, and rebellious to his true Prince, to whose obedience he is bound by oath, by nature, and by religion? No, they are only assured to be employed in all desperate enterprises, to be held in scorn and disdain ever among those whom they serve. And that ever traitor was either trusted or advanced I could never yet read, neither can I at this time remember any example.

And no man could have less becomed the place of an orator for such a purpose than this Morice of Desmond. For the Earl, his cousin, being one of the greatest subjects in that Kingdom of Ireland, having almost whole countries in his possession: so many goodly manors, castles, and lordships; the Count Palatine of Kerry, five hundred gentlemen of his own name and family to follow him, besides others (all which he possessed in peace for three or four hundred years), was in less than three years after his adhering to the Spaniards and rebellion beaten from all his holds, not so many as ten gentlemen of his name left living, himself taken and beheaded by a soldier of his own nation, and his land given by a Parliament to Her Majesty and possessed by the English: his other cousin, Sir John of Desmond, taken by Master John Zouch, and his body hanged over the gates of his native city to be devoured by ravens: the third brother, Sir James, hanged, drawn, and quartered in the same place. If he had withal vaunted of his success of his own house, no doubt the argument would have moved much and wrought great effect; which because he for that present forgot I thought it good to remember in his behalf.

For matter of religion it would require a particular volume if I should set down how irreligiously they cover their greedy and ambitious pretences with that veil of piety. But sure I am, that there is no kingdom or commonwealth in all Europe but if they be reformed they then invade it for religion sake: if it be, as they term, Catholic they pretend title, as if the Kings of Castile were the natural heirs of all the world; and so between both no kingdom is unsought. Where they dare not with their own forces to invade they basely entertain the traitors and vagabonds of all nations, seeking by those and by their runagate Jesuits to win parts, and have by that mean ruined many noble houses and others in this land, and have extinguished both their lives and families. What good, honour, or fortune ever man yet by them achieved is yet unheard of, or unwritten. And if our English Papists do but look into Portugal, against which they have no pretence of religion, how the nobility are put to death, imprisoned, their rich men made a prey, and all sorts of people captived, they shall find that the obedience even of the Turk is easy and a liberty in respect of the slavery and tyranny of Spain.

What have they done in Sicily, in Naples, Milan, and in the Low Countries; who hath there been spared for religion at all? And it cometh to my remembrance of a certain burgher of Antwerp, whose house being entered by a company of Spanish soldiers when they first sacked the city, he besought them to spare him and his goods being a good Catholic, and one of their own party and faction. The Spaniards answered that they knew him to be of a good conscience for himself, but his money, plate, jewels and goods were all heretical and therefore good prize. So they abused and tormented the foolish Fleming, who hoped that an Agnus Dei had been a sufficient target against all force of that holy and charitable nation. Neither have they at any time, as they protest, invaded the kingdoms of the Indies and Peru, and elsewhere, but only led thereunto rather to reduce the people to Christianity than for either gold or empery: when, as in one only island called Hispaniola, they have wasted thirty hundred thousand of the natural people, besides many millions else in other places of the Indies; a poor and harmless people created of God, and might have been won to His knowledge, as many of them were, and almost as many as ever were persuaded thereunto. The story whereof is at large written by a Bishop of their own nation, called Bartholomew de las Casas, and translated into English and many other languages, entitled 'The Spanish Cruelties'.

Who would therefore repose trust in such a nation of ravenous strangers, and especially in those Spaniards which more greedily thirst after English blood than after the lives of any other people of Europe for the many overthrows and dishonours they have received at our hands, whose weakness we have discovered to the world, and whose forces at home, abroad, in Europe, in India, by sea and land, we have, even with handfuls of men and ships, overthrown and dishonoured.

Let not therefore any Englishman, of what religion soever, have other opinion of the Spaniards but that those whom he seeketh to win of our nation he esteemeth base and traitorous, unworthy persons, or inconstant fools: and that he useth his pretence of religion for no other purpose but to bewitch us from the obedience of our natural Prince, thereby hoping in time to bring us to slavery and subjection, and then none shall be unto them so odious and disdained as the traitors themselves, who have sold their country to a stranger, and forsaken their faith and obedience contrary to nature and religion: and contrary to that humane and general honour, not only of Christians, but of heathen and irreligious nations, who have always sustained what labour soever, and embraced even death itself for their country, Prince, or commonwealth.

To conclude, it hath ever to this day pleased God to prosper and defend Her Majesty, to break the purposes of malicious enemies, of forsworn traitors, and of unjust practices and invasions. She hath ever been honoured of the worthiest kings, served by faithful subjects, and shall by the favour of God resist, repel, and confound all whatsoever attempts against her sacred person of kingdom. In the meantime let the Spaniard and traitor vaunt of their success, and we, her true and obedient vassals, guided by the shining light of her virtues, shall always love her, serve her, and obey her to the end of our lives.

GLOSSARY

The editor gratefully acknowledges his indebtedness in the compilation of this glossary to the following works, among others:

The Shorter Oxford English Dictionary (SOED), 3rd edition, 1964; *A Glossary of Shakespeare's Sea and Naval Terms, including Gunnery*, by A. F. Falconer, 1965; *A Handbook of English Costume in the Sixteenth Century*, by C. W. and Phillis Cunnington, 1954; *Chambers's World Gazetteer*, edited by T. C. Collocott and J. O. Thorne, 1965; *Voyages and Documents* by Richard Hakluyt, edited with an introduction and a glossary by Janet Hampden, 1958; *The Principal Navigations, Voyages* ... by Richard Hakluyt, Hakluyt Society edition, Vol. 12, General Index, 1905.

ADMIRAL, flagship.

ADVISO, announcement.

AGREEING with our climate: becoming acclimatised.

ALCAIDE, governor.

ANATOMY, a skeleton or a mummy.

APPOINTED, equipped, armed.

ARGOSY, a very large merchant vessel.

ARMADA, any fleet of warships or, occasionally, a single warship.

ARQUEBUS, a portable fire-arm of variable size; a kind of large musket.

ARTIFICIAL, skilful, workmanlike.

ASSAY, assault. AT ALL ASSAYS, in any attack, any danger.

BANQUET, dessert; sweetmeats and wine.

BARBARY, north-west Africa.

BARK, any sailing ship of moderate size.

BASE, 'a very small cannon, probably firing a six-ounce shot'.

BEHOVEFUL, advantageous.

BILL, halberd.

BOTIJO (Spanish), earthenware jar.

BOW, to. To bend.

BOW-SHOOT, BOW-SHOT, about 240 yards.

BRAVE, fine, beautiful, decorated.

BRAZIL, a wood used in dyeing cloth. The land of Brazil was named after it because very good dyewood was obtained there.

BREACH, the breaking of the sea on a shore.

BROWNBILL, a burnished axe.

BRUSTLING, crackling, rustling, roaring.

BUFF, buffalo.

BUSKIN, a boot reaching to the calf or the knee.

BY AND BY, at once.

CABRITO, goat.

CACIQUE, an Indian chieftain.

CALIVER, a long, light musket.

CANNON. The English cannon was probably a 7-inch gun firing a 40-lb. round shot. The Spanish cannon was larger, firing a 50-lb. shot.

CARAVEL, a small, light, fast ship, a Portuguese type.

CARGASON, cargo, bill of lading.

CARRACK, a large 'round ship'.

CAUSE, causeway, raised roadway.

CHAMLET or CAMLET. 'Probably a kind of mohair, or later camel-hair cloth, mixed with wool, silk or cotton, and having a watered appearance.' – C. W. & P. Cunnington: *A Handbook of English Costume in the Sixteenth Century.*

CHARGEABLE, responsible; expensive; troublesome.

CHARGED, high; having tall castles fore and aft.

CHASE, bow of a ship.

CHIRURGEON, surgeon.

CLIFT, split wood.

COCK-BOAT, a small boat, like a dinghy.

COD, pod.

COMMODIOUS, convenient, advantageous, profitable.

COMMODITY, advantage, profit.

COMPOSITION, agreement, treaty, compromise.

CONCEITS, ideas, fancies.

CONTAGIOUS, foul.

CONTRACTATION HOUSE, Exchange.

CORDOVAN SKIN, fine leather made in Cordova, Spain, or in the style of Cordova.

CORINTHS, currants.

CORREGIDOR, corrigidor, magistrate, sheriff.

CROSSBAR SHOT, cannon shot in the form of a bar or a cross.

CRUET, a small vessel holding wine or water for the celebration of the Eucharist.

CRUMBS, to gather up. To pick up strength.

CULVERIN, the longest-range gun in use. A long, muzzle-loading smooth bore gun, usually firing a round shot of about 17 lb. weight.

CUNNING, skilful, clever.

CUSTOMER, Customs House officer.

DAW, to. To bring back to consciousness.

DEFEND, to. To forbid.

DELIVER, QUICK TO, active, nimble.

DETRACT, to. To withdraw from.

DIGHT, dressed, dressed up, decorated.

DISBOCK, to. To flow out of or into.

DIURNAL, a day-by-day record.

DRAFT, chart.

DRUMBLER, a small fast vessel used as a transport or a fighting ship.

DUCAT, Spanish, worth about 5s. 10d. in Elizabethan money.

EASTERLAND, the territory of the Hanse merchants, on the Baltic.

ELCHIE, ambassador.

ELL, 45 inches.

EQUINOCTIAL, the Equator.

FACTORY, trading station.

FALCHION, a broad, curved sword.

FALCONET, a gun about $6\frac{1}{2}$ feet long, firing a $1\frac{1}{2}$ lb. shot.

FAT, cask.

FENCIBLE, easy to defend.

FIGU, plantain.

FINE, end.

FIRKIN, a small cask, containing about eight or nine gallons.

FISH, to. To mend a mast or spar by binding a splint to it.

FLEAD, FLEANE, flayed, skinned.

FLUX, dysentery.

FLY-BOAT, fast-sailing vessel.

FOIST, a small light galley with eighteen to twenty oars a side and two masts.

FRUMENTY or FURMENTY, a dish of wheat boiled in milk, and seasoned.

FURICANE, hurricane.

FURNITURE, equipment.

GABLE, cable.

GALLEASS, a large long vessel with a flush deck, with sails, auxiliary oars and broadside guns.

GALLIOT, a small galley.

GENERAL, commander of any expedition, maritime or military; flagship.

GLASS, gloss.

GOOSE-WING, 'one of the clews or lower corners of a ship's mainsail or foresail when the middle part is furled or tied up to the yard'. – SOED.

GRAVE, to, 'to clean a ship's bottom by burning off the accretions and paying it over with tar while aground on a beach or placed in a dock'. – SOED.

GROAT, fourpenny piece.

GUARDS (blue and green), stripes.

GUINEA, COAST OF, the west coast of Africa from Sierra Leone to Benin. There were Portuguese forts on this coast.

HALBERD, a kind of spear, about 6 feet long, with a head which could be used for both cutting and thrusting.

HARDLY, with difficulty.

HARQUEBUS, see Arquebus.

HARPING IRON, harpoon.

HOLD, fort.

HOUND, projection at the mast-head 'wherein the tyes do run to hoist the yards'. – Captain John Smith.

HOY, a flat-bottomed sailing vessel.

HULK, a cargo vessel, about twice the length of its beam; a carrack.

INGENIO, sugar mill.

INTEND, to. To attend to.

JEALOUSY, suspicion, mistrust.

JENNET, small Spanish horse.

JUT, a; a push, a knock.

KEMB, comb.

KERN, to; to make into grains, to granulate.

KINTAL, see quintal.

LARBOARD, now known as the port side.

LEAGUE, about three miles.

LARGE (of the wind), on the quarter.

LEESE, lose.

LEWD, unprincipled, vulgar, evil, foolish.

LIGIER, resident ambassador or commercial representative.

LIST, strip, edging.

LONGITUDE could not be calculated exactly until the chronometer was invented about 1760 by John Harrison.

LOWBELL, a small bell, used in fowling.

LUFF, to spring a; to bring the ship closer to the wind.

MAGUEY, American aloe.

MAIN, mainland.

MAIN, to; to lower (sails).

MAMMEE, a large tropical tree bearing a large fruit with a yellow bulk of pleasant taste – a mammee-apple.

MANKIND, 'mighty deer that seemed to be mankind'. ? male, i.e. stags.

MARK, thirteen shillings and eightpence. A sum of money, not a coin.

MART, market.

MATCH, slow-burning fuse for firing guns.

MEAN, moderate, medium.

MESS, a group of seamen, the unit for the distribution of rations.

MILLIO, millet.

MORSE, walrus.

OCCUPY, to follow one's occupation.

OPEN, in view of.

OVERSEEN, mistaken.

PAINFUL, diligent.

PANTOFLES, overshoes in the form of mules.

PART, partisan.

PARTISAN, a kind of spear about 9 feet long with a broad blade.

PATACHE, 'a small boat used for communications between the vessels of a fleet'. – SOED.

PEASON, peas.

PESO, 'piece of eight', worth about 4s. 3d. in Elizabethan money.

PILLED, pillaged.

PILOT, navigator.

PINE, pineapple.

PINNACE, a small ship or a boat, usually with oars as well as sails.

PINTADO, a cloth painted or printed in colours.

PIPE, (of wine, water, etc.), a very large cask, about half a tun.

PLANT, to; to colonize.

PLANTANO, plantain, similar to a banana.

POLICY, crafty device, stratagem, trick.

POLITICALLY, craftily, falsely.

POMPION, pumpkin.

POSY, a short inscription or motto.

PURCHASE, capture, plunder, prize.

QUINTAL, 100-lb. weight.

REAL OF PLATE, Spanish coin, worth about $6\frac{1}{2}d.$ of Elizabethan money.

RECEIPT, capacity.

REGIMENT, rule, government.

ROAD, anchorage, port.

ROAN CLOTH, a kind of linen made at Rouen.

ROYAL OF PLATE, see REAL OF PLATE.

RUDE, untutored, barbarous.

RUMMAGE, to. To stow cargo; to clean a ship thoroughly.

ST LAURENCE, island of; presumably Madagascar.

SERON, 'a bale or package (of exotic products, e.g. almonds, medicinal bark, cocoa) made up in an animal's hide'. – SOED.

SHIFT, to. To change (clothes).

SITH, SITHENS, since.

SLEEVELESS, useless.

SODDEN, boiled.

SORT (of files), a number of different kinds.

SPAN, about 9 inches.

SPEND, to (a mast, etc.). To lose.

SPOILED, despoiled, pillaged.

STATES, men of importance.

STEAD, help.

STIRK, a young bullock or heifer.

STOCK, the cross-bar of an anchor.

STONE BOW, 'a kind of cross-bow or catapult for shooting stones'. – *SOED.*

SUCCESS, fortune, good or bad.

SUCKETS, fruits preserved in syrup, or candied.

SUMACH, a preparation used in tanning and dyeing leather.

SWIMMER (of a fish), ? fin.

TABLES, pictures, flat surfaces.

TARGET, shield.

TIERCE, one-third.

TOWARDLY, promising.

TRADE, trail, footprints, tread.

TRAIN, a trap for catching wild animals, a decoy, a snare.

TROTTERO, messenger.

TUBERONES, sharks.

TURKY, turquoise.

TWELVE TIDE, the twelve days of Christmas. (?)

UNSTOCKED (of an anchor), without a cross-bar.

UTTER, outer; to offer for sale, to sell.

UTTERANCE, sale.

VAIL, to. To go down stream with the tide.

WAFT, to. To beckon, to wave (something) as a signal.

WANT, mole.

WATCHET, light blue, sky blue.

WAX (to), grow.

WOOD, mad.

WORM, snake, serpent, dragon.

ZABRA, 'a small vessel used off the coasts of Spain and Portugal'. – *SOED.*

ZEILAN, Ceylon.

ZOCOTORO, presumably Socotra.

INDEX